From the national debate over
THE REAL ANITA HILL

"[an] impressive investigative study . . . extremely damaging to Anita Hill's case . . . *The Real Anita Hill* is well written, carefully reasoned and powerful in its logic. It is a must reading for anyone who feels remotely touched by the case."

Christopher Lehmann-Haupt
The New York Times

"Sleaze with footnotes . . . a farrago of the preposterous and the vicious . . . this book is a model of the politics of character assassination."
Anthony Lewis
The New York Times

". . . this book is not, as some may have anticipated, a right-wing smear. It is . . . a serious work of investigative journalism that builds a case quietly and incrementally . . . the first salvo in a long and salutary search for the truth. . . ."

Jonathan Groner
Washington Post Book World

"Brock assembles an avalanche of evidence that Hill lied—about her career and her relations with Thomas. . . . To believe that Hill told the truth you must believe that dozens of people, with no common or even apparent motive to lie, did so. Brock's book will be persuasive to minds not sealed by the caulking of ideology."

George F. Will
Newsweek

"'The Real Anita Hill' . . . sink[s] beneath the weight of ideological bias . . . overwhelmingly one sided. . . . Mr. Brock laments the one-sided reporting during the hearings, and with some reason. Maybe someday someone will write an evenhanded account. This isn't it."

Anna Quindlen
The New York Times

"David Brock has written a book that can only be described as a bombshell. If, after digesting 'The Real Anita Hill,' the unofficial judges of scandal do not retroactively declare what happened to Clarence Thomas to be an outrage of historic proportions, then there is no honesty left in Washington."

Mona Charen
The Washington Times

"Like a prosecutor pouncing on every detail, Brock scours testimony from the Senate Judiciary Committee's hearings and special counsel's investigation, interviews witnesses who didn't testify, consults FBI records and scrutinizes every shred of Hill's background he can find. . . . While no one denies there were discrepancies in Hill's testimony, Brock comes up with some beauts that were overlooked or seen as inadmissible by the committee."

Patricia Holt
San Francisco Chronicle

"All nonfiction books contain errors, but this book is unusual in the extent to which its key arguments are based on them. . . . Once the sources are evaluated and the contradictory evidence is considered, Brock's arguments evaporate into a cloud of ill will."

Jane Mayer and Jill Abramson
The New Yorker

"Having read Mr. Brock's book, the Mayer and Abramson review and most of the other effusions concerning the Clarence Thomas controversy, I am convinced that the facts, reason and truth are overwhelmingly on the side of Justice Thomas and thus Mr. Brock's story."

Kenneth S. Tollet, Sr.
Howard University
(Letter to the *Washington Times*)

"Brock claims to have transcended partial perspective and found the truth, but instead of the truth he gives only his own perspective."

Kathleen M. Sullivan
New York Review of Books

"*The Real Anita Hill* takes every charge levelled by Ms. Hill . . . and destroys them (and her credibility) one by one. . . . Those who believed Anita Hill based on her testimony need to read this book and then offer Clarence Thomas an apology."

Cal Thomas
Los Angeles Times Syndicate

"[an] outrageous diatribe . . . backed by nothing more than its author's venomous bias."

William Kunstler
The Amsterdam News

"Beneath the veneer of investigative journalism, Brock's book is a hatchet job. It is weighted down with ideology, filled with conjecture, and one-sided. 'The Real Anita Hill' is a book which stoops but does not conquer."

Joel Connelly
Seattle Post-Intelligencer

"After reading David Brock's carefully researched book, *The Real Anita Hill*, those who wish to believe Professor Hill will have to believe that a small army of other people have lied when they flatly contradicted many parts of her story. Although the contents of this book are dynamite, there is no sensationalism, no strident political flourishes. There is only the slow but steady buildup of facts and careful analysis of claims and arguments on both sides of the Hill-Thomas controversy. But, in the end, it adds up to complete devastation of the testimony—and the media image—of Anita Hill."

Thomas Sowell
Forbes

"Our liberals and special interests apparently do not care that by opposing Brock's findings in 'The Real Anita Hill,' they are destroying much that liberalism labored for centuries to establish, for instance, the rules of evidence, of fair play and of objectivity, the principle of innocence until proven guilty, and the institution of a judiciary independent from politics."

R. Emmett Tyrell, Jr.
The American Spectator

"'The Real Anita Hill' . . . takes the testimony of Anita Hill and tears it to pieces. . . . I do not believe in any kind of harassment, sexual, color, religion, etc., but I do believe that Anita Hill was an unmitigated liar."

Louise Hopkins
Coatesville Record

"Brock's position seems influenced by his ideological stance. Although he promises a lot of answers, he fails to conclusively convince. Using unnamed sources and a lot of conjecture, Brock tries to build a case that Hill was not the reluctant but persuaded accuser who appeared to be a mild-mannered, straight-laced conservative Baptist."

Georgia Pabst
Milwaukee Journal

"Brock . . . debunks a lot of the myths that have been accepted as truth since October 1991, when Hill made her first public appearance. . . . Brock has done a solid job of reporting that should seriously weaken Hill's standing as a feminist icon."

Ray Locker
The Tampa Tribune Times

". . . [A]n excellent analysis of how Senate staff members persistently encouraged Hill to make her allegations against Thomas a formal part of the nomination battle. . . . 'The Real Anita Hill' is an important contribution to a debate that will certainly be with us for at least as long as 45 year-old Clarence Thomas continues to serve on the U.S. Supreme Court."

David Garrow
New York Newsday

". . . [A] powerful indictment of the little band of liberal activists and Senate staffers, aided and abetted by cronies in the media, who conspired to sink the Thomas nomination through a sustained campaign of leaks, smears, and misrepresentations."

Aram Bakshian, Jr.
California Political Review

"[An] explosive study. . . . David Brock makes short work of Anita Hill's entire tale . . . Brock's book has forced critics toward an honest effort to revisit the case."

Eric Brendel
New York Post

"[T]he Brock book . . . illustrates in a blatant way all that has gone wrong with what passes for the discourse of public affairs today . . . beneath the tissue-thin veneer of respectable writing, this book speaks—in the main— in filthy whispers . . . The real David Brock, author, is, it seems, a writer who treats conjecture as truth."

Lyle Denniston
Baltimore Sun

"It is to Brock's credit that his extensive investigation of Hill is not the right-wing polemic many expected. As the title of the book suggests, he considers Hill a villain, but a limited-purpose villain. In the end, the book is more measured and less shrill than the magazine article from which it grew, serving less as an indictment of Hill than as a cautionary fable warning against the morality of ends so often adopted by 'ideological warriors' of both the left and the right."

Philip Martin
Arkansas Democrat-Gazette

"Though Brock never deviates from cool logic and objectivity, he nonetheless achieves a dramatic impact that any novelist would envy. His devastating descriptions almost had me reading the book through spread fingers like a child at a horror movie."

Florence King
Washington Times

"When the deconstruction is complete, Brock's book will be revealed as a sham and a scandal, marking a journalistic standard so low that no reputable publishing house should have touched it."

Deirdre English
The Nation

"[E]xhaustively researched. . . . Brock's book does its greatest damage to Hill by carefully examining the testimony she and Thomas gave to the committee and investigators."

John Carlson
Seattle Times

"The detail contained in Brock's book is astonishing—there is an unreported or underreported revelation on almost every page. . . . I'll wager that most readers will find themselves turning the pages, as I did, saying to themselves, 'Gee, I didn't know that.'"

Richard Starr
Insight

"Brock himself is not exactly the objective investigator you read about on the book jacket. . . . More important, the book does not contain the long-awaited, long-suppressed facts about Hill. It's not, as the subtitle declares, 'The Untold Story.' It's the untrue story."

Ellen Goodman
Boston Globe

"Part detective story, part psychological study, 'The Real Anita Hill' is a crackling good mystery—with Thomas or the good name Thomas built over four decades as the only real victim. Read it and you'll finally get it."

David Reinhard
The Oregonian

"[A] wretched piece of journalism . . . riddled with inexcusable errors."

Molly Ivins
Nationally Syndicated Columnist

"Brock's sympathies for Thomas are apparent. But so is a striving for objectivity as he assembles and examines the evidence. By no means is this text all to be taken as gospel, but the essential facts put Anita Hill in a much different light. They do, that is, for the open-minded reader."

David DeBuisson
Greensboro News & Record

"Brock's work is discounted by those who point out he is a reporter for the conservative *American Spectator*. In the places where it counts, though, *The Real Anita Hill* appears to be objective. Read it and make up your own mind."

Harold Jackson
Birmingham News

"To pretend to be the victim of the very same person one is victimizing is both brazen and perverse. David Brock's timely book reassures us that the 'murder' of a good name eventually 'will out.'"

Esther Littmann
Detroit News

"David Brock . . . levels what has to be the best shot anyone will ever take at Anita Hill. Ultimately, he misses, but his book is a well written, thorough, and chilling attempt to destroy Hill on a multitude of levels."

Judith Timson
Toronto Globe and Mail

THE REAL ANITA HILL

THE REAL ANITA HILL

The Untold Story

DAVID BROCK

With a New Afterword

THE FREE PRESS
A Division of Macmillan, Inc.
NEW YORK

Maxwell Macmillan Canada
TORONTO

Maxwell Macmillan International
NEW YORK   OXFORD   SINGAPORE   SYDNEY

The Free Press
A Division of Macmillan, Inc.
866 Third Avenue, New York, N. Y. 10022

Maxwell Macmillan Canada, Inc.
1200 Eglinton Avenue East
Suite 200
Don Mills, Ontario M3C 3N1

Macmillan, Inc. is part of the Maxwell Communication Group of Companies.

First Free Press Paperback Edition 1994

Printed in the United States of America

printing number

1 2 3 4 5 6 7 8 9 10

Library of Congress Cataloging-in-Publication Data

Brock, David
        The real Anita Hill: the untold story / by David Brock.
            p.   cm.
        Includes bibliographical references.
        ISBN 0-02-904656-4
            1. Thomas, Clarence, 1948– . 2. Hill, Anita. 3. Judges—United
        States—Selection and appointment.   4. Sexual harassment of women—
        United States.   I. Title
        KF8745.T48B76   1993
        347.73'2634—dc20
        [347.3073534]   93–21724
                                                                             CIP

CONTENTS

Author's Note

Like most Americans, I tuned into the Thomas–Hill hearings with an open mind. At the time, I knew little about Clarence Thomas, and what I had seen during the first round of the U.S. Supreme Court confirmation hearings left me less than impressed and agnostic on the question of whether or not he should be confirmed. I also had no strong views on the merits of Thomas's conservative judicial philosophy, and on the issue that dominated the hearings, abortion rights, while ambivalent about the wisdom of relying on constitutional guarantees, I was pro-choice, while Thomas, at least as he was portrayed by his opponents, was not.

Watching Anita Hill's testimony with about ten other reporters and editors, I recall being one of two who believed that Clarence Thomas might well have been guilty as charged. The others were far more skeptical about Hill's allegations. By the end of the weekend, again like most Americans, I believed Thomas should not have been denied confirmation because Hill had not proven her case—but I was by no means convinced of the nominee's innocence. Intuitively, I did not believe the nominee's categorical denials, but I also did not think that solid evidence had been introduced to disprove it.

This book had its genesis a few weeks later in an assignment from the *American Spectator* to write about the leak of Hill's allegations to the media. At the time, I had been working on a book about the inner workings of the U.S. Congress, and my intention was to write a piece about the politics of leaks on Capitol Hill. It was never my intention to weigh in on one side or the other on the question of who was telling the truth.

In the initial weeks of reporting, however, I was surprised to discover that a number of promising leads were left unpursued by the major media, which seemed to be devoting its resources in the weeks following the hearing to digging up further evidence against Thomas.

The leads bore directly on the credibility and veracity of Anita Hill's sexual harassment allegations. In March 1992, the *Spectator* published "The Real Anita Hill," and the response to the piece convinced me that it should be expanded into a book.

Though readers may be struck by the book's seemingly single-minded focus on Hill, as opposed to Thomas, this should not lead anyone to conclude that only Hill's testimony was subjected to close scrutiny. Though he had been thoroughly investigated by the FBI and the Senate five times, and by at least four major news organizations even after he assumed his seat on the Supreme Court, Thomas was once again investigated in the course of the research for this book. Nothing was discovered to contradict his sworn testimony or corroborate Hill's charges, which is why the validity of her case against Thomas became the central focus. If the evidence had come out the other way, I was fully prepared to write a book that questioned Thomas's credibility and character and redeemed Hill's.

Some of this evidence has been obtained under the condition of anonymity for those who revealed it. To question or criticize Anita Hill is tantamount to breaking a potent political and cultural taboo, particularly in the university communities and legal circles in which these sources must continue to live and work. The sources spoke to me only because they believed the information was relevant to the credibility and veracity of Hill's testimony against Thomas and it is only in this spirit that the material is reported. Any aspects of Hill's personal life that bore no relation to the issues at hand have not been divulged.

I am under no illusion as to the difficulties that confront any author who seeks to reopen such a contentious issue. Many people on both sides of the controversy will be reluctant to revisit the divisive and disturbing events of that weekend of testimony; indeed, the Thomas–Hill case has become so disfigured by ideology and emotion that one has to wonder whether any reassessment of it can be honestly discussed. The very act of trying to do so will undoubtedly inspire reflexive charges of racism, sexism, and political motivation. Law professor Stephen Carter of Yale University, for example, in a *New Republic* review of recent books about the hearings, gave fresh evidence of the extent to which unfounded myths and rumors about both Clarence Thomas and Anita Hill have been enshrined as fact in the popular mind.* Coming as it did in this instance from a notably independent and judicious social critic, Carter's article renewed my doubts about the very possibility of opening these myths to objective inquiry, let alone dislodging them.

Carter's review attacked my *Spectator* article as the work of a "right wing journalist" who was trying to do "more of what the committee Republicans tried to do—that is, find people who will supply the evidence that Hill is either delusional or a fabricator, preferably both." He went on to suggest that I had cynically appealed to "popular stereotypes of black people as sensually obsessed, and women as vindictive and of black women as both." Only silence could inoculate an author against such unmerited attacks, and, I believe, it is precisely the fear of such attacks that best explains the deafening silence from my colleagues in the press on the facts of this case.

Were it not for Wlady Pleszczynski, the *Spectator*'s managing editor, this book would not have been written. Thanks to him and all of the folks at the magazine for opening their pages to me over the years.

Assistance from the John M. Olin Foundation and the Lynde and Harry Bradley Foundation enabled me to retain a research assistant, Hilary Adams, without whom my deadlines would never have been met.

I've been fortunate to work with two of the best literary agents a writer could have, Glen Hartley and Lynn Chu. Lynn's review of the early stages of the manuscript and her enthusiasm were particularly edifying. Tod Lindberg of the *Washington Times* also made helpful comments on an early draft of the manuscript.

I owe a special debt to my editor at the Free Press, Adam Bellow, whose perceptive and skillful editing was indispensable in the final stages of the writing. I would also like to thank Eileen De Wald, Managing Editor at the Free Press, for her exemplary commitment and professionalism.

My friend Ron Haft dispensed wise advice throughout the year, as did Bill Grey, who was the first to suggest that the "Real Anita Hill" article should be the basis for a book. I remain grateful to Bill for that encouragement and for much else.

Washington, DC
February 1993

---

*"The Candidate," *New Republic,* February 22, 1993, vol. 208, no. 8, issue 4075, pp. 29–35.

Introduction:
The Woman of the Year

And this is not a referendum on whether or not, whether or not sexual harassment is a grave offense. I said from the beginning, this is about whether or not sexual harassment occurred.
— *Senator Joseph Biden, October 10, 1991*

On Monday, October 7, 1991, Anita F. Hill announced in a press conference at the University of Oklahoma School of Law that she was ready and willing to testify in Congress about the inappropriate behavior to which Supreme Court nominee Clarence Thomas had allegedly subjected her a decade before. "I would be happy to cooperate in any investigation. If it means going and talking with the Senate, I am happy to do that."

Two weeks earlier, Hill had filed a confidential written statement with the Senate Judiciary Committee charging that Thomas had repeatedly pressed her for dates and discussed the contents of pornographic movies with her when she was his legal assistant in the administration of Ronald Reagan. Hours later, she gave a similar statement to the FBI. The Judiciary Committee, and then the bipartisan leadership of the Senate, weighed Hill's charges but concluded that the investigation could go no further if Hill's request for confidentiality was to be honored. The Senate vote on the Thomas nomination, therefore, would go forward.

Three days before the scheduled vote, however, the committee's decision was superseded when some person or persons unknown leaked the professor's allegations to the press, against the wishes of the Senate—and against the wishes of Anita Hill herself. And so, out-

1

doing the Army–McCarthy, Watergate, and Iran–Contra hearings, the most theatrical scandal in Washington history began to play itself out, a mix of race, ambition, passion, sex, political ideology, and, most of all, power.

Clarence Thomas, a sitting federal judge and the former chairman of the Equal Employment Opportunity Commission, the federal agency that polices sexual discrimination, had been closely examined in five FBI background checks and Senate confirmations during his thirteen-year career in Washington. The outspoken forty-three-year-old black conservative had made his share of enemies, but never before had even a hint of impropriety stuck to his name. His Supreme Court nomination had been assailed since it was announced in July, but before Hill's allegations were leaked more than the required fifty-one senators had announced in favor of the nomination.

As political protests from women's groups resounded through the capital, charging that the Senate had ignored and covered up Hill's allegations, the Thomas forces calculated that he might lose if the Senate voted without a further investigation of the charges. The Senators, in turn, believed that the political uproar necessitated hearing the allegations in a public forum.

After the leak, Thomas had issued a terse statement rejecting the allegations but had refused further comment. On the morning of Friday, October 12, he faced a Senate panel and a nationwide television audience:

> I have been racking my brains, and eating my insides out trying to think of what I could have said or done to Anita Hill to lead her to allege that I was interested in her in more than a professional way, and that I talked with her about pornographic movies or X-rated films . . . But I have not said or done the things that Anita Hill has alleged. God has gotten me through the days since September 25th, and He is my judge.

Next came Anita Hill, who entered the hearing room serenely, flanked by members of her family from rural Oklahoma. Not even the Democrats on the committee knew that what she was about to say would be so shocking and dramatic, compared with her earlier committee statement and FBI interview:

> He spoke about acts that he had seen in pornographic films involving such matters as women having sex with animals, and films showing group sex or rape scenes. He talked about porno-

graphic materials depicting individuals with large penises, or large breasts, involved in various sex acts . . .

On several occasions Thomas told me graphically of his own sexual prowess . . .

One of the oddest episodes I remember was an occasion in which Thomas was drinking a Coke in his office, he got up from the table, at which we were working, went over to his desk to get the Coke, looked at the can and asked, "Who has put pubic hair on my Coke?"

On other occasions he referred to the size of his own penis as being larger than normal and he also spoke on some occasions of the pleasures he had given to women with oral sex.

Perhaps the most memorable line of all came during questioning by committee chairman Joe Biden:

BIDEN: Again, it is difficult, but for the record, what substance did he bring up in this instance in the EEOC in his office? What was the content of what he said?

HILL: This was a reference to an individual who had a very large penis and he used the name that he had referred to in the pornographic material—

BIDEN: Do you recall what it was?

HILL: Yes, I do. The name that was referred to was Long Dong Silver.

When a visibly angry Thomas returned that evening to declare "I've heard enough lies" and then to denounce the proceedings as "a national disgrace" and a "high-tech lynching," the battle lines were indelibly drawn. The two accounts, sworn to under oath, were utterly irreconcilable. Thomas's denial was categorical. No dates, no movies, nothing. For her part, Hill had drastically raised the ante by transforming Thomas from a garden-variety workplace harasser into a sexual savage.

Indeed, one of the reasons the hearings provoked such a powerful public response was the fact that the accounts diverged so radically. The testimony seemed to rule out the most likely explanation of what had really happened—mixed signals, miscommunication, or even an affair gone sour between two young, attractive, single people in the workplace. No one could regard as normal discourse the things that Hill alleged Thomas had said and done; and Thomas had denied saying or doing *anything* in any event. In the Senate hearing room, in the press, and in offices and homes across America, the hearings would become a swearing contest, a case of "his word against hers," an epic struggle that would turn entirely on the question of personal credibility.

Not surprisingly, no one had witnessed the alleged behavior. While this made Hill's case difficult, Thomas was nevertheless placed in the more difficult position of having to prove a negative. Hill produced witnesses who remembered that she had complained of sexual harassment in the early 1980s. Thomas produced witnesses who reported that Hill had lavishly praised and repeatedly contacted him in the years following her alleged harassment. Hill's supporters described her as conservative—a straightlaced, deeply religious Republican who had no conceivable motive for coming forward other than a public-spirited concern for the honor and integrity of the nation's highest court. Thomas's supporters described him as a vigilant opponent of sexual harassment who conducted himself with an extraordinary degree of propriety and dignity at all times. Hill's supporters portrayed Thomas as a dangerous, ambitious, psychologically unbalanced, self-hating black, capable of boundless hypocrisy. Thomas's supporters, in turn, suggested that Hill was a fantasizing spinster put up to testifying by a sinister left-wing conspiracy. Most of the testimony, not to mention these reductive and insulting caricatures, did nothing to resolve the issues of fact at hand and only heightened public confusion.

The Senate, for its part, staged a show trial, allowing the sexual harassment charges—and the baseless innuendo that often passed for GOP countercharges—to be broadcast publicly but never settled. The very instant Hill's story broke, the pattern was set: all the players chose sides based on partisan loyalties and ideology, despite the unresolved questions and disturbing implications raised by the allegations. Neither side was willing to suspend judgment pending further investigation on the core question of who was telling the truth.

Before any evidence was adduced that the Judiciary Committee had in fact ignored Hill's charge for weeks before it was leaked to the media, organized groups of women came forward to condemn the committee for insensitivity to sexual harassment and demanded a full public venting of the allegations. A group of 120 women law professors, for example, released a statement calling for a public hearing, and seven female members of Congress marched from the House to the Senate with the same demand.

Charging that the men on the committee "just didn't get it," feminist activists formed an "Ad Hoc Committee on Public Education on Sexual Harassment." The group supplied each member of the Senate with a "fact sheet" on harassment that took Thomas's guilt for granted, and asserted on the basis of scant information that Hill's claim was a "typical case." Most of the professional activists, lawyers, and academics who have dedicated themselves to the issue of sexual harassment declared Hill's allegations manifestly true.

Meanwhile, Thomas's supporters in the Senate seemed scarcely more interested in moving beyond rhetorical manipulation to consideration of facts. They simply declared Hill's charges inherently false; Senator Strom Thurmond of South Carolina took the Senate floor the day after the allegations leaked to assert baldly that they had "no merit." Though no connection between Anita Hill and any anti-Thomas groups in Washington could be established, her allegations were quickly dismissed as a political plot to alter the composition of the Supreme Court. Senator Alan Simpson of Wyoming referred dismissively to "this sexual harassment crap," ominously warned that Hill would be "destroyed" in the process of coming forward, and later seemed to imply that she was a lesbian. Overreaching wildly, Senator Orrin Hatch of Utah charged that Hill's testimony had been inspired by the *Exorcist,* a novel about Satanic possession.

Unable to establish any motive, the Republicans produced a witness who barely knew Hill, but was nonetheless convinced that she harbored sexual fantasies about him. John Doggett's testimony, it turned out, seemed nothing more than an ordinary misunderstanding between the two about a canceled date. Waiting in the GOP wings was a psychiatrist who, though he had not examined the "patient," was prepared to testify that Hill had developed a "delusional system [with] elements of both erotomania and paranoia."[1] Though no one could explain why the alleged fantasy had lain dormant for ten years only to erupt upon Thomas's nomination to the Supreme Court, in the end many Republicans accepted Doggett's contention that Hill's testimony was the product of mental illness. This permitted the politically safe, but totally unsubstantiated, interpretation that Hill, though deluded, sincerely believed she was telling the truth. A press release from the office of GOP Senator Larry Pressler of South

Dakota illustrated well the moral obtuseness that interpretation permitted: "Pressler Votes for Thomas, Praises Hill."

Defending the Senate inquiry in a subsequent interview with the *Washington Post,* Senator Biden asserted, "There is nothing that we could have further investigated that would have enlightened us any more than we already knew."[2] This claim was fatuous, however. Biden had refused to subpoena the Senate staffers who had induced Hill to make her charges, and were later involved in leaking them. Questions about Thomas's personal life and about Hill's political beliefs were placed out of bounds. No testimony was heard from expert investigators of sexual harassment. When a former supervisor of Hill at the law firm where she worked in 1981 filed a sworn affidavit that directly contradicted her testimony about the circumstances of her departure from the firm, the Democrats quashed a Republican request to subpoena the firm's records, which could have settled the question. The committee struck a private deal with one potential witness who, according to media reports, might have also accused Thomas of sexual harassment, arranging for her *not* to appear, although her testimony might have damaged Hill. And a key discrepancy in the testimony of Hill's main witness, Susan Hoerchner, was inexplicably never pursued.

Supporters of both Thomas and Hill agreed in retrospect that the committee should have conducted a deliberate fact-finding mission rather than a hasty no-holds-barred smear session. GOP Senator John Danforth of Missouri, who had pressed to have the Senate bring in outside lawyers to handle questioning of witnesses, as occurred in the Iran–Contra investigation, expressed the view that Thomas was denied the chance to prove his innocence in an inquiry conducted with due process, rules of evidence, cross-examination of witnesses and the right to counsel. "There were not the minimal protections that common criminals get," Danforth said in a later interview. Senator Dennis DeConcini, Democrat of Arizona, found the process "inconceivable . . . I can't imagine anything more unfair to the man."

The supporters of Hill, who had her privacy rights revoked by the leakers before she even arrived in Washington, made the same argument. Decrying the "his word against hers" formulation that the hearings appeared to promote, Christine Littleton, a UCLA Law Professor, wrote:

> While it is true that much sexual harassment takes place out of the view of potential witnesses, it is not true that there is nothing else to investigate. The extremely short period (three days) between the decision

to air Professor Hill's allegations and the start of the public hearings provided almost no opportunity for the kind of investigation that might have settled doubts one way or the other.[3]

Once the allegations leaked, the committee could have opened a confidential inquiry conducted by trained investigators with subpoena power, met in executive session, and issued an authoritative report that either substantiated Hill's claims or cleared the air. Instead, the show trial proceeded, guaranteeing not only that the confrontation between the two witnesses would forever be seen through ideological blinders but also that the credibility of both Thomas and Hill would be forever left in question. Rhetoric, rumor, appearance, and prejudice would be the only bases for a conclusion that ultimately satisfied no one and condemned both the accused and the accuser. "It is a tragedy of major proportions," the columnist William Raspberry wrote, "that two splendid lives have been tarnished and that, absent some dramatic confession, cannot be restored."[4]

The performance of the media was no better. Once news of the charges broke, the media treated the Thomas–Hill scandal as a national referendum on sexual harassment rather than as a story about whether sexual harassment had been committed in this instance. A consensus quickly developed among ordinarily skeptical reporters that the allegations would be mythologized rather than investigated. Attention shifted from the merit of Hill's charges to the politically explosive issue of how the all-male Judiciary Committee had handled the allegations before the leak.

Though the media investigated the Iran–Contra affair for seven years, little journalistic effort was expended to advance the Thomas–Hill story on any front but the metaphysical. "The Thomas Nomination: The Senate and Sexism; Panel's Handling of Harassment Allegation Renews Questions About All-Male Club" was a typical front-page headline in the *New York Times*.[5] A year after the hearings, *Newsday*'s commemorative headline announced: "Men Still Don't Get It!"[6] Where were the stories about the facts of the relationship between Thomas and Hill when they worked together in the early 1980s? Where were the reporters trying to find out how Hill's allegations had been discovered and then leaked to the press, potentially in violation of the law? Why did a press corps that spent months delving into the most intimate aspects of the life of Clarence

Thomas make no effort to report even the most basic facts about Hill? In a long profile notable for its banality, the *Times* reported of Hill, "some of her closest friends here at the University of Oklahoma have trouble remembering any of her political beliefs beyond a commitment to the welfare of minority students on campus . . . she seems to have little interest in politics . . . several of her friends were stumped when asked about her private interests and beliefs."[7] Actually, it was the *New York Times* reporter who had so little interest in Hill's politics that he failed to wonder why her "closest friends" would know so little about her views.

Hill's credibility was not tested, but simply asserted to enhance the "he said, she said" melodrama. Certainly on the surface Hill appeared to be an impeccable witness. The *New York Times* called Hill "a credible woman . . . backed by credible witnesses." The *Washington Post* Style section carried a piece entitled "The Credible Accuser." *Time* magazine reported: "If Clarence Thomas had been a woman, he might have been Anita Hill."[8] But when one GOP senator, Pennsylvania's Arlen Specter, attempted to probe deeper, he was vilified in the media as if asking reasoned questions of an accuser were a crime. "A mean-spirited small town prosecutor," Anthony Lewis opined in the *New York Times*. Specter was declared "Public Enemy No. 2" (behind former President Bush) by the feminist leader Betty Friedan and targeted for defeat in the 1992 election.

Thus both the Senate and the press appeared content to regard the Thomas–Hill saga as a Rashomon-like standoff. *Rashomon,* the famous Japanese film directed by Akira Kurosawa, centers on the trial of a bandit who has been arrested for raping a woman in a forest in front of her husband, who is then murdered. The bandit, his accuser, a witness, and the dead man's ghost give four different and equally persuasive versions of the same events, demonstrating the perils of subjectivity and the elusiveness of absolute truth. In the end, Kurosawa seems to be saying, everyone is responsible, and no one is guilty.

Such formulations make compelling fiction; indeed, the conventions of drama demand that contradictions be resolved, and Kurosawa artfully exploited this psychic need to create a highly provocative and unsettling film. But in real life, real crimes are committed by actual people—sexual harassment, perjury, and the leaking of protected information among them. If, as seems apparent, increasing numbers of Americans believe that Clarence Thomas lied to get onto the Supreme Court and is therefore unqualified by character to hold his exalted position, serious damage has been done to the authority and dignity of the Court and to our whole system of justice, which depends on public confidence in the integrity of the federal bench.

For purposes of confirmation, Thomas won acquittal. He was confirmed on a vote of 52–48, the highest number of negative votes ever for a successful nominee. The decision was based not on a firm resolution of the case, but on the instant political reaction to the spellbinding weekend testimony, which drew some of the highest ratings in the history of television. National polls showed Americans believed Thomas over Hill by a two-to-one majority. There was no gap between women and men on the judgment, nor was there a meaningful difference between whites and blacks. Among blacks, support for Thomas's position was even higher after Anita Hill appeared than before, when Thomas had already won majority backing. The "men just don't get it" slogan notwithstanding, the Senate's two women, Democrat Barbara Mikulski of Maryland and Republican Nancy Kassebaum of Kansas, each voted with the majority of their political party.

The vote settled the confirmation question, but nothing else. Carol Gilligan, a Harvard psychologist, told *Newsweek* that the image of Anita Hill and the Senate Judiciary Committee would define the current age "the way Nick Ut's searing photo of a napalmed child captured the Vietnam era."[9] Spurred by the adverse outcome in the Senate, those who believed Anita Hill understandably refused to accept the judgment of the male-dominated body which they believed had failed to take her seriously in the first place, and took up her charge as a banner in a broader cultural conflict. The Anita Hill story thus took on an independent life, resonating profoundly through the country's political and popular culture, and she herself was soon transformed into "the woman of the year." Moved and inspired by her example, women ran for and were elected to positions of political authority in record numbers, and riveted the nation's attention on the widespread but largely hidden problem of sexual harassment in America's workplaces.

The 1992 political campaign was dubbed the "Year of the Woman" in the media. Emily's List, a group that gives seed money to women candidates, doubled its membership, raised three times what it had in the last political season, and became the largest Congressional political action committee. The "Anita Hill effect" was said to have been felt in Senate races in Illinois, where a virtually unknown black woman named Carol Moseley Braun knocked off incumbent Democrat (and

Thomas supporter) Alan Dixon in a primary and went on to become
the first black woman elected to the U.S. Senate; in Pennsylvania,
where Lynn Yeakel, a fundraiser for women's issues and a political
novice, won the Democrats' nod to take on Arlen Specter, and then
lost a close race in November; and in California, where Barbara
Boxer, one of the women from the House who had marched to the
Senate, and former San Francisco mayor Dianne Feinstein, won the
state's two Senate seats. A record forty-six women were elected to
the House of Representatives.[10] The Anita Hill effect may have also
influenced the presidential race, where a perceptible gender gap
among Republicans was said to have contributed to the victory of Bill
Clinton. Clinton, according to sociologist Michael Kimmel, is "Anita
Hill's revenge."[11]

Contrary to the dire predictions that were voiced when the Senate
rejected Hill's charges and confirmed Thomas ("Hill's experience
will deter victims, experts say," a banner headline in *USA Today* said),
the issue of sexual harassment took a front seat. Encouraged by Hill's
example, women came forward to reveal their own experiences. The
cataclysmic reaction to Hill's testimony made clear that sexual harassment occurs far too often, and that far too many women, fearful
of coming forward, have quietly tolerated such bullying. Even Ginni
Thomas, the wife of the new Supreme Court justice, said that she had
been sexually harassed on the job in 1986, before meeting her husband. "Every time a man and a woman are at the water cooler, Anita
Hill's right there between them," said Andrea Sankar, an anthropol-
ogist at Wayne State University in Detroit.

The Equal Employment Opportunity Commission reported that
10,522 people filed sexual harassment complaints in 1992, compared
with 6,883 in fiscal year 1991. After an attempt to whitewash the sexual assaults at Tailhook failed, the U.S. Navy became engulfed in a
sexual harassment scandal that led to the resignation of top naval of-
ficers. Fortune 500 companies offered re-vamped policies and special
sensitivity training on sexual harassment. Connecticut passed a law
requiring that all employers provide such policies and training. The
welcome shift was even said to have reached beyond the shores of the
United States. "France Rethinks Its Wink at Sexual Harassment," read
a *New York Times* headline.[12]

The "men's club" itself was rocked by sexual harassment charges.
Democrat Brock Adams of Washington declined to run again after
the *Seattle Times* published charges that he had molested a number of

women, and had raped at least one, and Senators Bob Packwood of Oregon and Daniel Inouye of Hawaii were investigated by the Senate Ethics Committee after several complaints of physical and verbal abuse were lodged against each of them. Senator Patty Murray of Washington, who won Brock Adams's seat in November, introduced legislation that for the first time would bring the Senate under the nation's sexual harassment laws.

Anita Hill, who had testified that she might have "made a mistake" in not speaking out against Thomas in 1982, was now not only an overnight authority on sexual harassment but, in the words of Marion Kaplan, the president of the New York Women's Foundation, a symbol of "a new and potent wave of feminism."[13] She was featured in *Glamour, Ms.,* on the cover of *Essence,* on *60 Minutes* and the *Today* show, and her story was dramatized sympathetically in episodes of two popular television series, *Murphy Brown* and *Designing Women.* The latter sitcom produced an episode called "The Strange Case of Clarence and Anita," described by its producer as a "valentine to all the women who believed Anita Hill was treated unfairly." Women in Minnesota announced a national drive to raise $250,000 to endow a chair for Hill at the University of Oklahoma, and Hill was appointed by Oklahoma's governor to a commission on the status of women.

Often garnering $10,000 to $12,000 an appearance, Hill spoke at Harvard, Yale, Penn, Rutgers, the University of California at San Diego, the University of New Mexico, and dozens of other schools. She was met by enthusiastic standing-room-only crowds, holding placards proclaiming "We Believe Anita" and "Graduate of Thelma and Louise Finishing School." Typical was a scene at Hamline University in St. Paul, Minnesota, where Hill told a crowd of more than 2,500 students, "We cannot stand back and expect that leadership will take the initiative on gender issues and race issues . . . And so what I want to do is challenge you to do what I have committed myself to do: to talk about these issues, to urge leadership on issues, to urge us to continue to move forward. We have a window of opportunity here. We have the world's attention." Hill then worked her way through a reception line, hearing over and over remarks like "you've really inspired me," "I'm very honored to meet you," and "you're a great person," according to an account in the Minneapolis *Star Tribune.* "I had anticipated coming so much," Wanda Rauma told the newspaper. "And I felt wholly fulfilled. I was surprised with the emotion I felt several times when she was talking. I felt this lump coming up and I don't know what that was all about." Women weren't the only ones moved. Student Derek Schmidt was quoted as saying, "I told her that I was not only shaking her hand for myself, but also for my mother and her colleagues."[14]

Hill received awards and cash bonuses from the American Civil Liberties Union, the American Trial Lawyers Association, and the National Women's Law Center, and was seen in the embrace of everyone from Barbra Streisand to Donna Shalala, now Health and Human Services Secretary. Representative Patricia Schroeder, the Colorado Democrat, recommended that Hill be named Attorney General. At the unaccredited New College of Law in San Francisco, Hill received an honorary doctorate of law, taking a place beside a previous recipient, Norma McCorveuy, the "Jane Roe" of *Roe* v. *Wade.* With *Ms.* magazine founder Gloria Steinem, Hill started a Coalition on Sexual Harassment and appeared at a conference entitled "Women Tell the Truth." Steinem described her dream: "After Clarence Thomas is impeached, President Eleanor Holmes Norton [Thomas's predecessor at the EEOC under Jimmy Carter] will name Anita Hill to the Supreme Court."[15]

At the 1992 convention of the American Bar Association, the future First Lady, Hillary Clinton, spoke to a luncheon session where Hill was presented with the Margaret Bent Women Lawyers Achievement Award. "All women who care about equality of opportunity, about integrity and morality in the workplace, are in Professor Hill's debt," said Mrs. Clinton. When dozens of lawyers resigned from the ABA to protest the award, ABA President J. Michael McWilliams issued an unlawyerly letter, explaining that the award was meant to honor Hill "for raising our nation's awareness" rather than to "attempt to address or recognize the specific allegations made."[16]

All the while, Hill remained silent about her own experience. She generally avoided interviews, talk shows, or uncontrolled question-and-answer sessions where she might be asked specific questions about the substance of her charges. She spoke instead, in the language of gender feminism, of the "powerlessness of women," and our "misogynist society." She argued that "having laws on the books isn't enough" and explained how harassment is rooted in young boys' heterosexual "rites of passage." Hill never renewed her charge against Thomas, never rebutted allegations of perjury and mental imbalance hurled at her during the hearings, never expressed disappointment that sexual harassment had not been enough to keep Thomas off the

Court, never publicly mentioned the name of Clarence Thomas again. "I can't say enough that we need to get beyond those hearings, because I think what those hearings come down to is me against him. And that we need to move beyond that," she told Ed Bradley of *60 Minutes.*

While Hill was canonized as the Rosa Parks of sexual harassment, Thomas, who had the not inconsiderable consolation of serving on the Supreme Court, continued to be demonized. The media was replete with stories and images casting Thomas's integrity as an open question. The supposition was that *Thomas* was somehow responsible for the fact that his confirmation had been a low point in modern political history. "His burden continues to be Sisyphean," *Newsweek* reported, "to erase the public's memory of him left by his lurid Senate confirmation hearing."[17] This, of course, he could not do; settling into a circumspect judicial rather than political role, Thomas did not comment on the allegations, or anything else, again.

". . . in spite of the support he received from the White House and his loud disclaimers of wrong doing, [Thomas's name] is irrevocably tarnished," Nellie Y. McKay wrote, approvingly, in a collection of essays on the scandal edited by the novelist Toni Morrison. "Until his death, ghostly shadows of Anita Hill's allegations will haunt his steps and more often than he may ever know cast doubts upon his public words. Anita Hill's case against Clarence Thomas did not close when the hearings were over; it rested."[18]

Thomas's implicit guilt became a staple of media commentary, popular culture, and Democratic rhetoric. While acknowledging the absence of new damaging facts to substantiate Hill's charges, NPRs Nina Totenberg, who broke the story, said in a spring 1992 speech at Stanford University that Thomas's career "may yet be ruined" by Hill's allegations. Totenberg observed that Thomas "faces constant references" to the hearings in evaluations of his work on the court. "Justice Thomas will certainly be scrutinized in a very uncomfortable way," she said.[19] Leading Democrats also accused Thomas of sexual harassment and perjury. At the 1992 Democratic National Convention, for example, Senator Barbara Mikulski boomed: "Never again will a woman who comes forward to tell her story before a committee of the U.S. Senate be assaulted for telling the truth." Mikulski later asserted that "the Year of the Woman" was really about "revenge for Anita Hill." In a prepublication news conference for his book *Advice and Consent* in June 1992, Senator Paul Simon of Illinois, a Democratic member of the Senate Judiciary Committee, said: "I think Anita Hill told the truth, Clarence Thomas did not."[20]

Thomas was hounded by protesters; he canceled an appearance at Seton Hall University's School of Law after the Women's Law Forum announced it would stage a candlelight vigil in protest. He was compared not only to Brock Adams (one cartoon showed a campaign poster papered over with the message "Brock Adams for the U.S. Supreme Court"), but to William Kennedy Smith, who was acquitted on a rape charge, and to Mike Tyson, who was convicted of rape. Garry Trudeau promoted in his cartoon strip the unsubstantiated story of a woman who claimed Thomas made sexual remarks to her at the EEOC seven years ago. The *Village Voice* ran a front-page photo of a pro-choice rally, showing a sign in huge block letters: "Clarence, Keep Your Horny Fingers Off Roe v. Wade."[21] The Long Dong Silver movie "Conquering Cock" was rereleased on video, bearing the logo: "The Supreme Court's Highest Rating, The All-Time Favorite of Justice Clarence Thomas!"

More disturbing was the thinly veiled attempt to use Hill's allegations to exert political pressure on Thomas's judicial decision-making. Paul Simon said that he was "still hoping" Thomas would "redeem himself" while on the court, implying that the sexual harassment cloud over Thomas's head might be lifted if he were to issue a few politically correct opinions. A Federal judge, A. Leon Higginbotham, issued an unprecedented "open letter" to Justice Thomas, instructing him on how to vote on the court to atone for his past sins.[22] A *New York Times* editorial assessing Thomas's first term on the bench connected the "rancor" surrounding the Thomas confirmation to a perceived lack of "judiciousness" in his Supreme Court votes.[23]

Such criticism only added to the mythical portrait of Clarence Thomas that had been painted by opponents during his often stormy tenure as a public official in Washington and, in the end, served as an incriminating backdrop for Hill's allegations. That portrait represented Thomas as an enemy of civil rights, a self-loathing black who acted as a hatchet man for Ronald Reagan, crippling the enforcement of civil rights laws. In this view, Thomas's overweening ambition, culminating in his Supreme Court nomination, had allegedly led him to abandon his roots and sacrifice the principles and beliefs that as a black American he was expected to hold. Moreover, he was considered unqualified for the posts he attained, a beneficiary of blatant racial pandering practiced by cynical Republican politicians who, like Thomas himself, were opposed to affirmative action for rank-and-file minorities. It was not a far step from these caricatures to the image of Thomas as an outlaw justice, a Jekyll-and-Hyde personality capable of repressing his massive guilt and thus lying to win confirmation.

Lance Morrow, a *Time* essayist who did not support the Thomas nomination, was one of the few observers who anticipated the political utility of Thomas's implicit guilt soon after the October hearings concluded:

> According to the polls, Americans around the country did not subscribe to the ideological conclusion to which so many in the woman's movement leaped—the appalling syllogism that: 1) sexual harassment is horrible and widespread (it has happened to me and to many I know); 2) Anita Hill (and only Hill, but that's enough because that's the way harassment happens) says he did it; therefore 3) Clarence Thomas is guilty as charged (without trial), should be kept off the Supreme Court, and bears the monstrous guilt of all men everywhere, so now that he is on the court all his future decisions, including any possible opinions on *Roe* v. *Wade*, are illegitimate, the product of his sick mind. And by extension, all future decisions by this conservative Supreme Court affecting women are contaminated by what Anita Hill claims to have happened ten years ago between a man and a woman in his office—words about pubic hair on a Coke and about a porn star with a large member.[24]

A third line of interpretation, which neither lionized Hill nor demonized Thomas, consisted of various "middle ground" theories. "With his mainstream cultural guard down, Judge Thomas on several misjudged occasions may have done something completely out of the cultural frame of his white, upper-middle class work world, but immediately recognizable to Professor Hill and most women of Southern working-class backgrounds, white or black, especially the latter," Harvard sociologist Orlando Patterson wrote in the *New York Times*.

> . . . I am convinced that Professor Hill perfectly understood the psychocultural context in which Judge Thomas allegedly regaled her with his Rabelaisian humor (possibly as a way of affirming their common origins), which is precisely why she never filed a complaint against him . . . If my interpretation is correct, Judge Thomas was justified in denying making the remarks, even if he had in fact made them, not only because the deliberate displacement of his remarks made them some-

thing else but on the utilitarian moral grounds that any admission would have immediately incurred a self-destructive and grossly unfair punishment.

Patterson's widely discussed theory understandably angered the staunch supporters of both Thomas and Hill. So did the social critic Camille Paglia's rejection of Hill's sexual harassment charge: "If Anita Hill was thrown for a loop by sexual banter, that's her problem." Though courageously dissenting from liberal orthodoxy on this question, neither Patterson nor Paglia could explain why, among the dozens of women from all walks of life with whom he had worked closely, Thomas had chosen to speak coarsely only to Anita Hill.[25] Yet the attention such pieces garnered showed that many, if not most, observers privately rejected the stark choice presented in the hearing that either the accused or the accuser was a psychopathic liar, and concluded that there were elements of truth and deception in both accounts. The powerful impression of sincerity made by both Thomas and Hill created tremendous pressure to resolve the conflicting stories, and each viewer did so in a highly idiosyncratic and often intuitive way.

The speculative middle-ground resolutions all began from the assumption that Thomas really said the things Hill claimed, though in a context that may have differed from the one presented in her testimony. This inevitably reinforced the notion that Thomas is—if not a sexual harasser—a liar nonetheless. Opinion among black Americans remained a well-spring of support for Thomas, but even most blacks apparently never accepted Thomas's testimony that *nothing* had happened of a sexual nature between himself and Hill that could have been the basis for her testimony. Jacquelyn Johnson Jackson, a medical sociologist at Duke University, wrote in the *Black Scholar:*

> About forty-eight of my black female and male friends and acquaintances (mostly social scientists) telephoned me from far and near during the Hill–Thomas cataclysm to see what I thought. We all agreed that Hill lied . . . Yet most of us think that something 'went down' between them. We do not dismiss sexual innuendoes by Thomas, but we question both Hill's situational descriptions of when they occurred and her own behavior toward him in those settings and her linguistic description of them.[26]

A Public Broadcasting Service documentary on how blacks viewed the hearings showed the community divided between those who supported Hill, and those who thought that for the sake of racial solidarity she should not have testified. "They said, 'My God, sexual harassment? He just talked to her.' They didn't want to hear about sexual harassment. No one said she was lying actually. It didn't matter," said the show's producer, Ofra Bikel. "The big thing was she should have shut up."[27]

Thus while the Senate and the press were happy to leave the Thomas–Hill contest unresolved, the issue of credibility *was* eventually settled, *de facto,* in favor of the Woman of the Year. As even Hill's critics were reluctant to assert Thomas's innocence, the burden of proof was subtly shifted from Hill onto Thomas. A year after the hearings ended, public opinion polls found that Hill had changed places with Thomas in perceived credibility. While national polls conducted at the time of the hearings showed that Americans—including women—believed Thomas's denials of Hill's charges by a 2–1 margin, a *Wall Street Journal* poll in October 1992 found that 44 percent of those surveyed believed Hill, while only 34 percent believed Thomas.[28] A December 1992 *Newsweek* poll found that 51 percent of women believed that Thomas had harassed Hill, compared with 27 percent in October 1991.[29] "Anita F. Hill was the loser in her battle with Clarence Thomas a year ago. But as time passes, she is looking more and more like the winner," the *Journal* reported on its front page.[30]

What no one seems to have noted, however, is that the year-later poll results measured not the public's closer reading and reflection on the facts of the Thomas–Hill case, but rather *distance* from the facts. Declaring the poll results evidence of a more settled and informed popular verdict is a misleading technique akin to polling a jury a year after they have heard testimony in a trial. No new facts had emerged since the hearings ended to justify this shift in judgment. Eight months after the hearings, the *Boston Globe* observed, "Since the days last fall in which witnesses rode rough and tumble over each others' reputation on national television, and perhaps because of the emotional fatigue caused by the extraordinary testimony, the matter of who was being truthful has been virtually boycotted by the media."[31] And one year later the *Journal* asked, "What factors have caused the profound change in public opinion to Prof. Hill's side? There have been no substantive new disclosures about the truth of either her allegations or Justice Thomas's flat denial."[32]

A special investigation of the scandal by the Senate focused on who leaked the Hill allegations to the media, rather than whether or not the allegations were true. "It was not part of our mandate to weigh the merits of the Thomas nomination or the truth of Anita Hill's allegations," the Senate special counsel, Peter Fleming, wrote. Unlike the Iran–Contra independent counsel, Lawrence Walsh, Fleming did not have prosecutorial power; he could bring no charges for false Congressional testimony. The question of "who leaked?" thus stood in for "who lied?"

This was not an unimportant question—indeed the leak produced the grossly unfair trial by publicity in the court of public opinion—but it too would be left unresolved. Because Congress exempted itself from the provisions of the Privacy Act, which makes it a crime for anyone to disclose confidential FBI reports, the leak was characterized as at worst a potential violation of Senate rules. "No crimes were committed," Biden was quick to say. Voting along party lines, the Senate rejected a Republican proposal that would have set the FBI immediately to work for thirty days to zero in on the leakers. Republican Senator Hank Brown of Colorado, the first to propose an investigation, called for the expulsion of any Senator found to have abetted the leak, and firing and charging with contempt of Congress for any guilty staffer. Brown released a draft proposal on October 8, but the Senate did not act until October 24. Rather than Brown's FBI investigation, the Senate approved the hiring of a special counsel, who had no more independence than a Senate staffer.

Peter Fleming did not start work until January 1992 and did not report until the following May. Moreover, his investigation was diluted by Senate Democrats who insisted that the leak of a Senate Ethics Committee report on the so-called Keating Five influence-peddling scandal also be examined. "It should have been done in the first thirty days. The delay gave everybody [on Capitol Hill] a chance to get their stories straight," Brown said in an interview. The lag left Fleming with little alternative but to subpoena testimony from the two reporters who broke the Hill story, National Public Radio's Nina Totenberg and Timothy Phelps of *Newsday*. Citing the First Amendment, the reporters refused to answer questions about their sources. Though the courts might well have enforced the Fleming subpoenas despite the reporters' claims, the Senate Rules Committee refused to take any action to compel the reporters' testimony, such as issuing contempt citations. The committee also quashed subpoenas requested by Fleming for the telephone records of the reporters.

In sum, the Senate sacrificed its ability to ensure witness confidentiality to the reporters' presumed first amendment rights. No Senator fought for the integrity of the institution, and a new form of confirmation terrorism was legitimized. "Whoever leaked the confidential FBI documents established a dangerous precedent in which anonymous character assassination can be an effective means of shortcircuiting the nomination process," Senator Mitch McConnell, Republican of Kentucky, said.[33]

The leaker or leakers got off scot-free.

Based on interviews with more than a hundred people and exhaustive searches of telephone and telefax records, Peter Fleming released his report on May 5, 1992. While failing to identify the leaker conclusively, the report demonstrated with devastating precision how "Senate staffers worked closely with interest groups not merely in an attempt to defeat Thomas but specifically in an effort to bring Hill's charges before the public," the Capitol Hill newspaper *Roll Call* observed. Perhaps because of its political import, the major media buried the Fleming report. A story appearing on page A18 of the *New York Times* deceptively suggested that the leak had sprung from *Republican* Senators.[34]

Hill's media image, therefore, is the only explanation for her "reversal of fortune" in the national opinion polls. The standard and prevailing image, which has gained acceptance not only with those who believed Hill but also among those who did not, holds that Hill came forward, of her own volition, simply to inform the Senate of Thomas's behavior, with no expressed intention of stopping his confirmation; that Hill's story was ignored by the Senate Judiciary Committee for weeks until a leak of her written allegations forced an investigation; that in her "swearing contest" with Thomas, Hill made no misrepresentations or omissions, and that therefore the two were of equal credibility (indeed, hers was greater since his was tainted by an evasive performance in the first round of hearings that struck many observers as dishonest); that Hill's charges against Thomas were first voiced ten years ago, as corroborated by four independent witnesses, and therefore could not have been concocted to derail the nomination, as some Republicans hastily charged; that Hill's case was "typical" of most authentic sexual harassment claims, and that questions by Republican senators suggesting otherwise were mean-spirited and abusive; that Republican strategists kept another credible Thomas accuser from offering testimony that would have established a pattern of abuse on his part, and covered up his affinity for pornography; and finally that Hill had no personal or political motivations to testify against Thomas, and thus had nothing to gain by doing so.[35]

But this image is based on a woefully thin factual foundation. Hill's discussions with the Judiciary Committee and other Senate staffers opposed to Thomas prior to the leak have never come into public view, nor have her crucial discussions about coming forward with her main witness, Susan Hoerchner. The mystery of who leaked and why—the very event that triggered Hill's public appearance—remains unsolved. There has been no attempt to compare Hill's sworn testimony with public records and the testimony of third parties to test its veracity. Nothing is known about Hill's witnesses, why they came forward, or the significance of their testimony. And little has been revealed about Anita Hill's background, beliefs, and character that might have established a motive.

These questions and others are as much a mystery now as they were in October 1991: Why did Hill wait ten years before notifying the authorities about Thomas's behavior? How did the Senate committee first learn of it? Did Hill have any reason to oppose the Thomas nomination? What really transpired between Thomas and Hill when the two worked together a decade ago? Did Thomas fit the profile of a typical sex harasser? If Thomas was not guilty, where could the salacious details in Hill's testimony have come from? Is Hill, after all, the right person to honor as the Rosa Parks of sexual harassment?

Neither Thomas nor Hill seems willing to lay these lingering doubts to rest. Neither consented to be interviewed for this book. Both appeared relieved that neither the Senate nor the White House pursued the perjury issue further. Hill declined to take a second turn on the witness stand, and when it was over Thomas was quickly sworn in, in an unusual private ceremony. Such an official inquiry, however, remains the best hope for laying the matter to rest, either with the impeachment of Thomas or the prosecution of Hill.

In the meantime, re-opening these questions will inevitably be a painful and unpleasant experience for the two people directly involved, as it may be for some readers. Neither Hill's nor especially Thomas's most avid supporters were particularly anxious to revisit these events, and their sentiments are not without foundation. The results of this inquiry present a much more complicated picture than the simplistic narratives advanced at the time of the hearings by either side, and supporters of both Thomas and Hill will find grounds to be troubled by it. Some of the evidence may seem as bizarre and as hard to believe as anything alleged in Hill's Senate testimony.

The untold story of the real Anita Hill is at odds with the myth of Anita Hill in every important respect, and therefore deserves a fair hearing from anyone who remains unsatisfied by the uninformed, politicized and emotional assertions that have characterized the pop history of the affair. In the course of this investigation, the official record of the Senate hearings will be examined more carefully than the Senators' histrionics and the distorting lights of national television cameras permitted at the time; evidence will be brought forth that has never before been made public, including sworn affidavits, confidential Senate interviews of witnesses, and sections of the FBI file on the Thomas nomination; numerous details from the Fleming report, veiled by a media black-out, will be unsheathed; and new information gleaned from extensive interviews will be reported.

This book is not about whether or not Clarence Thomas should have been confirmed to the Supreme Court. Nor does it seek to question whether sexual harassment is a serious offense. It is; and if buttressed by facts, it is an appropriate issue to raise in a judicial confirmation proceeding. Rather, it seeks to establish whether sexual harassment occurred *in this instance.* As chairman Biden said, that was the only question before the Senate, and we ought not to allow our just concern about the egregious problem of sexual harassment to silence further investigation and analysis of this case.

At this juncture, Anita Hill remains Thomas's sole accuser, and so the inquiry must focus on which of the two was the more reliable witness. The evidence will show that Hill misrepresented or suppressed various facts pertaining to her relationship with Thomas, her contacts with the Senate staff during the nomination proceedings, and her background, beliefs, and possible motives. The cumulative portrait indicates that Hill does not deserve the credence that she continues to be granted in so many quarters. As for Thomas, no evidence has been discovered to contradict his categorical denial that he committed sexual harassment, nor any aspect of his sworn testimony. By any reasonable evidentiary standard, he should be fully vindicated of Hill's charges.

How Anita Hill should be viewed and finally judged, however, is a separate and more difficult question. This book is certainly not an attempt to demonize Hill, who was as victimized and transformed by these events as Clarence Thomas, in ways that remain to be shown. Whether Hill's story and her subsequent Senate testimony was really a *lie,* in the sense of being knowingly false, and could thus be said to constitute perjury remains an open question, although some readers will probably be inclined to judge her harshly on the evidence. For others, the circumstances of Hill's "coming forward" as they will be revealed in these pages may tend to be exculpatory, relieving her to some extent of full responsibility for her actions, and shifting it at least partly onto those in Washington who pressured, cajoled, and induced her to testify. For those who share Hill's views and motives, on the other hand, or who believe that the undeniable benefits of her testimony in bringing new public awareness to bear on the issue of sexual harassment is finally more important than whether or not she was in fact harassed by Thomas, Hill's testimony may be justified, in retrospect, on the utilitarian moral grounds that govern public affairs.

Admittedly, the stated aim of settling the fundamental issue at hand may be unrealistic. Only two people know for certain whether or not Thomas sexually harassed Hill. As William Raspberry put it, the power of a sexual harassment charge, aired in the media and in a Senate proceeding with no rules of evidence, is such that, absent a dramatic confession from the accused or the accuser, no accumulation of facts or evidence, and no interpretation developed from those facts, is likely to foreclose spirited debate and contrary opinions.

In this sense, we may be left in a position analogous to the Alger Hiss affair, in that both cases may be larger than the facts. The nation has remained divided for more than 40 years over former Communist Whittaker Chambers's accusation that Alger Hiss, a top State Department official under Franklin Roosevelt, was a Soviet spy. As the Alger Hiss case was forever entwined in the politics of the Cold War, despite his conviction for perjury in 1950, Anita Hill's case will likely be forever wrapped in thick layers of sexual, racial, and judicial politics, in spite of the dictum "innocent until proven guilty," and regardless of the evidence.

Anita Hill herself acknowledged as much in a speech at Georgetown University on the first anniversary of Thomas's confirmation. She contended that her testimony failed to defeat the nomination because her account was deconstructed by the Senate and the press and then reconstructed in a "series of narratives" based on negative stereotypes of blacks, women, black women, career women, and single women. "Not only did the Senate fail to understand or to recognize me because of my lack of attachment to certain institutions, like marriage and patronage, they failed to relate to my race, my gender, my race and gender combined, and in combination with my education, my career choice, and my demeanor," Hill said. "Because I and my reality did not comport with what they accepted as their reality, I and my reality had to be reconstructed by the Senate committee with assistance from the press and others . . . through the questioning they tried to reconstruct my narrative and recreate their own narrative to explain what happened in my life."

Hill's speech, while it functions as an all-encompassing defense against *any* analysis of her case that does not accept her testimony at face value, does raise an important point. Certain Republican attacks on Anita Hill during her Senate testimony invoked all of the worst— and in Hill's case, false—images traditionally deployed against victims of sex-related crimes: either she asked for it; or she submitted to it out of burning career ambition; or she was suffering from frustrated romantic desires and "wishful thinking."

Hill was also correct in arguing that any effort to explain what really happened to bring herself and Thomas together in that dramatic historical moment involves "constructing narratives." Each fact requires interpretation. Every case rests on a theory. Ironically enough, though, Hill's complaint in this respect seems misdirected. For it is mainly her defenders (and Thomas's critics) who have taken up their pens to invent various narratives for understanding the scandal, solely through symbolism and literary convention, that demonstrate no better understanding of Hill's "reality" than did her Republican interrogators. Until now, there has been no effort to examine Hill's account on the evidence and to "reconstruct a narrative" dispassionately, and from a factual foundation. Readers will have to decide for themselves whether that alternative construction is persuasive.

1

The Shadow Senate

On the day before the scheduled public testimony of Clarence Thomas and Anita Hill, four Republican members of the Senate Judiciary Committee sent a private written request to the chairman, Joseph Biden, asking that U.S. Senate staffers also be called to appear under oath. When Biden refused the request, blocking the appearance of Senate staffers who were deeply involved in inducing Anita Hill to come forward with her sexual harassment allegations, a great deal of the background to the Anita Hill story was kept from public view.[1] That allowed a misleading image to be presented: an image of a woman who emerged voluntarily after ten years, pressured by nothing and no one but her own conscience, to tell a deep, dark truth about Clarence Thomas.

In a book of essays on the Thomas–Hill scandal collected by the author Toni Morrison, Nellie Y. McKay, a professor of American and Afro-American literature at the University of Wisconsin, encapsulated the conventional view of what lay behind Hill's Senate testimony: "That she agreed to make the allegations public when she did was testimony to her understanding of her civic duty in conjunction with her religious training and her sense of moral responsibility . . . she could do no less than tell the truth of her experiences as she knew them, as sordid as that was, and as difficult as she must have found the telling."[2]

Hill's supporters, of course, had no reason to question this account of how it all happened. "She stepped forward to clear her conscience; to break a silence long held because she believed so strongly that too much was at stake," said then-Senator Al Gore of Tennessee in the Senate debate on the nomination. "She had pushed these memories away through other confirmation hearings when Clarence Thomas came before the Congress. But this time, it was a nomination to the highest court in our land, a lifetime appointment that comes with an indelible impact on our future and our society. Anita Hill felt she had to, as she said yesterday, perform her duty as a citizen."[3]

Thomas's supporters, on the other hand, had a more urgent need to explain why he was being accused, falsely in their view, of sexual harassment. If Hill was lying, how and why did she end up making such a sensational charge on national television? But they advanced no explanation for how such a story could have originated, other than in a desperate eleventh-hour gambit to kill his nomination. "I believe these comments were made in an attempt to derail this nomination at the last minute," Senator Strom Thurmond insisted, while offering no evidence to support such a conspiratorial view.[4] "Left-wing interest groups, intent on derailing Clarence Thomas's nomination to the Supreme Court, knew they had to manufacture a bombshell relative to Thomas's character because they would not defeat him on the merits. Like aggressive public-interest lawyers, they picked their plaintiff and developed their facts," the conservative Free Congress Research and Educational Foundation charged.[5] Commenting on the Thomas camp's failure to provide any proof that the charge was concocted, Senator Bill Bradley of New Jersey said, "They set out to say she was part of a conspiracy of interest groups, the press, and U.S. Senate staff—all coordinating and keying off each other in a blatant smear—even though no one could explain the motive for her stepping forward or the connection between the groups and her powerful words."[6]

In Senator Alan Simpson's view, the story was "stuff from the moon." In a colloquy with Senator Biden, even the nominee was flummoxed. "Do you believe that interest groups went out and got Professor Hill to make up a story? Or do you believe Professor Hill had a story, untrue from your perspective, that, as referred to here, groups went out and found? Which do you believe?," Biden asked. "The story developed. I don't know how it got there," Thomas responded, satisfying no one.[7]

The questions of whether or not Hill's story was true and what motives she may have had for trying to stop the Thomas nomination cannot be seriously addressed without first accounting for how Hill's story "got there" in the first place. The answer to Biden's question can be discovered only by carefully reconstructing the curious events—the hushed telephone conversations, the political intrigues, the mixed signals, the sheer coincidences—of the summer of 1991. Hardly a last-minute invention, Anita Hill's story was being discussed within hours of Thomas's nomination in July 1991, and it first surfaced on Capitol Hill three weeks later, a full three months before her charges were leaked to the media and she testified publicly. At the outset, this seemed to result neither from Hill's urgent sense of moral and civic duty nor from a calculated conspiracy to defeat the Thomas nomination, but rather from a series of fortuitous circumstances that took on a life of their own.

The Thomas nomination itself was widely portrayed as a cold-blooded, cynical ploy by the Bush White House to replace a black liberal with a black conservative. "What happened was not a careful search for the best in the nation," Senator Paul Simon wrote in his book *Advice and Consent*. "The President wanted a black conservative, someone far enough to the right to satisfy both his hard-core rightists and African-Americans, and apparently did it."[8]

The truth of the matter was that George Bush had wanted to nominate Clarence Thomas to the Supreme Court well before it became known that the open seat would be Thurgood Marshall's.[9] When William Brennan stepped down from the Supreme Court in 1990, the initial instinct of the President was to nominate Thomas. C. Boyden Gray, Bush's counsel, and Attorney General Richard Thornburgh, however, objected that Thomas wasn't seasoned enough, having served on the Court of Appeals for the D.C. Circuit for only eight months. "If the president had no advisers, Thomas would have been nominated in 1990," one administration official involved in the selection process said. A little-known state judge from New Hampshire, David Souter, was selected instead.

So it was not unusual—nor is it evidence of political cynicism—that Thomas would have been at or near the top of the list when Thurgood Marshall, the first black American to sit on the court, stepped down on June 27, 1991. Had it been any other Justice, Thomas was still the most likely to have been picked.

Indeed, the fact that Marshall and Thomas were both black worked against, not for, Thomas's nomination prospects. "We were praying it wouldn't be Marshall's seat," one Thomas supporter in the administration said. Locked in a struggle with Congressional Democrats over racial quotas in the 1991 Civil Rights Act, Bush worried that nominating Thomas would ignite the charge of a quota appointment, as it later did.[10]

While Thomas was not therefore a "quota" appointment in the rigid sense that one black American was chosen to replace another for the "black seat," or to represent "black opinion," his racial heritage, and the trials and tribulations of his life, did constitute an asset for the high court in the President's view, as did his conservative judicial philosophy. Thus the White House strategy of emphasizing the nominee's background in presenting the nomination while denying that the choice was a quota appointment was faithful to the spirit in which he was chosen. But the denial of the quota charge seemed to constitute a denial that race had been a factor at all, and the White House, cowed by a decade of Republican rhetoric about a "colorblind society," never explained in a straightforward manner what role race had played. This opened the administration up to charges of hypocrisy that cast a pall over the nomination from almost the moment it was announced.

As for Thomas's conservatism, the virtual silence on this score from the nominee and his sponsors—consistent with the reluctance of Presidents to concede that philosophy and politics are part of the selection equation—only served to obscure the choice further.

After thoroughly reviewing Thomas's record on the appeals court, Gray sought to ascertain whether or not Thomas felt ready to accept the assignment, whether he had the confidence, and the iron stomach, it would take to get confirmed. Ironically enough, the one subject on which no one in the administration anticipated trouble was Thomas's personal background. Unlike the recent nominees, Anthony M. Kennedy and David Souter, who were new to Washington life, Thomas had been living under a microscope as a public official for a decade, and he had been through the same drill as recently as eighteen months before for his appeals court confirmation, which was approved overwhelmingly.

At 4 P.M. on the day that Thurgood Marshall resigned, Thomas was interviewed at the Justice Department by Gray and Thornburgh. Earlier in the day, Gray had called Thomas and asked him if he wanted to "take a walk." Thomas asked Gray to send a friend of his who worked in the White House counsel's office, Mark Paoletta, to come and get him, and Thomas was picked up in a Jeep Cherokee on a street corner near the appeals court and driven through a rarely used entrance to the Justice Department. Gray satisfied himself that Thomas was ready and pressed for his appointment.

Thornburgh wasn't so sure. Considering how judicial confirmations had become three-ring media circuses in recent years, the main question was whether or not Thomas was confirmable. Some officials in the Justice Department felt that Thomas—whose opposition to racial quotas and advocacy of self-help strategies for black empowerment was anathema to the civil rights establishment in Washington—was too controversial, perhaps another Robert Bork, who in 1987 had become one of a handful of Supreme Court nominees in history to be rejected by the Senate.

In an Oval Office meeting with the President on Friday, Gray argued that Thomas should be named outright. But the Attorney General prevailed in having the choice put off until another candidate, Judge Emilio Garza of the Court of Appeals for the Fifth Circuit in Texas, could be considered. Garza flew to Washington for an interview, and William Barr, the deputy attorney general, and Gray questioned him on Saturday morning. His interviewers found Garza and his legal writings to be less than impressive.

Nonetheless, over the weekend the Washington media became convinced that Garza, a Hispanic thought to be more moderate in his views than Thomas, would be the nominee. Like Justice Souter, dubbed the "Stealth nominee" in 1990 and chosen in part because his obscurity would make him easier to confirm, Garza had no "paper trail," no controversial record to contend with. And the Republicans, it was thought, stood to make more inroads with Hispanic voters than blacks. Yet in one of the few bold strokes of his presidency, Bush didn't follow this conventional wisdom. Word of Bush's "surprise" announcement at Kennebunkport, Maine, on Monday, July 1, that Thomas would be nominated to replace Marshall dominated the television news throughout the day.

Three time zones removed, in Norwalk, California, a woman named
Susan Hoerchner flicked on her TV set to learn that an outspoken
black conservative named Clarence Thomas had been named to the
court. Clarence Thomas? Wasn't that the man who had sexually harassed her friend Anita Hill a decade ago when she and Hill had
worked in Washington? Hoerchner described this critical moment
three months later, when she was interviewed by Senate lawyers before she testified for Hill. Hoerchner listened closely to the July 1 television report on Thomas's work history: sitting Federal judge on the
D.C. circuit, former Chairman of the EEOC, former Assistant Secretary of Education. "I just remember waiting for them to explain his
background and then yelling to my husband, 'He's the one!' "[11]

Soon thereafter Hoerchner picked up the phone and called directory assistance in Norman, Oklahoma, remembering that Hill was
a professor in the law school at the university there. The two women
hadn't spoken to one another in seven years, since crossing paths at
a professional seminar in 1984. Hoerchner's call on July 1 to Oklahoma was placed without a hitch, as the professor's home telephone
number was listed in the directory. Despite not having spoken to her
friend in years, Hoerchner cut directly to the chase. She asked if Hill
had heard the news that Clarence Thomas—that "pig," Hoerchner
called him—had been named to the Supreme Court. According to
the FBI interview of Anita Hill:

> Hill did not discuss the sex conversations with Hoerchner after the win-
> ter of 1981, until the announcement of Thomas's nomination for the
> Supreme Court. Hoerchner called Hill to tell her of this and said she
> could not believe it since he was such a "pig."[12]

According to Hoerchner's interview with the Senate staffers, she
asked Hill if she was going to say anything about Thomas, "and she
[Hill] did not answer that directly." Hoerchner was "really surprised."
She thought Hill would want to talk. Apparently, however, Hoerchner never explicitly asked Hill if Thomas was the man who had sexually harassed her a decade earlier. She simply assumed he was. In the
interview, which took place two days before Hoerchner testified, a
group of Democratic and Republican Senate committee staff lawyers
took turns questioning her. At one point, Hoerchner was asked:

> Q. Let me go back to one thing. You said you asked her, "Are
> you going to say anything?" Two questions. The first one is, is
> that as close as you can recall or paraphrase? Did you provide
> any more detail?

A. You know, she knew I knew. I knew she knew I knew.

Q. And what was it that you were referring to when you said, "Are you going to say anything?"

A. The sexual harassment that she told me about ten years previously.

This vague exchange between Hoerchner and Hill—amounting to little more than an exercise in telepathy—will later be seen to permit the interpretation that the sexual harassment that Hill told Hoerchner about ten years previously had nothing whatever to do with Clarence Thomas. Hill went along with Hoerchner's intimations that day on the phone, but she did not elaborate, for reasons that will shortly become evident.

A strawberry blonde with aviator-style glasses, Hoerchner then asked Hill to release her from an "oath" that she had taken ten years earlier never to discuss the matter with anyone else. Hill agreed to do so, thereby indicating an initial willingness to circulate the story, provided she did not have to do so herself. Was Hill willing to have her friend speak the truth on her behalf? Or had she for some reason knowingly allowed her friend to proceed based on a misapprehension?

Three weeks later, in late July, Hill called another old friend from Yale, Gary Liman Phillips, who was then a staff attorney with the Federal Communications Commission. The two had been friends in Washington in the early 1980s during the time that Hill was working for Clarence Thomas, first at the Department of Education and then at the EEOC. Since leaving Washington, Hill had maintained regular contact with Phillips, speaking by telephone every three or four months, and getting together for dinner when she would come back into town. When Phillips casually asked Hill what she thought about the Thomas nomination, Hill told him—for the first time in the history of their relationship—that she had left Washington in 1983 because Thomas had sexually harassed her.

When Phillips was interviewed as a potential witness by Judiciary Committee lawyers on the day in October that the Thomas–Hill hearings opened, he described that July call from Hill. (Phillips was never summoned to give public testimony.)

Q. When did you first come to know of Professor Hill's allegations of sexual harassment?

A. Shortly after Judge Thomas was nominated, Anita called me at work, just to say hello and to catch up, and we were just, you know, talking about things in general, how we were. Then I said, "You're probably sick of this question but what's your impression, what did you think?" and she then told me that the reason she left the EEOC was that she had been sexually harassed by Judge Thomas when she was there.

Q. Did she tell you the specific nature of her allegations or did she—well, go ahead.

A. No. And I didn't ask because, as I said, Anita was a very private person and she was respectful of other people's privacy, and I felt like this was probably awkward and an invasion of her privacy to press for lurid details. . . .

Q. Did she tell you she was going to go forward and tell anyone else of this during the nomination process?

A. She told me she was not. She told me she was not inclined to.[13]

Three weeks after the nomination, Hill was still unwilling to discuss her feelings about Thomas or to say much about what had happened ten years before. If the idea of seeing a sex harasser confirmed to the Supreme Court greatly troubled her conscience, as she later testified, she was not at this point willing to take action to stop it. The question was, why not? Did she have legitimate fears of the consequences of coming forward? Was she repressing an experience that was too painful to relive? Or was she trying to figure out how to implement Hoerchner's suggestion?

In neither conversation did Hill indicate an interest in directly approaching officials in Washington with a charge against Thomas. In fact, she specifically indicated the opposite to both Hoerchner and Phillips. Her friends had broached the subject of the Thomas nomination, not the other way around. And when it was brought up, Hill told them she was not inclined to talk about it. But if Hill had wanted this information to remain totally secret, why did she release Hoerchner from her oath? And why did she tell Gary Phillips, a Washington attorney with connections to Capitol Hill staffers?[14]

The story might have gone no farther than these phone conversations with Hoerchner and Phillips. Although it is not known who, if anyone, Hoerchner spoke to about the charge, Phillips told the interviewers that he soon relayed the information to two other people in Washington: his male roommate, who had once met Hill, and someone else whom Phillips identified only as a mutual friend.

   Within a few days of Hill's conversation with Phillips in late July, a still-unidentified guest at a Washington dinner party—a party also attended by Nan Aron and George Kassouf of the Alliance for Justice, a leading lobby in the anti-Thomas campaign—repeated the story. When the Thomas nomination came up in conversation, this guest remarked that he had heard about a woman who was teaching law in Oklahoma, who had worked for Thomas at the EEOC, and who claimed to have been sexually harassed by him.

   According to the report of special counsel Peter Fleming, the Senate's leak investigator in the Anita Hill affair:

> Both Aron and George Kassouf, director of the Alliance's Judicial Selection Project, told Senate staffers that the information had reached them from a friend of a friend of Hill's who had described her allegations at a dinner party. They refused to identify the friend, but did say it was a man living in Washington.[15]

   It is not clear whether "the man living in Washington" referred to here was the friend of Hill, in which case they were certainly speaking of Gary Phillips, or the friend of the friend of Hill, in which case they meant that a male friend of either Phillips or Susan Hoerchner passed along the story. In either case, the identity of the dinner party guest is not important to the sequence of events. What is important is that in July the harassment charge was divulged to a group of people in Washington who were eager to defeat the Clarence Thomas nomination, and furthermore that this occurred without Anita Hill's explicit knowledge or consent. If she wanted the charge to remain a secret, Hill apparently was quite naïve in having mentioned it at all to someone in Washington, where gossip travels at the speed of light. On the other hand, if Hill had wanted to get the rumor mill churning without taking responsibility for initiating anything, she must be judged to have been very shrewd indeed.[16]

   This much was certain: The Anita Hill story took on a life of its own as the result of this fortuitous development. If Nan Aron and George Kassouf had stayed home that Friday night in July, the Clarence Thomas sexual harassment story might well have evaporated in the midsummer heat. It also seems certain that whatever Hill's thoughts were, she had little idea what she was unleashing in her murky conversations in early July about sexual harassment. Nor could she anticipate to what lengths the Thomas opposition would go in order to stop him.

This was the first time that *any* story about Clarence Thomas and sexual harassment had entered the collective consciousness of the Washington Beltway. Once it did, and particularly as the campaign against Thomas faltered on all other fronts, the charge was bound to be used as ammunition in the war against the nominee. The forces arrayed against Thomas would have it no other way. The only question was how and when. On July 28, an article in the *Boston Globe* reported: "The major civil rights and civil liberties organizations, many of them led by veterans of the Bork battles, are sharing research and coordinating strategy . . . The official said, for instance, that opposition groups have been withholding some damaging information about Thomas's record, and will time its release to achieve maximum impact."[17] Whether the reference was to Anita Hill's charges or to something else, at a minimum the quote betrayed the partisan mindset of the anti-Thomas camp. The opposition was planning an October Surprise.

The Clarence Thomas–Anita Hill conflagration was the capstone of a gradually escalating political and cultural war between liberals and conservatives for control of the nation's courts that began more than thirty years ago. This war had been the inevitable consequence of a shift in the flow of power toward the courts and away from the political branches. Under Chief Justices Earl Warren and Warren Burger, the judiciary had come to be seen as a political instrument. Political confirmations were the logical result.[18]

For three decades the courts had given important victories to the supporters of liberal social policies: establishing a constitutional right to abortion, upholding the constitutionality of and even mandating racial quotas and school busing, outlawing the death penalty and school prayer, and expanding the rights of criminal suspects and prisoners. Not coincidentally, the lion's share of these victories came in areas—abortion on demand, quotas, capital punishment—where victory might not be won through the political process. Controlling the outcome of the courts' pronouncements so that the "good guy" plaintiffs won, whether they be labor unions, civil rights groups, consumer advocates, or the disabled, became the key to the political fortunes of contemporary liberalism.

The problem was that Presidents appointed federal judges. While the presidency had been in the hands of Republicans for twenty of the twenty-four years before President Clinton's election in 1992, decades of liberal jurisprudence did not trigger a backlash among conservatives until the election of 1980. The appointees of Presidents Nixon and Ford had done nothing to disturb the liberal gains in the courts and had even enhanced them in many areas. But President Reagan came to office pledging to reverse the power shift by appointing judges whose narrow reading of the Constitution would return many of the culturally divisive questions—none more so than the abortion rights guaranteed in *Roe* v. *Wade,* settled in favor of liberals by the courts—back to Congress and to state legislatures, where liberals feared that they would lose these court-provided rights. There was disagreement among conservatives about the validity of many of these "rights," but there was a broad consensus that if they were to be provided, this should come through the political process rather than be discerned in the Constitution by unelected judges.

Understandably, Reagan, and later George Bush, ran up against the big organizations—the abortion-rights lobby, the American Civil Liberties Union, the NAACP Legal Defense Fund, the Women's Legal Defense Fund, the Ralph Nader "public interest" groups, labor unions, trial lawyers—that were litigating and winning their battles in the courts. These groups were motivated by their fervent belief in rights for workers, women, minorities, and gays; redistributing wealth; preserving the environment; deterring police misconduct; and a host of other causes. Since years of liberal jurisprudence had helped secure these goals, over time these groups developed a vested interest in the makeup of the judiciary, and they fought hard to protect that interest when it was threatened.

Consider, for example, the political and financial impact on the civil rights organizations once the courts, rather than require racial quotas, began to stand in the way of implementing them. Their constituents, the mostly middle-class blacks and women who benefit from quota regimes, would suffer directly from such decisions. And much of their business—litigating employment discrimination cases, lobbying government and private industry to adopt quotas, consulting on how best to put quotas in force—would vanish. To cite another consideration, abortion rights groups could more simply and cost-effectively campaign to hold onto a fragile majority on the Supreme Court than take their case to fifty state legislatures.

To maintain their eroding position in the courts in the Reagan–Bush era, the lobbying and litigating groups had only one place to turn: the U.S. Senate, which under the Constitution must confirm executive nominations for the judiciary. The groups needed fifty-one votes in the Senate to block judges whom they viewed as ideologically unacceptable. Though this task became easier when the Democrats won control of the Senate in 1987, at least a dozen Democratic Senators were considered to be swing voters whose socially conservative constituents favored judges who, like the Republicans in the White House, advocated a restrained judicial role. Thus the liberals could never hope to attain the votes they needed to stop conservative nominees without radically altering the traditional nature of the judicial confirmation process. They accomplished this by shifting the locus of power in judicial confirmations from the Senate, with its constitutional advice and consent powers, to a loose coalition of special-interest lobby groups, zealous Senate staffers, and a scandal-hungry press corps: a coalition worthy of the name the "Shadow Senate."

The Shadow Senate consisted of a dozen or so key operatives who organized or facilitated the opposition to conservative judicial nominees, from Chief Justice William Rehnquist in 1986 and Robert Bork in 1987 to Clarence Thomas in 1991. Such ideological warriors, to be sure, were not an unknown breed in Washington, on either side of the political aisle. The closest approximation of the liberal Shadow Senate, in fact, may have been the hard-charging shadow government that emerged in the Iran–Contra affair, a cast of characters who were willing to stretch the rules and mislead Congress for the sake of foreign policy ends in which they strongly believed. The Shadow Senators, too, were men and women of great zeal and good motives. However, like Oliver North and Richard Secord, in the Anita Hill case they finally went too far.

In the political pressure cooker, the opposition to judicial nominees started *outside* the Senate, not inside. One of the leading figures in generating this pressure was Nan Aron, the executive director of the Alliance for Justice. A veteran activist, Aron had been an EEOC trial lawyer in the 1970s under Eleanor Holmes Norton, and then a member of the ACLU's National Prison Project, before joining the Alliance in 1979. A self-styled coalition of public interest law groups whose stated aim was to achieve social change through litigation, the Alliance was the nerve center of the opposition campaigns, establishing in 1985 a Judicial Selection Project to monitor the Reagan Administration's appointments. As it happened, Aron's group, the first to pick up the Anita Hill rumor, was the functional equivalent of an opposition research team in the judgeship wars. Their free-lance investigations, however, were conducted with none of the probity, and none of the regard for the rules of evidence and due process, that official investigations by the Justice Department, the FBI, or even the U.S. Senate usually display.

Judicial candidates could be sunk by the Alliance before any Senator had a chance to make a judgment. Mere rumors circulated to Democratic Judiciary Committee staffers by the Alliance sometimes sufficed to doom candidates before they were even nominated. The Alliance's own literature described its mode of operation:

> When the Alliance received word that U.S. Magistrate William Turnoff was being considered for the Southern District of Florida, the [Judicial Selection] Project immediately launched an investigation. Several public interest attorneys who appeared before Turnoff questioned his courtroom demeanor and respect for the rights of women.[19]

Turnoff wasn't nominated. The Alliance also boasted of having twice blocked the pending judicial nominations of Michael Horowitz. His offense: "As former legal counsel to OMB chief David Stockman, Horowitz was one of the principal architects of the Reagan drive to dismantle the government regulatory apparatus." In addition, Horowitz was cited by the Alliance for a "celebrated temper, and closed-mindedness."[20]

Aron had more leeway to go after Clarence Thomas than the mainline liberal groups; the Alliance drew more of its sponsorship from groups like NOW and from a cluster of Ralph Nader organizations like the Center for Law in the Public Interest, than from the traditional civil rights groups like the NAACP or the labor unions, which were slower to oppose the Thomas nomination. The Nader groups, in turn, were supported in part by the Association of Trial Lawyers of America. In areas of the law like employment discrimination and product liability, the trial lawyers had a huge financial stake in the disposition of judges, who were to determine the viability of their claims as well as the availability of punitive damage awards, where lawyers take as much as one-third to one-half.

The Alliance for Justice had been the only special-interest group to fight vigorously against Thomas's circuit court nomination in 1989. Part of the fight had been conducted publicly, but a good deal of it was waged behind closed doors. Just before he was nominated, the Alliance sent a secret memo arguing against Thomas's qualifications to the American Bar Association's Standing Committee on the Federal Judiciary. This is the body that decides a nominee's ABA rating, whose stated bases are integrity and competence.[21] The memo may have been influential in the ABA's decision to give Thomas a midlevel "qualified" rating in 1989.

Though the ABA had been criticized by Republicans in recent years for acting as a cat's paw for the organized Left, its official ratings, while not taken as seriously as they once were, were still important because they generated headlines. The Alliance, therefore, tried hard to influence the ABA. As a matter of standard practice, the ABA provided the Alliance for Justice with the names of potential nominees supplied to it by the White House for evaluation in a prescreening procedure before nominations were made. That inside information permitted the Alliance—which passed the names along to other groups in the Shadow Senate like People for the American Way, the NAACP, and the Women's Legal Defense Fund—an early opportunity to influence ABA decisions on judicial qualifications and thus to determine who did or did not get nominated by the President. This was a rather breathtaking example of how a marginal pressure group was able to affect the deliberations of a mainstream institution like the ABA.[22]

While the Alliance continually faulted the Bush Administration for appointing too many white men to the courts—"I can't believe the administration can't find 50 conservative blacks or 50 conservative women," the Alliance's George Kassouf said in March 1991[23]—that changed when Clarence Thomas came along, and the group concluded that this conservative black nominee was unqualified to be a judge. For the Supreme Court nomination, the ABA gave the Alliance for Justice the empirical gloss it needed to impugn Thomas's abilities. The ABA had three rankings for Supreme Court nominees— well-qualified, qualified, and not qualified. The ABA's rating committee, whose membership included the Boston attorney Alice Richmond, a vocal abortion rights supporter, gave Thomas an overall "qualified" rating, with two members voting that he was "not qualified," and one member not voting. The ABA panel's rating for Thomas was the lowest that any successful Supreme Court nominee had received since the ratings began forty-five years ago.[24] On the issue of the nominee's integrity that would later be raised in the Anita Hill hearings, however, the committee, after conducting more than a thousand interviews with professional colleagues of Thomas, was effusive in its praise. "Virtually all comments on Judge Thomas's integrity, character, and general reputation were highly favorable. Many people who know Judge Thomas remarked, as did one United States Court of Appeals judge, that he is a 'good, caring human being,' " the ABA's report said.[25]

As a result, Thomas's qualifications became a major theme of his detractors, at least among those who were white. Most black leaders, in contrast, barely mentioned the criticism because they believed it had a racist edge. Indeed, it was an awkward spectacle to see white advocates of quotas based on race denouncing a black man as an unqualified racial token.

Though it may have been a hypocritical argument, this objection was grounded in the legitimate concern that Thomas lacked the seasoning and legal wisdom that were desirable in a Supreme Court nominee, since he was quite young, had been a judge for only eighteen months, and had practiced law for only a short time in the late 1970s. However, it deserves to be acknowledged that if there was to be such a standard, it ought to have been applied universally. Justice Souter, for instance, had not written his first court opinion as a federal judge when he was named to the high court. Joseph Story, John Marshall, Louis Brandeis, and Felix Frankfurter, regarded as four of the greatest justices in history, had never been judges at all before they went on the high court. More recently, neither Earl Warren, Byron White, Lewis Powell, nor William Rehnquist had any judicial experience prior to their high court appointments. Justice Potter Stewart had been the Deputy Mayor of Cleveland. The qualifications issue had never dogged any of them.[26]

Certainly in relative terms Thomas was qualified for the Supreme Court, as he has subsequently demonstrated. Whether or not he was, as President Bush said in introducing the nominee, the "best qualified" for the post was a manufactured issue arising from Bush's notorious use of imprecise language. Bush's prepared statement had said that Thomas was "the best man for the job," a thoroughly defensible assertion, implying as it did an element of political calculation. In response to a question, Bush then defensively said Thomas was "the best qualified," an impromptu bit of presidential hyperbole that was disingenuously seized upon by Thomas's opponents. After all, everyone in judicial circles knew that the nominees who are the "best qualified" on paper are routinely passed over by Presidents. And when superbly qualified nominees are chosen, they may be rejected by the Senate because they do not meet the Senate's subjective criteria. "They said Thomas had no scholarship, hadn't written many opinions," said Senator Alan Simpson, the GOP minority whip and

Judiciary Committee member. "I loved that one. It was hypocrisy. I would say, 'Oh, we had one of those. His name was Bork.' "[27]

Such fine distinctions, of course, count for nothing in Washington. Thus the President's "best qualified" claim was blown out of proportion and ingrained in the nation's memory. It became a source of derision, and, perhaps, genuinely insulted feelings among many black jurists, lawyers and legal academics who were technically better qualified than Thomas but would not necessarily bring his conservative view of the judiciary or his fierce independence to the court.

Aron and her group were the most deeply hidden operatives in the judge's war. Higher up in public profile were such other interest-group leaders as Kate Michelman of the National Abortion Rights Action League, the top abortion-rights lobby in Washington. NARAL, a grass roots, direct-mail-funded organization with chapters in forty-four states, had ample resources to pour into advertising campaigns against judges it opposed. Michelman frequently testified against judicial nominees before the Senate, most dramatically in the Thomas case, when she told the moving story of her own decision to have an abortion in 1970. Living in Pennsylvania at the time, Michelman had had to locate a husband who left her pregnant and financially destitute to obtain his written permission to have the procedure. Unlike Nan Aron, Michelman had access not only to the Senate staff but directly to prominent liberal Senators.

There was also Ralph Neas, a veteran Capitol staffer who was the head strategist for the Leadership Conference on Civil Rights. This coalition of 180 civil rights and religious groups had its roots in the civil rights struggles of the 1950s and 1960s. It pursued a wide-ranging legislative agenda on Capitol Hill that extended well beyond judicial nominations. A liberal Republican, Neas was known as a self-promoter who picked his fights carefully and did not like to lose. Generally the leading organizer of the opposition's efforts on judges, Neas convened daily strategy sessions so that the array of liberal groups could coordinate their activities.

Rounding out the circle were Judith Lichtman, a top-flight feminist lawyer who ran the Women's Legal Defense Fund, a litigating and lobbying organization dedicated to eradicating "gender discrimination," including sexual harassment and legal restrictions on abortion; Molly Yard and Eleanor Smeal of NOW; and Art Kropp and Melanne Verveer of People for the American Way, a 250,000-member organization founded in 1980 by television producer Norman Lear specifically to use the medium of television to fight for "constitutional liberties," which to PAW meant preserving liberal control of the courts.[28]

These and other interest-group leaders worked hand-in-glove with ideologically sympathetic Senate staffers, like Ricki Seidman, Senator Ted Kennedy's investigator on the Senate Labor Committee, who had previously been legal director of People for the American Way. Seidman had designed PAW's advertising strategy against Judge Bork. His supporters had charged that one notorious ad contained ninety-nine misstatements of fact. Before working for PAW, Seidman had been a professional private eye. Just as Kennedy had brought a man named Anthony Podesta from People for the American Way to his staff during the Bork confirmation, Seidman joined Kennedy's staff within days of Thomas's nomination in July. At a reported salary of $82,000, Seidman was assigned to one of Kennedy's Labor Committee subcommittees.[29]

Another very involved Senate staffer was James Brudney, a Yale Law School graduate who had clerked for Supreme Court Justice Harry Blackmun and had practiced law in a downtown Washington firm. He joined Senator Howard Metzenbaum's Labor Committee staff in 1985, developing a reputation as one of the most effective staffers on the hill, particularly on behalf of worker's rights. Brudney was smart, diligent, and patient in his work. In a speech on the Senate floor, thanking Brudney for his efforts on a labor bill, Metzenbaum highlighted his ideals and accomplishments:

> I wish to compliment him publicly for all that he has done for workers in this country. Without Jim Brudney there probably would not have been a plant-closing law or the Older Workers Benefit Protection Act. He has made substantial contributions on minimum wage, and civil rights, and worker safety, and other labor legislation.
>
> He is, indeed, a committed young man. He has fought hard. He has worked over weekends. He has worked late at night. He has given of himself.[30]

Many of Brudney's colleagues, however, believed he fought too hard, sometimes relying on questionable means to attain his ideological ends.

Ultimately, Brudney would be to the Thomas–Hill scandal what Oliver North had been to Iran–Contra. Like North, Brudney was a low-profile Washington staffer who seemed to act with little regard for advancing his own career, making money, or gaining public recognition. He was willing to work quietly and patiently, and with great dedication, for what, in his view, was the good of the country. In pursuit of his ideals, in this case protection of America's workers, ethnic minorities, and women from Clarence Thomas's rigid view of the Constitution, Brudney would employ strategies and tactics that took him outside the bounds of established process. Just as many conservatives lionized Oliver North and overlooked his disregard for the letter of the law, many liberals who believed that Thomas should not have been seated on the high court because of the sexual harassment issue or other matters have Brudney to thank for applying all of his energies in their behalf.

Like most instrumentalists, in politics as elsewhere, Brudney was known for cutting ethical corners and compromising personal relationships to achieve desired results. Everyone, it seemed, had a story about Brudney, though no one wanted to criticize him publicly. EEOC officials spoke of making deals with Brudney, only to have him go back on his word. Labor Department nominees told of being left in confirmation limbo until policy concessions were extracted. Lobbyists recalled informal meetings where Brudney, a legendary note-taker, wrote everything down and later claimed legislative language had been agreed to. If the lobbyists balked, Brudney would suggest they might lose future access. Fellow Senate staffers discovered they had been undercut in private conversations between Brudney and their bosses. Friends of Brudney on other Senators' staffs described how they were misled on occasion to secure their Senators' votes.

Evidently driven by a mix of ideology and power, Brudney was part of a new class of zealots on Congressional staffs, which had doubled in size during the 1970s. They existed mainly to cause trouble for the executive branch, working with lobbyists and the Washington press corps to do just that. Acting through his Senate patron Metzenbaum, Brudney was able to fashion a minor career out of antagonizing Clarence Thomas, who was unfortunate enough to have headed the agency that Metzenbaum was charged with overseeing from Capitol Hill. During Thomas's reconfirmation as EEOC chairman in 1986, for example, Metzenbaum required that the EEOC submit to the Senate Labor Committee regular reports on all cases coming to the EEOC that might be amenable to a racial quotas remedy. In this way, EEOC policy-makers could be second-guessed by Metzenbaum staffers at every turn. While at the EEOC, Clarence Thomas complained often about bullying staffers like Brudney, who were trying, he said, to run his agency from the hill. "We have been hounded and harassed by staffers. . . . They call late at night," Thomas said in one 1989 interview. "They demand documents. There have been incredible abuses. . . . Where are the checks and balances?"[31]

One of the best illustrations of how Brudney, allied with a special interest lobby, harassed Thomas came in the area of age discrimination. Metzenbaum, Brudney, and the anti-Thomas groups expended a good deal of effort publicizing the false charge that under Thomas's chairmanship the EEOC had allowed 13,000 discrimination cases to lapse beyond the statute of limitations period, leaving the elderly plaintiffs with no way to press their claims in court. The issue was important to the American Association of Retired Persons, one of the most powerful lobbies in Washington. (As with many such grassroots organizations, the headquarters staff of the AARP was far more activist than its membership.)

The facts were really otherwise. Thomas computerized the antiquated agency operations in 1987. At that time he discovered that nine hundred or so age discrimination cases had accidentally been allowed to lapse. He made the information public immediately and supported legislation to extend the statute of limitations for those cases. The figure 13,000 was an invention of the partisan opposition; it was simply an estimate of the number of claims that might, during the same period, have lapsed. But claims become cases only when they are deemed to have merit. In any event, many of these cases would have been the responsibility of state agencies, not the EEOC.[32]

The AARP took its complaint to the Senate Select Committee on Aging, whose chairman, former Senator John Melcher of Montana, launched a sixteen-month investigation that included massive documents requests and unprecedented subpoenas for confidential EEOC records, which were then leaked to reporters. When Melcher was defeated in 1988, Metzenbaum took up the slack for the AARP, making the age discrimination cases a central issue in Thomas's appellate court confirmation. It was a measure of Metzenbaum's and Brudney's success that the issue also haunted Thomas throughout his Supreme Court confirmation. The NAACP's report on the Thomas nomination charged, "During his tenure at EEOC, the agency failed to process over 13,000 age discrimination cases."[33] This misperception that Thomas had little regard for the law would later enhance the brief against him by Anita Hill—and, indeed, the age discrimination canard would be continually cited by her supporters in the months after the hearings as evidence of his disposition to disregard sexual harassment laws as well.

"Brudney told me that they wanted to get off the age discrimination thing, but they couldn't because the AARP had 30 million members," Ricky Silberman, the EEOC's vice chairman, said.[34] According to Silberman, the AARP's real complaint was an EEOC rule promulgated in 1987 that said early retirement plans offered by employers did not constitute age discrimination, a position the AARP vehemently opposed. "The groups would disagree with a policy, and then take the battle to the hill," Silberman said. Brudney would seek to have this favor returned during Thomas's appeals court confirmation, when he tried, ultimately unsuccessfully, to get the AARP to oppose the nominee. Consequently, Brudney's boss Metzenbaum and Nan Aron were left out on a limb as Thomas's only declared foes.

To score a political point against Thomas's EEOC, Brudney even exploited his third-grade classmate, Jeff Zuckerman.[35] In 1986, Zuckerman, who remembered Brudney as "little Jimmy" from New York, was nominated by Thomas to be general counsel of the agency, a position that required Senate confirmation. Like the struggles over the Justice Department nominations of Edwin Meese and William Bradford Reynolds, this was another instance in which Congress was able to deny the President the ability to appoint the people he wanted to carry out his policies, particularly in civil rights. Zuckerman was raked over the coals by Metzenbaum for his opposition to racial quotas and his opinion that it was appropriate for employers to make layoffs among employees eligible for pensions, which the AARP considered age discrimination. "I am absolutely shocked!" Metzenbaum exclaimed at one point in the Zuckerman hearings, referring to the pension eligibility question.

Zuckerman was told that Senate staffers called his former secretary from the Justice Department, a black woman, to find out if he had ever said anything to her that might support a charge of racism.[36] Staffers slipped Ted Kennedy the damaging information that Zuckerman read the works of Thomas Sowell, a conservative black intellectual whose work had also been important in shaping the views of Clarence Thomas. In a public hearing, Kennedy demanded to know the name of an EEOC staffer to whom Zuckerman had loaned one of Sowell's books. In the end, Zuckerman's nomination was rejected by the Labor Committee.

Brudney and his allies could not have succeeded in politicizing the judicial nomination process without the complicity of an idelologically sympathetic press corps. Nina Totenberg, who became a nationally prominent journalist on the strength of her legendary scoops, set the tone for the coverage of judges as though they were political candidates. Her brand of legal reportage stemmed from either an inability or an unwillingness to regard the judiciary as anything but a third political branch of government.

Totenberg had already scalped one Supreme Court nominee, Judge Douglas Ginsburg, in November 1987. A sitting federal judge on the D.C. Circuit, Ginsburg had been nominated for the high court after Bork's defeat. Totenberg reported that Ginsburg had used marijuana in the 1960s and 1970s while he was a student and then a law professor. The *Washington Post* followed the Totenberg story, the White House folded its cards, and Ginsburg withdrew.

Though it may surprise her many listeners, Totenberg—not unlike James Brudney—would stretch the ethical standards of her profession to get a story. Larry Sabato's study of "attack journalism," *Feeding Frenzy,* explained how Totenberg worked with the special-interest groups to conceal the true source of the Ginsburg story. According to Sabato, a political scientist, the story of Ginsburg's marijuana use was passed by a bitter ex-girlfriend of the nominee to one of the liberal groups in Washington working against the Ginsburg nomination. Totenberg got two of Ginsburg's former Harvard colleagues to confirm the story and attributed it to them.[37] (Totenberg was later the subject of a story in the Washington *City Paper* about her own use of marijuana. Totenberg at first denied it, but then admitted she had used the drug.)[38]

Totenberg's guerrilla tactics would be the subject of even more criticism in the Anita Hill episode. In her initial discussions with Hill, when Totenberg was trying to persuade her to talk, she told Hill that she herself had been sexually harassed when she worked for the *National Observer* newspaper in the early 1970s. That was apparently a way of establishing common ground with Hill. But when a profile of Totenberg in the *Washington Post* a few days after she broke the Anita Hill story reported this,[39] Al Hunt, the Washington bureau chief of the *Wall Street Journal,* wrote an article taking issue with Totenberg's sexual harassment claim. Hunt said he wrote the piece "because she said she was fired over sexual harassment, which simply wasn't the case."[40]

Hunt, a former staffer of the *National Observer*—which, like the *Journal,* is published by Dow Jones—reported that Totenberg had actually been fired for plagiarism. A profile of former House speaker Tip

O'Neill written by Totenberg contained "substantial and identical quotations" out of a previously published *Washington Post* profile, according to Hunt. The author of the 1973 *Post* story was quoted by Hunt as saying: "There is strong evidence this was a serious case of plagiarism or a rewrite job." Lionel Linder, the former editor of the now defunct *Observer,* said, "it was clear that she plagiarized."

Totenberg was hardly unbiased in her coverage of the courts. Six months after the Thomas–Hill imbroglio, she gave a lecture at Stanford University mocking Senator Biden; special counsel Peter Fleming, who was handling the leak investigation; and Justice Clarence Thomas. "Chairman Biden does not believe in investigating nominees," she said. "There is no evidence that Senator Biden has the leadership capacity to resist the president consistently. I think he's gutless."[41]

Nor was she notably modest. Totenberg called special counsel Peter Fleming a "fool" and said he issued a "stupid report," because he had failed to identify the leaker. In an interesting analogy, she revealed that her strategy for winning the public debate about whether she should be forced to reveal her sources to the leak investigators was to "scream bloody murder, scream rape." Totenberg added that the American Bar Association had given Thomas a qualified rather than an unqualified rating "because he was black, and because the bar did not want to give an unqualified rating" to a black man.

Totenberg's hubris so angered Simpson that he chased her into the parking lot after a *Nightline* broadcast on the Anita Hill allegations, waving a book on journalistic ethics. Never at a loss for words, Totenberg shouted, "You big shit. Fuck you," according to the Senator.

The second reporter who, simultaneously with Totenberg, broke the Hill story was Timothy Phelps of *Newsday.* New to Washington, Phelps was understandably eager to make a name for himself. "A journalist could make a career coup by sinking a Supreme Court nominee," he later wrote in his book on the Thomas nomination, *Capitol Games.*[42] As his book also showed, Phelps was not very knowledgeable about the judiciary. Though few in Washington read *Newsday,* Phelps was nonetheless a favored outlet of the Shadow Senate for negative stories, because he was likely to run them. His stories could then be clipped and perhaps placed in one of the more influential newspapers or newsmagazines, or maybe a member of the Senate would develop an interest in it.

This is just what happened with Phelps's favorite anti-Thomas story, which concerned Thomas's friendship with Jay Parker, a black conservative think-tank president who had also been a paid lobbyist for South Africa in the mid-1980s. Phelps's story that Thomas had defended his friend's lobbying activities struck those who knew him as plain silly. According to a former EEOC legal adviser, Clint Bolick, "When Bill Keyes [another Thomas friend] signed a big contract to represent South Africa, I saw Clarence Thomas hit the roof. The idea that he would have a moment's sympathy for anyone flacking for South Africa is ridiculous."[43]

Phelps worked the Thomas–Parker connection into several pieces throughout the summer. In the first round of hearings, Senator Paul Simon took up the matter. When Thomas testified under questioning from Simon that he could not have defended Parker because he had not even known that Parker had been a paid lobbyist for South Africa, Phelps found an anonymous source to contradict Thomas's account. The next day at the hearing, Simon asked Thomas about the Phelps followup. Phelps then wrote a third story in *Newsday* based on Simon's questions:

> Thomas told Senator Paul Simon (D–Ill.) he "did not recall" a 1986 staff meeting reported in *Newsday* Thursday in which, according to a former assistant who asked not to be identified, he had defended his good friend James (Jay) Parker from charges that he was hypocritical for taking money to lobby for South Africa.
>
> Thomas had testified Wednesday and said again yesterday that he did not know Parker, a black conservative, had represented South Africa.[44]

Phelps , like Totenberg, was willing to bend the rules to get a story. As he showed in *Capitol Games*, he also shares with Totenberg a view of the judiciary as a political battlefield expressing nothing but the biases and interests of antagonistic parties. Phelps's own biases are hardly concealed. In his book, he endorsed the political goals of the Shadow Senate and opposed the Reagan-Bush emphasis on conservative jurisprudence as self-evidently wicked. Thus he was inclined to support any means required to stop Thomas, whom he seemed to hold in particular disdain. Anyone who failed to share Phelps's view of Thomas, particularly fellow liberals, was vilified. The central villains in his book are Ted Kennedy and Benjamin Hooks of the NAACP, who failed to oppose the nominee with adequate fervor.[45]

Americans have always believed that the courts should be free to interpret the laws without political pressure from other branches of gov-

ernment, much less organized political lobbies, unelected Senate
staffers, and members of the media elite. When challenged on the validity of their approach to the judiciary, the liberal combatants in the
judicial war argued that they were merely trying to check a hard-line
conservative effort to pack the courts. There was little doubt, in fact,
that the courts under Reagan and Bush moved in a more conservative direction. Together, they appointed about 60 percent of the federal judiciary in twelve years. Yet this was nothing new. There has
always been an element of politics in judicial selection, as in the confirmation process. Presidents could be counted on to choose judges
who shared their general political and philosophical outlook, and
Senators would occasionally vote against nominees on the basis of politics and philosophy.

But there is politics, and then there's *politics*. Whether or not one
agrees that it was a good idea to do so, the Reagan–Bush effort to
bring a more conservative approach to the law was squarely within
the presidential prerogative as exercised throughout our history, just
as President Clinton will have the authority to remake the judiciary
in line with his own view of the law. Beginning in the mid-1980s, however, the nature of the Senate's opposition to presidential nominations clearly departed from the role of advice and consent envisioned
by the Constitution. If liberals wanted to defeat conservative nominees, they were free to do so in the Senate chamber. But because they
could not muster a political majority to secure this aim, they turned
to other means.

This trend had come to a head in the nomination of Robert Bork
in 1987.[46] An eminent former law professor and circuit judge, Bork
was a lightning rod for liberal opposition because, with his outspoken academic record in favor of judicial restraint, he came to sym-
bolize the Reagan move to rein in the "imperial judiciary." Bork's
writings and opinions were powerful arguments for a jurisprudence
of original intent, the idea that judges should adhere closely to the
language and intentions of the Founding Fathers in interpreting the
law. Like many other legal scholars of differing political views who
question the wisdom of judges taking an activist approach to legal interpretation, Bork viewed much of the jurisprudence of the Warren
and Burger eras as an illegitimate usurpation of policy-making power
by the judiciary from the other branches of government and the
states, which in his view undermined the diverse structural balance
between state and federal systems, as well as the checks and balances
within the federal system of American government.

After serious debate and reflection, had the majority of the Senate decided in their wisdom to vote down Robert Bork (or Clarence Thomas, for that matter) because they didn't like what he stood for, they would have only been doing their jobs. What was new, and corrupting, about the Bork experience was that his opponents understood from the outset that Bork's views alone were not enough to defeat him within the walls of the U.S. Senate. A dour, rotund, chain-smoking intellectual with a craggy gray beard and the somewhat arrogant manner of the opinionated academic intellectual, Bork would be demonized instead in a negative publicity barrage calculated to explode the senatorial deliberative procedure, turn up the heat on Senators, and force them to oppose a nominee out of sheer self-interest.

Senators' decisions on judicial nominations, as on everything else, were determined by money and votes, as parceled out by organized labor, the civil rights establishment, and the abortion-rights lobby to the Democrats who controlled the Senate. Traditionally, civil-rights and abortion had not been near the top of labor's political agenda; the unions' efforts had been directed far more at the legislative than the judicial process. But that all changed as blacks and women, especially in the public sector unions, came to represent a significant portion of union membership, and employment discrimination suits and arbitrations became an important source of leverage and power against employers. The key to the operation was organized labor's coffers. When judicial selection became a matter of political survival for the special-interest groups, the activists squeezed votes out of the Democratic Senators with threats of primary election challenges—to be backed by a powerful combination of labor money and the votes of blacks and feminists.

Incumbents will do just about anything to avoid expensive and time-consuming primary challenges. In a Democratic primary, the black vote and a small percentage of the white vote can take a Senator out. Particularly vulnerable to this combination were a number of Southern Democrats who were elected by carrying the black vote overwhelmingly but only a minority of the white vote. For instance, black voters, about one-fourth of the Alabama electorate, gave more than 90 percent of their vote to Senator Howell Heflin in 1984 and to Senator Richard Shelby in 1986. Neither won a majority of the white vote. The Bork nomination was defeated by the Shadow Senate's sophisticated use of this Southern strategy. "I know of two Democratic senators who told me we know Bork is worthy, he's one of the

finest nominees to come before the committee, but we've been
threatened by primaries. Anyone who voted for Bork would have a
primary," Republican Senator Orrin Hatch of Utah recalled.[47]

To make the primary threat real, public opinion had to be turned
against the judicial nominee. The Bork proceedings, therefore, were
conducted by Bork's opponents as a hardball political campaign, replete with multimillion-dollar media buys, celebrity endorsements,
direct mail, opinion polls, and phone banks. A serious debate about
judicial philosophy was obscured behind a cloud of innuendo and
distortion. By the time the White House and the nominee realized
what was happening, it was too late.

On employment discrimination and other civil rights issues,
Robert Bork had compiled a moderate to liberal record as Solicitor
General in the Nixon Administration. He had no announced view on
affirmative action, the litmus test of the civil rights professionals. But
the votes of Southern Democratic Senators could be captured only if
their black constituents turned on Bork, and those constituents were
unmoved by the abortion and privacy issues that animated upper-
middle-class whites. So Bork was portrayed as a racist. Just after the
nomination was announced, Ted Kennedy picked up the phone and
woke up the Reverend Joseph Lowery on the eve of the Southern
Christian Leadership Conference's annual convention to tell him
that the racist Bork must be stopped. Lowery conveyed the message
to the SCLC membership, who took it back to local black churches
throughout the country. Kennedy also persuaded Southern black
politicians like Barbara Jordan, Andrew Young and the black mayors
of New Orleans, Tuskegee, and Birmingham to come out early against
Bork. At the NAACP annual convention a few weeks later, Benjamin
Hooks vowed to fight Bork "until hell freezes over."[48]

The racism charge rested largely on a 1963 article in the *New Republic,* in which Bork had called the proposed civil rights bill giving
all races equal access to hotel bars, restaurants, and other private business establishments a "departure from the freedom of the individual
to decide with whom he will deal." Of course, a number of current
members of the U.S. Senate had opposed the bill at the time, too.
Bork later repudiated the article in his 1973 hearing on his appointment to the post of Solicitor General. Yet fourteen years later,
Kennedy continued to insist that the *real* Robert Bork favored "forcing blacks to sit at segregated lunch counters." A second racism
charge was based on Bork's holding in a case involving poll taxes.
Newsweek pointed out that People for the American Way had "dis-

torted" the judge's record: "He didn't 'defend' poll taxes, he disagreed with the court's reasoning in striking one down."[49]

A second line of attack concerned Bork's previously announced view of *Roe.* "I am convinced, as I think almost all constitutional scholars are, that *Roe* v. *Wade* is an unconstitutional decision, a serious and wholly unjustifiable judicial usurpation of state legislative authority," then-Professor Bork drily informed a Senate hearing in 1981. Contrary to Ted Kennedy's assertion that Bork would force women into "back-alley abortions," Bork never advocated banning abortion. Bork's disagreement with the legal reasoning of *Roe*—a view shared by many liberal legal scholars as well as conservatives—was presented to the public as tantamount to making abortion illegal.

But even the judge's views on *Roe* were not enough to generate mass opposition to his nomination. The problem for Bork's foes was that their judicial agenda simply didn't impress the majority of Americans or the Senate. So proxy issues had to be found and skillfully deployed. In the Bork nomination, the nominee's views on privacy and birth control stood in for abortion. People for the American Way mounted an advertising campaign charging that Bork stood for "no privacy." Bork had been critical of the undefined right to privacy divined by the Supreme Court in the 1965 case *Griswold* v. *Connecticut,* where the court struck down an archaic Connecticut law that restricted the use of contraceptives by married couples. Bork's view was that any number of specific constitutional provisions, including the First, Fourth and Fifth Amendments, establish various, but limited, rights of privacy. His objection, voiced in the Senate hearing, was to the generalized formulation of the right as enunciated in *Griswold,* which was very broad and failed to define the scope of the privacy right being protected. His quarrel with the rationale of cases involving "privacy" left Bork open to attack as a man poised to outlaw contraception and to send the mounted police into marital bedrooms.

Planned Parenthood and PAW produced ads that charged that Bork favored strict controls on pregnancy via mass sterilization and quotas on family size. In the Senate, Howard Metzenbaum absurdly charged that Bork had "put women to the choice of work or be sterilized." Once again, Bork's legal reasoning and views on judicial power in a case involving worker sterilization at the American Cyanamid Company were distorted for public consumption into extreme policy views he was said to hold.[50] The legal experts conducting the anti-Bork campaign knew quite well that they were perpetrating a fraud on the public, which could hardly be expected to parse the refined, but critical, distinction between a method of judicial reasoning and the result in a particular case.

This is not to say that Bork deserved to have his appointment to the Supreme Court confirmed. What Bork deserved was a fair process and a serious inquiry, and the opposition ensured that he got neither. Bork would have relished a debate on the grounds of Constitutional principle and philosophy, which might have forced the Senate to reject him because he was too strict an adherent of judicial restraint or had too cavalier an attitude toward the precedential force of the Warren-era law, not because he was a racist and a sterilizer of women. As it turned out, few Senators had the courage to say that they opposed Bork because they simply disagreed with his judicial views. To use a term that soon gained currency among liberals themselves, he was "borked"—in other words, defeated by the Shadow Senate's caricature of his record.

The precedent those hearings set was that judges—who until then had been regarded as impartial and nonpartisan adjudicators of the law whether they had "liberal" or "conservative" inclinations—would ever after be treated like candidates for political office. This was a transformation so deep that while it seemed to be a change only in the *manner* that judges were opposed, it was in reality a campaign to change the very nature of judging, and with it the law. In this way the campaign for "politically correct" courts—a campaign that ultimately culminated in the Anita Hill scandal—threatened to turn the rule of law into nothing but a results-oriented political exercise.

The aim of borking was to make a nominee appear to be *unfit* for the bench if he or she had ever taken any action, written any public or private opinion, or made any quotable statement that contradicted the position of the liberal groups. Political and philosophical disagreements were turned into questions of character. A climate of fear and intellectual intimidation was thereby fostered: a judge writing an opinion based not on a reading of the law but to achieve the politically popular result; or a young legal scholar tailoring an argument for the audience. This pernicious effect is perhaps most pronounced in the most scrutinized of all venues, the Supreme Court. When the court upheld *Roe* v. *Wade* in June 1992, legal circles were awash with the story that Justice Anthony Kennedy, who had voted to overturn *Roe* as recently as 1989, switched his vote for political rather than jurisprudential reasons when, with the replacement of Justice Marshall with Thomas, he would have cast the fifth vote to overturn the decision.[51]

In a speech on the Senate floor during the debate on the Thomas nomination, Senator Mitch McConnell put it well:

> Increasingly, the confirmation process resembles a national Supreme Court election: Polls are taken, millions of dollars are raised, TV ads are run, press conferences are held, direct mail is sent out by the truckload, and spin-doctors appear on the nightly news discussing who won the last round . . . the process has been hijacked by the beltway special interest machine, which clamors for one result or another, depending on each group's narrow self-serving agenda. I do not think that is what the framers of the Constitution envisioned when they drafted the advice and consent clause. . . . While even the Soviet Union is dismantling its KGB, in America, the liberal thought-police are poring over old journals, speeches, and newsclippings—looking for evidence of treason against liberal doctrine.[52]

High-minded colloquies on judicial philosophy disappeared from the confirmation proceedings. Nominees were forced to take policy positions on issues, or positions were invented for them with cut-and-paste jobs on old speeches or articles. And there were no more rules for the game. As in rough-and-tumble political campaigns, which often turn on manipulating voters with negative images, all that mattered was winning.

For the negative ads, the press releases, and the sound bites, the opposing groups needed dirt. Regardless of what the law required, did the nominee ever issue a legal opinion where a black, a woman, or an elderly person lost a claim? If he served in a political job, what was his record? What were his private political thoughts? Did he publish a controversial article thirty years ago? Did he have a sixty-year-old unenforceable racial covenant on his house? Any tax problems? Did he belong to an all-male club? Who are his friends? Did he have a cross word with someone ten years ago? Does he have a temper? What church does he attend? Does he attend church? What do his ex-wife or old girlfriends have to say? Why is he still single? Does he drink? What library books and video tapes has he borrowed? Has he smoked marijuana? Did he inhale?

The witch hunt, conducted by people who liked to consider themselves "liberal," was as intolerant and mindless as it was relentless. Any hint of political incorrectness, any unsubstantiated rumor, any whiff of scandal would suffice. In the Bork case, the opposition distorted the nominee's "paper trail"—his writings, speeches, and legal opinions—giving the anti-Bork campaign a veneer of credibility, since it appeared to be based on matters of principle. Like Bork's, Thomas's story was to be as much about the politics of judicial nominations as about the honesty and integrity of his enemies. But the borking of Clarence Thomas, an extension of the ideological war, would be accomplished by blatant character assassination.

After hearing the rumor about sexual harassment at a dinner in mid-July, Nan Aron and George Kassouf, the top Alliance for Justice officials, immediately went into action. Having failed to defeat Thomas in 1989, when he would have been easier to stop, this time Aron and Kassouf would go for broke. The charge of sexual harassment had a special potency for a black nominee but the racist undertone would seemingly be negated by the fact that the accuser was also black. "They resorted to the old taboo, a black man and sex," said Harry Singleton, a close friend of Thomas.[53]

However, contrary to what many Republicans believed—including, apparently, Thomas himself—the Anita Hill story was not invented by the Thomas opposition. There is no evidence to suggest that someone in Washington decided to cook up a charge to bring Thomas down. Though somewhat nebulous in form, the charge already existed when it was intercepted by the Alliance for Justice, quite by chance, and then quickly handed off to Senate staff. Aron and Kassouf found Anita Hill easily; there weren't many women who had worked for Thomas at the EEOC who were now law professors in Oklahoma. Neither Aron nor Kassouf spoke with Hill, however. They merely located her. According to the report of Senate special counsel Peter Fleming, Aron passed the information to Bill Corr, Senator Metzenbaum's chief Judiciary Committee staffer on his subcommittee on antitrust.

It was not by happenstance that Aron approached the Metzenbaum staff. Metzenbaum's shop had been a thorn in Thomas's side throughout his tenure at the EEOC, faithfully carrying water for every group that opposed EEOC policies in the 1980s. Metzenbaum was also one of two members of the Senate Labor Committee, along with Paul Simon, to vote against Thomas's reconfirmation as EEOC chairman in 1986, and the only Senator on the Judiciary Committee to oppose his appellate court nomination.

The structure of the Judiciary Committee was somewhat unique on Capitol Hill. While the chairman appointed the majority staff, power was decentralized. Each Senator on the committee had his own staff, tucked away in one of the many subcommittees, giving him a research and investigative arm independent of the chairman. That way, he could pursue his own agenda.

An energetic seventy-five-year-old legislator who had made his fortune running a parking lot franchise in Ohio, Metzenbaum commanded the most effective strike force on Capitol Hill. Known as "labor's poodle" for his work on behalf of Big Labor, Metzenbaum seemed to show up everywhere on Capitol Hill. In the fall of 1991, while leading the charge against Thomas, Metzenbaum was also the chief inquisitor of the Bush Administration's nominee to head the CIA, Robert Gates. "He's a hard worker. When no one else will make the calls, he will," one GOP Senate staffer said.[54]

With his combative reputation, Metzenbaum was not especially well-liked by his clubby colleagues on either side of the aisle. "I didn't go to the U.S. Senate to be loved," he once said. "I have taken hard-line positions and I have no apology for any of them."[55] The interest groups knew that he could get the job done like no one else. Metz, as he was called, helped engineer the unprecedented seventy-day lag between Reagan's nomination of Bork and the start of the Senate Judiciary hearings, giving the opposition groups plenty of time to saturate the public with anti-Bork material. Metzenbaum aides also intimidated a pro-Bork witness, a black law professor, into canceling a scheduled appearance in support of the judge.[56]

The operating style of the Senator from Ohio could best be seen in the bloodletting over the 1989 nomination of William Lucas for Assistant Attorney General for civil rights in the Bush Justice Department.[57] In many ways, the Lucas fight set as much of a precedent for the Thomas nomination as did Bork's defeat. A lifelong Democrat, Lucas had a distinguished career in law enforcement as the first black elected Sheriff of Wayne County, Michigan, the jurisdiction in which Detroit is located. Lucas later ran successfully for Wayne County Executive, then went into private practice in Detroit. In 1985 he switched parties and became a Republican. He was defeated in a race for governor in 1986.

As they would in the Thomas case, the civil rights groups divided on the Lucas nomination, thereby bolstering his chances of confirmation. Jesse Jackson, Atlanta Mayor Andrew Young, and other black leaders endorsed Lucas, while the Washington-based civil rights groups opposed him because he was not a civil rights lawyer, and was therefore "unqualified." Republican Senator Charles Grassley of Iowa, however, said that Lucas's main flaw was being "a black Republican, worse yet a black conservative Republican, worse yet a Democrat turned black conservative Republican." As recently as 1982, Senator Kennedy had effusively complimented then-Democrat Lucas for his creativity, integrity, and vision.

At the outset of the Lucas hearings, which had been delayed for weeks while the committee pored over the thousands of pages of documents it had subpoenaed, Orrin Hatch vowed, "I'm laying down the gauntlet. We're not going to let you be smeared." Lucas appeared headed for confirmation, but the Republicans suspected a last-minute surprise. It was sprung by Metzenbaum, who had made a black art of using "ethics" charges to trump political opponents.[58] On the first day of the hearings Metzenbaum produced a Customs Service Record showing that Lucas and his wife had been fined for failing to declare $4,000 in merchandise purchased on a family trip to Asia. "Bush's Nominee for Top Rights Job Runs Into Trouble," the *New York Times* reported the next day. Lucas had mentioned the matter to Metzenbaum when he was first nominated, but Metz held it in his vest pocket for weeks, until the moment when it would have maximum negative impact. The Lucas nomination was killed in the Judiciary Committee on a 7–7 vote. Citing the Customs charge, Senator Howell Heflin of Alabama cast the deciding "no" vote.

When Metzenbaum and his staff later applied this tactic in the Anita Hill matter—using an ethics charge to stand in for a political disagreement—the *New York Times* columnist William Safire dubbed it "Metzenbaumism."[59] Metzenbaum even sprung one of these surprises before a national television audience in the Thomas–Hill hearings. Late Sunday night of that memorable weekend, in an effort to discredit one of Thomas's witnesses, John Doggett, a black lawyer from Texas, Metzenbaum began reading from the transcript of a telephone interview between Judiciary Committee staff and Doggett on the sexual harassment claims of a woman about Doggett himself. The unsworn sexual harassment claim was eight years old and had surfaced when Democratic committee staffers started checking into Doggett's background after learning he was going to testify. The staffers then sprung the woman's allegation on the witness during his interview in an apparent effort to intimidate him into canceling his public testimony.

Metzenbaum began reading from the transcript of the Doggett interview, during which Doggett was asked about the charge. Sneaking the unsubstantiated and uncorroborated allegation into the record in this manner was a violation of committee rules. Senator Biden finally intervened:

Senator, I would hope you would not read from his statement of questions asked of him. It's a little bit like if someone asked me over the telephone, "Are you still beating your wife?" And I answer, "yes" or "no," it doesn't matter. I'm still in trouble. And then someone says, "I'm only reading from your statement, Mr. Biden. You're the one that mentioned your wife" . . . I want the record to show that I don't think anything that is unsworn . . . is anything but garbage.

Revealing the extent to which he was scripted by staffers like Jim Brudney, Metzenbaum later explained in a *New York Times* interview, "I don't think I was at my savviest at that moment. My staff gave me some questions and I went with them rather than reflecting on the propriety of doing so."[60]

Bill Corr took Nan Aron's tip about Anita Hill to Gail Laster, a young black attorney on Metzenbaum's Labor Committee staff. The Labor staff knew the intricacies of the EEOC far better than the judiciary people, since Labor was the legislative committee responsible for overseeing the civil rights agency. Laster would check out the allegation.

The Labor Committee, whose staffers played a decisive role in the Clarence Thomas nomination, was under the tight control of the Democratic Party's left wing, with none other than Ted Kennedy presiding.[61] The committee was a little like the old Soviet Politburo—the Republicans never won a vote. A Republican victory was declared when none of the Republicans defected to vote with the Democrats. While the prevailing mood on the Judiciary Committee between Democrats and Republicans was polite and professional, the Labor staffers were schooled in all the dirty tricks of partisan warfare. The Democrats were even known to spy on their Republican counterparts from their glass-enclosed offices, which looked directly into a bank of glass-enclosed GOP offices on the opposite side of the Hart Senate Office Building. The Democrats would then telephone the executive branch officials or lobbyists who had been seen meeting with the Republicans and would sabotage any legislative deals that might have been struck.

Two other Labor Committee liberals, Paul Simon and the ubiquitous Metzenbaum, sat with Kennedy on Judiciary, where they constituted a powerful, though not dictatorial, presence. The cluster of liberal groups whose interests the trio and their multimillion-dollar staff organizations served on the Labor Committee had a keen interest in the outcome of Supreme Court decisions. Thus Kennedy,

Metzenbaum, and Simon were captives of the special interests in their role on the Judiciary Committee. They exercised virtually no independent judgment on nominees.

Chairman Biden therefore operated on a short leash. A committee chairman has no authority if he does not control his committee. To cultivate the perception of authority, Biden was forced to move to the left. Always in the back of Biden's mind was the knowledge that Kennedy could have asserted seniority and become the chairman of the Judiciary Committee back in 1987, when the Democrats took control of the Senate and the politics of confirming judges became explosive. Kennedy chose to take Labor, the traditional province of the old liberal coalition, the civil rights groups, and the labor unions.

During the Bork fight, both Biden and Simon were planning to run for President in 1988. Accordingly, they had to placate the labor unions that would fill their campaign coffers. Because Kennedy had taken such a high-profile position on the subject, Biden was under pressure to oppose Bork early. When Justice Antonin Scalia was confirmed in 1986, Biden had said that if Bork was sent up next, "I'd have to vote for him." Within a week after the nomination, Biden met with Kennedy and then summoned several interest-group leaders to his office, promising to lead the fight *against* Bork.

Biden would be tempted occasionally to veer off the prescribed track, if he had the backing of Howell Heflin of Alabama or Dennis DeConcini of Arizona, two Democrats who often broke ranks and voted with the Republicans on judicial nominations. The more conservative politics of their home states sometimes required it. DeConcini, a former prosecutor and advocate of tough law enforcement who was the first Democrat to be elected to the Senate from his state in three decades, was an easy read and a fairly reliable vote for Republican nominees.

Senator Heflin, the committee's legendary swing vote, was another matter entirely. A former Chief Judge of the Alabama Supreme Court, Heflin still liked to be called "judge" as part of the aura of judiciousness and objectivity that he cultivated, though he was actually one of the most cagily political members of the committee. His style was to wait until the very last moment before declaring his intentions, taking every opportunity to see which way the wind was blowing back in Alabama. His constituency was mainly conservative, but Alabama also had a large black population that could be mobilized by the civil rights groups. Heflin's campaigns also took in a good deal of cash from the tort liability lawyers who had a financial stake in judicial selection.[62]

Heflin's longtime position was that he did not believe in ideological tests for judicial nominees. The search for proxy reasons to vote against them led the judge down some peculiar paths. In 1987 Heflin actually questioned Bork about why he had a beard ("give us an explanation relative to the beard"),[63] as well as the nominee's youthful flirtation with socialism. In his socially conservative home state, Heflin made sly references to Bork's alleged agnosticism. "This is a strange individual, this man Bork," Heflin said, playing on the oddness of the name itself to raise doubts about the nominee.

With the backing of DeConcini and Heflin, Biden was able to draw the line at the tactics that Metzenbaum, Kennedy, and Simon countenanced among their staffers, particularly their Labor aides, who were out of Biden's field of vision. That is why the Labor Committee figured so prominently in the Clarence Thomas–Anita Hill story, as the Judiciary and Labor committees clashed repeatedly over the handling of Hill's allegations. The Judiciary Committee staff under Biden insisted on adhering to established procedures designed to ensure fairness for all concerned. The Labor Committee staff was like Oliver North's NSC, more concerned with results than with process.

For details on Anita Hill, in late July Gail Laster first called Nan Aron of the Alliance of Justice, who was the proximate source of the rumor. Aron gave Laster Hill's name and telephone number and also suggested that she call two other women who had worked for Thomas at the time and who might also be able to link Thomas to sexual harassment. Laster first called the two women: Judy Winston, an American University professor, and Allyson Duncan, a professor at the University of North Carolina at Chapel Hill. They gave Thomas such a clean bill of health on the issue of his personal conduct that Laster did not bother calling Hill.

2

The Borking
of Clarence Thomas

By late July the Anita Hill rumor had made its way to Capitol Hill, but it would not be pursued in earnest until the effort to defeat the nomination flagged on all other fronts. The skill of the Thomas camp in blunting the attacks of the opposition through the summer and early fall would lead Democratic Senate staffers to force Anita Hill's story into play.

From virtually the day Thomas was nominated, the opposition, emboldened by the 1987 defeat of Judge Bork, signalled that it would pull no punches. NOW President Patricia Ireland announced "We're going to bork him."[1] Flo Kennedy, another feminist leader, declared, "We have to bork Thomas. We don't wait—we don't wait for questions, we don't wait for the senators, and we kick ass and take names. . . . We're going to kill him politically. This little creep, where did he come from?"[2]

For these activists—the abortion rights lobby and groups that, like the Alliance for Justice and People for the American Way, were founded to wage political campaigns against conservative judges—the individual views, philosophy, and record of Clarence Thomas were never really at issue; the long-term strategic plan was to block conservative judicial nominees from the court. Nina Totenberg reflected this view when she reported in July that not only Thomas but the next—as yet unnamed!—nominee would be borked as well: "Gradually Clarence Thomas opponents are coming to the conclusion that the only way to get a justice more to their liking is to beat *two successive* nominees and to force a more moderate choice on the president closer to the election."[3]

But Thomas posed an even bigger threat to the liberal establishment than Bork had: He was not only a conservative, but a black conservative. The Washington-based civil rights litigators and lobbyists needed to destroy Clarence Thomas because his intellectual apostasy threatened to sap their political power, derived from their claim to speak for the political and moral aspirations of *all* black Americans.[4] Whether Thomas was confirmed or not, many liberal black leaders wanted to hobble his effectiveness as a high-profile role model and spokesman at a time when they were beginning to lose their claim to represent mainstream black opinion. Character assassination thus became an end in itself, which was exactly the effect that the Anita Hill allegation ultimately had.

In many ways, the battle over the court confirmation was a battle to define the "real Clarence Thomas." The top strategists for the nominee sought to emphasize his personal background and strong character over his philosophical outlook and controversial stands on the problems of black America, which had the effect of presenting Thomas as something of an empty suit. The opposition viewed Thomas as a toady for the conservative right-wing who changed his positions to advance his career. Despite these stark contrasts, both sides seemed to agree that the nomination would be won or lost on the issue of Thomas's character.

There was general agreement as well about the facts of his early life, but there would be heated debate about whether Thomas's career represented the fulfillment of his beginnings, or their betrayal in a quest for power. Thomas was born in Pinpoint, Georgia, a small town outside Savannah, in 1948.[5] Thomas's father left the family when Thomas was still a young child. His mother, Leola, who shelled crabs to support her family, lived in a small frame house with her aunt and uncle. The household included Thomas, his older sister, and his younger brother as well. The house had no indoor plumbing and shared an outhouse with several neighbors. At the age of eight, Thomas went with his brother to live with their maternal grandparents, Myers and Christine Anderson, who had an ice delivery and fuel oil business. Thomas attended a segregated Catholic school. After school he worked with his grandfather on the oil truck. Myers Anderson instilled in the young man the need to be self-sufficient, "to do for yourselves," Thomas once recalled.

"I grew up under state enforced segregation, which is as close to totalitarianism as I would like to get," Thomas said in one speech. "My household . . . was strong, stable, and conservative. In fact, it was far more conservative than many who fashion themselves conservative today. God was central. School, discipline, and hard work, and knowing right from wrong, were of the highest priority. Crime, welfare, slothfulness, and alcohol were enemies. But these were not issues to be debated by keen intellectuals, bellowed about by rousing orators, or dissected by pollsters and researchers. They were a way of life: they marked the path of survival and escape from squalor."

In the eleventh grade, Thomas transferred to St. John Vianney Minor Seminary near Savannah, where he was the only black student in his class. Under his picture in his high school yearbook was the line: "Blew that exam, only got a 98." Thomas attended his first year of college at the Immaculate Conception Seminary in Missouri and then transferred to Holy Cross College in his sophomore year. Thomas later said that he decided not to enter the priesthood when he heard a fellow seminarian react to the shooting of Martin Luther King, Jr., by saying, "God, I hope the SOB dies."

An academically demanding institution, Holy Cross graduated Thomas with honors in 1971. At Holy Cross, where he majored in English, Thomas developed a lifelong interest in black nationalist themes, reading Malcolm X and following the activities of the Black Panthers. The day after graduation, Thomas, by then a stocky young man sporting a goatee, married Kathy Ambush, a student at a nearby black Catholic school for women. A few years later they had a son, whom they gave a Muslim name, Jamal.

In the fall Thomas enrolled in Yale Law School. Thomas's experience at Yale helped shape his later views on the ill effects of racial preferences. According to Jeffrey Zuckerman, a former aide to Thomas at the EEOC, "At Yale, it was the first time white liberals were thinking he got there because he was black, whereas up to that point, in places like Pinpoint, it was that he got where he was *despite* being black."

On graduating, Thomas interviewed with a number of high-priced law firms but found the process dispiriting. Even though his law school grades were among the highest in his class, he was grilled about his academic performance going back to grade school, on the presumption that he couldn't have gotten through Yale on sheer brain-power. "People meeting me for the first time would automatically dismiss my thinking as second-rate," Thomas told the *Atlantic* in 1987. This was the same veiled racial discrimination that reemerged after his Supreme Court nomination.

Newsday's Tim Phelps, among other critics, has alleged that Thomas gravitated to Washington early in his career seeking to ingratiate himself with the conservative movement and betray his "black roots" as a way of satisfying a ferocious personal ambition. In fact, Thomas's first job was as a $13,000-a-year lawyer in the office of Missouri's then-Attorney General, a moderate Republican named John Danforth. Working for Danforth, Thomas represented the state in a wide variety of cases before the courts, including the Supreme Court of Missouri. He liked and respected Danforth for not treating him differently from any other lawyer on his staff. After working in the law department of the Monsanto Company in St. Louis for two years, Thomas moved to Washington in 1979 to work on the staff of Danforth, who had been elected to the Senate. Working on energy and environmental issues, he also became a Republican.

Thomas began to make enemies from the moment he accepted a civil rights post in the Reagan Administration in 1981, as the Assistant Secretary for Civil Rights at the Department of Education. A man of genuine independence, he had not wanted to work in civil rights because he saw it as the stereotypical post for a black lawyer. In a 1980 interview, Thomas had told the *Washington Post:* "If I ever worked for the EEOC or did anything directly connected with blacks, my career would be irreparably ruined. The monkey would be on my back again to prove that I didn't have the job because I'm black." Though he would have been happier as an assistant secretary in the energy department, Thomas had caught the eye of Reagan transition officials, who wanted to place conservative blacks in civil rights posts. The thirty-two-year-old Thomas, in a pragmatic bow to political reality, accepted the appointment.

Despite his critics' efforts to portray Thomas as a right-wing ideologue, his views on race relations were not conventionally conservative, particularly in his earlier years in Washington. "He is a very principled person, but there is no ideology there," Clint Bolick, a former EEOC special assistant, said. "If he has a concrete philosophy, it is a rugged individualism that he adheres to in his own way."[6] That is evidently what got him into hot water with the civil rights groups: He had views independent from theirs. Taking the time to argue with

Thomas meant his ideas deserved consideration, acknowledging a split in black opinion. Instead, the groups shut him out, refusing to see in Thomas anything but an extension of the "anti–civil rights" agenda of the Reagan Administration.

But the gap between Thomas and the black establishment had cultural as well as political roots. "He thought the [Andrew] Youngs and the [Julian] Bonds, the elite blacks, were as far removed as whites from his social background," John Marini, a former special assistant to Thomas at the EEOC, recalls.[7] The black elite also tended to be lighter-skinned than Thomas, who often recalled how he had been called "America's blackest child" in his youth. Harry Singleton, a friend of Thomas from Yale who also hailed from humble black roots, said: "It was very strange to hear the elitist blacks saying Clarence hadn't had the 'black experience.' "[8] Jeffrey Zuckerman recalled a time when Representative Gus Hawkins, Chairman of the House Committee on Education and Labor, gave Thomas a hectoring lecture that suggested Thomas was a traitor to his race. "I later said 'I can't believe a white guy would talk to you like that,' " Zuckerman recounts. "He [Thomas] just roared and roared."[9] Hawkins was an extremely light-skinned black man.

If he did not have his mind made up about the wisdom of various solutions, Thomas did have a deeply felt view that the professional civil rights activists were neglecting the core problems that kept blacks from advancing in American society—education, economic empowerment, drug abuse, teenage pregnancy—an apostasy which explains in part why the civil rights leadership became so set against the prospect of his being confirmed that they would stoop to any slander to stop him. Thomas charged that they promoted integrationist remedies like forced busing, gaining reparations for historic discrimination through racial quotas in employment and education, and increasing government entitlements, and then set themselves up as brokers of these government benefits that in the end did nothing to break the cycle of black poverty and underachievement. Further, he maintained that the civil rights groups' desegregation strategies mainly benefited middle-class blacks who were already in a position to take advantage of the access to white neighborhoods or corporate jobs. And, not coincidentally, he observed, the professional civil rights groups were filled with such middle-class blacks. "Thomas was asking whether numerical remedies had benefited low income blacks, and I remember Elaine Jones [of the NAACP] once saying, 'You can't even ask that question,' " Zuckerman reports.[10]

"If quotas help you, fine," Thomas said in one speech. "If they made your life wonderful, fine. If they get you a BMW or a Mercedes, say that is why you want quotas. Man, quotas are for the black middle-class. But look at what's happening to the masses. They are just where they were before these policies."

Not surprisingly, such forthright views were not the ones that the White House especially wished to tout during the Supreme Court nomination. This allowed the opposition to define Thomas's views on race as something akin to an old-time segregationist's. Though Thomas opposed racial preferences to guarantee equal results, he also supported affirmative action designed to encourage equal opportunity. While the Reaganites tended to cast the quota issue as one of reverse discrimination against whites, Thomas's emphasis was a more affirming one for black Americans. In a 1989 interview, he said: "I believe in affirmative action. My problem is with preferential treatment, because in there it assumes that I am not the equal of someone else, and if I'm not the equal, then I'm inferior."

One of Thomas's noted activities at the Education Department—where he first met Anita Hill when she came to work for him in the fall of 1981—was an objection to the Reagan administration's policy of encouraging the nation's historically all-black colleges to integrate. Thomas disagreed with the implication that black colleges were not as good as integrated ones. They were doing a fine job of educating young blacks, he argued, and integration for its own sake should not take precedence over that mission. The black leadership feared that Thomas's argument gave comfort to those who opposed integration—as did Anita Hill, unbeknownst to almost everyone at the time she came forward to testify against Thomas.

In the same vein, Thomas raised hackles in criticizing the Supreme Court's opinion in *Brown* v. *Board of Education,* the landmark decision that declared segregation illegal in the public schools. Thomas believed the court had relied on sociological data that assumed any all-black school had to be inferior to any integrated school. He argued, as Thurgood Marshall had in litigating the 1954 case on behalf of the NAACP, that the Court should have reached the same result by relying on the Fourteenth Amendment's requirement that states treat persons equally regardless of race or color. During the Supreme Court confirmation, his opponents falsely asserted that he opposed the *Brown* decision.

But in his early days in Washington at Education, Thomas did more to prove his iconoclasm by attacking not the civil rights groups but the Reagan Administration. Thomas's maverick streak was another facet of his persona that neither his conservative fans nor his liberal detractors wished to focus attention on. Many liberal blacks portrayed Thomas as an Uncle Tom—a devastating defamation of his character that later made it possible to suggest that he was capable of just about any immoral act. Yet to take one example, Thomas argued publicly that the Administration "blew it" when it supported tax exemptions for Bob Jones University, a private school that discriminated against blacks. And in one speech, Thomas said that some officials of the Reagan Administration were setting a "negative agenda" on civil rights. "Yes, there are a lot of racists in the administration," he remarked.

In another speech, to the conservative Heritage Foundation in 1987, given when he was chairman of the EEOC—a highly visible position—Thomas again criticized the Reagan Administration for failing to promote a positive civil rights agenda and to take into account the views of its own black appointees:

> It often seemed that to be accepted within conservative ranks and to be treated with some degree of acceptance, a black was required to become a caricature of sorts, providing side shows of antiblack quips and attacks. . . . It is not surprising with these attitudes that there was a general refusal to listen to the opinions of black conservatives. In fact, it appeared often that our white counterparts actually hid from our advice. There was a general sense that we were being avoided and circumvented.[11]

The well-earned animosity toward Thomas among some elements of the right surfaced in his Supreme Court confirmation. In an article in the conservative magazine *Chronicles,* Llewellyn Rockwell called Thomas a "racial victimologist" and a "pre-1975 liberal," and even mocked his life story, as recounted in his Senate testimony. "As to the outhouse, a fixture for many white and black Southerners of the time," Rockwell wrote, "there is only one way it can become 'unworkable and unusable.' When nobody cleans it out."[12]

Thomas's complexity and open-mindedness counted for nothing with the civil rights groups (though it was noted and appreciated by his assistant Anita Hill, as will later become evident). The cold shoulder turned to rage when in 1982 Thomas moved from Education, where he had a much narrower scope of influence, to the chairmanship of the Equal Employment Opportunity Commission, the government agency charged by the 1964 Civil Rights Act with enforcing the nation's antidiscrimination laws in the workplace.

Thomas was chosen by no design of his own, by the way; the Administration turned to him when its first choice, William Bell, could not get confirmed by the Senate. Thomas had no such difficulty.

Anita Hill in tow, Thomas moved from the Department of Education to the EEOC on May 17, 1982. Coincidentally, on that same day, the U.S. General Accounting Office, Congress's investigative arm, released a severely critical report on the EEOC's management under Thomas's predecessor, Eleanor Holmes Norton, who would later lead the attack on the Thomas Supreme Court nomination and help to make Thomas's record at the EEOC an issue. The GAO described the agency Thomas inherited as "beset by acrimony, improper employee conduct, poor performance and favoritism." A million dollars of employee travel advances remained uncollected. "Even the building itself was a disaster," Joe Schutt, the EEOC's director of audit, recalled. "People didn't want to come to work. There was mold growing in the halls. Carbon monoxide was coming in from the garage. Thomas cleaned it up."[13]

Thomas soon locked horns with the civil rights groups when he let it be known that, as chairman of the agency, he would run it as he saw fit. "Clarence used to say that when he came in, the NAACP thought it was their agency," Marini said. "They had access to private meetings, and he basically told them they would have no more access than any other private group."[14] Ricky Silberman, the EEOC's vice chairman, explained: "The civil rights establishment would like policy made through the civil service staff rather than through the politically appointed commissioners."[15] There was also a patronage angle. "Before Thomas came in, if you were a product of the civil rights movement and you wanted a job, all you had to do was ask," Phyllis Berry-Myers, who directed Congressional relations at the EEOC, said.[16] Thomas professionalized the agency, bringing in people who were skilled in a law enforcement model, rather than civil rights advocates who pursued the more far-reaching goals of social justice and integration of the nation's workforce.

The root of the problem was a philosophical disagreement about racial quotas between Thomas and the traditional civil rights constituencies of the EEOC, which, in turn had ramifications for the way Thomas managed the agency. Every time Thomas made a decision his adversaries did not agree with, the civil rights groups would declare a national emergency—the "end of civil rights"—and thereby create a perception about Thomas that would follow him into the

Supreme Court battle. Eventually the NAACP board called for Thomas's resignation, angering Thomas in their refusal to concede that both he and they supported expanded civil rights, but differed on how to achieve this.

Along with the U.S. Department of Labor, the EEOC in the 1970s was a principal vehicle through which the civil rights groups imposed racial quotas on the nation's businesses. The quotas, a means of ending employment discrimination, were designed to ensure proportional representation of minorities in the workforce. The EEOC developed big class-action lawsuits against employers, based largely on statistical analyses that showed too few blacks had been hired in proportion to their representation in the general population. The cases often were never formally brought, and therefore no money damages were won for the charging parties, nor was there any way of knowing if the employers had actually discriminated. The threatened companies often would agree to adopt "goals and timetables," or federally imposed quotas, for minority hiring to achieve proportional representation. Though it was a rather cynical approach to enforcing employment discrimination laws—Thomas believed it amounted to no enforcement at all—the civil rights industry and the Washington media were pleased.

Thomas focused on attaining real relief, like back pay and damages, for those who had been discriminated against instead of stretching the concept of discrimination. "His view was 'nail the discriminator and make it hurt.' Quotas don't hurt. The EEOC changed from an advocacy group into an effective law enforcement agency," Clint Bolick said. "Under Eleanor Holmes Norton, you couldn't tell the Lawyers Committee for Civil Rights from the EEOC."[17]

Under Norton, the agency had adopted a so-called rapid charge approach to enforcement. Geared toward negotiated no-fault settlements, the agency made no effort to distinguish between charges that had merit and those that did not. Thomas, on the contrary, required that each discrimination case be investigated. If it failed conciliation, it would be presented to the commission and considered for litigation. This law enforcement thrust inevitably meant that in addition to the big class-action suits, individual claims of discrimination—cases that were too small to make a political point, provided no work for the civil rights industry, and did not make a splash in the press— would also be taken seriously. Oddly enough for groups that prided themselves on the defense of individual rights, the civil rights activists chose to paint the new attention to individual cases as another attack by the Reagan Administration on the cause of civil rights.

The results spoke for themselves: The number of discrimination charges considered for litigation authorization rose from 401 in 1982 to 764 in 1988. The number of cases where litigation authorization was granted rose from 241 to 554 in the same time period. More monetary relief for charging parties was won during Thomas's tenure; in 1980 the figure was $78 million for the year, while in 1984 it was $145 million. By 1987 the previously critical *Washington Post* ran what amounted to an editorial retraction, taking back its earlier judgment that Thomas had dismantled the EEOC and gutted its effectiveness.[18]

The interests of the civil rights groups, of course, were served by portraying Thomas's actions in the most extreme terms, even though his policies as chairman were on the whole quite moderate, particularly in the early EEOC years when he clashed repeatedly with the Reagan Justice Department, which wanted to roll back affirmative action plans already in place around the country. Thomas opposed upsetting the status quo in this fashion. Early in his tenure, he also fought the orders of the Administration that he rewrite the agency guidelines that required employers to take race and sex into account in making hiring decisions.

Thomas was able to separate his personal views about affirmative action from his responsibilities as the chairman of a law enforcement agency, a quality that his colleagues later said would make him a fine candidate for the bench. Class action suits filed by the EEOC remained relatively constant throughout the years, up to and including Thomas's tenure. And the EEOC continued to use goals and timetables as a remedy in discrimination cases, though most often as redress when actual discrimination had been shown, not simply to correct statistical disparities.

The tenor of the agency did become more conservative over time, partly as a result of the changing membership on the commission, which grew more conservative as President Reagan made more of the appointments, and the direction of the federal courts, which became more hostile to quota approaches as the 1980s wore on. Then, too, the management mess that Norton had left behind had been cleaned up, and Thomas was freer to concentrate on policy and less bound by plans and procedures already in place.

These facts allowed Thomas's opponents to portray him as an unprincipled political chameleon and a traitor to the civil rights movement. But people who knew him well attested that while his position on various policy issues may have been flexible through the years, as he gained experience and honed his political philosophy, his core values never changed.

Willie King, an EEOC official who had worked with Martin Luther King, said, "After Thomas learned that I worked in the cotton fields, tobacco fields, vegetable fields in Georgia, and worked directly with Martin Luther King, Jr., we regularly talked about the accomplishments of the civil rights movement. Occasionally, he would bring some young protégé to my office and say to me, 'Willie, tell them about the civil rights movement.' Thomas saw the agency and its mission as a direct result of the civil rights struggle."[19]

By 1986, Thomas was so out of sync with the Reaganites that he was certain he would not be reappointed chairman, though in the end he was. "He was spurned and vilified by the left and the right, but despite the advice of a lot of people he decided to stay," Thomas's friend from his Holy Cross College days, Dick Leon, said. "He told me he had told his grandfather that he would finish what he started."[20]

Thomas was reconfirmed on a 14–2 vote—with Metzenbaum and Simon dissenting—by the Senate Labor committee. In a telling statement, Metzenbaum said Thomas "has failed to show the kind of leadership which the civil-rights community is entitled to." Metzenbaum and Brudney would continue to oppose Thomas tooth and nail until, in 1991, they found a lethal weapon in Anita Hill's sexual harassment charge.

In 1989, President Bush nominated Thomas for the seat held by Robert Bork on the federal appeals court in Washington, following Bork's retirement. Contrary to the portrait sketched by critics of a man who had schemed for years to get a court appointment, Thomas in fact had done little if anything to lay the groundwork for the nomination.

After he was satisfied that the agency's business was back on track, Thomas, in another illustration of how he was able to separate his own political and philosophical interests from his duties as chairman, began to do more public speaking and writing on a variety of approaches to the problems facing black Americans. He hired speechwriters who helped him explore new intellectual terrain, including libertarian and natural law philosophies, and who often penned slashing polemics for Thomas to deliver. Though by this point he had matured into a more recondite conservative, and was a favorite of

Washington's conservative activist circuit, Thomas remained independent, curious and open to new ideas—some of which were voiced merely as trial balloons. This is just the kind of experimentation and rhetorical showmanship that judge-bashing confirmations are designed to exploit. "Some of the speeches we wrote were quite provocative," one speech writer said. "There's no way he could have been thinking about a judicial confirmation."

"I had talked to him about becoming a judge when I don't think it was foremost in his mind," said Judge Laurence Silberman, who eventually sat with Thomas on the D.C. circuit court. "His disposition was initially to be against the idea. He said, 'Look, I'm an administrator.' I did my best to convince him that he would love it. He talked about going into the corporate world, but I said 'Clarence Thomas, I don't think you care about money,' and he said, 'I guess you're right.' He certainly didn't lust after it."[21]

When Thomas was nominated in late October, defeating him immediately rose to the top of the Shadow Senate's agenda, because many in Washington saw the circuit court as a likely stepping stone for a Supreme Court appointment. The D.C. Circuit is the most influential of all of the federal circuits, ruling on major constitutional cases and having jurisdiction over administrative and regulatory law. The opposition believed that Thomas would be easier to beat in a contest for a lower-profile court post waged inside the Beltway—where only the interest goups and the press would be engaged—than he would be in the retail politics of a Supreme Court confirmation, where the nomination of a black conservative could be expected to split the civil rights community.

The Alliance for Justice, which tried to sabotage the nomination before it was made with a secret September memo to the ABA, led the battle. In the memo the Alliance had argued that the nominee was unqualified because he had displayed a "disdain for the rule of law" in adopting policies on racial quotas with which the Alliance disagreed. Thomas's writings were also faulted on essentially political grounds. Finally, the Alliance found Thomas's temperament unsatisfactory, owing to his having shown "extreme hostility to Congressional oversight" and having made an "insensitive" comment about his sister ten years prior—a charge that would resurface again in his Supreme Court confirmation. Criticizing the culture of welfare dependency, Thomas had said his sister "gets mad when the mailman is late with her welfare check. That's how dependent she is."

Other members of the anti-Bork coalition did not join the Alliance.

The abortion groups, focused exclusively on *Roe* v. *Wade,* do not generally take positions on lower court appointments. And despite the efforts of Jim Brudney, Thomas's critics at the AARP decided not to break with its tradition of staying neutral on judgeships. This left only the civil rights groups. "Clarence Thomas has one thing that is going against him, and that is he is a black lawyer of fairly conservative political and judicial philosophy," Jack Danforth said. Fourteen Democratic chairmen of House subcommittees, including most of the Congressional Black Caucus, opposed Thomas on the basis of a "questionable enforcement record" at the EEOC.[22] This was neutralized, however, when fifty-two members of the House wrote their own letter two days later stating, "The record of the EEOC speaks for itself, however, we would like to point out that the number of discrimination cases processed since Mr. Thomas became Chairman has increased significantly, as has the number of actions filed. . . . Claims to the contrary are nothing more than political posturing."

The Leadership Conference on Civil Rights could not reach a consensus, so it stayed neutral. The NAACP's position was in doubt until Thomas met privately with a top official of the group. Althea T. L. Simmons, the NAACP Washington bureau director, and renowned civil rights activist, met with Thomas in her hospital room, where she lay dying, on the eve of his confirmation hearings. Simmons persuaded the NAACP board to stay neutral. "He has not forgotten his roots or black folk," Simmons later told *Jet* magazine. "I gained a new meaning of Clarence Thomas and felt that he will help us. He's a very dedicated man."[23]

Simmons's endorsement, along with a letter of support from William T. Coleman, Jr., chairman of the NAACP Legal Defense and Education Fund who would play a secret role in opposition to his Supreme Court confirmation, sealed Thomas's confirmation victory. An unprecedented five months later, after a careful scrutiny by Metzenbaum and Brudney of more than a thousand pages of documents on Thomas's EEOC record, the Judiciary Committee voted out the Thomas nomination with only one dissent, that of Metzenbaum. The Senate then confirmed Thomas on a voice vote.

Having had the benefit not only of a trial run eighteen months before but also of the Bork experience, the White House strategy for confirming Thomas to the high court was more elaborate, and far more self-consciously political, than any other in recent history. (A 1987 *Washington Post* headline had proclaimed: "Reagan Wants Confirmation of Bork to be Apolitical.")[24] The Republicans were not slow learners. After being caught flatfooted by the bare-knuckle fight over Bork, they began to develop antiborking techniques.

The first of these was to draw attention to Thomas's personal background. A black man from humble origins, Thomas would be difficult to caricature negatively. And the facts of his life story would be helpful in splitting the civil rights establishment, which had spoken with one voice in opposing Bork. From a liberal viewpoint, Thomas was objectionable because of his unorthodox views on civil rights, particularly his opposition to racial quotas. Yet no matter how similar his views were to those of white conservatives like Bork, Thomas could not be called a racist. This denied the opposition its most effective means for discrediting conservative nominees in the eyes of black and liberal Americans. Black opponents were left to attack Thomas's character by labeling him a self-hating black or a race-traitor.

As if on cue, Thomas's fellow black leaders—the same people who were virtually silent during the nominations of conservative nominees like Scalia, Souter, and Anthony Kennedy—uttered some of the most ferocious statements ever made about a judicial nominee. They charged that Thomas was inhuman; that he was evil; that he was not really black; and, more conventionally, that he was an Uncle Tom. "Judge Thomas is a strange creature," the Reverend Jesse Jackson said.[25] Dean Haywood Burns of the City University of New York Law School implied in the *New York Times* that Thomas was a viper who deserved only death: "Well, if it moves like a snake, coils like a snake, hisses like a snake, then . . . What's that you say, Grandma? Get you a sharp hoe?"[26] Representative Major Owens of the Congressional Black Caucus called Thomas a "monstrous negative role model" and compared black reaction to his nomination with "how the French would have felt if the collaborative Marshal Petain had been awarded a medal after World War II, or if in Norway Quisling had been made a high official of government."[27]

A Harvard professor, Derrick Bell, appearing on *Nightline,* said Thomas "looks black" but "thinks white." Howard University's professor Ronald Walters said that blackness "ultimately means more than color; it also means a set of values from which Thomas is apparently estranged." Judge Bruce Wright of New York called Thomas "emotionally white." Carl Rowan wrote in his column that Thomas "is the best only at his ability to bootlick for Ronald Reagan and George Bush."[28]

The columnist Barbara Reynolds wrote in *USA Today* that Thomas "strikes me as a man who would get a note from his boss before singing 'we shall overcome'. . . . If he is influenced by his wife, a white conservative who lobbied against comparable pay for women, he will be anti-women's issues." On the subject of black "self-hate," she wrote: "That can result in a rejection of black culture, causes, friends, even black spouses," though she did allow that "if Hugo Black, who once was a member of the KKK, could become a distinguished liberal justice, there is hope that a Negro could turn black."[29] (No one who criticized Thomas's mixed marriage saw fit to mention that Thurgood Marshall's second wife was not black).

Some commentators even suggested that any black who dissented from the views of the liberal black establishment was mentally ill, an image that laid the basis for the later view of Thomas as a Jekyll-and-Hyde personality able to repress and deny his "dark side," just as he denied his black roots to succeed in the white power structure. In a *Time* essay, Jack White dismissed the notion that "Thomas or any other black who disagrees with racial preferences and hiring quotas is suffering from a mental disorder," then went on to quote two eminent black psychiatrists, Alvin Poussaint and Price Cobbs, who implied that Thomas might have contracted "Token Black Syndrome."[30]

The *St. Louis Post-Dispatch,* and then the *New York Times,* reported that Thomas had kept a Confederate flag on his desk when he was an Assistant Attorney General in Missouri in 1975 and 1976. Representative William Clay, a Missouri Democrat, claimed that the flag showed Thomas's lack of respect for black values. Haywood Burns said the flag showed that Thomas "has appropriated the values and philosophy of those responsible for the vertical relationship of white over black, rich over poor." The flag in question was actually the state flag of Georgia.[31]

Next came an attempt to make Thomas appear hypocritical for criticizing affirmative action policies, since he himself had benefited from them. The Black Caucus's Charles Rangel of New York said that Thomas had "dedicated his life to seeing to it that those benefits ended with him."[32] During the period that Thomas attended college and law school, however, neither school utilized group-based, quota-type affirmative action programs. Rather, they employed recruitment-type affirmative action, actively seeking out minority applicants who were fully qualified, including Thomas. Thomas had criticized the former, not the latter, form of affirmative action. Graduating in the top 7 percent of his class at Holy Cross, Thomas was no less qualified than top white graduates who went on to Harvard and Yale graduate schools.

Just prior to Thomas's appointment, the former EEOC Chairman, Eleanor Holmes Norton, said: "I would like to see an African-American, but not an African-American at odds with the views of Justice Marshall." Professor Bell, too, said he would have preferred a "conservative white male appointee" to Thomas. And in Senate testimony, John Conyers of Michigan, a Congressional Black Caucus member, spoke of fears of "being placed in the position [where] a member of the Supreme Court . . . will . . . be quoted extensively and used against us."[33]

What frightened the black establishment about Thomas was clear from their own words. Thomas threatened to make nonliberal views legitimate in the black community. He was too powerful an alternative role model. Moreover, Thomas was not alone in preaching the virtues of self-reliance and community-based solutions, and the black leadership knew it. That is why no debate could be permitted, why black dissidents had to be ostracized and tarred as race-traitors. They might persuade other blacks that it was okay to speak their minds: According to a 1992 poll by the Joint Center for Economic Studies, a full 33 percent of American blacks called themselves conservative, and 30 percent said they were moderates.[34]

Once the silence was shattered the rationale for what Stephen Carter has called "diversity affirmative action"—based on the idea that there is one way to "think black"—would begin to collapse. The civil rights leadership would lose its ability to speak for black voters, its clout in the policy-making councils of the Democratic Party, and the benefits that come with the affirmative action system. White liberal politicians had a huge stake in keeping blacks on the intellectual plantation as well. If the civil rights establishment lost its hold on the black vote—about 20 percent of the Democratic vote nationally—the whole Democratic party could come crashing down.

This attack on Thomas was not effective, however, because it was not unified. Thomas's racial heritage created a special problem for him but also a special opportunity that recent conservative white nominees had not enjoyed. The civil rights groups could not bork a black nominee without risking a backlash from their own constituents, who were expressing overwhelming approval of the Thomas nomination as well as growing dissatisfaction with the civil rights leadership in nationwide polls. While the Congressional Black Caucus was voting 24–1 to oppose Thomas in mid-July on the grounds that he was a "dangerous thinker," the results of a *USA Today* poll showed that only 17 percent of black Americans were against him.[35]

The National Urban League announced on July 21 that it would stay neutral on the Thomas Supreme Court nomination, the first of the major civil rights groups to declare its intentions. When informed of league Chairman John Jacob's announcement, Senator Kennedy growled, "Oh shit!," according to Senate staffers. Kennedy knew this would be the first hotly contested nomination with no monolithic civil rights position. The level of pressure exerted on Southern Democratic Senators with significant black constituencies might not be enough to extract their votes.

Throughout July the Leadership Conference on Civil Rights, the NAACP, and the NAACP Legal Defense and Education Fund remained silent, putting the Congressional Black Caucus in an embarrassing position. According to one member, the Caucus leapt blindly to its decision to oppose Thomas in mid-July at the bitter insistence of Eleanor Holmes Norton, who evidently seems to have harbored a grudge against Thomas for exposing her as a bureaucratic bungler when he succeeded her at the EEOC.[36] Now the District of Columbia's delegate to the House of Representatives, and widely spoken of as a possible candidate for a Supreme Court seat herself, Norton would later lead a charge of female legislators from the House across the Capitol to the Senate, demanding that the vote on the Thomas nomination be put off because the Judiciary Committee had not taken Anita Hill's sexual harassment charge seriously. How seriously Norton herself took such charges is evident from an account given by an EEOC official with firsthand knowledge of complaints filed against one of her political cronies during the Carter years, who had been accused of sexual harassment seventeen times by a number of female co-workers over the years. Norton transferred the man out of one of the EEOC's district offices and brought him for a time to Washington headquarters before sending him back to work with some of the same women who had filed the charges.[37]

By late July Caucus members enlisted the help of sympathetic officials at the AFL-CIO, itself internally divided, in bending the civil rights groups into an anti-Thomas posture. Big Labor, a major financial backer of the NAACP, pressured unionists on the NAACP board, according to sources within the AFL-CIO. In short order five labor leaders who sat on the NAACP board sent a letter to their fellow board members demanding a vote against Thomas. While the final vote was a lopsided 49–1 against, the month-long delay had a devastating effect on the opposition. For one thing, the AFL-CIO was frozen until the NAACP acted because it didn't want to be out front in opposing a black nominee. The union came out against the nomination later the same day. The delay also kept Ralph Neas's Leadership Conference on Civil Rights in check, since the NAACP's Chairman Ben Hooks happened to be serving that year as the chairman of the conference, a coalition of predominantly liberal groups including the American Civil Liberties Union, the National Council of Churches, and the National Education Association.[38]

Through July and early August Neas, the executive director of the conference, was growing anxious about his ability to deliver his organization into the anti-Thomas column. Prior to the Thomas nomination, there had always been unanimity among conference members before a position against a nomination was taken. This time there would clearly be holdouts among the members, and Neas dreaded the prospect of sitting on the sidelines in a high-stakes nomination battle. With no leadership from the civil rights groups in July, Art Kropp of People for the American Way, Kate Michelman of NARAL, and Nan Aron of the Alliance for Justice were running the daily planning sessions.[39]

On August 7 Neas announced that a consensus of the executive committee of the conference had been reached to oppose the nomination. Denying the obvious, Neas claimed that the Thomas struggle was not about "liberalism versus conservatism or about those who support affirmative action and those who do not." Something was suspicious about this "consensus," however. No vote had been taken of either the twenty-five-member executive committee or the membership. Since more than half the executive committee represented organizations like NOW and the Women's Legal Defense Fund, which had already come out against the nomination, Neas's consensus was actually meaningless, except in one respect. The conference statement contained an unprecedented disclaimer listing member organizations that dissociated themselves from the "consensus" position: Anti-Defamation League, U.S. Catholic Conference, American Jewish Committee, League of Women Voters, Jewish War Veterans, and National Urban League.[40]

Cracks were opening in the NAACP's wall of opposition, too. Margaret Bush Wilson, the former NAACP chairman, wrote a column in the *Washington Post* describing the nominee as a "thoughtful and caring man. . . . Let the record show that the NAACP's former national board chair respectfully disagrees with its position."[41] Federal Judge Jack Tanner, the Pacific Northwest's first black U.S. District judge and a former NAACP official, also endorsed Thomas. Robert Woodson, a spokesman for a coalition of black businessmen, said: "They're demanding that Thomas be politically correct. They're looking at life through an elitist perspective."[42]

Several local branches of the NAACP were opposing the national board, a rare if not unprecedented division in the ranks. Branches from Compton, California, to East St. Louis, Illinois, to Liberty County, Georgia, were instructed by the national organization that they had to revoke their support of the nominee or face expulsion. A working-class city south of Los Angeles, Compton had a larger percentage of blacks living in its borders than any city in California. The chapter president, Royce Esters, a Democrat who listed Thurgood Marshall and Martin Luther King among his heroes, said that Thomas "is talking about self-help, and I don't see anything wrong with that." He went on, "I'm astounded. I heard they're supposed to get me at high noon, just like in the movies. We're not gonna resign. We're going to fight them." The national board backed down, perhaps seeing that it had more to lose than the Thomas nomination by pressing the point.[43]

Fireworks were also set off at the National Bar Association, which represented 13,000 black lawyers nationwide. The judicial selection committee had voted Thomas down 6–5, only to be reversed by the Board of Governors 23–21.[44] The group ended up not taking an official stand on the nomination. Lowery's Southern Christian Leadership Conference, so easily incited by Ted Kennedy's bluster against Bork in 1987, stayed neutral for months and then endorsed the nominee toward the end of the confirmation hearings.

Most important in swinging the key bloc of Southern Democrats in Thomas's favor were the black voices throughout the South singing Thomas's praises: C. D. Coleman, the senior Bishop of the National Christian Methodist Church; Tyrone Brooks, a veteran civil rights activist and Georgia State Legislator; the North Carolina–based Black Elks Lodge, with twice the membership of the NAACP; the South Carolina Legislative Black Caucus; Frankie Muse Freeman of St. Louis, a former member of the U.S. Commission on Civil Rights; many presidents of black colleges; and the majority of black newspapers.

Thomas was endorsed by the D.C. Black Police Caucus, the National Association of Black Women Attorneys, and the National Black Nurses Association. He was glowingly profiled in *Jet* magazine. The African-American Freedom Alliance placed ads in Southern newspapers directed at black readers. One carried the headline: "Where We Sit Will Always Be a Measure of Our Standing in Society." Another said: "Like Bull Connor, They Are Siccing the Dogs on an Innocent Man." The Reverend Henry Delaney of Christ Methodist Episcopal Church in Savannah met with 128 ministers throughout the south to lobby for the nominee.[45] On the day the NAACP announced its opposition, forty-five black friends, relatives, and neighbors from Savannah and Pinpoint, Georgia, rode ten hours by bus to have breakfast with Thomas and then spent the day lobbying on Capitol Hill.

This was the black grassroots—nonpoliticized blacks who were ignored by the political establishment, especially the national press corps. They were the true saviors of the Thomas confirmation, like the very dark-skinned people, most of them women, who lined the Senate halls cheering and crying and praying and denouncing the "lynching of our black men" when Thomas faced the Anita Hill tribunal. Had it not been for significant black support in both rounds of hearings, Thomas likely would not have been confirmed. Many liberal blacks who celebrated racial solidarity in other contexts hated to see their fellow blacks rally around Thomas and attacked them as fools and dupes.

The split in black opinion and the underlying White House focus on Thomas's background made it virtually impossible for liberal white Democratic Senators to assail the nominee, not least because they themselves were strong proponents of appointing more blacks to high office. Senator Kennedy, for instance, had held a special hearing a few years back when he had decided President Reagan was not nominating enough women and black nominees to the courts. How was he supposed to lambaste the second black in American history to be nominated to the Supreme Court? In his opening statement in the Thomas nomination hearings, Kennedy said: "In many ways he exemplifies the promise of the Constitution and the American ideal of equal opportunity." Senator Danforth scribbled the phrase onto a note card and passed it to Ken Duberstein, the former chief of staff to President Reagan who had been brought in by the White House to handle the Thomas nomination. *We're going to win it,* Danforth remembered thinking.

Danforth and Duberstein were not taking anything for granted, however. While in theory they were opposed to the idea of running confirmations like elections, Thomas's supporters—an antiborking brigade—did what they had to do to get him confirmed, even if it meant playing by the opposition's rules. The first leg of Thomas's antiborking strategy was to divide the civil rights opposition by playing up his personal background, which some viewed as a cynical tactic; the second leg was to answer each and every charge—as would a presidential candidate—the moment that the flow of negative stories and charges began.

In July and August—before most of the public was paying attention—Senators Danforth and Hatch made a series of speeches on the Senate floor defending Thomas's record against charges from the interest groups and the media. The conservative Free Congress Foundation, though hopelessly outgunned in terms of money and manpower and influence, matched the anti-Thomas groups press release for press release. "If we were going to lose, it wasn't going to be because we made the same mistakes as last time. The anti-Bork coalition used written documents and reports that were shopped around to the press and in the Senate. This time, we did the same," Tom Jipping, head of Free Congress's judicial selection project, said.[46]

Televangelist Pat Robertson's Christian Coalition aired television spots in support of Thomas, and its members generated 100,000 petitions, letters, and phone calls to the Senate. A host of organizations were enlisted to endorse Thomas and take the edge off the interest-group campaign: the American Association of Black Women Entrepreneurs, Americans for Tax Reform, Hispanic American Builders Association, National Catholic Education Association, Cuban American National Foundation, Knights of Columbus, Association of Retired Americans, Asian Pacific Chamber of Commerce, American Indian Alliance.[47] Thomas's supporters also checked the organized opposition of women. An *ad hoc* group of Republican activists, Women for Judge Thomas, held a press conference on the same day that the Women's Legal Defense Fund announced its opposition. The press took the bait; the next day's headlines tilted Thomas's way by reporting that "women's groups" were split on the Thomas nomination.[48]

Without White House approval, some conservative supporters went so far as to launch a preemptive borking of the Democrats. Sponsored by Citizens United and the Conservative Victory Committee, a sensational television ad aired shortly before the first round of hearings. Designed by Floyd Brown, the independent operative who produced the Willie Horton attack ads against Michael Dukakis in the 1988 presidential campaign, the ad dredged up Chairman Biden's plagiarism of a speech by the British politician Neil Kinnock, which, when it was first revealed in 1988, had caused Biden to withdraw from the presidential race. The ad also pointed out Senator Alan Cranston's involvement in the Keating Five savings-and-loan scandal.[49] The voice-over announced that Senator Kennedy had "left the scene of the accident at Chappaquiddick." A newspaper tabloid headline appeared across the screen: "Teddy's Sexy Romp," a reference to the drunken Easter weekend festivities at the Kennedy's Palm Beach estate in 1991 that led to rape charges against Kennedy's nephew. Kennedy had reportedly been roaming around the estate in the middle of the night without his pants on.[50]

A former Reagan White House aide, Gary Bauer, started the Citizens' Committee to Confirm Clarence Thomas and raised half a million dollars to lobby for the nominee. "The other side perfected a way to destroy nominees by making charge after charge after charge. The charges against Thomas tended to be answered within twenty-four hours," Bauer said.[51] His groups ran television ads in Southern states showing mud being thrown in Thomas's face.

The image was apt. Having just been through a grinding appeals court confirmation with the same committee eighteen months before, Thomas was inoculated against the opposition's more valid arguments. His tenure on the appeals court, meanwhile, had been short and uncontroversial. He had not written the kinds of opinions whose results could easily be misrepresented, the way Metzenbaum and PAW had used a Bork ruling to charge that the nominee had advocated the sterilization of women. Even the Alliance for Justice, in its July 1 report on the Thomas nomination, concluded: "His decisions do not reflect an overly idealogical [sic] tilt." On July 29, when the Alliance announced its formal opposition to Thomas and released its report, the judgment that his judicial opinions were not ideological was notably absent.[52]

Exasperation, even desperation, therefore characterized the anti-Thomas campaign from the outset, a sharp contrast to the frenzied optimism of the battle against Bork. As it intensified, the desperation glaringly revealed how liberals—defeating nominees they disagreed with—had come to sanction ugly and dishonest means. In the absence of substantive avenues of attack, false and misleading "ethics" charges would be raised to discredit this nominee. The idea was to throw out enough charges, half-truths, and rumors on which to hang fifty-one negative votes.

The borking machinery was already in place when Thomas was nominated. "The structure exists to defeat him," PAW's John Gomperts said. "It's just the will. Once the determination is made, the constellation of activists and organizations who work on a range of issues can be very powerful."[53] The machinery, however, needed grease to get cranking. In July the Association of the Bar of the City of New York, which almost lost its tax-exempt status for campaigning against Bork, began calling federal judges in search of damaging information on Thomas.[54] Reporters stole into Thomas's garage, after his son had left the door open, and combed through Thomas's books and other personal belongings.[55]

Ed Watkins, an official of the EEOC employee's union in New York, had callers asking, "Where's the dirt? Give us the dirt!" A staffer for People for the American Way sneaked into an off-limits section of the EEOC library and rifled through the Thomas archives.[55] A man who identified himself as "Senator Metzenbaum's counsel" telephoned Floyd Hayes, a professor of political science at Indiana University, who had been a special assistant to Thomas at the EEOC. "He was looking for dirt. The tenor of the questions was very negative," Hayes said. "It was a negative investigation of Clarence Thomas. I'm not a conservative, but when I wasn't saying anything negative, he got off the phone."[57]

Juan Williams, a *Washington Post* columnist, recounted how the interest groups had called and asked if he had turned up any dirt on Thomas that he hadn't published in a long profile on Thomas in 1987 in the *Atlantic*. Williams was clearly appalled. "Here is indiscriminate, mean-spirited mudslinging supported by the so-called civil rights groups and women's organizations," Williams wrote.[58]

Clint Bolick was called by Timothy Phelps of *Newsday*, who would later break the Anita Hill story. "He wanted to know if there were any affairs, any moral improprieties. I was kind of taken aback, because if there was anything unassailable about Clarence, it was his personal life," Bolick recalled.[59] According to Ricky Silberman, 90 percent of the reporters calling over the summer, including Phelps, whispered: "Why did he marry a white woman?"[60]

The press obliged the campaign for politicized courts by covering Thomas as a political candidate. The *Boston Globe* reported that Thomas had gotten a medical deferment from the draft during the Vietnam War. The nominee quickly explained that he suffered from curvature of the spine.[61] The White House, in a preemptive strike, informed the *Washington Post* that Thomas had "taken several puffs" of marijuana in college, something Thomas had divulged himself during his appellate court confirmation.[62] *Newsday* had an item about a federal tax lien placed on Thomas in 1984 for failing to pay $2,150.59 in taxes in 1982. Thomas acknowledged a mistake in calculating an income-averaging formula on his return, but he had been unaware of the lien, and in any case had long since paid the money owed.

The *Dallas Times Herald* reported that Thomas had praised Louis Farrakhan, leader of the Nation of Islam, in two 1983 speeches.[63] Jeffrey Zuckerman immediately dispatched letters to the editor explaining that at the time Farrakhan was not widely known to be an anti-Semite; the Anti-Defamation League of B'nai B'rith had not publicly called attention to Farrakhan's anti-Semitism until 1984. Upon further investigation, it turned out that Farrakhan's name was invoked by Thomas as an exemplar of the black self-help movement, in a passage written by Armstrong Williams, an EEOC aide. The Thomas camp was soon circulating a 1989 magazine interview in which Thomas was asked whether hate groups "such as skinheads . . . represent a growing trend of racism." He responded: "Of course, you never want to have hate groups in your society—whether it's Farrakhan or the skinheads."[64]

Another charge in the early days of July surfaced only indirectly in the press. Thomas's first wife, Kathy, it was rumored, had divorced him in 1984 after suffering beatings at his hand. Reporters who pored over the legal papers, however, found that the divorce had been uncontested and that Thomas had gotten custody of the couple's son, Jamal. To put out this fire, Nelson W. Ambush, Kathy's father, told the *Boston Herald*, "I'm very proud of Clarence. My whole family is." Ambush went on to say that Thomas had been a "wonderful" single parent to Jamal and that the divorce was "no knock-down, drag-out fight. They were congenial and have remained so."[65] Nevertheless, NOW operatives continued to try to confirm the hurtful rumors. "If you're a women's activist group, how can you not do that?" Kim Gandy of NOW later remarked to the *Washington Post*.[66]

Other stories were marketed to the press by the Shadow Senate. A precooked story broke once every ten days or so, in a steady rhythm, throughout the summer. One negative story never sat on another, and they were given as exclusives to one media outlet for maximum play. People for the American Way assigned four full-time staffers, several interns, and four "field organizers" to the research effort. The group filed Freedom of Information requests for reams of EEOC documents and for copies of videotapes of all of Thomas's speeches while he headed both the EEOC and the Office for Civil Rights at Education.[67] The videotapes were sought to follow up a rumor, never substantiated, that Thomas once disparaged the mentally ill by imitating a chicken during a speech.[68]

When PAW obtained Thomas's EEOC travel records through the FOIA they were leaked to the *Boston Globe*. PAW claimed that Thomas had violated agency travel rules in charging the government for a number of trips over the years during which Thomas delivered "political" speeches unrelated to the mission of the EEOC. Thomas had records to show that he had conducted EEOC business on each occasion. Taking his cue, Metzenbaum charged that the travel vouchers raised questions about "the nominee's integrity."[69]

The Nation Institute's "Supreme Court Watch" floated the allegation that as an appeals court judge, Thomas had committed an ethical breach by failing to recuse himself from ruling on a case that may have boosted the stock holdings of his Senate patron, Jack Danforth. The Thomas opinion threw out a $10 million fine that had been levied against Ralston–Purina for making false health claims about Purina Puppy Chow. Ralston–Purina was founded by Danforth's grandfather, and the Senator owned about $7 million in company stock. Danforth, however, said that he and Thomas had never spoken about the case, and even lawyers for Alpo, the dog food company that had sued Ralston–Purina, told the press the complaint was unwarranted.

Yet *Newsweek* ran a gossipy item on its "Periscope" page about the case. On the Sunday that the magazine hit the newsstands, a release went out from the Institute using the short clip from *Newsweek* to attract other media attention. Early in the week two long pieces appeared in *USA Today*,[70] though even the promoters of the story seemed to sense its lameness. "It's not the silver bullet," Stephen Gillers, a New York University law professor and an adviser to the Nation Institute, said. Gillers was often quoted in the press as a "legal ethics expert," with his Nation Institute affiliation unacknowledged.

The abortion-rights lobby was having no better luck positioning Thomas as an abortion foe given that his record on the issue was a blank slate. They were left having to base firm claims about his position on the most tenuous grounds. Marcia Greenberger of the National Women's Law Center stated that Thomas believed abortion was a matter for "legislatures to decide." The document she cited, called "Notes on Original Intent," actually was a memo written to Thomas by a commission aide mistakenly taken to be notes for a Thomas speech.

During a July 16 press briefing in one of the Senate office buildings, Kate Michelman of NARAL claimed that Thomas had a "clear record" of opposing abortion and the right to privacy. She asserted that Thomas would vote to overrule both *Roe* v. *Wade*—which Thomas later did, though not on the grounds that Michelman predicted he would—and *Griswold* v. *Connecticut*, the 1965 case that discerned an undefined right of privacy in the Constitution—which Thomas later endorsed in his confirmation hearings. Challenged in a letter from pro-choice Senator Hank Brown of Colorado to provide evidence for these assertions,[71] Michelman could point only to a speech given by Thomas to the conservative Heritage Foundation in 1987, where he favorably cited an article by Lewis Lehrman in the *American Spectator*, "Natural Right and the Right to Life."[72] NARAL discovered the article and brought it to the attention of Phelps at *Newsday*.[73] In the speech, Thomas had called Lehrman's conclusion that the life of an unborn fetus was protected by natural law a "splendid example" of applying natural law reasoning. The citation actually had been suggested to Thomas by an aide, Ken Masugi, in the car on the drive across town to Heritage, as a way of invoking natural law principles— binding laws or principles derived from nature that are said to exist even in the absence of positive law—before a presumably skeptical conservative audience gathered in an auditorium named for Lehrman's father. Gracious comments of this sort are simply par for the course at such events.

The attempt to portray Thomas as an ideological foe of abortion also took on bigoted overtones, and along with the natural law flap contributed to the opposition's characterization of Thomas as "an extreme right winger." Referring to Thomas's Catholic upbringing, Virginia's Governor Doug Wilder asked, "How much allegiance is there to the Pope?"[74] Ellen Convisser, a NOW official, echoed Wilder's remarks.[75] The Women's Legal Defense Fund argued that "critical questions about the separation of church and state" would arise if a religious person were appointed to the Court. The National Women's Law Center asserted that "Thomas's views of natural law include a strong religious emphasis." After it was reported in the *Los Angeles Times* that Thomas was no longer Catholic but had joined a charismatic Episcopal church, Senator Simon said, "He attends an Episcopal church that has made a crusade out of the [anti-abortion] stand."[76]

As Simon's statement indicated, the abortion issue would dominate the confirmation hearings in September. When Chairman Biden began the first round of testimony on September 10 with a convoluted question on natural law ("there is good natural law, there is bad natural law"), Ricky Silberman, who was seated behind NARAL's Kate Michelman, overheard her say, "Why is he asking *that*? That's not the good stuff!"[77]

The third and final leg of the antiborking strategy was to deflect as much of the "good stuff" as possible by foiling the committee's game of forcing the nominee into commitments on how he would rule as a judge. Bork's testimony showed that the committee's intent was to set ideological snares for nominees by getting them to adopt positions on particular cases, rather than to conduct a serious dialogue about constitutional philosophy.

Thomas was able to sidestep these snares, but in so doing he created the impression that his refusal to discuss his views on many Constitutional issues—particularly *Roe* v. *Wade*—amounted to lying. What turned out to be a successful strategy in the first round of hearings produced a view of Thomas as evasive and calculating, which undermined his position when facing Anita Hill. Thomas would be penalized in the court of public opinion for playing the insider confirmation game too well.

The Constitution provides that the President shall nominate, and "by and with the Advice and Consent of the Senate, shall appoint . . . Judges of the Supreme Court." Until Harlan F. Stone in 1925, Supreme Court nominees had not even appeared before the Senate. After Stone, there was no regular procedure until John Marshall Harlan testified before the Judiciary Committee in 1954. All nominees thereafter testified.[78]

In the years following, Senators from both parties began to take an increasingly politicized posture in judicial confirmations. Nominees were questioned by both liberal and conservative Senators on judicial philosophy in general. In the 1950s and 1960s, conservatives tried to determine nominees' views on judicial restraint and *stare decisis* (respect for settled law). Still, ability and integrity were the overriding concerns of the Senate in confirmation proceedings, and almost every rejected appointment involved a legitimate issue of competence or ethics. By 1987 the Senate had rejected a total of eleven Supreme Court nominees in history, and only three since 1930.[79] There was little or no historical precedent for the Senate to focus the inquiry on specific questions about judicial philosophy, politics, or "legal policy"—until the rejection of Bork.

In the era of liberal ascendancy in the courts in the 1960s and 1970s, liberal Senators were especially vocal in arguing for the traditional view that a nominee should not be kept off the bench on the basis of his or her views. They said a nominee should not have to answer questions under oath on matters that could conceivably come before the court, because it necessarily compromised their independence and neutrality with respect to future litigants. If a nominee were to gain a Senator's vote by promising to rule in a certain way and the facts of a case later dictated a contrary outcome, the judge's position would be seriously compromised whether or not he abided by his confirmation pledge.

When Thurgood Marshall was nominated to the high court in 1967, Ted Kennedy said that "any nominee to the Supreme Court would have to defer any comments on any matters which are either before the court or very likely to be before the court. This is a procedure which, I believe, is based on sound legal precedent." Joe Biden, commenting on the nomination of former Democratic Representative Abner Mikva to the D.C. Circuit Court of Appeals in 1977, said, "I frankly do not know how we could approve anyone who ever served in a policy position, who has taken a position on any issue, if the rationale for disqualifying you is that you have taken strong positions. That is certainly not proof of your inability to be objective and avoid being a policymaker on the bench." At the 1980 confirmation hearings of Ruth Bader Ginsburg, appointed by President Carter to be a judge on the D.C. Circuit Court, Howard Metzenbaum said that if a nominee "has the integrity, temperament, ability, that can make a good or great jurist . . . then regardless of our agreement or disagreement with his or her particular views, shouldn't we under those circumstances send that nomination to the floor with our recommendation?"[80]

The Democrats also strongly rejected litmus-test questions. "I believe there is something basically un-American about saying that a person should or should not be confirmed for the Supreme Court . . . based on somebody's view that they are wrong on one issue," said Metzenbaum. Senator Patrick Leahy of Vermont argued: "A commitment on a future vote must never be the price of nomination or confirmation." And Kennedy said, "It is even more offensive to suggest that a potential justice must pass the litmus-test of any single-issue group." All three statements were made in 1981, when Sandra Day O'Connor's nomination was under attack by antiabortion activists who insisted on their own litmus test.[81]

As recently as 1986, Antonin Scalia followed this bipartisan tradition in refusing to be boxed in by questions long considered inappropriate. Scalia stonewalled on every litmus-test question he was asked, even refusing to take a position on *Marbury* v. *Madison*, the seminal Supreme Court decision from 1803, and he was confirmed 98–0. But that was the year before the Democrats took control of the Senate and the interest groups began running the Judiciary Committee from the wings. If the liberal Senators were correct in arguing for twenty years that pinning down a nominee on a specific case or issue placed the rule of law in jeopardy, their 180-degree shift during the Bork confirmation had to have been an unprincipled response to Republican domination of judicial appointments, a political prerogative won fair and square at the ballot box.

Senators, of course, were well within their constitutional prerogatives to ask nominees anything they wanted, proper or not. The Senators could also oppose a nominee for any reason, good or bad: because they didn't like what he stood for, or the way he parted his hair. Since the politicians could be expected to press for as many commitments as they could extract, the nominee had to protect his judicial independence by refusing to answer improper questions. The public at large, for the most part, did not understand this dynamic. Therefore, the more adept the nominee proved at sidestepping these improper queries, the more it appeared that the *nominee*, not the Senators, was doing something wrong.

This was the double bind that Thomas found himself in. In the wake of the transforming Bork hearings, no nominee could hope to take the Scalia approach of declining to answer. Bork, on the other hand, had been too candid, in effect giving the committee the rope with which to hang him. After Bork, shrewd judicial nominees who wanted to beat the confirmation process began behaving like political candidates—waffling, dodging, even flip-flopping.

As a matter of both self-preservation *and* principle, Thomas took artful dodging to a new level, proving adept at inventing ways *not* to answer questions. This was a deliberate strategy designed to do nothing more than win confirmation, and it was executed flawlessly. As the *Wall Street Journal* commented at the time, Thomas "could have engaged the committee in a forthright exchange of opinion about his past views, in which case the committee's Democrats and probably Arlen Specter would have pounded him for days and ultimately destroyed his nomination."[82]

Contrary to the widespread notion, even among some of his supporters, that Thomas was a creature of his White House handlers, the nominee himself directed virtually all aspects of the confirmation strategy. He had agreed that emphasizing his background over his beliefs would provide the most effective introduction to the committee and the public. He had personally courted black leaders over the summer, hoping to gain their support and split the opposition. And he instantly provided the information needed to rebut each new charge aired by the critics. (To the extent that Thomas's role was recognized, the opposition criticized him for unseemly politicking. Yet given the charged confirmation process, such a savvy campaign was essential.)

As the hearings opened, Thomas made certain that his supporters were strategically placed to counter the public relations offensive of the opposition. While Thomas testified, they huddled in the conference room of GOP Senator Thad Cochran of Mississippi, watching the proceedings on television. At each break they escorted Thomas's Senate sponsor Danforth, the ordained Episcopal minister known as St. Jack, to the set of microphones outside the hearing room. Danforth's reputation for forthrightness and integrity, combined with the fact that he had distanced himself from the White House position during the heated debate over the 1991 civil rights act reauthorization, made him a particularly effective spokesman, just as the moderate GOP Senator Warren Rudman's sponsorship had been helpful to Justice Souter. A Senator always attracts the television cameras; Danforth talked through the breaks in the hearings, denying Kate Michelman and Ralph Neas the opportunity to "spin" the story their way.

More important was Thomas's decision not to use the hearings to expound at length on his beliefs and principles, beyond a general endorsement of judicial restraint, as some of his conservative supporters were urging. Thomas took the view that judges were not meant to perform a political function, and therefore his prior policy views and political philosophy were not relevant to the hearings. Just as he separated his personal beliefs from his role in enforcing civil rights laws, he would not read his preferences into the law as a judge. Besides, such an effort could easily backfire in an arena controlled by Senate liberals and a hostile press, he calculated. He was ahead: Why aim to do anything more than get confirmed?

At one point in the hearing Thomas acknowledged this strategy openly:

THOMAS: . . . what I have attempted to do is not agree or disagree with existing cases.

BIDEN: You are doing very well at that.

THOMAS: The point that I am making or that I have tried to make is that I do not approach these cases with any desire to change

them, and I have tried to indicate that, to the extent that individuals feel, well, I am foreclosed from a—

BIDEN: If you had a desire to change it, would you tell us?

THOMAS: I don't think so.

Yet this was not only the expedient position; it was also the principled one. If Thomas had treated the committee to long and detailed
lectures on his views on the doctrinal bases of various cases, he would
have undermined the open-mindedness that litigants are entitled to
expect from judges. The success of liberals in politicizing the confirmation process was so complete that even many conservatives were
privately clamoring for Thomas to adopt positions in the hearings attacking *Roe* or affirmative action, or embracing libertarianism, natural rights theory, or other pet ideologies of the Right.

Conservative activists, Thomas's friends, and the viewing public outside the Washington Beltway may have been sorely disappointed with
his stance in the hearings, but this reflected a distorted expectation.
While they had a point that the Clarence Thomas of the hearings was
not the "real one"—he came across as a wooden figure with few strong
opinions—judicial confirmations were not supposed to be elections,
with the nominee paraded before the klieg lights to show off his forensic skills, telegenic manner, or even his political theorizing.

Moreover, the nominee was determined to do everything he could
in good conscience to beat the committee at its own farcical game.
This required careful, deliberate, and narrow responses on judicial
philosophy, not a demonstration of high-flown inspirational oratory
or soul-baring. Thomas sensed correctly that the less he said, the easier it was for Senators—as a group, not exactly the bravest souls in
Washington—to support him. Though scarcely noticed at the time,
Thomas knew how to slide through committee hearings even if it
meant submerging part of himself. Though he had successfully kept
his politics out of his work on the D.C. Circuit Court, Thomas was a
political animal, and why this should have been held against him in
Washington of all places is a wonder. Unlike David Souter, who had
taken a similar tack in 1991, Thomas was a veteran of Capitol Hill testimony, having appeared before various committees more than sixty
times in the course of his career. His smoke-blowing skills came naturally; he did not have to be handled or coached to be unresponsive
to congressional baiting. Though he held strong convictions, Thomas
knew how the system worked, and he was not about to fall on his
sword. "You could always tell when he was going to the hill," said Clint

Bolick of Thomas's days at the EEOC. "He would get quiet and moody. He would say he was going to be taken out to the woodshed and get his whupping."[83]

"His ability to go through the first hearing, and to so assiduously avoid confrontation, was to a certain extent a reflection of what blacks in this country have gone through for years and a part of him just knew how to do it," said Ricky Silberman.[84] Some in the Thomas camp called this the "nice Negro" strategy, to thwart the "mad Negro" strategy of the other side. "One of the opponents' strategies was to bait and coerce Thomas into showing some type of intemperance. That he didn't have the requisite judicial temperament," Singleton said. "That's why they asked him the same questions over and over again."[85]

Hence another irony of the anti-Thomas campaign: Having converted Supreme Court nomination proceedings into no-holds-barred political campaigns in the Bork battle, Thomas's opponents were now faced with a great political candidate, a man with well-honed survival skills, a loyal cadre of supporters, a bulging Rolodex, and a silver tongue—a virtual Teflon nominee.

It was this tactic of repeatedly asking Thomas the same questions again and again that triggered his undoing—at least as a matter of public perception—in the first round of hearings. A scripted line of questioning designed to trap Thomas into saying something about *Roe* v. *Wade* that would destroy his confirmation prospects ended by his allowing the opposition to question his sincerity. "His credibility was destroyed, and he needed that credibility later on," Bolick said.

The Thomas strategy of saying as little as possible about his prior political record and making no commitments on how he would rule as a judge was modeled on the confirmation of David Souter. A state judge in New Hampshire, Souter was thought to be unborkable. His only writings were legal opinions—briefs written when he was Attorney General of New Hampshire—and his 1961 thesis from Harvard. There were no written texts of speeches or articles. With no grounds to attack the nominee, the civil rights troops stayed on the sidelines for weeks, until a furious Ted Kennedy finally started working the phones. Things got so desperate that, according to a *Wall Street Journal* report, Metzenbaum "demanded to see a demographic profile of Camp Mahew, a New Hampshire summer camp to which Mr. Souter had contributed."

The Souter hearings began according to script. Flashing his

patented smile, Joe Biden welcomed the nominee and told him not to take personally the contretemps that were to follow. Next came Senator Strom Thurmond. Ninety years old, with bright orange hair, Thurmond rambled through the same set of staff-written questions he asked every Supreme Court nominee: "Jedge, what is your view of *stare decisis?*"

The battle always began with Ted Kennedy, who asked Souter a critical line of questions about his alleged role while he was Attorney General in the 1970s in a former Governor of New Hampshire's refusal to supply the federal government with statistics on the racial composition of the state's workforce.[86] Souter's proper, all-purpose reply to such questions was, "I was acting as an advocate, as a lawyer, in asserting a position on behalf of a client." In a similar vein, Thomas would later explain that the views he held as a policy-maker and "part-time political theorist" would have little if any bearing on adjudicating cases as a judge. Many liberals scoffed at this, because they did not believe in such distinctions between politics and law as Souter and Thomas were drawing.

But Souter fumbled the Kennedy query because he did not recognize the case, leaving the impression that he had refused to comply with the federal affirmative action mandate. When it came time for Orrin Hatch to begin his questioning, he quickly led Souter to correct the record:

HATCH: Who was the attorney general at that time?

SOUTER: My esteemed former colleague, Senator Rudman. I would not want to suggest that Senator Rudman counseled any executive decision on that.

HATCH: No. I am not trying to embarrass Senator Rudman here. But the point is that as I understand it Senator Rudman was then the attorney general when the Department of Justice sued the State of New Hampshire for this information in 1975?

SOUTER: That is correct.

HATCH: And I understand, his name and Assistant Attorney General Edward A. Haffer were on the answer to the Federal Government's lawsuit and they signed that particular answer, if you can recall.

SOUTER: I believe that was correct.

HATCH: Was your name on that answer?

SOUTER: I do not remember. I do not specifically remember.

HATCH: The answer is no, I do not think that you were.

SOUTER: You are a better student of my history than I am.

"I threw him leading questions that allowed him to smash every-thing Ted Kennedy said right into the ground," Orrin Hatch said. "Kennedy was prostrate. And we didn't see one more vicious attack like that." When his turn came, Metzenbaum cracked, "Well, you con-vinced me that Warren Rudman shouldn't be on the Supreme Court." Souter later told Hatch he had never seen a better rehabilitation of a witness. As Souter attested, Hatch had emerged as the most effec-tive rehabilitator of Republican nominees, a one-man truth squad, or "Dr. Hatch," as some called him. After his daylong emotion-laden ses-sion questioning Thomas during the Anita Hill hearings, Nina Toten-berg told Hatch: "Senator, you just saved his ass."[87]

The Souter strategy worked well for Thomas, though it had been a better fit for the nominee who originated it, a blander character, who had a far less provocative public record, and thus had the good fortune to avoid an all-out clash with the interest-group partisans and a series of litmus-test questions from the committee Democrats. A sec-ond problem was that the Souter strategy did not fully anticipate the fact that Thomas would be held to a different standard.

In Biden's opening round of questioning in the Thomas hearings, the Senator took a leaf from Kennedy's book in trying to bork the nominee. Biden asked Thomas about a quote from a speech in which he said he found the libertarian arguments of the Harvard Govern-ment professor Stephen Macedo attractive. Biden had taken the quote out of its context to make Thomas look like a judicial radical; the full quote was passed along to Senator Hatch. When his turn came to question the nominee, Hatch began:

> In all due respect, let me just start with the Chairman's excerpt that he cited to you earlier. That excerpt from the Pacific Research Institute speech is, in my view, completely out of context. Let me read it to you:
> "I find attractive the arguments of scholars, such as Stephen Macedo, who defend an activist Supreme Court which would strike down laws restricting property rights. But the libertarian argument overlooks"—you immediately take on that statement—"but the liber-tarian argument overlooks the place of the Supreme Court in the scheme of the separation of powers. One does not strengthen self-gov-ernment and the rule of law by having the non-democratic branch of government make policy."

The Republicans were learning. Yet they did not expect that in Thomas's case, the opposition would dramatically raise the stakes. Thomas would be forced to face the abortion question—which NARAL's Kate Michelman had called the "good stuff"—more squarely than David Souter had in 1990. Michelman was adamant that "Thomas should be held to a higher standard than Souter" on the abortion question.[88] NOW's president Molly Yard had tried to persuade Chairman Biden to adopt a litmus test for the Souter nomination, but Souter had slipped onto the court without having to commit himself. Souter had then ruled in *Rust* v. *Sullivan* that the federal government could legally bar abortion counseling for pregnant women in federally funded clinics. NARAL and NOW were determined to prevent that kind of judicial outcome again. "Judy Lichtman [of the Women's Legal Defense Fund] told me we just can't afford another decision like that," Ricky Silberman recalled.[89]

Though he frequently denounced the Bush Administration for applying an antiabortion litmus test in deciding whom to nominate for the court, Metzenbaum took his cue from NARAL and adopted a proabortion litmus test for Thomas, declaring: "I'm through reading tea leaves and voting in the dark. . . . I will not support yet another Reagan–Bush nominee who remains silent" on the abortion question. Senator Patrick Leahy of Vermont also embraced the *Roe* test for Thomas. So did Paul Simon, who confirmed that the liberal standard for judicial nominees was now the same as that for candidates for political office. Simon, whose wife, Jeanne, sat with abortion-rights activists in the audience during much of the hearings, asked, "Would we elect a President or Senator who told us that he or she had never discussed the *Roe* v. *Wade* decision and had no thoughts on it? Should we approve a Supreme Court nominee who gives us that answer?" A former newspaper editor who affects a professorial air with his bow ties and horn-rimmed glasses, Simon was especially persistent in insisting on politically acceptable responses throughout the hearing. In this vein, Simon distinguished himself during the Souter hearings by suggesting that the bachelor judge spend some time on an Indian reservation for "sensitivity" training.

Toward the end of the hearing, Hatch pointed out that Thomas had been asked more than seventy questions relating to his stance on abortion, as against thirty or so for Souter: "What are we going to have, 64,000 questions on abortion?"[90] This litmus-test questioning only amplified the fact that Thomas's replies were purposely unresponsive, making the nominee appear stubbornly deceptive, when in reality he was simply trying to avoid falling into the trap the abortion-rights lobby had set for him.

A nominee could not "pass" such a litmus test. If he or she announced a predisposition on abortion, the nominee would surely alienate enough Senators on one side to doom his nomination, not to mention prejudicing the judicial position to which he or she aspired. Even the liberal *Washington Post* editorial page recognized that the test was designed to produce a no-win situation for the nominee: "Naturally, Judge Thomas's opponents, no matter what their objection to his candidacy, would like him to answer the abortion question because no matter how he answers he could alienate enough senators to kill his nomination."[91]

When Leahy asked, "Judge, does a fetus have a constitutional status as a person?" Thomas answered: "Senator, I cannot think of any cases that have held that. I would have to go back and rethink that. I cannot think of any cases that have held that." Thomas hadn't answered the question. When Leahy asked Thomas whether he had discussed *Roe* or heard discussions about the decision when it came down, Thomas said: "*I cannot remember* personally engaging in those discussions." The battered nominee continued to avoid the abortion questions:

> *I don't recall* commenting one way or the other.
>
> *I can't recall* saying one way or the other . . .
>
> I don't have a position *to share with you here today* on whether or not that case was properly decided.

The repetition gave viewers the impression that the Senator's palpable exasperation was due to Thomas's recalcitrance, when it was actually due to Leahy's inability to entrap the nominee. Leahy finally asked:

> LEAHY: Have you ever had any discussion of *Roe* v. *Wade* other than in this room? In the 17 or 18 years it's been there?
>
> THOMAS: Only, I guess senator, in the fact that in the most general sense that other individuals express concerns. One way or the other and you listen and you try to be thoughtful. If you're asking me whether I ever *debated the contents of it,* the answer to that is no, senator.

The litmus-testers had finally gotten what they wanted: An answer that could be twisted to the nominee's disadvantage in the court of public opinion. Veterans of congressional hearings know that if you ask any nominee enough questions with the intent of manufacturing a "character issue," you will eventually succeed in eliciting an answer that is incomplete, inconsistent, or misleading. This was the congressional equivalent of the old adage that determined prosecutors can find a way to indict ham sandwiches.

The confirmation shorthand for the *Roe* exchange was that Thomas had never discussed *Roe* in his life. "He badly bruised his credibility by insisting he had never discussed the merits of *Roe* v. *Wade,* the abortion landmark, with anyone, ever," the *New York Times* editorialized.[92] Mary McGrory wrote in the *Washington Post* that Thomas had "insist[ed] that he had never discussed the abortion decision with anyone."[93] Hoping to nail Thomas on a perjury charge, Neas's Leadership Conference on Civil Rights and Eleanor Smeal's Fund for a Feminist Majority took out a paid advertisement in the *Legal Times* looking for anyone who might have ever discussed *Roe* v. *Wade* with Thomas to come forward.[94]

No one did. Hence there was no evidence for the charge, leveled by Simon and others after Thomas won confirmation, that he had lied to the committee; but as the unsubstantiated Anita Hill charge showed, liberals like Simon did not require any evidence before convicting Thomas of perjury. "Whether it was his expressed assertion that he had no opinion on the *Roe* v. *Wade* decision, or his claim that the White House advisers did not shape his answers in any way, or his dramatic shifts in position on everything from natural law to Oliver Wendell Holmes, some of us on the committee came away with the feeling that he had not been straight with us. He had shaped his answers to please us, rather than telling the truth," Simon wrote in *Advice and Consent.*[95] "If Thomas was not telling the whole truth about *Roe,* as common sense would seem to indicate, it meant he was willing to dissemble to get onto the Supreme Court," Tim Phelps, echoing Simon, wrote in *Capitol Games.*[96] "Judge Thomas's bland, unblinking denial of ever having discussed *Roe* v. *Wade,* along with his claim to have evolved no position, or even thoughts he was prepared to share with the Senate, on the most troubling and contentious moral and legal question of the day, should have" disqualified him, Michael Thelwell, a member of the department of Afro-American Studies at the University of Massachusetts, wrote. "That had to be either outright perjury or else admission of an intellectual torpor so profound as to constitute in itself grounds for disqualification."[97]

In fact, these accusations are unfounded. Thomas never said that he had had no discussions about *Roe.* He simply sidestepped Leahy's question altogether by saying he had never "debated the contents of it." This construction had a precise meaning among lawyers: Thomas was saying he had not debated the legal contents, or the jurisprudence, of *Roe*. In other words, Thomas may have discussed abortion or even *Roe* in layman's terms while expressing no critique of the ruling's legal basis. That Thomas would have done so seemed odd only to laymen; lawyers know that few are really able to debate the ruling's arcane jurisprudence. Embroiled in an equally hot controversy every day of his professional life at Education and the EEOC—affirmative action—why would Thomas have gone out of his way to stake out a position on an issue where he had no professional interest and that would only earn him more enemies? Unlike Bork, Thomas was not a constitutional scholar, so he would not necessarily be expected to have developed a view on the legal wisdom of *Roe*.

This kind of technical hair-splitting—debating the contents of a decision versus discussing abortion—was a perfect riposte within the cynical forum of the Judiciary Committee hearing. In fact, when David Souter had given similarly unresponsive answers to a line of questioning on abortion in his confirmation hearings, the *Washington Post*, in its news pages, wrote in a nonpejorative manner of Souter's "brilliant ambiguity."[98] But because of the Democrats' litmus test for Thomas, which required him to answer the abortion questions dozens of more times in dozens of different ways, the nominee's critics were able to create the impression among the public that his calculated refusal to engage the issue amounted to a shameless public lie.

The *Roe* episode, of course, did not take on cosmic significance until Anita Hill challenged Thomas in a battle of credibility. At that point, Simon and others cited the *Roe* exchange as a central reason to believe Hill was telling the truth about sexual harassment. Before Anita Hill the slick, tell-them-nothing strategy pursued by Thomas may not have been intellectually stimulating, but it had worked.

There was, to be sure, a last-ditch effort to turn Thomas's restraint against him by accusing him of a "confirmation conversion," the predictable end-point of the opposition's strategy. Everyone knew that nominees, some more skillfully than others, would refuse to discuss positions as if they were candidates for county supervisor. When efforts to pin down the nominee failed, the unrevealing answers would be labeled a "confirmation conversion," making it appear as though an evasive and deceptive nominee had renounced his or her record or prior writings. In high dudgeon, the Senators would then accuse the nominees of shamelessly pandering to the committee in order to win confirmation.

"Who is the *real* Robert H. Bork?" Senator Kennedy asked in 1987.

"Which is the *real* David Souter?" Senator Paul Simon asked in 1990.

"What is the *real* Clarence Thomas like?" Senator Howell Heflin asked in 1991.

But even this usually reliable gimmick fell flat when used against Thomas. Indeed, as the hearings drew to a close in late September, despite the character question his opponents were able to disingenuously raise as a result of the *Roe* exchange, his confirmation seemed a near-certainty. Two Republicans who had voted against Bork, John Warner of Virginia and Arlen Specter of Pennsylvania, were backing Thomas, and important swing Democrats like Bennett Johnston of Louisiana, David Boren of Oklahoma, Harry Reid of Nevada, and Dennis DeConcini of Arizona, a member of the Judiciary Committee, began announcing for him too. So alarmed were the Thomas opponents that word went out in the Democratic cloakroom to stop announcing before the Senate floor debate. A few blocks down Pennsylvania Avenue, the top Justice Department official handling the nomination, J. Michael Luttig, decided to go to Hawaii on vacation in late September. He thought it was all over.

Notwithstanding what Luttig and others concluded, some of the nominee's other influential supporters were uneasy. "I did a *Nightline* toward the end of round one of the hearings with Ralph Neas and Nina Totenberg," Gary Bauer recalled.[99] "What struck me was how upbeat Neas was even though it did not appear that things were going well for him at all. He said 'It's not over, we're still going to get him.' "

Was this just bluster, or did Neas know something the Republicans did not?

As it happened, plots were unfolding below the surface. William Coleman, Jr., a millionaire at the pinnacle of Washington's political establishment, was about as far from Pinpoint, Georgia, as one could get. Coleman chaired the NAACP Legal Defense and Education Fund (a group that had given Anita Hill her Yale scholarship). A senior partner in the law firm of O'Melveny & Myers and a board member of several major corporations, Coleman was a liberal Republican who had served as President Ford's Transportation Secretary. During the Thomas confirmation battle, Coleman was attending White House meetings in an attempt to help hammer out an agreement over the civil rights bill pending on Capitol Hill. The dominant issue was whether or not it would encourage employers to adopt racial quotas in hiring. Coleman appalled White House Counsel Boyden Gray by declaring in a meeting that what young black Americans needed most was a "generation of proportional hiring."

Many believed that Coleman's public testimony against Robert Bork sealed the nominee's fate in 1987. Though he had been a member of the ABA committee that unanimously found Bork well qualified for his appeals court nomination, Coleman revised that view in the heat of battle. In a display of political rather than legal commentary, Coleman said that Bork's views were "negative" and that the nominee "always comes out the wrong way" in his opinions.[100]

The Coleman question was probably more important than any other for the White House. In early July, a deal was struck. Coleman promised that he would not become a public spokesman for the position of the Defense Fund's board, which was sure to be negative. In exchange for his silence, the White House promised not to release the text of a highly laudatory letter Coleman had written to President Bush, at Thomas's request, during Thomas's appeals court nomination.[101] In the October 31, 1989 letter, which never surfaced during the nomination fight, Coleman had written:

> I understand that you are going to nominate the Honorable Clarence Thomas, Chairman of the Equal Employment Opportunity Commission, as a Judge of the United States Court of Appeals for the District of Columbia. I think this is a fine appointment and that Mr. Thomas will add further luster and judicial ability to the Court.
>
> I have known Mr. Thomas since 1975 or 1976 as he was a student at Yale Law School at the same time two of my three children were at the Yale Law School. His starts and advantages in life at the beginning were in no way equal to that of my children's. I saw a young man, however, who was determined to be a first rate lawyer and legal scholar and I think his career so far has demonstrated that he has met every challenge placed before him. He is equal to and has the courage to decide legal issues according to the statutes and precedents and what he thinks the Supreme Court would do in those areas where the law is not yet fully settled and clear. To these talents he adds the drive and understanding of human frailties which those who have not always had it easy had to have to reach important positions of public service.[102]

During the summer Thomas paid courtesy calls to Coleman, as he had with other movers and shakers on the judicial circuit. Thomas knew he was in the political fight of his life; he'd seen what happened to the defenseless and impolitic Robert Bork, and he was not above lobbying for support. This pragmatic streak—which had led Thomas to take a civil rights position in the Reagan administration in the early 1980s when he first came to Washington—would be viewed in the worst possible light by critics who saw it as evidence that because he worked hard to get confirmed within the new rules, he would do *anything* to get confirmed. The opposition knew that this conclusion, though unreasonable, would nonetheless strike a responsive public chord.

Throughout July and August Coleman was sticking to his side of the bargain. Meanwhile, Coleman made a side deal with his daughter Lovida, a close friend of Clarence Thomas from their days at Yale Law School and a supporter of his nomination. The father–daughter split was a microcosm of the division on Thomas within the nation's black community. Lovida agreed to stay neutral on the nomination if her father did the same.[103] What Coleman did not tell his daughter was that he had already arranged to stay neutral with the White House, leading Lovida to think that she was trading her silence for her father's. A well-connected attorney in her own right who later became a counsel to the Bush–Quayle campaign, Lovida, thus neutralized by her father, declined to join a group formed in July in favor of the nomination, Women for Judge Thomas.

In mid-August Coleman's group released its report on Thomas. A section on Thomas's "lack of moderation" gave as evidence his praise for Robert Bork's character and his friendship with Jay A. Parker, the president of the Lincoln Institute, the right-wing black think tank. Without Coleman's imprimatur, however, the report was just another piece of paper. Except for a few tics, the reports of the major anti-Thomas groups were identical.[104]

During the first round of Thomas's testimony in early September, Coleman began to move off the deal he had struck with his daughter, though he remained in technical compliance with his White House deal to say nothing against Thomas publicly. Outfitted in his signature expensive dark blue suit with a crisp white pocket square, Coleman watched the proceedings with Justice Thurgood Marshall, his close friend, in the Justice's elaborate chambers at the Supreme Court, across the street from the Capitol. Dons of the civil rights establishment, Coleman and Marshall had litigated *Brown* v. *Board of Education* together almost forty years earlier. Marshall was not quite so dapper as his friend—during the press conference announcing his retirement he had worn white socks with his black suit—nor was he nearly as smooth. Marshall denounced Thomas in his shoot-from-the-hip fashion. In a reference to the adage that one should never speak ill of the dead, Marshall had told ABC's Sam Donaldson in a 1990 interview that President Bush was "dead." On announcing his resignation in June, Marshall warned against "picking the wrong Negro" to replace him, and, in a veiled reference to Thomas, said that a "snake is a snake"—white or black. During the Thomas hearings, Marshall was still formally a member of the Supreme Court. Yet, in a clear violation of judicial ethics, he implored Coleman to do something to stop the Clarence Thomas nomination.[105] Coleman bobbed into action, targeting the vote of the undecided Senator Heflin on the theory that if he got Heflin, he'd also get Biden, who was undecided and personally leaning toward Thomas—a judicial double-play. Biden would never be able to position himself to the right of Heflin, who was regarded as the most important moderate swing vote on the Democrat side of the aisle. Thus Heflin's vote against Thomas would lock the committee in a 7–7 tie, assuming that Senator Dennis DeConcini of Arizona voted for Thomas, and the committee's Gang of Five—Kennedy, Metzenbaum, Simon, Patrick Leahy of Vermont, and Herb Kohl of Wisconsin—voted against. Along with an NAACP defense fund lobbyist, Elaine Jones, Coleman began working Heflin over in private sessions.[106]

There was also a scheme brewing on Thomas's own circuit court to sink the nominee. On the morning before the Judiciary Committee vote on the nomination, the *Legal Times,* a Washington newspaper on legal affairs, reported that Thomas had drafted, but withheld, a Circuit Court opinion in *Lamprecht* v. *FCC,* a controversial case dealing with the Federal Communications Commission's affirmative action program for women.[107] To promote diversity in programming, the FCC gave minorities and women an enhanced opportunity to get broadcast licenses through a complicated formula for awarding such licenses. The program for minorities had already been challenged and upheld by the Supreme Court in 1990.

Thomas drafted the majority opinion for a three-judge panel, which struck down the gender-preference program as unconstitutional because the judges found no evidence that the preference actually made a difference in the programming.

Several clerks on the eleven-judge appeals court, and perhaps even a judge, wanted so badly to stop Thomas that they leaked the draft opinion to *Legal Times*—the cardinal sin of the judiciary, which can function as a nonpolitical branch of government only if its deliberations are kept confidential. The newspaper cited seven sources who had "read the ruling closely" in the D.C. Court of Appeals. "The logical conclusion is that the opinion would have been issued but for the fact that Judge Thomas wanted to wait until after the Senate confirms him," one source said.

Generally considered the most political of the federal courts, the D.C. Circuit Court was turned upside down by the leak.[108] In an opinion concurring with Thomas's, Judge James Buckley called for an investigation into the leak. He wrote of a "willful breach of trust" and concluded that it is "essential that we prevent this disease from invading the judiciary." Five of Buckley's fellow judges joined the call for an investigation.

The Chief Judge on the Circuit Court, selected by seniority, was Abner Mikva, a former liberal U.S. Representative appointed to the bench by President Carter. Judge Mikva also happened to be the dissenter in the *Lamprecht* case, so Mikva's clerks would have had access to the opinion throughout the course of its drafting. They had been the main suspects in the leak. Curiously, in a written statement responding to Buckley's call for an inquiry, Mikva admitted having spoken to the reporter for the *Legal Times*, but only *after* the reporter already had the story.

As Chief Judge, Mikva was able to block any formal inquiry, and he did. In his statement, he claimed that one of Judge Thomas's clerks had circulated the *Lamprecht* opinion to the clerks of several other judges on the court, making any investigation difficult and unlikely to produce a result. Things got even more byzantine when Mikva conveyed the impression in his statement that the matter had already been fully investigated to no avail by Judge David Sentelle, whom Mikva had asked to determine who had access to the drafts. Joining Judges Buckley and Silberman in calling for a formal inquiry, Judge Sentelle issued his own statement to the effect that his inquiry had only skimmed the surface: "All findings that are reported to the chief judge were preliminary and tentative in nature and were intended by me as the basis for a possible investigation, not the result of one." Finally Silberman, in a written statement, accused Mikva of issuing a "misleading" account. "I think the chief judge's statement is misleading in several respects. Now that he has opened up the subject, he should disclose the full truth of the court's decision-making process on this terribly serious matter."

As with the later unauthorized disclosure of Anita Hill's charges, the leakers of the *Lamprecht* decision got off scot-free. Since the business of journalism thrives on leaks, the press tends not to investigate leakers. The *Lamprecht* leakers, however, misfired. Only Arlen Specter was sufficiently troubled by the opposition's accusations to ask Thomas about them, and he accepted Thomas's statement that the decision had not been released because it was not yet complete. When the 2–1 opinion was officially announced four months later, on February 19, 1992, Judge Buckley wrote that, in fact, the court's opinion had not been completed, and was not ready for release, at the time it was leaked.[109] The opinion contained a citation from December 1991, two months after the time the leakers had said it was finished.[110]

As the hearings ended on an optimistic note for the nominee and the vote approached, such stealthy tactics were the only ones left. Despite all the mud-slinging, the campaign against Thomas was more significant for what had *not* happened than for what had. The opposition never developed a theme. The criticisms of Thomas's record were a dull repeat of the circuit court confirmation, and the anti-Bork coalition had not coalesced because of divisions among blacks. Though it would later detract from his credibility, the Thomas strategy in the hearings seemed to work like a charm.

There were no paid advertisements against Thomas, no phone banks, no direct mail, no midnight telephone calls from Ted Kennedy. NARAL had spent more than $50,000 on ads, but none of them mentioned Thomas by name. The Alliance for Justice and the Leadership Conference on Civil Rights pooled their funds and hired a few grassroots organizers in a half-dozen states, but no interest in a Bork-like campaign was sparked. Ted Kennedy had not replicated his famous "in Robert Bork's America" speech, and no Democratic Senator was willing to lead the opposition, a thankless task that would eventually fall to Howard Metzenbaum.

Since the groups had not piled on at the beginning, the more time that passed, the more politically risky opposing Thomas was. Bill Coleman, for example, had moved against Bork only when the odds had shifted decisively against the nominee after weeks of attacks from the special-interest groups. Thomas looked like a winner from the outset, a self-reinforcing proposition.

The opposition, in short, had met its match. Or so it appeared. By beating the permanent opposition at its own game, by refusing to be borked, Thomas stood on the brink of Senate confirmation. Neither side had fully succeeded in defining the "real Clarence Thomas"; he seemed more enigmatic after the hearings than before. Thomas's strategy had been to reveal his core values and judicial principles, while limiting his points of vulnerability. This had the effect of checking the opposition, skirting controversy, and picking up votes, but left even his close supporters somewhat disillusioned and wondering if they knew who the "real" Thomas was.

If even Thomas's supporters admitted to such doubts, the battle to define Thomas's image was not over. While the opposition had failed to define Thomas substantively as an abortion foe, a follower of natural law or libertarian philosophy, an enemy of civil rights, or a judicial radical, this failure produced another, more subtle, advance. The confirmation process had become a no-win proposition for the nominee. The politicking and positioning required by irresponsible liberal tactics left Thomas vulnerable on the issue of personal character.

As in elective politics, when the enemy is not being beaten on the merits, the dirty tricks are rolled out. Where Bork had been the victim of a grassroots mobilization, only an inside job could now doom Thomas. If Bork had been hammered, Thomas would get the stiletto.

3

The Tempting of Anita Hill

The prevailing view of Anita Hill is that of a courageous woman who approached the Senate with a sexual harassment charge against a powerful political figure after repressing her experience for ten years and then wrestling with her conscience for months following his Supreme Court nomination. Hill then came forward of her own volition, placing her career and reputation in peril for the sake of the high court's integrity. When she finally spoke up, she was not taken seriously by an all-male committee, which first showed little interest in investigating the charge and then tried to sweep it under the rug. Hill was thus a victim of male-dominated society twice over, once when she was sexually harassed by her boss, and again when she came forward and was disbelieved by the "men's club" that runs the U.S. Senate.

At the time, a front-page news story in the *Washington Post* criticized "the male-dominated chamber's apparent lack of zeal in investigating the charge and initial unwillingness to delay the nomination long enough to examine its merits."[1] *Time* headlined an article on Hill's charges: "The Ultimate Men's Club: As Pampered Denizens of a Virtually All-Male Bastion, Many Senators Were Slow to Grasp the Seriousness of the Sexual Harassment Issue."[2] "Congress wanted to ignore the statements of Anita Hill," according to Judith Resnik, a law professor at the University of Southern California.[3]

"The contempt and verbal abuse heaped upon Anita Hill by the white male Judiciary Committee during the Thomas confirmation hearings was ironically quite similar to the kind of abuse she had received from Thomas himself a decade before. . . . In terms of the Thomas and Hill confrontation, what was termed by reactionary white conservatives as a 'high-tech lynching' of Clarence Thomas was in actuality a public gang rape of Anita Hill, and by extension, a violent assault upon all women of African descent," Barbara Ransby wrote a year later.[4] Gloria T. Hull, a professor of women's studies at the University of California at Santa Cruz and a member of a group formed to protest the Thomas nomination, African American Women in Defense of Ourselves, described Hill this way: "I believe that she is a brave woman who did us all a great service. And she is certainly not responsible for the macho morals and ethical barbarism which block appreciation of her fine behavior . . . being a nice, good girl got Anita Hill what all 'good girls' usually get: nothing—but further abuse."[5]

The actual record of Hill's complex dealings with the Senate shows that much of this portrait of Hill's decision to come forward with her story to the Senate Judiciary Committee is false. Anita Hill, extremely reluctant to involve herself in any official way, did not approach anyone. U.S. Senate staffers came to her. Indeed, Hill never really "came forward" at all. More accurately, she was drawn forward by a group of fervently committed Senate staffers who wanted to use her charge to beat the Thomas nomination. Through their zealous efforts, these staffers sucked Hill into the borking machinery.

Once caught, Hill's subsequent aim of making a charge against Thomas on terms that were acceptable to her accounted for a series of hitches along the way to the filing of an official allegation. What looked like an inadequate response to her charges by the Committee was really the result of Hill's unwillingness to "come forward"—evidenced by her extreme caution, and her efforts to shield her identity. As soon as she made the claim, the Judiciary Committee did everything it could within proper bounds and established procedures to treat Hill's charge with the seriousness that it deserved.

The process of Hill's "coming forward" should thus be viewed not as a demonstration of her personal responsibility and courage, but rather as a series of delicate proddings and half-steps that over the course of several weeks developed an inexorable momentum.

By mid-August Thomas's supporters were confident that they had weathered the storm over the nomination. Tom Jipping, head of the judicial selection project at the conservative Free Congress Research and Education Foundation, wrote in a memo to his boss, Paul Weyrich, the New Right leader, on August 7: "It seems to me that unless they cook up some kind of ethics charge or discovery, they cannot beat him with what they have so far." That was the consensus, too, on Capitol Hill, where a few blocks from Weyrich's offices, staffers to Senator Metzenbaum met to compare notes on the nomination fight. With the Senate in summer recess, mid-August is normally a time for catching up on paperwork and taking leisurely lunches: except during a Supreme Court nomination. Over the summer, Thomas was required to submit more than 32,000 documents to the Senate. A special Metzenbaum document request read, in part:

> I. Provide all documents generated within EEOC's Washington D.C. headquarters which addressed, discussed, or served as the basis for each of the following:
>> (a) the development or issuance of the EEOC Compliance Manual section issued in 1983 addressing investigation charges involving fetal protection policies . . .
>
> II. Provide all documents (a) prepared by, or on behalf of Chairman Thomas, or (b) transmitted to Chairman Thomas, or (c) that describe or refer to the involvement or position of Chairman Thomas, regarding each of the following:
>> (a) The EEOC's decision to participate (as a party or otherwise), or not to participate in, each stage of the following cases:
>> 1) *Wright v. Olin Corp.* . . . .
>> 2) *Zuniga v. Kleberg Co. Hospital* . . .
>> 3) *Hayes v. Shelby Memorial Hospital* . . .
>> 4) *UAW v. Johnson Controls, Inc.*[6]

While they provided everything from the name of the gym where Thomas worked out to his personal correspondence with a magazine on whose board he sat, the massive document requests weren't turning up anything damning.[7]

Back in Norman, Oklahoma, Professor Hill was preparing for the school year to begin. Whether or not she was hoping the doubts that she had planted with Gary Phillips about Thomas would circulate in Washington and harm his nomination prospects, she certainly did not expect that her conversations about sexual harassment in early

July would within a matter of weeks place her in the middle of an iron triangle of Senate staffers, liberal interest groups, and the media, and eventually lead to a grueling public hearing. No match for the Shadow Senate, she was unaware that the information she had privately shared with Susan Hoerchner and Gary Phillips had already reached the Alliance for Justice and had been passed on to Metzenbaum's office, where another old friend of Hill was working night and day to stop the Thomas nomination.

In the Metzenbaum staff meeting, Gail Laster, who had been given the sexual harassment lead a month ago by Nan Aron of the Alliance for Justice, was grasping at straws. A host of borking strategies had failed, making an approach to Anita Hill all but inevitable. Laster mentioned that she had not fully checked out the rumor, since she had not called Hill directly. Laster's boss on the Labor Committee was James Brudney, who, in another apparent coincidence, happened to be a close friend of Anita Hill from Yale. Curiously, Laster, not Brudney, made the first call to Hill.[8]

With the Thomas confirmation hearings scheduled to open on September 10, Laster finally phoned Hill at the University of Oklahoma on the fifth—the first known contact between Hill and the Senate. Laster did not ask Hill if she had been sexually harassed by Thomas. Senate special counsel Peter Fleming, who investigated the unauthorized leak of Hill's charges to the press, reported on the entirely oblique initial exchange between Hill and Laster:

> Laster referred to an allegation that Thomas had harassed female employees. Hill responded that Laster should investigate the charge. Laster asked Hill for names of possible leads. Hill said that she would think about it. Laster never asked Hill whether she had been harassed by Thomas. Hill did not volunteer.

On hearing this, Jim Brudney, in consultation with Bill Corr, the Metzenbaum aide on the Judiciary Committee who was the original point of contact for the Alliance for Justice on the Hill matter, pulled Laster back. Hill would have to be drawn forward carefully, perhaps by someone she knew and trusted, like Brudney himself. If Brudney was planning an approach, he was certainly not advertising his involvement in opposition efforts against Thomas. David Kyllo, who handled Congressional relations at the EEOC, asked Brudney in late August if he was working on the nomination. "He told me he was not," Kyllo said. "Later, when Anita Hill was testifying and I saw Brudney sitting behind Senator Metzenbaum, I wondered why he had lied."

For her part Hill seemed to want to keep the rumor alive while distancing herself from it—much the same impulse she obeyed when she initially told Susan Hoerchner that although she was not going to say anything, Hoerchner could be released from her vow of silence. Hill would later make much of her own reluctance to testify against Thomas, as though that were proof of her lack of ill will toward the nominee. At the outset, however, Hill's reluctance must be seen for what it actually was. Hill was reluctant to attach her name to the rumor; she was reluctant to take official action; and she was certainly reluctant to confront Thomas publicly. But Hill's subtle encouragement of Laster showed that she was not so reluctant to have those who were investigating his nomination identify Thomas as a sexual harasser.

In a speech on the Senate floor, Senator Metzenbaum later supplied a chronology of these events:

> As a result of her news conference today [October 7], some confusion seems to have arisen as to who first contacted Professor Hill and when that contact occurred. It is not very complicated as it was a routine inquiry by my staff. In preparation for the confirmation hearings on the Thomas nomination, several members of my staff made inquiries of literally dozens of former colleagues and individuals who had worked with Clarence Thomas over the years. . . . Anita Hill was one of three women who worked with Thomas at the EEOC who were contacted by my staff. They were asked about a range of women's issues, including rumors of sexual harassment at the agency.[9]

Metzenbaum evidently meant to convey the impression that his staff had somehow stumbled upon Hill in a general canvass of the EEOC. But as the Fleming report showed, this was not really a "routine inquiry." Nor did Metzenbaum mention that the information had come to his staff from Nan Aron and the Alliance for Justice, which perhaps would have compromised the image of Anita Hill as a lone actor with no apparent motive that Metzenbaum and his allies were promoting.

At the same time that the Brudney–Laster operation was proceeding, Metzenbaum's investigator—some Senators employ their own gumshoes—was conducting her own inquiry into Thomas's background. Bonnie Goldstein heard about Hill from the Alliance for Justice also. The Alliance apparently had been spreading the rumor around town without even having spoken with Hill. Goldstein passed Anita Hill's name to Senator Kennedy's investigator, Ricki Seidman. The former PAW official and professional private eye would know how to handle the information. Seidman first checked back with the Alliance for Justice, then called Anita Hill on September 6. When

Seidman raised the subject of sexual harassment, Hill said she would not talk about it. "When Seidman asked why, Hill made some oblique comments about victims of sexual harassment," Fleming reported.

But Hill did agree to speak with Seidman again, taking a half-step forward. Seidman called Hill again on September 9. Securing assurances of confidentiality and privacy from Seidman, Hill took the first of a series of conditional steps towards making a charge against Thomas. "Hill said she had decided to talk about the harassment issue, but had not yet decided how far she wanted the information to go," according to Fleming. For the first time, Hill then "described without any great specificity, a pattern of alleged conduct by Thomas consisting of repeated requests for dates and sexual comments." In a cover story similar to Metzenbaum's, Kennedy later released a misleading statement about Seidman's contacts with Hill, calling them part of a systematic review of former EEOC employees.[10]

Hill's responses to these suggestions were predictable, the kind that anyone in her position might have registered. Seidman obviously knew something about Thomas, Hill, and sexual harassment, but Hill didn't know how much. Having already spoken herself with Phillips and Hoerchner, and having told Hoerchner she could talk to others about Thomas, Hill was past the point where she could deny Seidman's suggestion that she might have been sexually harassed by Thomas. A denial would have undermined her credibility with whomever she had already told. Once something so striking is said, it cannot simply be taken back. In this way, Hill naïvely wandered into a situation from which she was unable to extricate herself.

Every time Hill took a step, she tried to set up an obstacle, only to be overcome by the skillful Washington operators who were handling her. Seidman had gotten her to acknowledge the sexual harassment story, but that was all Hill was willing to do. If the charge was to be entertained, Hill would have to make it to the Judiciary Committee, and Seidman, a Labor Committee staffer, needed help in encouraging Hill to take the next step toward a sworn allegation. Between September 6 and 9, Seidman learned that Hill and her Labor Committee colleague Jim Brudney had attended Yale Law School at the same time. Seidman suggested to Hill that she "might be more comfortable discussing the matter with a person she knew, identifying Brudney"—a tactic reminiscent of how defectors are "brought in" by the opposing side's intelligence agency.

Senator Hank Brown, a Republican member of the Judiciary Committee from Colorado, said he personally spoke to Hill three days before her public testimony on October 11.[11] In the conversation with Brown, Hill described the calls from Laster and Seidman. According to what Hill told Brown, Laster had mentioned sexual harassment but did not let on she had heard that Hill had been a victim. Seidman had gone a step further in her September 6 call to Hill, letting Hill know that she had heard *Hill* had been harassed. This had prompted Hill to briefly describe the alleged behavior for the first time on September 9.

This is not surprising under the circumstances. Seidman had employed a technique known to any skilled investigator, or journalist. By allowing the person being questioned to know that the investigator knows something about what the subject has said or done, he creates the impression that he knows more than he actually does, often eliciting a nervous explanation, even a confession. Though she undoubtedly used a reassuring tone, Seidman probably unnerved Hill by telling her that she had heard Hill had been harassed by Thomas and by further revealing that she already knew of Hill's personal link to Brudney. Thus Hill was shaken from her position.

Brudney was able to intervene because he had special influence with Hill, having known her at Yale, where he was one year ahead of her in law school, and then in Washington in the early 1980s. (At Yale, Brudney also had been a friend of Susan Hoerchner's brother, who was in his law school class). According to Diane Holt, Thomas's long-time personal secretary and a friend of Hill from the EEOC office, Hill spoke often of going out on the town with the bearded, bespectacled Brudney—to dinner, to the theater, to see a movie. "She also mentioned several times having spent the weekend at his apartment, in Foggy Bottom I think it was," Holt said.[12] "Brudney used to call all the time at the EEOC. He was one of her best friends," said Armstrong Williams, a former special assistant to Thomas, who spoke often with Hill at the EEOC.[13] At the time, in 1982 and 1983, Brudney was not yet on the Senate staff.[14]

That he later was in a position to use his relationship with Hill to damage Clarence Thomas was yet another fortuitous circumstance that would be crucial to the flow of events in the Thomas–Hill scandal. If Brudney had not been a close friend of Hill, he probably would never have been able to persuade her as he did. From Hill's viewpoint, the decision to speak with Brudney was not necessarily an indication that she intended to make a formal charge, but simply an effort to seek the advice and guidance of someone she knew and trusted. This was a gesture that Brudney would exploit and finally betray.

According to Fleming, when Brudney called Hill on September 10, "Hill began the conversation by saying she did not wish to testify publicly." Fleming did not describe what else was said in the Brudney–Hill call, though the result was clear: For some reason, in the hours after she spoke to Brudney, Hill decided to talk with the Judiciary Committee, though under the severe constraint of anonymity.

According to Brown, Brudney took Seidman's prodding further, suggesting to Hill that "rumors were flying in Washington that she'd been harassed by Thomas, that lots of people knew about it." Was this why Brudney had waited until Hill had been approached by two total strangers and asked about the rumors before calling her himself? In a statement on the Senate floor after Hill's charges had been leaked to the media, Brown described the staff calls, drawing on the information gleaned from his own conversation with Hill:

> First, they told her there were widespread rumors about sexual harassment at the EEOC and implied to her the rumors concerned her. In effect, they implied that she needed to set the record straight because of what was being said about her. . . . Professor Hill confirms those characterizations were a fundamental factor in her coming forward.[15]

In the Senate hearing, Brown questioned Hill about the call from Brudney, bringing out exactly how Brudney's comments influenced Hill's thinking.

> BROWN: . . . Now, could you share your view of what those rumors or what they had suggested to you in those calls?
>
> HILL: . . . I did not want the committee to rely on rumors. I did not want the rumors to perhaps circulate through the press without at least considering the possibilities or exploring the possibilities through the committee process of coming forward.

By the time Brudney spoke to Hill, she had already been led into acknowledging the charge to Seidman. When Brudney suggested that the story was making its way through Washington political circles, Hill appears to have been convinced that she could gain control of the story by telling it to the committee herself in confidence, rather than have it circulate unchecked at the level of rumor and perhaps spin beyond her control. Of course, given the explosive nature of the charge, there was already great risk involved, no matter what Hill did or did not do.

In addition to Hill's concern with losing control of the situation, however, there was another critical dimension to the Hill and Brudney discussion. Brudney was employing a classic pressure tactic. On one level, he was backing Hill into a corner, alarming her about Washington rumors. But on another level, he was enticing her forward, playing to an assumed desire on her part to stop the nomination. Though Hill had not mentioned the sexual harassment charge to Brudney ever before, he had been close to Hill during the entire time she worked for Thomas. Presumably, therefore, he knew something about Hill's true feelings toward Thomas and must have surmised that she would be predisposed to help the cause.

Hill's friend Brudney had not known about the harassment before hearing of it through the Alliance for Justice. Hill maintained that the reason she waited ten years to come forward with her charge was that she had never before been asked by anyone in an official capacity what she thought of Thomas. When Senate staffers approached her, she said, "I felt I had a duty to report." But while Hill did not tell Brudney about the harassment while it was allegedly occurring in the early 1980s, the meticulously thorough Metzenbaum aide must have asked Hill about Thomas when he was trying to derail Thomas's reconfirmation to the EEOC in 1986, and then again in 1989 when he wanted to do the same to his appeals court nomination.

The question remains: Why did she acquiesce to the pressure from Senate staffers? Why was Hill willing to say something now, when she had said nothing on those prior occasions? Had her sense of privacy and reticence prevailed? Or did this suggest that the charge was developed after 1989? Was Hill simply too uncertain and confused to rebuff these probing conversations? Or was she in fact willing to contemplate "coming forward," but only with a guarantee that her identity could be shielded?

Hill's own account of the Brudney conversation indicates that her concern was not with the ethical or moral dilemma of whether or not to tell her story, but rather with the tactical question of *how* to tell it without exposure. Hill did not seem completely unwilling to talk; she seemed preoccupied with ensuring that no one would know she was the one talking.

A second concern she evinced at this time was determining whether Thomas's alleged behavior would have constituted sexual harassment. If Thomas really said and did the things she later described in her Senate testimony, the question that arises is how Hill, who has taught sexual harassment law, could have had any doubt on this score. Was it possible that the behavior she initially described to

Brudney was far less obnoxious than the behavior of which she would later accuse Thomas?

Under questioning from Senator Specter, Hill described the Brudney call in her Senate testimony:

> HILL: Well we discussed a number of different issues. We discussed one, what he knew about the law on sexual harassment. We discussed what he knew about the process for bringing information forward to the committee. And in the course of our conversations Mr. Brudney asked me what were specifics about what it was that I had experienced.
>
> In addition, we talked about the process for going forward. What might happen if I did bring information to the committee. That included that an investigation might take place, that I might be questioned by the committee in closed session. It even included something to the effect that the information might be presented to the candidate, or excuse me, *the nominee might not wish to continue the process.* [Emphasis added.]

> SPECTER: Mr. Brudney said to you that the nominee, Judge Thomas, might not wish to continue the process if you came forward with a statement on the factors which you have testified about?

> HILL: Well, I am not sure that that is exactly what he said. I think what he said was, depending on an investigation, a Senate, whether the Senate went into closed session and so forth, it might be that he might not wish to continue the process.

> SPECTER: So Mr. Brudney did tell you that Judge Thomas might not wish to continue to go forward with his nomination, if you came forward?

> HILL: Yes.

A more striking piece of evidence on this portion of the Brudney call was reported by *USA Today* on October 9, 1991. After speaking with Brudney in mid-September, Hill sought advice from another Washington friend, Keith Henderson, who had worked for the Senate Judiciary Committee in the early 1980s. *USA Today* reported:

> Anita Hill was told by Senate staffers her signed affidavit alleging sexual harassment by Clarence Thomas would be the instrument that "quietly and behind-the-scenes" would force him to withdraw his name.

Keith Henderson, a 10-year-friend of Hill and a former Senate Judiciary Committee staffer, says Hill was advised by Senate staffers that her charge would be kept secret and her name kept from public scrutiny.

"They would approach Judge Thomas with the information and he would withdraw and not turn this into a big story," Henderson says.[16]

Henderson has refused to comment further on the call, but the Senate staff interview of Gary Phillips shed some light on it. Through Phillips, Henderson had met Hill in 1981. Phillips was asked in the interview:

Q. When did you know that she had told someone other than you about her allegations?

A. I had a conversation with Keith Henderson and he told me that he had spoken to Anita and that Anita had told him that she had been contacted by Senate staff and that she had agreed to provide them with the information that she had told me about, and that she had done so with *the idea that the matter would be handled discreetly by the Senate Judiciary Committee.* [Emphasis added.]

Evidently Brudney had offered Hill a carrot: Come forward now, "quietly and behind the scenes," and Thomas would withdraw. *Throw the rock, and no one will see who threw it.* In that instant, the entire situation was transformed. Brief conversations with some friends, followed by hesitant, vague, and noncommittal encounters with two Senate staffers (Laster and Seidman), had suddenly mushroomed into an opportunity to stop the Supreme Court nomination by making an anonymous charge. Anonymity, of course, meant that the deed could be accomplished at no risk to Hill herself.

Yet even that tempting prospect would not be enough to make Hill move. She had to be shown a stick: *People in Washington are talking about you. If the press gets hold of the story, it will become known anyway, in a highly public and embarrassing way.* In other words, Hill had to be convinced that coming forward *then* was the only course that would allow her to avoid publicity. If she moved first, she could control the process, maintain anonymity, and prompt Thomas's quick withdrawal—or so she was led to expect. On this premise, Hill inched forward again. "Having very little choice, I chose the official route," Hill later told a press conference. She telephoned Brudney later the same day to say that she was willing to approach the Judiciary Committee.

The next morning, Brudney called Harriet Grant, the chief of Biden's Judiciary Committee nominations unit, to tell her that a woman who had worked for Clarence Thomas at the Department of Education and the EEOC was prepared to describe allegations about sexual misconduct, but the woman did not want to testify publicly. Hill believed Brudney had promised that her identity could be completely shielded, but Hill did not realize that Brudney, a Labor Committee staffer, was in no position to deliver on such a promise. Brudney, however, must have known that an anonymous charge would preclude any investigation.

Grant did things by the book. As nominations clerk, she had seen all sorts of anonymous, unsubstantiated charges flow in against nominees. This was in the nature of the business, particularly with high-profile nominations. From Grant's point of view, there was nothing unusual about Hill's allegations, especially since, at that point, none of the spectacular details that would later become public were being voiced. In the Senate debate on the Thomas nomination, GOP Senator Malcolm Wallop stated: "Virtually every nominee before this body has an FBI investigative report which is available to Senate members and a limited number of staff. An FBI report contains a vast amount of information—much of which is nothing more than baseless allegations."[17] Senator Danforth added:

> . . . what is happening now is grossly unfair—grossly unfair to Clarence Thomas. What is fair, Mr. President, is the normal process of the U.S. Senate. What is fair is what each one of us has experienced when we reviewed FBI files of a whole variety of nominees that come before the Senate. We review those files and many of them contain various allegations against nominees. Many files have various statements, some of which related to sexual activity. When that happens, we usually share it with other members of our committee quietly, try to reach our best conclusion, and then have a vote in the committee and that is the end of it.[18]

Indeed, contending that current members of the high court could not have been confirmed if the Senate aired unsubstantiated rumors, Justice Scalia was quoted shortly before Thomas was confirmed for the court as saying that one of his brethren "still gets letters from a woman in the mid-West who claims he's the father of her child."[19]

Harriet Grant did not call Hill, citing a Judiciary Committee investigating procedure that contact must be initiated by the person making the complaint. Unlike Seidman and Brudney, the Judiciary Committee aides were not in the habit of soliciting accusations against nominees. Brudney therefore called Hill and told her to call Grant. Thus, despite Grant's reservations, the accusation *was* solicited.

Hill called Grant on September 12. According to Grant's contemporaneous notes from that conversation, Hill emphasized that it would be "important" to have other women making similar charges against Thomas. Hill had said the same thing to Ricki Seidman when the two first spoke on September 6. As she later acknowledged in a press conference, Hill was aware that in the overwhelming majority of sexual harassment cases, a pattern of harassment against more than one victim is established. This is not always true, of course, but it is particularly important in establishing a claim when a case is lacking in other evidence—if there is no physical evidence, no witnesses, and no contemporaneous corroboration. Thus Hill's interest in having other women also come forward may have been a sign that she recognized her own case was weak. It may also have been a means of placing an impossible condition in the path of her own testimony, in order to avoid being called.

Hill also had other concerns. She told Grant that she wanted to remain anonymous; not even Thomas was to know her name, though it had been years since Thomas could have exacted any kind of direct or indirect retribution, and she now had a lifetime tenured position at the University of Oklahoma. Finally, Hill said that she was telling Grant about the charge in order to "remove responsibility" and "take it out of [her] hands." This statement makes it clear that Hill hoped, simply by talking to Grant, she could end her involvement.

When Biden was briefed on the sexual harassment allegation after Grant spoke with Hill, he realized that no investigation could begin unless Hill agreed to drop her insistence on anonymity. Despite what Hill believed after speaking with Brudney, anonymous charges could not be pursued. Fundamental fairness demanded that the accused be confronted with the charge and allowed to respond before it could be taken seriously. A formal investigation could then be opened. The Judiciary Committee's procedures for handling charges of this type could not be taken lightly by the chairman. Presumption of innocence, due process, rules of evidence—these were basic tenets of the American system of justice.

This is not a view held by Biden—or other male Senators—alone. Shortly after winning election to the Senate from Illinois on the coattails of the Woman of the Year, Carol Moseley Braun faced a sexual harassment controversy involving her campaign manager and boyfriend. Several weeks before the election, the Braun campaign conducted a confidential investigation of the allegations that found them to be unsubstantiated and took no further action. When word of the confidential investigation reached the media in mid-December, and one of the manager's anonymous accusers charged Braun with a cover-up, the Senator told the press: "As I've said before, the people who were interviewed were staffers, were interviewed in confidence. I see no reason to, I have no choice but to honor their desire that their comments be confidential." She went on to attack anonymous complaints as McCarthyite. "I'm old enough to remember the days when somebody could be accused of being a communist with nobody coming forward. I'm old enough to remember what it did to people's lives."

Hill's insistence on anonymity and Biden's insistence on going by the rules created a standoff. Meanwhile, time was running out. The confirmation hearings were well under way by this time in September, and what is more they were proceeding very well for the nominee. Thomas had begun testifying on September 10, the day that Brudney first called Hill. He testified for a record five days, concluding on September 14. Garnering only minor cuts and bruises, he was well on his way toward confirmation. This only compounded the pressure on Brudney to produce Anita Hill.

In fact, some observers of the confirmation made a connection between the Democrats' failure to exploit Thomas's position on abortion rights and the filing of a sexual harassment charge by Hill. In an essay in *Black Scholar,* a quarterly review published by the University of Michigan, Sarah E. Wright observed: "They concentrated their fire on Thomas's position regarding *Roe v. Wade.* They calculated that white feminists were the strongest liberal pressure group. But Thomas would not make a target of himself, would not take a stand, to the Democrats' frustration. . . . Anita F. Hill was [then] brought forward."[20] Ricky Silberman also saw a link: The opposition "defeated Robert Bork on the abortion issue, and five years later set their sights on Clarence Thomas. But he refused to engage on abortion, so they trotted out the gender warrior's ultimate weapon: Anita Hill's accusation of sexual harassment."[21]

Brudney began burning up the phone lines to Norman, Oklahoma, trying to move Hill off her position. He made thirteen calls to Hill in the thirteen days from September 10 to September 23. When asked to account for the phone calls by Fleming, Brudney tried to portray himself as a neutral friend and adviser to Hill during the period. Fleming wrote:

> Although enjoined not to encourage Hill in pressing her charges [presumably by Harriet Grant], Brudney says that he felt responsible for Hill because he had placed her in a difficult situation and she was upset with the committee's perceived inaction. Most importantly, neither Brudney nor his [Labor Committee] colleagues wanted Hill to feel Brudney had deserted her.

Hill, however, was not upset with "the committee's perceived inaction," as Brudney claimed. When Fleming interviewed her, Hill said that while she did not wish to proceed, Brudney was pushing her in that direction:

> [Hill] disagrees with Brudney's claim that he was entirely neutral. Although she clearly takes responsibility for her own decision, Hill recalls Brudney's stance as more persistent and says she told him on several occasions that it was her decision to make [whether to drop her anonymity demand]. From Hill's perspective, the difference in approach was her own experience that allegations of sexual harassment are often disbelieved, whereas Brudney was confident that Hill's statements, with evidence of a contemporaneous complaint to a friend in 1981, would be credited.

Though Hill continued to maintain the position that her charge alone would not be enough to establish that Thomas was a sexual harasser, she eventually yielded. Had it not been for Brudney's dogged persistence, it appears that Hill would never have met the committee's requirement that she allow herself to be identified for purposes of an investigation. Thus even at this late stage of events, Hill's charge—if one can really call it that—would have died on the vine.

Brudney's influence alone, however, was clearly not enough to persuade Hill to drop her insistence on anonymity. There were others in the wings, though less is known about their role in these events, particularly that of Susan Hoerchner. Hoerchner helped to persuade Hill to file the charge, and she nudged it through the Senate at key moments throughout September.

According to Hoerchner, she had not spoken to Hill at all since the July 1 call, when she had asked if Hill was going to say anything about that "pig" Thomas. Hoerchner may or may not have had contacts over the summer with Senate staffers or interest groups: she did say in an interview with Senate staff that she had been acquainted with Jim Brudney through her brother, who had been in Brudney's class at Yale. Hoerchner's past employment at a public interest law group that was a member of the Alliance for Justice coalition would later be revealed as well. These facts suggested that Hoerchner had connections to the anti-Thomas campaign at the time she was released from her vow of silence.

When Hill and Hoerchner spoke again in early September, Hoerchner gave Hill the same advice as Ricki Seidman had: Talk with Brudney. In the interview with the Senate committee, Hoerchner was asked:

Q. Did you give any instructions to Ms. Hill that may have related to Brudney?

A. Instructions?

Q. Did you ever ask Ms. Hill or tell Ms. Hill that it might be good if she talked to Jim Brudney?

A. I did early . . . because she had known him and had said that she trusted him, trusted his confidentiality.

Contrary to Hoerchner's later claims not to have advised Hill, this clearly constituted "advice." After Hill's initial talk with Brudney on September 10, in fact, Hill and Hoerchner had several telephone conversations until the night before Hill filed an official statement with the Judiciary Committee, charging that Clarence Thomas had asked her for dates and discussed pornography with her in the early 1980s. Having put the show in motion, Hoerchner was waiting backstage to play her part as Hill's corroborating witness. In her typically diffuse style, Hoerchner described to the Senate lawyers the anxious tenor of her contacts with Hill in September: "I had the feeling I was calling her," Hoerchner said. "At first it wasn't, I would say—let me see— either once a week or every week and a half, just to see if she knew what had happened or if someone was going to call me [for corroboration] and, you know, [I would] say 'hello' immediately."

A few days after Hill first spoke with Brudney and Grant, Brudney was trying to bridge the divide between Biden's staff and Hill on the anonymity issue. Brudney called Hill early on Friday, September 13, and again on Sunday evening, September 15. He had assured Hill that her complaint, along with corroboration from Hoerchner, would be credited. Though Hill's allegation was not moving through official channels, because she would not allow her name to be divulged, perhaps the corroborating witness would spark the committee's interest. Interestingly, there seems to have been no effort on the part of either Hill or Brudney to identify corroborating witnesses other than Hoerchner. Why hadn't Hill called former colleagues from the EEOC or any of the people who eventually offered corroborating testimony to see if any of them could back up her account? Why did Hill believe that only Hoerchner could corroborate the story, especially since other people did later appear?

After these consultations with Brudney, Hill called Hoerchner on September 16 and suggested for the first time that she call Harriet Grant to corroborate the sexual harassment story. Hoerchner called Washington on September 17. While she too insisted on remaining anonymous, she told Grant she could corroborate that in a telephone call in the spring of 1981, Hill had told her that she was being sexually harassed at work. The fact that Hill was not working for Clarence Thomas in the spring of 1981 seemed to slip by unnoticed, not least by Hoerchner herself. When Hoerchner told this to the FBI the following week, a couple of lawyers in the Justice Department read the FBI report and recognized the incompatibility of the dates for what it might be: A gaping hole in the Anita Hill story.

Apparently neither Hill nor Hoerchner, both Yale-educated lawyers, was troubled that lodging anonymous charges ran counter to the tenets of the American legal system. The two seemed to think that disseminating the information clandestinely would satisfy the Senate investigators and fulfill their political purpose. To this end, Hoerchner was fanning the flames with other unidentified parties, in the hope that neither she nor Hill would have to come forward. Hoerchner was clearly assuming, as everyone apparently did, that Thomas was guilty of the charge and would undoubtedly withdraw once it was circulated:

Q. Did you subsequent to that conversation [July 1] with Anita Hill, did you have another conversation . . . ?

A. Oh, yes. Sure. I would check with her [Hill] every so often for a status update. My feeling was—I talked to Harriet Grant. I was putting out the information. You know, if there was a question someone would contact. Either it would be believed, accepted, rejected, or more information requested. We thought it was all over.

But it was not nearly over. "Putting out the information" was not enough. The Judiciary Committee was adhering to its standard process. And Hill would not relinquish anonymity, despite Brudney's efforts. Thus Anita Hill herself, not the committee, was responsible for the fact that her charge was not immediately investigated when she relayed it to Biden staffer Harriet Grant on September 12.

By this point, Brudney knew that Hill had misinterpreted their initial discussion, and had concluded that she could proceed in total anonymity. Since Hill would not abandon that position, Brudney argued that Grant had misunderstood Hill's request. He contended that Hill was willing to identify herself to the nominee and the FBI, if only the committee would engage Hill in further talks. He persuaded Ellen Lovell and Ann Harkins, two lawyers who worked on the Judiciary Committee for Senator Patrick Leahy of Vermont, to try to get the committee more deeply involved. The pair met with Grant and two of Grant's superiors, Ted Kaufman, Senator Biden's chief of staff, and Jeff Peck, the Judiciary Committee staff director. Fleming reported:

> They told the Biden staffers of Brudney's concerns and suggested placing another call to Hill for the purpose of determining whether she in fact meant to cut off all committee activity through her request for total anonymity. Having calculated that ten persons already knew of Hill's allegations, Harkins warned disclosure could embarrass the committee if nothing more was done.
>
> Grant responded that Hill had appeared to be equivocal and uncertain in publicizing her allegations. Kaufman was adamant that, given her request for confidentiality, it would be wrong to push Hill in any way.

Clearly, Chairman Biden and his staff were ensnared in a Catch-22. Ideologically opposed to Thomas but not necessarily against his confirmation, concerned about the sexual harassment story yet responsible for guaranteeing a reasoned and reasonable confirmation process, the Biden staffers rejected the Brudney-inspired promptings of the Leahy aides. In an interview with the *Washington Post* after Hill's charges were leaked, Biden explained his thinking: It "would have been immoral to have done that, going out and pushing her and cajoling her would have been wrong to do. That would be thrusting an incredible burden on someone who is going to go through a difficult decision that is going to have a dramatic impact on her life."[22]

On September 19, nine days after she had first told her story to Brudney, Hill, having finally decided to abide by the rules, called Harriet Grant again. Hill told Grant that she did not want to abandon the sexual harassment matter, though she was still applying brakes by only inviting exploration of her options. What could she do so that the charge could be considered officially by the committee? "She wanted all members of the committee to know about her concerns; and, if her name needed to be used to achieve that goal, she wanted to know. She also wanted to be apprised of her 'options,' because she did not want to 'abandon' her concerns," according to the Biden chronology of committee contacts with Hill.

After stalling for more than a week, Hill had agreed to move from anonymity to confidentiality in order to prompt consideration of the charge. Clarence Thomas and the members of the committee—but only they—could be informed that she was the accuser. This distinction made an enormous difference, as GOP Senator Kit Bond of Missouri later explained on the Senate floor. "[W]e must differentiate between confidential and anonymous. Anonymous charges cannot be given credence because to do so is extraordinarily unfair to the accused—as they have no way of defending themselves. Thus Professor Hill's early requests for anonymity meant that the process of checking into her allegations could not proceed. However, confidentiality—which implies full and fair hearing of the facts, but not in public—is certainly a legitimate approach to take."[23]

What had occurred to change Hill's mind? In his frustration with the delay, Brudney had called Susan Deller Ross, who runs a legal clinic on sexual harassment at the Georgetown University Law Center, and asked her to intervene with Hill. Ross and Hill spoke for the first time on September 18, the day before Hill changed her mind. With Hill's permission, Ross in turn had sought the counsel of Judith Lichtman, president of the Women's Legal Defense Fund, a group fighting the Thomas nomination. In helping Ross to bring Hill forward, Lichtman—more than any other interest group leader—became the *eminence grise* of the Hill affair.

Ross and Lichtman knew each other well; Lichtman sat on an advisory board of one of Ross's sexual harassment law programs at Georgetown as did two other committed opponents of Clarence Thomas: Marcia Greenberger of the National Women's Law Center, which later gave an award to Anita Hill, and D.C. Delegate Eleanor Holmes Norton. Shortly after Hill's charges leaked, the *New York Times,* without mentioning Ross by name, reported on the relationship between Ross and these anti-Thomas partisans: "Some officials of the liberal interest groups that have been lobbying against the nomination said they had indirect contact with Professor Hill, through an intermediary they would not identify during the period when she was considering whether to cooperate with the committee."[24] There can be little doubt that Ross, who became the Hill team's expert on sexual harassment during the public hearings, encouraged Hill to file the charge.[25]

In conversations with Hoerchner, Ross, and, indirectly, Lichtman, Hill became convinced that the charge should be leveled. But when Hill called Grant on September 19 to say she wanted to go ahead, Grant told her that the first step was for the committee to report the confidential allegations to the FBI for investigation. This was standard committee procedure, and an indication that if Hill would put her name to the charge, the committee was ready to make it a top priority. This is also something that she should have learned from Brudney if in fact their first discussion focused on the official procedures for bringing a harassment charge before the committee, as Hill testified.

But the prospect of an FBI investigation apparently worried Hill, who at first agreed to the interview and then called back to say she had changed her mind. The Biden chronology summarized events:

> At the close of the [first] conversation, Professor Hill stated that while she had "no problems" talking with the FBI, she wanted to think about its "utility." She told committee staff she would call later that day with her decision on whether to proceed.
>
> Late that afternoon . . . Professor Hill again spoke with committee staff and explained that she was "not able to give an answer" about whether the matter should be turned over to the FBI. She asked that staff contact her on September 21. On September 21, full committee staff spoke with Professor Hill for the sixth time. She stated: "She did not want to go through with the FBI investigation, because she was skeptical about its utility, but that if she could think of an alternate route, or another 'option,' she would contact staff."

Why was Hill reluctant to be interviewed? Hill told Grant she was concerned that the FBI interviewers might "distort" her allegations. She also said that publicity was not her "agenda," according to Grant's notes. What kind of "distortion" she feared and how a confidential FBI interview would constitute "publicity," was not apparent. In any event, Hill's choice of words—"utility," "option," "agenda"—seemed to indicate a careful effort to protect herself and forestall action.

Anita Hill, not the Senate committee, was responsible for this second delay. Hill's decision not to cooperate with an FBI investigation derailed the process just two days after she had agreed to satisfy the committee's requirement that she give her name.

On the very day that Hill shied away from the FBI inquiry, the Thomas confirmation hearings ended. Was Hill stalling again—as she had for almost two weeks over the anonymity issue—to keep the harassment charge from coming out in the hearings? Once the hearings were over, perhaps she was hoping that it would be too late to come forward. If that is what Hill was thinking, she would not be let off the hook so easily.

With the committee hearings ended and the vote on the nomination just one week away, a frantic round of telephone calls ensued over the weekend of September 21. Ross, Hoerchner, and Brudney spoke to Hill several times. When Hill told Hoerchner that she did not want the FBI called in—again despite her claims that she never "advised" Hill—Hoerchner suggested that she file a signed statement with the Judiciary Committee as a way of avoiding or at least delaying an investigation. Hoerchner told the Senate interviewers:

> And I had talked to her sometime before that, before I knew the FBI was trying to get in touch with me and before she had consented to the interview. And she said that she was told that her only option was to be investigated by the FBI, and we both thought it was odd, and I thought there should have been some alternative where she could make a statement with her name being used, as some sort of an intermediate measure.

Hill later told the FBI that her contacts with Susan Hoerchner were decisive when she was considering whether or not to file the committee statement that weekend:

> She advised the interviewing agents that she made the decision to prepare the statement after several telephone conversations with her personal friend, Susan Hoerchner. The last telephone conversation

between her and Hoerchner was on a Sunday night prior to her preparation of her statement.

Hill also called Brudney that Sunday night:

She told Brudney—who she had not spoken with since Tuesday—she was trying to decide whether to submit to an [FBI] interview. She also told him she had been working on a statement which she could submit to the FBI if she decided to go forward with the FBI interview. She said she was concerned that her story be told "in her own words." Brudney says he neither encouraged nor advised Hill in connection with either her statement or the FBI process.

On Sunday evening, Sept. 22, Brudney telephoned Hill at home. They spoke for a half hour. Hill said she had not yet decided to go forward with an FBI interview, but had drafted a statement. Brudney says he called Hill on Sunday evening because he felt that he had been somewhat abrupt with her the prior afternoon. Again, Brudney says Hill did not request his advice, and he did not provide any advice.

On Monday, September 23, Harriet Grant walked over to the Judiciary Committee's telefax machine and picked up a four-page typewritten statement, dated and signed by Anita F. Hill.[26] At that moment, Brudney's prior assurances to Hill were exposed for what they had been all along. Making the charge was not a way of maintaining control, as Brudney had led Hill to believe, but a virtual guarantee of losing it. There was no going back. Once the charges existed in writing, committee staffers with their own agendas could vent them without her knowledge or consent. When confronted with the written statement, Hill would have to either verify it or undermine her own character by disowning it. Orrin Hatch later explained the tactic in a speech on the Senate floor: "I am concerned because I have seen some of the staff operate. Once witnesses make a statement or are pushed into making certain statements . . . then that person is stuck with the statements."[27]

It had been a long and winding road to September 23. During the public testimony of Thomas in early and mid-September, the Metzenbaum and Kennedy aides, and then Biden's aide Harriet Grant, had spoken with Anita Hill several times. Committee aides began whispering about a "mystery" witness who might testify behind a screen. "We were picking up signals that the Kennedy and Metzenbaum staffers thought they had a show-stopper. We didn't know what it was," one Justice Department official said.

But Biden could not touch an anonymous charge. After fourteen days on the fence, on September 23, Hill filed a confidential statement, supplying her name and agreeing to an FBI interview. (She refiled the statement two days later, on September 25. The substance had not changed, but the new statement was cleansed of the grammatical errors and misspellings in Hill's first draft.) The day she filed her statement, the very moment Hill agreed to speak with the FBI and agreed that Thomas could be informed of her identity, the Judiciary Committee ordered an investigation of Hill's charges. Once Hill had put her name to the allegation, the committee moved swiftly to check it out.

Still, despite these indisputable facts, Hill prevailed in forming the public's perception of what had happened behind closed doors. In a press conference in Oklahoma before she flew to Washington, Hill maintained that the committee was to blame for the delay in airing her charges. "I don't believe that they were necessarily taken seriously," she said . . . "I can only say that I think this is part of the frustration that I am experiencing—that these kinds of claims and statements are not taken seriously, that this is not an issue that men can deal with necessarily without a lot of different supporting documentation, and that just does not happen in most cases." When she was specifically asked whether or not her request for anonymity had impeded the investigation, Hill said: "To say that I perhaps delayed is not true." The *New York Times*'s account of Hill's press conference reported: "She said she had struggled for nearly two weeks last month to put before the 14 male members of the committee a confidential account of being verbally harassed by Judge Thomas when she was his assistant from 1981 to 1983, first at the Education Department and later at the EEOC."[28]

Nina Totenberg and other reporters unquestioningly adopted Hill's version of events in their reporting. "Several senators contacted by NPR say they are troubled by the Hill allegations and the long delay in investigating them *by Chairman Biden*," Totenberg reported.[29] At another point, Totenberg said, "Biden simply never got it—never understood that sexual harassment was a serious charge."[30] Even eight months after the hearings concluded, Timothy Phelps of *Newsday*, having presumably reviewed the record for his June 1992 book *Capitol Games*, was asked on *Good Morning America* why the committee had not immediately begun an investigation of the Hill charges in early September. "Well, frankly, I think that sexual harassment was not at that time an issue that the mostly white men in the U.S. Senate considered to be really important," Phelps replied.[31]

In reality, however, between September 9 and September 19, Hill had refused to identify herself in order to allow an investigation to proceed. The committee would not accept her first request, total anonymity, an unacceptable precondition in *any* case of this nature. When Hill agreed to shift from anonymity to confidentiality, she objected to an FBI investigation, even though she had been told previously that it was standard procedure. This accounted for another four-day delay.

Obviously, and perhaps understandably, facing down her sexual harasser in a hostile public forum was the last thing Hill ever wanted to do. Hill's motive in coming forward has been portrayed as extremely high-minded, and her hesitation in doing so has been ascribed to personal delicacy, an instinct for privacy, and an unwillingness to generate vulgar publicity. Yet in an exchange with Specter during her public testimony, Hill disclosed that the real reason for her hesitation was a desire to control the process:

> SPECTER: Is that what you meant, when you responded earlier to Senator Biden, that the situation would be controlled "so that it would not get to this point in the hearings?"
>
> HILL: Of the public hearing. In entering into these conversations with the staff members, what I was trying to do was control this information, yes, so that it would not get to this point.

Earlier Hill had told Biden, "The desire was never to get to this point. The desire—and I thought that I could do things and if I were cautious enough and I could control it so that it would not get to this point, but I was mistaken."

Missing from the way Hill conducted her negotiations with the committee was any sense of responsibility to come forward, even if it meant facing the accused, signing her name to the allegation, and submitting to an FBI investigation. Was it not worth the risk of perhaps being victimized by the process in order to keep a sexual harasser, a man so contemptuous of civil rights laws—indeed in this case a profoundly cynical person who posed as a champion of protections for women in the workplace while harassing his own employee—off the highest court in the land? Why was there no effort by Hill—a professor of law—to balance her personal interests against the need to preserve the integrity of the Supreme Court? Why *did* the Senate have to come to her, dragging her along every step of the way? While Hill's desire not to go public was certainly understandable, why was anonymity even within the Senate, which had properly and confidentially handled many such allegations over the years, so important to Hill? Why didn't she want even Thomas to know her name? Why would a truth-teller negotiate so many veils of secrecy?

These nagging questions seemed to trouble Senator Nancy Kassebaum of Kansas when she addressed the Senate on the Thomas nomination.

> Apparently [Hill] agreed to provide a statement under the condition that her name would not be disclosed to the public, to the full Senate or . . . even to Judge Thomas himself. . . . If this is true, I find it difficult to comprehend what was intended in these charges. Is it possible that Professor Hill, an experienced attorney and law professor, believed that Judge Thomas's appointment could be killed in secret? Was she led to believe the mere raising of these charges could force the judge to withdraw or lead the committee to reject his nomination with no explanation to the full Senate or public?[32]

In fact, there was a fairly recent Washington precedent for such a scenario. In 1989, former Texas Senator John Tower withdrew his nomination as defense secretary after confidential allegations regarding excessive drinking and sexual harassment were made to the Senate. The charges appeared to have been serious, since they generated concern and opposition among Senators and ultimately doomed the nomination. But they were not aired in detail, Tower's accusers did not go public, and the allegations were never substantiated. The critical difference in the Thomas case was the nominee's decision not to withdraw, and the subsequent decision of his opponents to move the unsubstantiated charges from the Senate chambers onto the front-page of *Newsday,* and NPR's airwaves.

Hill was interviewed by the FBI the evening of Monday, September 23. Two agents—one a male, the other a female—arrived at her modest three-bedroom ranch-style home on South Berry Street in Norman, Oklahoma. After the interview she promptly called Brudney to tell him what had transpired, and also to inform him that Susan Hoerchner was scheduled to be interviewed that night in California. Before Hoerchner agreed to be interviewed, she also called Brudney for advice.

The FBI interviews generated what is known as an FD 302 report. These reports consist of unprocessed, or raw, data and typically draw no conclusions. By Wednesday, Clarence Thomas, now that he could be told who had made the charge against him, was confronted for the first time by the FBI as well.[33] Thomas emphatically denied each of Hill's allegations. Two former EEOC employees, Nancy Fitch and Allyson Duncan, were also interviewed. Like virtually *everyone* who knew both Thomas and Hill, Fitch and Duncan said they believed Thomas. But more important was what Thomas did *not* do. He did not immediately withdraw his nomination when confronted with the charge. The strategy of making an allegation "quietly and behind the scenes" that would lead the nominee to withdraw had therefore failed.

How should Thomas's failure to withdraw be interpreted? If Thomas *had* sexually harassed Anita Hill, as the Shadow Senate seemed convinced, the behind-the-scenes strategy of forcing him to withdraw would almost certainly have worked. Consider as an analogy the case of Douglas Ginsburg, the circuit judge nominated to the high court after the defeat of Bork. When his embittered girlfriend leaked a story of his marijuana use to Nina Totenberg, Ginsburg pulled out and returned to a productive career on the appellate court. The charge against Ginsburg, while of debatable relevance, was true. Like Ginsburg, Thomas already had a life-tenured position on the D.C. circuit. And before the Hill charges leaked, he still had his good name. Thus while Thomas's obvious motive for lying was a seat on the Supreme Court, if he was guilty of even the least of the charges, there was great risk involved in pressing ahead with confirmation in a public hearing, and even more in categorically denying the charges under oath. How did he know Hill had not kept a diary, or written a poignant letter to her parents recounting the harassment? What if someone had seen or heard him harassing Hill in the EEOC cafeteria, one very public place where she claimed the harassment occurred? In short, his own belief that he was innocent is the best explanation of how he could have been confident that her case would not be strong enough to defeat him.

Meanwhile, two days had passed since Hill filed her statement and talked with the FBI, and she still had heard nothing from the Judiciary Committee. According to the chronology released by Senator Biden, on Wednesday, with the committee vote two days away, Hill again called Harriet Grant. The Biden staff had planned to brief the Democratic committee members on the Hill statement and the FBI report before Friday's committee vote. But Hill now wanted them to go further:

For the first time, she then stated that she wanted the statement "distributed" to committee members. Committee staff explained that while the information would be brought to the attention of committee members, staff could not guarantee how that information would be disseminated—whether her statement would be "distributed" or communicated by oral briefing. . . . She concluded the conversation by stating that she wanted her statement "distributed," and that she would "take on faith that [staff] will do everything that [it] can to abide by [her] wishes."

Hill was not happy with Grant's response. She called Brudney to complain that her statement might not be "distributed" to the members of the committee. At that point, having been persuaded to make the allegation formally, Hill seemed to have shed much of her earlier reticence in dealing with Washington. Since Thomas had not thrown in the towel, Hill's concern now seemed to be that her confidential statement should reach the right people, achieving maximum impact within the Judiciary Committee forum. Having agonized for so many days about whether and how to come forward, Hill wanted to be sure that she had not gotten in so deep for naught. She now wanted to see the process through.

Brudney, of course, shared this concern. If the statement was not circulated, there was no chance that it would prompt one of the committee members to call for further investigation—the last hope for stopping the nomination. He therefore told staffers of Ted Kennedy that a formal statement had been received and that Hill had been interviewed by the FBI. The Kennedy aides in turn told their boss, and they also told the two aides to Senator Leahy who had earlier intervened on Brudney's behalf. Leahy immediately asked for an oral briefing on the charges. Kennedy, meanwhile, mentioned Hill's allegation to Paul Simon.

On Thursday, with the committee vote scheduled for Friday, September 27, Biden orally briefed the committee Democrats. He talked with Kennedy and Metzenbaum. He pulled Herb Kohl of Wisconsin, Howell Heflin, and Simon into a corridor off the Senate floor to let them know about the charge. Biden also talked with Senator Dennis DeConcini, the only Democrat on the committee publicly supporting Thomas. DeConcini asked to see the FBI report, as did Simon.

Simon's interest was piqued earlier Thursday morning, when Susan Kaplan, his chief counsel, received a telephone call from Sonia

Jarvis, who had been Anita Hill's roommate in Washington in the early 1980s. After filing her statement with the committee on Monday, Hill had called Jarvis, to whom she had not spoken in some time, to say that she had leveled a charge against Clarence Thomas and to ask if she could help bring the charge to the committee's attention. Now the director of the Black Voter Participation Project in Washington, Jarvis had lived with Hill near the Capitol during the entire time the alleged incidents took place; yet Hill had never mentioned them to Jarvis before. Jarvis told Kaplan that Hill was concerned that her statement was not going to be distributed to the committee Senators. Kaplan, who knew generally that a charge had been filed, arranged for Simon to speak with Hill directly.

Why Jarvis called Simon's office, rather than another Senator's, is not known. According to his 1992 book *Advice and Consent,* Simon agreed to call Hill to assess her bona fides. The two discussed the committee's handling of her statement.[34] "The possibility of distributing her statement to all members of the Senate was raised, but Hill decided against such distribution when Simon said it was impossible to keep her name out of the public eye," Fleming reported. By then, it was clear to Simon, if not to Hill, that the signed statement and the inconclusive FBI report would not be enough to force Thomas to withdraw or to cause an official postponement in the committee vote.

Hill's demand for confidentiality, therefore, was now a hurdle for those who wanted to bring up the charge against Thomas. She had moved from anonymity to confidentiality, allowing a preliminary investigation to go forward in the apparent hope of forcing Thomas to pull out. When that did not happen, the allegation remained a confidential matter within the committee; Hill had laid down a ground rule under which no one but the nominee and the members of the committee was to know her name. But if the charge was to do Thomas any harm at this late hour, it would have to be publicized, requiring Hill to rescind her condition.

Simon wrote in *Advice and Consent* that he did not give Hill any advice one way or the other on this issue in their telephone conversation. However, an account of the Simon call in *U.S. News* reported: "When he heard of the allegations, Simon was disturbed enough to call Hill himself. She asked that he distribute copies of her statement about Thomas to all members of the Senate, while keeping her name anonymous; he explained it was 'impossible' and *tried to persuade her to testify.* When he failed, Simon still sought no delay in the committee vote."[35] In a book on judicial confirmations, *A Matter of Principle,*

Mark Gitenstein, a former Biden Judiciary Committee counsel, gave a similar account of Simon's talk with Hill: "Paul Simon called Hill and asked her if it would be possible to reveal her name [publicly]. Simon told Biden of his conversation with Hill before the committee vote."[36]

On the other side of the aisle, Senator Thurmond had decided, in autocratic fashion, not to brief the Republicans on the Hill allegations, because in his view they were unmerited. Two of Thurmond's staffers, Duke Short and Melissa Riley, had received copies of the Hill statement earlier in the week from the Biden staff, but they kept them in a committee vault, telling no one about them.

Three other committee Republicans heard about the charge informally. On the Senate floor, Thurmond told Orrin Hatch about the allegation. Hatch called Thomas instantly, and Thomas told him that what Hill was alleging had simply never happened.[37]

Alan Simpson found out about the allegations from Biden and Kennedy. "I saw [Biden and Kennedy] having a very animated discussion in the back of the chamber and went up and asked them what that was all about," Simpson recalled. "And they said there was somebody making a sexual harassment charge against Thomas. And I said 'What else? We get all kinds of *stuff* in here.' Joe was terrifically concerned because the woman kept saying she wanted confidentiality, and if she wasn't going to come out, they weren't going to force her." Neither Hatch nor Simpson saw the Hill statement or the FBI report before the vote. The only Republican other than Thurmond who saw the FBI file was Arlen Specter, who heard about the charge from DeConcini on Thursday night and promptly asked to review the Hill report.[38]

Such committee machinations, of course, begged the question of why the Hill allegation neither affected the outcome of the vote in the Judiciary Committee nor moved any member of the committee to postpone the vote to permit further investigation and perhaps a reopening of the hearings. This is also the question that angered so many women and animated the media at the time of the hearings, making the committee's inaction seem as scandalous as the Hill allegations themselves.

On the morning of the committee vote, the Thomas nomination appeared headed for a 7–7 tie vote in the committee. The apparent outcome surprised the White House, which was hoping for an 8–6 or even a 9–5 in favor. The decision of Howell Heflin to go against the nomination was announced late Thursday. The statement was vintage

Heflin, citing Thomas for everything but the real sticking point, his philosophy. "Judge Thomas's answers and explanations about previous speeches, articles, and positions raised thoughts of inconsistencies, ambiguities, contradictions, lack of scholarship, lack of conviction, and instability," Heflin said.

As late as Thursday Biden's staff told reporters that he had not decided which way to vote. Biden had told one Republican Senator earlier in the week that he would probably vote in favor of Thomas. But the Heflin announcement made it politically impossible for Biden to do so. In a move virtually unheard of for the lumbering judge, he had jumped into the pool ahead of Biden, forcing the Chairman's hand—precisely the judicial double-play envisioned by Bill Coleman of the NAACP Legal Defense and Education Fund. Coleman and the NAACP lobbyist Elaine Jones had met with Heflin shortly before his decision was made. "I think Heflin decided to give his vote to the [civil rights] groups since Thomas was going to be confirmed anyway," one veteran Heflin-watcher on the Senate staff said.

The shift in the committee, however, was not related to Hill's allegation. After the allegations leaked to the press, many women's activists would later use this fact to argue that the committee had "covered up" the Hill charges. Obscured first by a layer of judicial politics, then by the politics of race, the Thomas nomination would finally be wrapped in a particularly virulent strain of sexual politics. "It's back to what did they know and when did they know it," the feminist leader Eleanor Smeal said.[39] "The Senate's reaction is fairly typical of organizations run by men," Claudia Withers of the Women's Legal Defense Fund said. "They just didn't get it."[40]

"The Senate was attempting to continue as if it was business in the usual way, when they should have been responding to this extraordinarily serious complaint," Lichtman told the *New York Times*—a complaint that, as the *Times* never saw fit to report, Lichtman had a major hand in eliciting. "This is a microcosm of the problem, endemic in society, about the way working women are viewed."[41] (According to Biden's adviser Gitenstein, Lichtman privately held a different view, one that is more consistent with the record. He reported that Lichtman "told Biden in a private meeting after the story broke that he had handled Hill's request for confidentiality correctly").[42]

The media also helped whip up the feminist frenzy. "From the beginning the Senate—especially Judiciary Committee Chairman Joseph Biden, Democrat of Delaware—bungled the matter, seemingly hoping it would simply disappear," the *Wall Street Journal* reported. "To some, its response to the potentially explosive charges seemed a textbook example of how male-dominated institutions are often paralyzed by allegations of sexual harassment in the workplace, and how ill-informed even lawmakers are about the sensitive subject."[43]

Such feminist boilerplate obscured the real reasons why the allegation did not affect the committee vote. On Friday, Biden decided to circulate to every committee Democrat a physical copy of Hill's statement. Biden thus went the extra step to comply with Hill's wish that her statement be "distributed." The intervention of the Harvard law professor Laurence Tribe seems to have accounted for this. According to the Fleming report, Harvard's Professor Charles Ogletree, who became Anita Hill's counsel during the second round of hearings, had been contacted the day before the committee was to vote by two of Hill's friends for advice on how to draw the committee's attention to her charge. Ogletree, in turn, had called his colleague Tribe on Friday morning. Tribe promptly called Biden's chief Judiciary Committee counsel, and his former student, Ron Klain, and told him that Hill's friends were concerned that her allegation had not been distributed to the committee.[44]

The copies of the closely guarded Hill statement were placed in sealed envelopes and marked by Judiciary Committee Democratic staff for "Senators' eyes only." They were then hand-carried by Biden staffers to the Democratic Senators, each of whom read the statement, placed it back in the envelope, and returned it to the Biden staff. All the copies then were shredded at the Senate Intelligence Committee offices except the original telefax from Hill, which remained sealed in a Judiciary Committee vault.

Under committee rules, after reading the Hill statement, any member could have automatically been granted a one-week postponement for any item on the committee's agenda. One Senator might have put off the Thomas vote for a week and called for a closed or executive session to hear more about the charge. But no one did. The question is, why not?

First of all, the facts did not seem to warrant it. No one stopped to think that one of the reasons Hill's charge did not derail the confirmation train was that the committee members simply did not believe it was credible—a judgment that the American people would eventually reach as well, after much pain had been inflicted on both the accused and his accuser. Hill had come forward after ten years of silence. She had left a secure job at one government agency to follow

Thomas to another, contrary to the response displayed by most harassment victims of avoiding the harasser. The FBI investigation found no evidence to confirm or support Hill's account of Thomas's behavior. The sole contemporaneous corroboration for the charge, that of Susan Hoerchner, was less than compelling. Two women who had worked closely with both Thomas and Hill—including one, Nancy Fitch, who had been a close friend of Hill—told the FBI they believed Thomas.

For his part, Thomas vehemently denied all of the charges to the FBI. Everything known by the Senate about Thomas up to that point—the collective forty-three years of his life—militated against the credibility of the allegation. Thomas had many political enemies on Capitol Hill, but no one had ever questioned his personal character. Certainly no one had ever charged him with sexual harassment before (or since).

The second and less subjective reason why no one on the committee called for a postponement of the vote and a further investigation was that Hill was still insisting on confidentiality—that her name be known only within the committee. The next step would have been a full-scale committee investigation. If the committee proceeded further, even in closed session, maintaining the witness's confidentiality would be an insurmountable challenge. Once it was known to all the Senators, the entire Senate staff, and the national press corps that the vote had been postponed at the last moment, every reporter in town would have jumped on the story. Senators outside the committee would have insisted on knowing what was going on. And once the Thomas forces found out why the vote had been put off, the nominee would have had the right to respond to the charge in any way he saw fit—even by calling a press conference.

Thus any move for a delay would have inevitably meant disclosing Hill's name to the public. That is why Simon had called Hill and asked if her name could be revealed. Even Thomas's most adamant detractors on the committee were not willing to expose Hill against her wishes, even if it meant forgoing the last chance to stop Thomas. "The fact is, they were in a terrible box because she would not allow her name to be used," Gitenstein told the *National Law Journal.* "It is a pretty serious thing to breach someone's promised confidentiality."[45] There was also an institutional consideration. Bruce Fein, a legal affairs commentator who opposed Thomas's confirmation, wrote in the *ABA Journal:* "Certainly Congress' ability to guarantee confidentiality is vital. Fear of retaliation, embarrassment, or unwanted publicity would prompt many to refuse to provide legislative committees with evidence—whether on organized crime, terrorism, or the qualifications of Supreme Court nominees—if their identities were public."[46]

In a speech on the Senate floor, Biden explained the committee's decision:

> We continued to honor her request, which was that no one in the U.S. Senate be made aware of her allegations beyond the members of the committee unless we were able to guarantee that her name would never be mentioned, that no one would ever know, a guarantee that could not and I would add should not have been made. So, consequently, the committee was unable to move any further with the investigation beyond what the FBI had done. I took her charges seriously, as we did on the committee, but we also took her request not to have anyone outside the committee aware of this seriously.[47]

Howard Metzenbaum explained the committee's desire to protect Hill this way: "I did not seek to delay the committee vote nor to raise the issue publicly or with my colleagues because it was my understanding that Ms. Hill wished that only the committee members be notified of her allegations. I believed each member would decide for himself and that Professor Hill's confidentiality needed to be protected."[48]

In other words, the investigation could go no further because *Anita Hill would not permit it*. The only way the sexual harassment charge could have been taken more seriously would have been for Hill to lift her confidentiality demand, which she evidently had no intention of doing.

Regardless of Hill's intentions, matters did not end there. The people who had spent weeks to bring Hill forward only to have their strategy fail were unwilling to accept the decision of Biden, Metzenbaum, and the other Senators to respect her confidentiality. Accordingly, their quiet, behind-the-scenes strategy advanced to a more desperate and destructive phase.

4

Trial by Leak

Timothy Phelps of *Newsday* was apparently the only reporter who noticed that while the Judiciary Committee sent the Thomas nomination to the Senate floor, all was not well: Something disturbing had appeared on the committee's radar screen. In his September 28 story reporting the 7–7 committee vote, Phelps wrote:

> Biden, who said he cast the tie vote [against Thomas] "with a heavy heart" yesterday, said he was in favor of an early [floor] vote. He also admonished opponents to stay away from "personal" attacks, an apparent reference to what sources said was a reopening of the FBI background investigation on Thomas to check opponents' allegations of personal misconduct.[1]

Opponents' allegations? Well, yes. Nan Aron of the Alliance for Justice discovered Anita Hill. A Kennedy aide, Ricki Seidman, got her to confirm Aron's rumor. Jim Brudney, a Metzenbaum staffer, induced her to contact the committee and to make an anonymous charge. When that wasn't enough, Susan Hoerchner, Susan Deller Ross, Judith Lichtman, and Brudney persuaded her to put the charge in writing and then to agree to an FBI check.

But all of that *still* was not enough. Thomas wasn't backing out. And no one on the Judiciary Committee was willing to stop the show officially. The Senate's constitutional confirmation process was not yielding the desired results. And Anita Hill—contrary to the popular view of her as a woman who courageously refused to be "silenced" by an insensitive club of powerful white men—declined to take the final step of going public with her charges. Frustrated that their plan to kill the nomination had been foiled, first by Thomas's refusal to withdraw and then by the committee's decision (in compliance with Hill's confidentiality request) not to reopen the confirmation hearings, the Shadow Senate would not accept the collective judgment of fourteen U.S. Senators, including seven who opposed the nomination on other grounds. Nor would they respect Anita Hill's confidentiality rights.

Now not only Thomas but also Hill would be sacrificed to achieve the overriding ends of the special-interest groups. Hill's confidential allegations would be leaked to the press—an unprecedented violation of Senate rules that enraged Senators on both sides of the aisle and prompted a five-month investigation to determine who had leaked this information. "I find no evidence that Professor Hill is part of some dark conspiracy," Senator Nancy Kassebaum said on the Senate floor, "but there are real questions now about whether she was used by others in an effort to subvert the Senate's confirmation process."[2] The investigation was ultimately inconclusive, and the identities of those who leaked the charges have remained a mystery until now.

During debate on the leak investigation, Senator Thad Cochran of Mississippi explained why the allegations leaked:

> [S]omebody would not take no for an answer. Someone on the inside knew that there was one last chance to derail the Thomas nomination. Further investigation was unnecessary, the truth of the allegation immaterial. What was important was that the allegation existed. If only it could be made known to the public, Judge Thomas still could be railroaded. So despite committee assurances to Professor Hill that her confidentiality would be respected, despite the opportunity to delay the vote or ask for hearings in executive session, one or more persons on the inside went straight to the media.[3]

As Cochran noted, it no longer mattered to Thomas's critics, if it ever had, whether the charge was true. Thomas's invocation of the term "lynching" to describe his predicament—while much derided by his enemies—in fact had a precise historical meaning: In a lynching the guilt or innocence of the accused was irrelevant. Thomas was already guilty—and he would be figuratively killed—because he was a conservative black, not because he was a sex harasser. Since Thomas would never be able to prove a negative in the court of public opinion, the leak ensured that his reputation would be destroyed even if he was confirmed.

The hope of the opposition, of course, was to vent the sexual harassment charge publicly, creating a cloud of doubt over Thomas's head. They would then claim this was reason enough to vote down the nomination. The charge would not have to be substantiated, only publicized. Perfectly capturing the essence of this strategy, Lichtman said, in a letter to members of the Senate after the Hill charges became public: "To earn a lifetime appointment to the highest court in the land, a candidate must be beyond reproach. Both Judge Thomas's long and troubling substantive record and the compelling evidence of sexual harassment illustrate that this nominee is not beyond reproach. So long as *any* doubt exists as to Judge Thomas's fitness to serve on the Supreme Court, the Senate is duty bound to reject the nomination."[4] Clear evidence exists, however, that this "doubt" was fostered by the anti-Thomas camp, not least by the efforts of Lichtman herself.

By the weekend following the September 27 Judiciary Committee vote, the opposition had shifted into high gear. Senate staffers told their contacts in the anti-Thomas groups that their bosses had failed to postpone the vote after being briefed on the sexual harassment allegations. The groups began lobbying the liberal Senators to reconsider their decision. Favored reporters were alerted that the Anita Hill story might be a last chance to sink Thomas. Together they would increase the pressure on Hill to go public.

The action began the day before the committee vote, when Bill Corr and Jim Brudney of Senator Metzenbaum's office telephoned two lobbyists outside the Senate and discussed the confidential Hill statement. This would certainly qualify as the first "leak" of the committee's confidential material. The two were Judith Lichtman, who had urged Hill to come forward through the sexual harassment expert Susan Deller Ross, and Wade Henderson of the Washington office of the NAACP, who had not previously known of Hill. Corr and Brudney later said the reason they placed the calls was to let the groups know that, contrary to what was likely to be their first instinct, they should not look to Metzenbaum's staff to promote the charges beyond the confines of the committee. Their hands were tied by the Senator, who became concerned that Brudney had gotten too close to Hill after Biden told him that Brudney was mentioned in the FBI report.[5]

Henderson was skittish about the harassment allegation, believing that it played on a racist stereotype—a stance the civil rights groups would maintain, at least publicly, throughout the second set of hearings. On the other hand, typical of the white middle-class feminists who unconditionally embraced Hill, Lichtman went ballistic trying to air the allegation. According to a note taken by Bill Corr and furnished to Fleming, Lichtman declared in a telephone conversation with Corr that she was "going after [the] affidavit." Lichtman denied this when later deposed by Fleming, but she confirmed that in a conversation with Ross she had suggested taking the story to Nina Totenberg. Lichtman also considered calling Senators outside the Judiciary Committee and ratting on the committee Senators, but Ross persuaded her, for the moment, to protect Hill's confidentiality.

Any notion that there was a well-coordinated "conspiracy" to leak Hill's statement or FBI interview should be dispelled. Some of the interest group members were genuinely dismayed that the committee had not seen fit to reopen the hearings and consider Hill's charge more closely, while others, to be sure, simply could not pass up the last chance to stop Thomas. But they were unsure how to proceed and concerned about the consequences of doing so. No one, save perhaps Lichtman, seemed eager to take Hill's charge to the press without Hill's acquiescence. And even Lichtman, in a conversation with Ricki Seidman and Ralph Neas, worried openly that the Shadow Senate would be accused of "ginning up" the allegations as a last-ditch political ploy.

The crucial factor in forcing the story public was time. The final vote on the Senate floor was drawing perilously near, perhaps as soon as Friday, October 4. On Wednesday, October 2, a strategy session for the impending vote was convened in the offices of Senator Metzenbaum. The Fleming report described the scene:

> In attendance were Senators Metzenbaum, Simon, and Kennedy, certain of their staffers and various representatives from groups opposing the nominee. Although there was no discussion of Hill or her allegations at the meeting itself, various staffers recall allusions to the issue in hallway conversations after the meeting concluded. [Simon aide Susan] Kaplan, for example, overheard a snippet of conversation between Senator Simon and Kate Michelman, the head of NARAL, about the "Oklahoma thing." Brudney had a similar conversation with Henderson.

In his book *Advice and Consent,* Paul Simon also reported hushed midweek discussions among Senators and interest groups. While no committee member had exercised his right to call for further investigation of Hill's charges during the committee's official deliberations the prior week, Simon seemed to be holding out hope that the charges might still somehow slip out:

> When we returned [from the weekend recess], there was more discussion among senators privately about the vote on Thomas . . . and the general feeling was that Thomas would make it, but that that could change if Anita Hill went public . . .
>
> In the middle of the week, I received a call from a lobbyist working against the nomination to discuss a couple of key Thomas votes. I remember ending the conversation by saying, "There is still one matter that has not been disclosed that could make a difference in the Senate vote if it became public." She startled me by responding, "Do you mean the statement of the woman from Oklahoma?" That was the first I had heard of anyone outside the Senate knowing about it. Obviously, it was getting around Washington.[6]

In Simon's statement to Fleming, he identified this caller as Kate Michelman. When questioned by Fleming, however, Michelman denied knowing of Hill before the story broke publicly. If Simon is to be believed, Michelman not only knew about Hill's existence, but also the fact that she had filed a statement with the committee. In fact, there is evidence that Hill's charge was filtering down through NARAL's ranks the week before it became publicly known. Three or four days *before* the Hill story broke, the head of NARAL's Chicago office called an abortion-rights supporter in the Chicago suburbs, who had been previously approached to do some fundraising for NARAL. The NARAL official told the woman, "We have such exciting news to tell you. We have this woman who's going to come forward, Anita Hill, and Thomas won't make it. She's going to come forward, and she'll be good for fundraising. We've been working on her since July." According to Senator Danforth, the woman, upset by the ecstatic tone of the NARAL official, subsequently reported the call to him.[7] (There is no evidence that NARAL itself was literally "working on" Hill since July. This was an apparent reference to the fact that the Alliance for Justice and the Metzenbaum staff—with whom NARAL formed a common front—first identified Hill in mid-July.)

With Senators Kennedy and Metzenbaum, Paul Simon was a member of the liberal trio on the Judiciary Committee. Due to his affable demeanor and professorial image, he was a favorite of the interest groups, and he was rewarded handsomely for his efforts on their behalf by large infusions of campaign money from Hollywood's liberal political activists. Simon also had close connections to the abortion-rights movement through his wife, Jeanne, who actively opposed the nomination. Simon played a special role in the Anita Hill affair because Ted Kennedy, with his reputation for womanizing, could not credibly press the harassment allegation. As for Howard Metzenbaum, Brudney's repeated contacts with Hill in the days before she filed her statement seemed to lead the Senator to conclude that he had better not get too close to the matter himself.

While Anita Hill was not openly discussed in the Wednesday meeting in Metzenbaum's office, a decision related to her committee statement did emerge from the session: The floor vote should be postponed for as long as possible, in the apparent belief that the contents would become known, by hook or by crook, in a matter of days, and Thomas might still be beaten.

The 7–7 Judiciary Committee vote the prior Friday was an invitation to Thomas's opponents to apply redoubled pressure. Two days after he had been briefed on Hill's sexual harassment charges, Metzenbaum laid the groundwork for this stalling strategy:

> Two and one half months ago, Judge Thomas's nomination was regarded as a lock—even two weeks ago it was still regarded as a sure thing. But today, Judge Thomas was unable to muster support from a majority of the Judiciary Committee. Much is being made about the need to rush our deliberation to put Judge Thomas on the court by October 7, but another few days does not matter when you are talking about a man who could be on the court for 40 years.[8]

Metzenbaum also told the *Washington Post,* "In this business, it's never over till it's over."[9]

The lobbyists, too, joined the chorus. "Time is now very important," said Lichtman, who had been told by Brudney of Hill's statement the day before she called for delay. "The fact . . . seven members found his record so troubling they couldn't find it within themselves to vote for him suggests senators should take their time."[10] And People for the American Way said: "The conventional wisdom on this nomination just went out the window."[11]

"Contrary to White House propaganda, the nomination of Clarence Thomas is not a done deal," Ralph Neas of the Civil Rights Leadership Conference announced. According to a report in the *Wall*

Street Journal, "Mr. Neas said he and other liberal lobbyists believe they can persuade some senators who have already announced their support for Judge Thomas to switch sides."[12] Neas must have been referring to the possibility of making Hill's charges public.

By Thursday, Majority Leader George Mitchell and Minority Leader Robert Dole—having been briefed on the charges leveled by Hill and concluded, as had the Judiciary Committee, that they should not be aired publicly—were attempting to get an agreement of the Senators to hold the Thomas vote on Thursday, October 3, or Friday, before a scheduled ten-day recess of the Senate. To do so, the leadership had to obtain the members' unanimous consent.

But this proved difficult in the face of the liberals' filibuster. Senate sources later confirmed that at least one objection to the unanimous consent request had been lodged by Metzenbaum. With Metzenbaum's objection to scheduling the vote on Friday, October 4, the opposition would have four extra days to get the story out. The Senate decided not to take an anticipated ten-day recess, and the vote was scheduled for the following Tuesday, October 8. One more weekend news cycle.

"Every effort was made to invoke the rules and to delay the matter and to try to get it past last Friday, because I guess they presumed that there would be an interim 10-day recess and there would be a full two weeks where Judge Thomas could be smeared while all of us were out of town," Orrin Hatch recalled on the Senate floor on October 8.[13]

The day after the leak was published, Senator Dole said:

> And I know what some on the other side said, oh, they would like to have another weekend. I have been around here a while. I knew last weekend when we did not vote on Friday what was going to happen on Saturday and Sunday, and it did. There is always somebody out there willing to collaborate and to print classified, or to go on the radio with classified information, and they did.[14]

Senator Simpson, a deft tactician himself, also knew exactly what Metzenbaum and his allies were up to:

> The fact is that the FBI report on the matter was submitted to the Senate Judiciary Committee and the ranking member and the chairman and various members before the vote. That is a fact. No one chose to delay it in any way, to create a stumbling block or an obstacle with it, except—except—I carefully recall the negotiations last week for a unanimous consent agreement, and it was said that we would start on that Thursday morning, and that we would finish by Friday evening, even if we went late, to which there was an objection, unnamed, oddly

enough, just to fit the scenario of the Saturday slap and the Sunday slap and the Monday slap. So that when we get to six o'clock tomorrow night, it will be a full feeding frenzy.[15]

There were two ways of making use of the much-needed extra time to get the story out. The first was to persuade Hill to go public on her own. Nan Aron of the Alliance for Justice called Hill's former Washington roommate, Sonia Jarvis, whom she did not know, and asked if Hill would go public. But Hill told Jarvis to call Aron back and tell her no. Such a course was out of the question as far as Hill was concerned.

On Wednesday, October 2, Hill and Brudney spoke for thirty-three minutes, in what may have been yet another attempt by Brudney subtly to influence Hill's position. Though the committee had already decided it would not pursue Hill's allegation further, Brudney was not satisfied. The next morning, Brudney spoke to Ricki Seidman about his conversation with Hill. Peter Fleming reported:

> According to Seidman, Brudney said he had spoken with Hill *about whether Hill was going to publicize her allegations.* Seidman's impression from this conversation with Brudney was that Hill was undecided about what, if anything, she would do. [Emphasis added.]

The other course open to the anti-Thomas forces would be to take the choice away from Hill—to "out" her. The potentially illegal leaking to the media of a physical copy of Hill's committee statement or the FBI report does not seem to have been a foreordained plan. The initial plan for outing Hill was to tip off a few reporters to the existence of the documents and to have them call Hill and ask about them. Once Hill spoke on the record, reporters would have their story and no one in Washington would be implicated in the event.

But once again, things would be terribly complicated for the Thomas foes. Thomas had not withdrawn when confronted with Hill's charges, as they had expected. And now, rather than simply decide to give up her confidentiality and make the charge publicly before Thomas was confirmed, Hill refused to speak on the record until the reporters had obtained *copies* of her statement to the Judiciary Committee independently.

On advice from Charles Ogletree, Hill told the reporters who contacted her that she would not comment until she was certain that they had copies of the statement. That way, she would not be bluffed into becoming the source for the story. Whether Hill fully realized it or not, the strategy recommended by Ogletree, a prominent opponent of the Thomas nomination, would not prevent publication of the story, but would only prevent Hill from being seen as having taken the story to the press. Had Ogletree manipulated Hill into a position where she would eventually be compelled to confirm the allegation? Or was Hill fully prepared to do this, provided that her intentions would be camouflaged?

In any event, Ogletree's precondition not only indicated to the reporters that they were onto a hot story but actually necessitated the leak. Nina Totenberg ultimately obtained a copy of Hill's committee statement from someone in the Senate, and she interviewed Hill on the air. Timothy Phelps of *Newsday* never got a copy, but, after being briefed on the contents of the FBI report by someone in the Senate, ran a story without Hill's cooperation. (Neither reporter obtained a physical copy of any part of the FBI file.) The obsessive focus at the time of the hearings on the "leaker" obscured the fact that there were two reporters, two stories, and *two* leakers.

The Anita Hill story was broken in print in the October 6 issue of *Newsday* by Phelps, the paper's Supreme Court correspondent.[16] Phelps later said, in an appearance on ABC's "Nightline," that he had heard a sexual harassment rumor about Thomas and Hill as early as mid-July, just after the Alliance for Justice and the Metzenbaum staffers had learned of it. But he promised this source that if he approached Hill, he would not ask directly about sexual harassment. When he called Hill a number of times over the summer to soften her up—asking her about Thomas's political views, among other things—Hill had volunteered nothing about sexual harassment.

By the day of the committee vote, Phelps had noticed a wrinkle in the proceedings, as he indicated in his September 28 dispatch. Like Totenberg, he was picking up scuttlebutt from the groups that a law professor in Oklahoma had made a sexual harassment charge against Thomas. On Wednesday, October 2, the day that the Metzenbaum group met and decided to delay the floor vote, Phelps was working in the Senate press gallery when he got a message that a Senator wished to speak with him. Phelps soon appeared in the chamber, just off the Senate floor. Here is how he told the story in his book, *Capitol Games:*

> The senator, an opponent of Thomas, had a tip for me regarding a
> news article I had written earlier about the nominee. It proved to be

of little use; but when asked if he had any hopes of stopping the nomination, he gave me a straightforward answer.

"Not unless someone with important information who is insisting
on keeping it confidential comes forward publicly," the senator said.

For me this was a lightning bolt, a chance to confirm that at least
some of the senators knew about Hill's allegations of sexual harassment and thought them serious enough to potentially derail the
Thomas nomination. "You mean the law professor from Oklahoma?"
I asked.

His eyes opened in amazement. "How did you know about that?"[17]

Later in the book, Phelps wrote: "The conversation also superseded my obligation not to call Anita Hill and ask her about sexual
harassment. The subject had been broached with me, albeit unintentionally and indirectly, by a senator."[18] In other words, the initial
tip to Phelps, confirming that Hill's charge had come before the committee, came from a U.S. Senator who opposed the Thomas nomination. The Senator apparently did not realize that he was setting
Phelps's wheels in motion.

Phelps did not openly reveal the identity of this Senator in his book,
nor did he cooperate with special counsel Fleming in identifying his
sources (the Senate refused to enforce the subpoenas Fleming issued
to Phelps and Totenberg, which would have compelled them to talk).
According to both Phelps and Fleming, Phelps spoke to a U.S. Senator on Wednesday, October 2, three days before Phelps broke the
story. When Phelps was writing his book, the Fleming report had not
yet been released. In telling the story of his discussion with the unnamed Senator, Phelps supplied the details of the conversation. Fleming did not report the contents of the conversation between Phelps
and the Senator, but in interviews with Senate staffers he was able to
discover the name of the Senator who spoke with Phelps on October
2: Paul Simon. Had Phelps known that Fleming would stumble upon
the Senator's name, it's a safe bet he would have never implicated the
Senator in the confirmation of the rumor. (Simon had probably summoned Phelps to discuss a story of mutual interest: the Jay
Parker–South Africa connection.)[19]

Simon told Fleming that he did not remember whether or not he'd
spoken to Phelps during this period. But Ricki Seidman of Senator
Kennedy's staff recounted a conversation with Phelps on Thursday,
October 3, in which he told her he had spoken to Simon the day before. According to Seidman's deposition, Phelps told Seidman that
"he thought he might be onto something" after the chat with Simon.

Released by the Simon conversation from his earlier commitment not to talk to Hill about sexual harassment, Phelps called Hill on Friday and again on Saturday, but she was not cooperative, refusing to talk unless she knew he had her statement. Phelps called Ricki Seidman as well on both Friday and Saturday, seeking a copy of the statement, which he never was able to obtain.

At this late hour Hill was undoubtedly anguished at the prospect of the story's breaking. Hill may have believed that by refusing to talk until the reporters had her statement, she was setting so difficult a precondition that she was in effect blocking the story from coming out. In retrospect, however, there were surer ways for Hill to have tried to thwart publication. Hill could have told Phelps, "I don't know what you're talking about," or "I'm not commenting under any circumstances." She could have let the phone ring off the hook. Instead, all she said was she would not comment until Phelps had her statement, and she told Nina Totenberg the same thing. To a skilled reporter, this was more of a challenge than a roadblock.

But had Hill refused to cooperate at all, she would have lost any chance of influencing what the reporters wrote. As Hill's careful negotiations with the Judiciary Committee showed, "controlling the process" was always foremost in her mind. In her insistence that the reporters obtain copies of her statement before she spoke to them, Hill seemed more concerned with *how* the story got out than she was with stopping it. Perhaps Hill drew the reasonable conclusion that the story was going to break with or without her, and her precondition was designed to afford her the opportunity to put her own spin on it. Realistically, this was about the most Hill could aim for. If someone on the inside in Washington was determined to leak her allegations, as seemed clear from the reporters' dogged inquiries, she would be coerced into either confirming or denying them. For the sake of her own credibility, she would have no choice but to confirm.

On Saturday Phelps called Hill again, but she would not budge. He then had an unknown number of telephone conversations with Paul Simon, who was out of town at a class reunion at Dana College in Blair, Nebraska, which Simon had attended for two years. While again refraining from naming Simon, Phelps wrote in *Capitol Games* that the same Senator who had called him off the Senate floor on Wednesday (Paul Simon) was now offering to leak Hill's charges to him. Simon's plan was for Phelps to call Hill, ask her to call Simon, and give Simon permission to leak the allegations. Hill told Phelps she would not go along with Simon's suggestion—a clear sign that given the choice she did not want the charges known publicly, even if a U.S. Senator was willing to do the dirty work—but the exchange showed that Simon was willing to leak. Phelps called Simon back and told him there was no deal.

At some point late Saturday afternoon, after Phelps's Sunday deadline had passed, someone—a "trustworthy" source, Phelps later wrote, without a trace of irony—described to Phelps the general thrust of the allegations Hill had made to the FBI, effectively robbing Hill of her rights under the Privacy Act, breaking a vital Senate rule on the disclosure of confidential material that carried the penalty of expulsion of a Senator from the body, or the firing of a staff member, and blackening Thomas's name forever.

That evening, Phelps tapped out his story for the Sunday editions. It began:

> An Oklahoma University law professor has recently told the FBI that she was sexually harassed by Supreme Court nominee Clarence Thomas while working for him at the Equal Employment Opportunity Commission.
>
> The professor, Anita F. Hill, told the FBI that Thomas repeatedly discussed sexual matters with her in a suggestive way while she worked for the job discrimination monitoring agency in Washington, according to a source who has seen her statement to the FBI.[20]

The first version of the Phelps story quoted by name only Simon, who called for a postponement of the Tuesday floor vote until the Hill allegations could be further investigated. In later editions, a longer Phelps story carried a statement from the White House, a quote from Anita Hill, and quotes from two Republican Senators on the committee, Orrin Hatch and Alan Simpson.[21]

In determining the identity of the source of Phelps's story, the same technique used to identify the unnamed Senator who called Phelps off the Senate floor—Paul Simon—can be employed: Lay the information that Fleming discovered without Phelps's cooperation over the information that Phelps revealed without knowing what Fleming would find independently, and there is only *one* person who could have been the leaker.

Phelps's story, unlike Totenberg's, was replete with references to the FBI and the FBI report. In the story, Phelps described his source as "someone who has seen her statement to the FBI." In *Capitol Games,* which went to press before the leak report was released, Phelps wrote: "I had a source who had seen the FBI report."[22] This information in *Capitol Games* was precisely the piece of the puzzle that Fleming lacked. Fleming had been unsure whether Phelps's source had seen the FBI report or had seen only Hill's statement to the committee, which was also furnished to the FBI. Citing Phelps's reference in *Newsday* to "a source who has seen her statement to the FBI," Fleming wrote:

> This language lends itself to two interpretations which were brought to Phelps' attention in deposition and which he refused to clarify. First, the language could refer to a source who had seen the FBI's form FD-302 report of its interview of Hill on Sept. 23. Second, the language also could mean a source who had seen Hill's statement to the Judiciary Committee, and knew a copy of that statement had been given to the FBI.

Fleming overlooked a passage at the end of the Phelps story that should have clarified this perceived ambiguity. Phelps quoted one unnamed U.S. Senator, "an opponent of Thomas who *read the* [FBI] *report and an accompanying statement* by Hill" (emphasis added). This phrase showed that Phelps did in fact appreciate the distinction between the FBI report of its interview of Hill, and Hill's Judiciary Committee statement. Thus Phelps's identification of "a source who has seen her statement to the FBI" in *Newsday* undoubtedly meant that the source had seen the report of Hill's FBI interview. This was the point that Phelps confirmed in *Capitol Games.*[23]

At the time of the leak it was apparent to many Senators that the Phelps source had seen the FBI file, and therefore had to be a Senator on the Judiciary Committee rather than a Senate staffer, since the staffers had no access to the report. During the Senate hearing, Hatch said Hill's charges had been "leaked to the press by *somebody on this committee,* in violation of law, in violation of the Senate ethics, in violation of a stringent rule formulated because these FBI reports contain raw data." In a Senate floor statement defending himself against a charge by Hatch that he was the leaker, Howard Metzenbaum said:

> As every senator knows, but the public may not, the FBI file is a closely held document. A senator must ask to see it. It is brought to the senator's office by a top aide to the chairman who sits there with you while you read it. No one but senators may read the FBI file and when the senator is finished reading, the committee staffer takes it away.
>
> I want to add a few more facts to the mix here. Over the weekend, I finally read the *Newsday* article of Oct. 6. The source for this story was an individual who had seen the FBI report. . . .
>
> I did not see the FBI report until the day after the story broke. I repeat, I did not see the FBI report until the day after the story broke.[24]

Yet Fleming concluded that the "evidence indicates that Phelps's source was a person who had seen Hill's statement, but had *not* seen the FBI report." Under the Fleming interpretation, it would have been almost impossible to draw a conclusion as to who had leaked the story, since more than two dozen Senators and staffers had seen Hill's committee statement. Thus, Fleming's conclusion—a conclusion happily repeated by the media to keep the Anita Hill tale sheathed in ambiguity—was that he could not find Phelps's source.

But what if Fleming had known that Phelps's source had *"seen the FBI report,"* as Phelps wrote in *Capitol Games*? According to the leak investigation, only five people on Capitol Hill read the FBI report before the Phelps story ran, all of them U.S. Senators. Senators Biden, Simon, Thurmond, DeConcini, and Specter had all reviewed the FBI report. As Fleming noted, the latter three supported Thomas and would have had no motive to leak. And Biden "clearly had no reason to disclose the allegations which would subject him to the criticism he subsequently received," Fleming noted.

Motivation aside, Fleming reported that none of these four had spoken to Phelps during the period in question. Had Fleming only been sure that Phelps's source had seen the FBI report, he would have been able to identify the leaker as the fifth Senator, who had read the FBI report before the Judiciary Committee vote and had been the only person who read the report and also spoke with Tim Phelps before Phelps broke the story: Paul Simon. (Fleming was on the right track: He asked *Newsday* to turn over any "tape recordings or notes of any conversation with Senator Paul Simon," but *Newsday* refused.)

Unless Phelps was plain wrong about whether or not his source had seen the FBI report, he inadvertently pointed the finger at Simon in his book, because he did not know what Fleming would find: that only five people had read the FBI report, and that only one of those five had spoken with him before he broke the story.[25] Not until the Fleming report was published—after Phelps's book went to press—was it revealed who had or had not seen the FBI report. That so few people had seen it was a surprise even to close observers; thus Phelps likely was unaware that he was disclosing the final piece of the puzzle.

Phelps later went out of his way to draw attention away from the leaker, first in a conversation with a Metzenbaum aide, and then in *Capitol Games*. Several weeks after the story broke, in a conversation with Metzenbaum's aide Bill Corr, Phelps tried to shift the blame for the leak onto Senators Hatch and Simpson, both of whom he had interviewed on Saturday evening before filing his story. According to the Fleming report, Phelps "made the statement that he had used one of the oldest tricks in the reporter's book of calling someone and stating that you know something, and having the other person, by responding, confirm that they knew it, and that he had done that in his conversations with Senator Hatch and Senator Simpson." Fleming, however, concluded that this was not true, "because neither [Hatch nor Simpson] had seen Hill's statement or the FBI report prior to October 6. . . . We do not believe that Phelps' source for the quoted remarks could have been a Republican."

To take the heat off his source, and to turn it up under Hatch and Simpson, Phelps may have altered the chronology of his late Saturday telephone calls in *Capitol Games*. According to Phelps, he called Hatch, Simpson, and Simon, in that order. But according to Fleming, Phelps called Simon *before* he called Hatch and Simpson (he may have called him afterward, as well). The Fleming report stated:

> Phelps was persistent in asking about the contents of the FBI report; the senator [Simon] recalls telling him at least three times that he could not divulge information from FBI documents. . . . The call to Simon probably concluded shortly before 6 P.M. Phelps then made a series of calls to other senators on the committee, including Senators Hatch and Simpson. . . .

If Fleming is correct about the sequence, it appears that Phelps was able to wear Simon down in this call and get him to briefly describe the allegations in the FBI report. The later calls to Hatch and Simpson would then have been attempts to elicit comment on a story Phelps already had. Phelps may have claimed in his book that Simon had been called last so that Simon would not be identified as the leaker.[26]

Pursuant to some circumstantial clues, Simon was accused of leaking shortly after the Phelps story ran. Simon was the only Senator quoted by name in Phelps's first edition. (Quoting someone by name in a piece in which they are also an unnamed source is sometimes a device to throw leak-hunters off the trail.) In the *Newsday* story, Simon called for a postponement of the Senate's scheduled vote based on the Hill charge. And Simon had been the only Senator in committee to vote against sending the Thomas nomination to the floor. This was a vote to kill the nomination; at a 7–7 tie, failing to send the nomination to the floor would have automatically killed it.

Finally, in one of the most curious moments in the affair, Simon misinformed both Phelps and Totenberg about the state of his knowledge regarding the allegations and when he saw the FBI file. Simon said he had not known about the allegations or read the FBI file before the committee vote on September 27, yet in fact he had read the FBI report and had even spoken to Hill by telephone on September 26. Here was the exchange with Nina Totenberg:

> SIMON: I did not know about it until after our vote, and—and I heard about it and then asked to see it [the FBI report].
>
> TOTENBERG: Do you know why nobody on the committee knew about it, or many people on the committee didn't know about it . . .
>
> SIMON: I think . . .
>
> TOTENBERG: . . . until after the vote?
>
> SIMON: I think that is a question you'd have to direct to the chairman.
>
> TOTENBERG: Are you mad?
>
> SIMON: No, it's—it's—it's a judgment call.[27]

Simon changed his story when, at about 2 A.M. on Sunday morning, he was on the phone discussing the story Phelps had broken at 9 P.M. Saturday with yet another reporter. The reporter was interviewing a White House official when her call-waiting signal came on. Paul Simon was calling. "Why don't you ask Senator Simon if he remembers seeing that FBI report before the vote," the official told the reporter. The reporter then told the Senator that the White House had already seen Phelps's copy—which had gone out from *Newsday* over the news wires late Saturday night—and had smelled something fishy in Simon's claim not to have known of the allegations before the committee vote. Simon backpedaled furiously, admitting he'd known of the Hill charges all along. "He's backing off his story," the reporter told the White House official after speaking with Simon.

Simon denied several times that he was the culprit. In the Thomas–Hill hearings, he said:

> First, not to the panel, but on a talk show this morning one of the commentators said that I was the source for the leak of the affidavit. That is just absolutely false. I don't operate that way. . . . Neither I nor my staff leaked the documents.

Simon denied the accusation shortly thereafter to the *Washington Times,* which quoted unnamed Judiciary Committee members as fingering Simon, though providing no evidence.[28]

The leak itself was not a crime because Congress is exempt from the provisions of the Privacy Act. However, it was a violation of Senate rules that is considered grounds for expulsion from the Senate. In addition, if Simon made a false statement to Congressional investigator Fleming in denying the leak, as the evidence strongly suggests, he violated the False Statements Act, a federal crime. Fleming wrote:

> Simon denied he was the unidentified source. He spoke on the record to both Totenberg and Phelps, but limited his comments to procedural matters. He expressly refused to discuss the contents of the FBI report, and we have no reason to believe he would then go off the record and discuss Hill's statement.

After the Fleming report was released in April, Simon issued the following statement: "I'm pleased that the report confirms that my staff and I were not the sources of any unauthorized information provided to the press."[29]

The question remains as to why Simon, a member of the Judiciary Committee who had the right to postpone the vote on the Thomas nomination, did not take this official route if he believed that Hill's charge should have been pursued further. The reasons that his colleagues did not do so—that they found the charges lacking in credibility, and that they wanted to protect Hill's confidentiality—obviously did not hold sway with the Senator from Illinois. Simon had suggested to Hill that she might go public in a telephone conversation before the committee vote, but Hill demurred. Was Simon simply unwilling to take the heat that he would have drawn if he had been the only one to ask for a delay in the Thomas vote? Or was he persuaded in the week following the committee vote, in his conversations with Kate Michelman and others, that Hill's confidentiality and the Senate's rules were less important than stopping Thomas, either for political reasons or because Simon believed that Thomas was a sex harasser. If that was the case, he may have concluded that concern for the court's integrity overrode procedural fairness.

During the first week in October, Nina Totenberg was working the Anita Hill story too. As Phelps had, Totenberg first heard about the allegations in July. But it was not until the "quiet and behind-the-scenes" Judiciary Committee gambit failed in late September that she was dispatched to unmask Hill.

Totenberg first called Hill on Thursday, October 3, using the dubious story of her own sexual harassment at the *National Observer* to entice her to talk. But Totenberg faced the same problem as Phelps: Hill wouldn't talk to anyone who did not possess a copy of Hill's Judiciary Committee statement. Unlike Phelps, however, Totenberg succeeded in getting Hill to cooperate, because she eventually met Hill's precondition. Totenberg's source, therefore, had to be someone who had not simply read the statement or the FBI file, such as Simon, but who could have provided her with an actual copy of it.

According to a written statement made by Totenberg to Fleming:

> During the continuing process of covering the Thomas nomination, I obtained the contents of an affidavit filed by Professor Anita Hill with the Senate Judiciary Committee. At no time did I receive a copy of any FBI report with respect to the Thomas nomination.[30]

On Friday Totenberg called Seidman, who had also been talking with Phelps in those few days before the Hill story broke. Totenberg then phoned Paul Simon in Nebraska. Neither Seidman nor Simon had copies of the Hill statement. She then called Senator Leahy in Vermont, who had resigned from the Senate Intelligence Committee in 1986 after admitting that he leaked a copy of the Iran–Contra committee report to NBC News, but he did not have a copy of Hill's statement either.[31]

Totenberg called Hill twice on Friday, threatening that she was "going with the story." Hill wouldn't talk, but she seemed to recognize the inevitable and so gave Totenberg the names of several character references. She also gave Totenberg the name of Susan Hoerchner as her corroborating witness. Totenberg then reported to Ricki Seidman that she was still having trouble getting the interview.

Late Friday night Hill called Totenberg and said once more that she was not willing to talk about the allegation. Perhaps this was one final effort on Hill's part to persuade Totenberg to relent. "Every witness who had contact with Hill during the time leading up to the October 6 disclosures has told us that Hill had no desire to go public with her allegations and indeed feared that possibility," Fleming wrote. A full year later, in a speech on a college campus in Minnesota, Hill explained her intention to have the committee consider the allegation behind closed doors. She never thought her confidential statement would end up on the evening news. "All I can say is that I did everything in that situation that I could to get the information to the fact-finders in as productive and professional a way as possible.

And through a series of circumstances which I do not understand even today . . . all of the things that I had tried to do really were out the window and I was thrust before the cameras."[32]

On Saturday morning Hill began preparing for the story to break nonetheless. She began calling family members and alerting them that the story—a story she had never told any member of her family previously—was about to blow.

Meanwhile, Totenberg was frantically trying to get a copy of the statement. After speaking with Hill again to no avail, Totenberg called Seidman and popped the big question: Do you know who has a copy? Seidman immediately called Metzenbaum's counsel Jim Brudney, locating him at the Library of Congress at midday Saturday. According to Seidman's deposition, she told Brudney that Hill would not give Totenberg a copy of her statement, and that Totenberg needed it badly in order to get Hill on the record. Brudney told Fleming "he did not recall Seidman saying Totenberg was looking for Hill's statement," which may have been a convenient memory lapse.

Within the hour, Totenberg was on the phone again to Hill. Totenberg now had the statement, and began reading from it. "Confronted with words from her affidavit, Hill agreed to cooperate and answered Totenberg's questions," Fleming wrote.

After the interview, Totenberg called two people who had a keen interest in her progress to tell them that she had the story, which would run on NPR Sunday morning—Ricki Seidman and Judith Lichtman. Soon thereafter Brudney was informed of Totenberg's progress too, presumably by Seidman. Throughout the machinations, the careful Brudney had spoken with Totenberg only indirectly through Seidman.

After the NPR story ran, Totenberg destroyed her copy of the Hill statement and notes pertaining to the leak. She wasn't the only one shredding a copy of that particular document. The leaker's copy was shredded, too. What he didn't know was that the physical copy of Hill's statement had been so closely guarded by the Judiciary Committee—copies were hand-carried in sealed envelopes marked "senators' eyes only," retrieved, and destroyed—that the identity of the leaker would turn on the fact that he was the only person on Capitol Hill who had a personal copy of Hill's statement.

Two days after Anita Hill faxed her statement to the Judiciary Committee on September 23, she received another in the series of calls from Jim Brudney, who asked her for a copy of her statement. Only the Biden staff had a copy, and Brudney couldn't ask for it without raising suspicions, since he was not even on the right committee to receive the information.

According to Fleming's interview with Hill, Brudney called on September 25 and told her he was writing a memo for Metzenbaum on sexual harassment, and wanted to know the details of the allegations she had made to the committee. This was a ruse on Brudney's part. According to Hill's public testimony, she had already provided Brudney the details in their phone call of September 10. Hill testified: "And in the course of our conversations, Mr. Brudney asked me what were specifics about what it was that I had experienced." Furthermore, according to the Fleming report's account of the September Hill–Brudney call, "Brudney took extensive notes of this conversation." In other words, Brudney already had the details.

Hill told Fleming she questioned Brudney about why he needed the statement, and whether it was proper to send a copy outside committee channels. Brudney assured her that the statement would be kept confidential, and she then faxed him an exact copy. When asked about this episode by Fleming, Brudney confirmed that he had obtained a copy of the statement from Hill, but he denied asking for it. "He denies asking specifically for the statement, although he assumes what he later received was a draft of the statement to the committee," Fleming wrote.

Brudney composed the harassment memo for Metzenbaum. Then he placed the statement not in a Senate vault or a locked filing cabinet but in his briefcase. Fleming reported: "He offers no explanation for why he retained his copy of Hill's statement—obviously a sensitive document—after its purpose had been exhausted with the completion of his memorandum on sexual harassment on Wednesday Sept. 25." (Fleming lays the groundwork for a theory that Brudney leaked, but stops short of explicitly drawing that conclusion.)[33]

On the Saturday ten days later when Totenberg called Seidman and asked her for the affidavit, and when Seidman called Brudney at the Library of Congress and told him Totenberg was looking for it, the statement was lying right there in Brudney's briefcase. Thus Brudney's was the only copy that could have been duplicated and then delivered to Totenberg, a violation of Senate rules that carries the penalty of dismissal from the Senate staff. (The other copy would have been Hill's own, but Fleming reported after a search of telefax and postal records that "we have found no evidence that, prior to Oct. 6,

1991, Hill provided a copy of her statement to any person or organization other than the Judiciary Committee and Brudney.")[34]

The evidence strongly suggests that Brudney committed a grave ethical lapse in leaking Hill's statement, an action which, if he had not been a Senate employee exempt from the provisions of the Privacy Act, would have been a federal crime. This was compounded by his sworn statement of denial to Fleming, which, if false, would also be a federal crime. Though it is evident that a number of people in the Thomas opposition gave conflicting accounts of their roles to the Congressional investigator, there has been no attempt to date to prosecute anyone under the False Statements Act. In the Iran–Contra scandal, high-ranking officials of the Reagan Administration were prosecuted for misleading or failing to fully inform Congress about sensitive and highly contentious foreign-policy operations during their unsworn Congressional testimony. Yet a number of statements made to Congressional investigator Fleming by Simon, Brudney, Lichtman, Michelman, and others in the Thomas opposition during their sworn depositions—specifically regarding the leak under investigation—would, if false, be far more blatant violations of the False Statements Act and the perjury statute than anything prosecuted in the Iran–Contra affair.[35]

The day after the Totenberg story ran, a nervous Joel Johnson, Metzenbaum's administrative assistant, asked Brudney if he still had the copy of the Hill statement that Brudney had mentioned to him earlier. Johnson then took the copy and destroyed it. Metzenbaum rushed to the Senate floor to announce that afternoon that his staff played no role in the leak: "Mr. President, in response to some inferences made here on the floor and elsewhere, I want to make it very clear that my office had absolutely no involvement in the release of any information dealing with Professor Hill. There is no evidence of this and that is because none exists. It is simply not the case." During the hearings, Metzenbaum reiterated: "But I want to make it clear today to you, Judge Thomas, and to any of the rest of the world that neither this Senator nor any of my staff have been the source of any leaks to the press on this matter."[36]

That would have been the end of the story if Fleming had not gone to work. Hill divulged to Fleming the story of how Brudney had extracted the extra copy of her statement from her. A good friend to the end, Brudney then tried to frame Hill for the Totenberg leak. Brudney told Fleming about a call Hill had made to him shortly before the Totenberg story ran. According to Brudney, Hill told him that she "had been talking to Nina Totenberg and friends in D.C. and was considering giving her allegations to Senator Leahy for circulation to the full Senate." Hill said she never told Brudney that. When Fleming checked Hill's telephone records to see if she had been calling friends in Washington during the time in question, it turned out that she had not.

Shortly after the Fleming report was released in 1992, Brudney resigned from the Senate staff to teach law at Ohio State University in Howard Metzenbaum's home state.

When the Phelps and Totenberg stories ran on Sunday, their effect was not immediately clear. Perhaps the Anita Hill story would be a one-day story, just as the other attacks on the nominee had faded fast. On Monday only Paul Simon was calling for a postponement of the vote scheduled the next day. The lobby groups, of course, were working hard to mau-mau the Senate into reopening the nomination hearings. The ubiquitous Lichtman met with Majority Leader George Mitchell in his office to press for a postponement of the Tuesday vote, but the leadership was committed to a schedule for voting. "This isn't going to be a big story," Senator Danforth confidently told the press.[37]

Not until Monday afternoon, when Hill held a televised press conference at the OU law school, did the story begin to spread. "There was no way of putting the genie back in the jar after that press conference," Senator Simpson recalled.[38] Once Simon and Brudney made the decision to throw Hill to the wolves and leak her charges, she moved into a more decisive mode, declaring that she would be available to come to Washington to testify.

More than the leak itself, Hill's stance on Monday led to the hemorrhaging of Thomas's support throughout the day Tuesday. Thomas paced around the pool of the Georgetown home of Judge Silberman and his wife Ricky, the vice chairman of the EEOC. He smoked cigars and spoke on a portable telephone with his Senate patron, Jack Danforth, throughout the afternoon. When it was clear that they could not be sure of fifty-one votes for confirmation, Thomas and his advisers agreed to postpone the vote to allow the Senate to hear Hill's testimony.

By the next evening, a feminist heroine literally overnight, Anita Hill arrived in Washington to prepare her Senate testimony, accompanied by her friend Shirley Wiegand, an OU law professor. Though this was shielded from the public at the time, leading figures in the campaign against conservative judges coordinated the strategy for her appearance before the committee. One of Hill's two chief legal advisers, John Frank of Phoenix, had opposed the elevation of William Rehnquist as chief justice, and had written memos to Senators against Robert Bork. The other, Harvard's Ogletree, drafted the NAACP's report opposing the Thomas nomination. These two attorneys were in charge of Hill's preparatory sessions at the law firm of Pepper, Hamilton & Scheetz on Thursday, the day before Hill testified. (A third lawyer present, President Carter's White House counsel Lloyd Cutler, bowed out early and did not appear as a Hill adviser during the weekend testimony.)

Also involved in various capacities were Susan Deller Ross, who had initially consulted with Hill at Brudney's behest before she made her charge; Patricia King, a professor of law at Georgetown, who was a member of the board of directors of Judith Lichtman's Women's Legal Defense Fund; political consultant Nikki Heidepriem, who had been recruited into the anti-Bork campaign by Nan Aron of the Alliance for Justice, was also a member of the board of directors of Women's Legal Defense Fund, and had done consulting work for NARAL; and Judith Resnik, a professor at the University of Southern California and a close associate of Aron's who had testified against Bork's nomination, helped Hill obtain legal advice and founded the Ad Hoc Committee on Public Education on Sexual Harassment, which lobbied the Senate to postpone the Thomas vote. Hill also consulted with public relations experts Wendy Sherman, a former aide to Democratic Senator Mikulski and consultant to Emily's List, the group that would later reap the contributions from her testimony; and Louise Hilsen, a former press secretary to Democratic Representative Eckart. Lichtman spoke to Hill's lawyers by telephone.[39]

Up to the point when the charges were leaked, the Senate's confirmation process, albeit imperfect, had worked. Thomas had survived the opposition's three-month campaign against him. He had testified for five days before the Judiciary Committee, an unprecedented length of time for a Supreme Court nominee. Hill's charge was filed, investigated, and considered. The committee went no farther because there was so little evidence to support the charge, and because the accuser wished it to remain confidential. The committee then sent the nomination to the floor. By Friday, October 4, two days before the Hill story broke, fifty-four senators had publicly announced in favor of the Thomas nomination, four more than Thomas needed.

Respect for civil liberties and formal procedures was once a central tenet of liberalism. But for the liberals of the Shadow Senate, both those who leaked and those who used the leak for their own political ends, the committee's procedures—procedures designed precisely to prevent character assassination, to ensure that unsubstantiated charges like Hill's were not displayed across the front pages of the nation's newspapers—did not matter. The informed, collective judgment of a committee of fourteen U.S. Senators of every political stripe did not matter. Senate rules governing confidential information did not matter. Hill's privacy rights did not matter. Thomas's right not to be destroyed by an uncorroborated charge did not matter. All that mattered was winning the political point. The leakers had come to believe that their ends—preventing Thomas, a conservative ideologue and now an accused sexual harasser, from taking a seat on the nation's highest court—justified the most illiberal of tactics. In so doing, they sacrificed the truth—as a close examination of Hill's Senate testimony will show.

5

In Her Own Words

Well, I think that if you start to look at each individual problem with this statement, then you're not going to be satisfied that it's true, but I think the statement has to be taken as a whole.
Anita Hill to Senator Arlen Specter, October 11, 1991

Observers of the Clarence Thomas–Anita Hill hearings came away concluding that one of the two—if not both—had lied about whether or not Thomas had sexually harassed Hill. But no one could be confident that they would ever know who. Neither Hill nor Thomas had documentary evidence that could settle the question definitively. Besides, the Senate inquiry and media coverage encouraged the idea that there was no way to prove which one lied by focusing on the soap opera aspects of the case rather than rigorously scrutinizing the testimony of each witness.

The absence of hard evidence turned the hearings into a fascinating but ultimately unsatisfying exercise in speculation. A parade of witnesses and commentators said that Hill *would* not lie, that a victim of sexual harassment *would* not stay in contact with the harasser, that Thomas *would* not act obnoxiously toward Hill, that a harasser *would* not just harass one person and never commit the offense again. By the end of the weekend, such observations began to sound like Jeffrey Dahmer's neighbors, saying what a nice, quiet young man he was. Thomas's friends and associates could not believe he was a sexual harasser; and Hill's friends and associates were just as sure she would not lie.

Thus the event would be characterized, forever more, as a case of her word against his. On the day before the Senate confirmation vote, a front-page story in the *Wall Street Journal* bore the heading: "Unsolved Mysteries: Even if Confirmed Judge Thomas Will Be Under Cloud of Doubt—Senate Hearings Fail to Prove That He or Prof. Anita Hill Is the More Believable."[1] Eight months later Timothy Phelps, whose book *Capitol Games* was sympathetic to Hill while uncovering not one new piece of information to support her case, wrote: "The Senate, while spending vast amounts of money to investigate the leaks, had made no effort to investigate who had lied under oath to the Judiciary Committee, Hill or Thomas."[2] And in a one-year anniversary article on the Thomas–Hill scandal in October 1992, the *Washington Post* reported: "Because the case essentially hinged on Hill's word against Thomas's, the truth may never be known."[3]

Certainly, a negative can never be proved. Yet the truth about whose word was more believable could have been found: It lay not in what Hill and Thomas *would or would not* have done, but in comparing what Hill and Thomas *said* they did with the accounts of other witnesses and various third parties. If the Senate and the press had been truly interested in moving beyond the stalemated "he said, she said" formulation, they would have tested Thomas's and Hill's stories for truthfulness and correctness at every point where they intersected with the account of a third party or with any verifiable fact. As Dr. Morris E. Chafetz wrote in a letter to the editor of the *Wall Street Journal* shortly after the Thomas–Hill hearings, "Motives be damned. Let's find out who's the perjurer." In other words, the central charge of sexual harassment could in effect have been proved or disproved by assessing the credibility and veracity of those parts of the testimony that did *not* turn on Thomas's word versus Hill's.

At this writing, no aspect of Thomas's statement has been challenged, in any way by anyone—before, during, or after the hearings—except in Hill's own testimony. Thomas's testimony—which lasted twice as long as Hill's—on how he comported himself at the agency, and on his relations with Anita Hill during and after she left his employ, was fully corroborated by other parties. More important, no one came forward, or has come forward since, to contradict anything Thomas has said.

When Anita Hill's testimony is scrutinized in a similar fashion, at numerous points where her word can be checked against someone else's or with a written record, her sworn testimony and public statements either conflict with the facts or omit certain incidents entirely. While some of these problems with Hill's story were evident during the hearings, Thomas's supporters sought to indict Hill with such a broad brush that they overlooked or failed to exploit several factual errors or misrepresentations in Hill's testimony. At the same time Hill's partisans succeeded in drawing attention away from the question of her truthfulness on specific matters by centering attention exclusively on the evils of sexual harassment in general. Perhaps they sensed that, taken together, the exposure of Hill's deceptions, deflections, and incorrect statements, most of which were made to enhance her image as a victim, would have precluded unbiased observers from crediting her account of sexual harassment by Thomas.

The question to which the committee devoted more time and attention than any other was why Hill had decided to follow Thomas to the EEOC in May 1982 after he had allegedly sexually harassed her, frequently and in vile ways, while she worked for him at the Department of Education. For many, the question seemed to encapsulate the political and cultural divide evident throughout the entire affair. For Thomas's supporters, her decision to follow her victimizer was said to be so incomprehensible that it undermined the entire case that she had been harassed. Sexual harassment victims, they claimed, would never follow their harassers to another job in the manner that Hill did. She "went to the EEOC with Judge Thomas to work for him there. This is clearly after—allegedly—he had sexually harassed her. . . . I ask my colleagues, is this behavior of this person, accompanying Judge Thomas to another job, indicative of someone who has been sexually harassed? I think the behavior is inconsistent with the allegation," Senator Hatch maintained.[4]

"These unfounded allegations, Ms. Hill says, occurred while she worked with Judge Thomas at the Department of Education," Senator Strom Thurmond said in Senate debate. "When Judge Thomas left the Department of Education to assume the chairmanship of the

EEOC, Ms. Hill chose—she herself chose—to go there with him. I find it hard to understand why Ms. Hill would follow Judge Thomas if the statements about what happened at the Department of Education are credible."[5]

For Hill's supporters, on the other hand, her move to the EEOC was seen as a symbol of Hill's essential powerlessness. Many victims of harassment, they contended, typically cannot sacrifice their jobs simply to escape their harassers. Responding to Senator Thurmond, Senator Simon said: "She said she moved from the Department of Education to the Equal Opportunity Employment Commission because the harassing had stopped sometime before the transfer. And she said, 'I was 25 years old and needed a job.' And that is the reason for that." Others saw it as an expression of the "battered woman" syndrome, emphasizing her passivity as a woman in a man's world. In Toni Morrison's book of essays on the Thomas–Hill scandal, Princeton University's Claudia Brodsky Lacour wrote of the

> . . . willful ignorance of the no-win decision innumerable people make, or try to make, or try to put off making daily: Whether to give up the job, the place, the people, the future one holds dear, denying one's own mental capacities, independence, and desires (what are left of them, what one remembers of them) just to get away. They will find themselves disgusting if they let their tormentor get his way, not—once again—by touching their body (never forget the obscene phone caller), but by forcing them to flee, to change anything they would not have changed if they were free to keep it: their white collar career or their cash register at the supermarket, it doesn't matter in the slightest.[6]

Such speculation about how a typical sexual harassment victim would have—or should have—behaved in Hill's situation obscured the only relevant question: Whether Hill had told the truth about her own decision to go to the EEOC. Did Hill follow Thomas because she feared for her job? Did she make the move with great reluctance and even foreboding? Was Hill really unaware of having other options, as she claimed?

Hill testified that Thomas had harassed her over the course of several months at the Department of Education. She then made a number of claims about the circumstances of her decision to accompany Thomas to the EEOC as a special assistant after she had endured the harassment. Hill said that during the time she was deliberating, Thomas's offensive behavior had stopped, and she hoped it would not continue. She said she did not know that as a Schedule A attorney at Education, she would have been assured continued employment at the agency after Thomas left—and she implied that Thomas himself had misinformed her that she would not have a job if she did not go with him. Finally, she said she did not know who Thomas's successor would be, and, rather than inquire, assumed that he or she would want to hire their own special assistant, leaving her out of a job.

In the opening round of Hill's testimony, Chairman Biden broached the topic of why Hill decided to move from the Education Department to the EEOC.

BIDEN: Can you describe to us how it was that you came to move over to the EEOC with Judge Thomas?

HILL: Well, my understanding of—I did not have much notice that Judge Thomas was moving over to the EEOC. My understanding from him at that time was that I could go with him to the EEOC, that I did not have—since I was his special assistant, that I did not have a position at the Office for Education, but that I was welcome to go with him to the EEOC.

It was a very tough decision, because this behavior occurred. However, at the time that I went to the EEOC, there was a period—or prior to the time we went to the EEOC, there was a period where the incidents had ceased, and so after some consideration of the job opportunities in the area, as well as the fact that I was not assured that my job at Education was going to be protected, I made a decision to move to the EEOC.

BIDEN: Were you not assured of that because you were a political appointee, or were you not assured of it because—tell me why you weren't assured of that.

HILL: Well, there were two reasons, really. One was that I was a special assistant of a political appointee, and, therefore, I assumed and I was told that that position may not continue to exist. I didn't know who was going to be taking over the position. I had not been interviewed to become a special assistant of the new individual, so I assumed they would want to hire their own, as Judge Thomas had done.

In the afternoon session, armed with the knowledge that Hill had been a career employee of the department, meaning that she in fact had job security whether she knew it or not, Arlen Specter pursued the point further.

A former Pennsylvania prosecutor, designated by the Republicans on the committee to question Hill, Specter, perhaps more than any other Senator, drew the ire of feminists for his performance in the hearings. At the Clinton inaugural, more than a year after the hearings had ended and Specter had won re-election in a close race with a candidate heavily backed by Emily's List, Barbra Streisand found herself in an elevator with Specter and said, "I don't like the way you treated Anita Hill."

A liberal pro-choice Republican, Specter had outraged conservatives in equal numbers by opposing Judge Bork's confirmation in 1987. For this reason, when the subject of who would question Anita Hill came up in a caucus of committee Republicans, some of the senators, including Thurmond and Danforth, did not trust Specter with the assignment, according to Senators who were present. The natural choice in terms of ability and loyalty was Utah's Hatch, but even Hatch himself feared that if he was unleashed on Hill, he would have done her more good than harm by generating sympathy for her.

In Hatch's view, Specter's liberal credentials made him the ideal interrogator. Specter also was faced with a challenge from the Right in the Pennsylvania GOP Senate primary, and this would be an opportunity to regain some lost ground with conservatives. Finally, his GOP colleagues thought that Specter would be so flattered that they trusted him with an important task that he would likely overcompensate, knocking the ball out of the park. Specter had an ego so big it stood out even on a committee of giant-sized egos.

On balance, however, Specter appeared to be a more thorough prosecutor than he actually was. Much of the outrage, in fact, seemed to be directed at Specter's highly skeptical, plodding manner in grilling the witness. In addition, as the only senator on either side of the aisle who moved the hearings onto the grounds of fact, he did more than anyone to highlight Hill's credibility problems. But in the final analysis, Specter, whose forensic skills were actually somewhat rusty, too often missed opportunities to nail down discrepancies in Hill's testimony.

In the federal government a career—or Schedule A—lawyer cannot be fired without cause, and is not reliant for his or her job on which political party controls the executive branch. A legal assistant to a political appointee—a Schedule C employee—would expect to either move with the boss if he or she went to another position, hook up with another political appointee, or else lose the job. Hill was not in this situation because she had Schedule A status throughout her government career. Yet when challenged by Specter, Hill denied knowing that she had had a career position.

SPECTER: I am shifting now, Professor Hill, to a key issue regarding your testimony that you moved with Judge Thomas from the Department of Education to EEOC because you needed the job. That is your testimony, correct?

HILL: Well, I think that is your summary of my testimony.

SPECTER: Well, is my summary accurate?

HILL: Well, I said that I moved to EEOC because I did not have another job. This position that—I was not sure whether I would have a position at the Department of Education. I suppose that could be translated into I needed the job.

SPECTER: Okay. I am informed, Professor Hill, that you were a Schedule A attorney and in that capacity could stay on at the Department of Education. Is that correct?

HILL: I believe I was a Schedule A attorney but, as I explained it, I was the assistant chair of—oh, excuse me—assistant to the Assistant Secretary of Education. That I had not been interviewed by anyone who was to take over that position for that job. I was not even informed that I could stay on as a Schedule A attorney, as well as, I stated before, the agency was subject to being abolished.

Under continued questioning from Specter, Hill began to cite other reasons why she may have gone to the EEOC with Thomas, including that "she enjoyed the work," and that she had wanted "to do civil rights work."

But Specter wouldn't relent:

SPECTER: . . . but your statements in your earlier testimony involved the conclusions that you would have lost your job, and I am now—

HILL: That was one of the factors.

SPECTER: Excuse me?

HILL: That was one of the factors.

SPECTER: That was one of the factors, and I am now asking you about the correctness of that in light of the fact that you were a Schedule A attorney, and while you would not have been Judge Thomas's assistant or perhaps the assistant of the Assistant Secretary, as a Class A attorney you could have in fact kept your job, had you wanted to stay there.

HILL: That really was not my understanding, sir. At the time I understood that my job was going to be lost. That was my understanding.

After a series of objections from Senators Metzenbaum, Kennedy, and Leahy to Specter's attempt to introduce evidence on this question—an indication that they were not interested in getting at the truth—from a sworn affidavit filed by Harry Singleton, who replaced Thomas as the Assistant Secretary of Civil Rights at Education, the Senator returned one final time to elicit an unambiguous answer from the witness:

SPECTER: Professor Hill, did you know that, as a Class A attorney, you could have stayed on at the Department of Education?

HILL: No, I did not know at that time.

SPECTER: Did you make an inquiry of his successor, Mr. Singleton, as to what your status would be?

HILL: No, I did not. I'm not even sure that I knew who his successor would be at that time.

At a subsequent point, Leahy pursued the same line of questioning in an effort to help Hill by placing responsibility for her ignorance about her job status on officials of the Education Department.

LEAHY: Now, did anybody tell you that you could stay and have a job at the Department of Education?

HILL: Nobody told me that.

Was it possible, as Hill maintained, that a Yale-educated lawyer would not know whether or not she was a career employee with job security, or a political appointee whose job would have ended if Thomas left the department? According to Phyllis Berry-Myers, who had worked at Education and at the EEOC during the same time as Hill, it was not. Berry testified that Hill had no reason to fear for her job at Education, because she would have been fully informed of her rights and her permanent status at the time of employment eight months earlier and would have signed a document spelling out her career status as well.

I was aware of only excepted service hiring decisions made in the office of Civil Rights, and that is the office that Clarence Thomas headed at that time, and Anita Hill was hired in that office as a Schedule A employee.

Federal personnel procedures require a lot of specific knowledge and a lot of paperwork, and I do not profess to be a Federal personnel expert. But I can attest to the procedures required by our office and the office of personnel at that time.

At the end of such procedures, a new employee would have no doubt whatsoever regarding their status, their grade, their pay, their benefits, their promotion rights, employment rights, and obligation as a Federal employee and as an employee in the department.

A new employee would know whether their employment is classified as permanent or temporary, protected or nonprotected, and those kinds of things. Each new employee must sign a form that contains such information, before employment can begin.

The document prepared on Hill's first day of employment specified "career tenure."[7] In further comments in an interview, Berry-Myers said that Hill surely knew she was a career employee because Berry-Myers was unable to obtain White House clearance for a political appointment for her. Hill's job as a special assistant would normally have been classified as political, but such a classification required some evidence of prior political activity on behalf of the Administration in office, or the party, and Hill had none. "I tried but I couldn't get her cleared as political, and I told her that a number of times.[8] So we hired her as career, and she obviously knew the difference," Berry-Myers said.[9]

The strongest evidence refuting Hill's version of the circumstances surrounding her job change came from two people who were never called to testify before the Judiciary Committee. Because the committee had only forty-eight hours to locate potential witnesses and had no access to Hill's and Thomas's testimony before it was delivered, people with relevant factual testimony were either never contacted or kept off the witness list in favor of witnesses whose testimony turned out to be of less importance. Senator Specter, for example, insisted that John Doggett be called, over the objections of top White House officials who did not believe his testimony would be probative. In any event, the independent recollections of these two former Education Department officials were diametrically opposed to Hill's sworn testimony about the events. They said that Hill not only knew her rights at Education but, contrary to the impression of reluctance she tried to create in her testimony, was very positive and even enthusiastic about joining Thomas at the EEOC.

Andrew Fishel was the head of the personnel office in the civil rights division of the Department of Education during Hill's tenure there. In an interview, he said that when Hill arrived at the department in late August 1981, he personally briefed her on her status as a Schedule A attorney, informing her that she could not be dismissed without cause and that she could keep her job at the agency regardless of the status of her boss. A year later, in 1982, Fishel continued, "We also had a discussion just prior to her leaving and going over to the EEOC," Fishel continued. "I was curious about what kind of appointment she was going to. She told me she was going over as a Schedule A. She said she liked being a Schedule A because she was not subject to dismissal. She clearly knew she could have kept her job at Education when she went to EEOC. She said she was personally and professionally flattered to be going with Thomas, that it was a great career move. She showed no hesitancy."[10]

Hill's insistence that she was hesitant about going with Thomas raised the question of why she had not, as she testified, made any inquiries about staying on at Education. She testified that she made no such inquiries because she did not know who Thomas's successor would be "at that time." Harry Singleton, Thomas's successor as Assistant Secretary for Civil Rights at Education, flatly and angrily contradicted Hill's testimony on several points. According to Singleton, Hill not only knew that he was Thomas's replacement—which Hill denied in her sworn testimony—but also turned down his offer to stay at Education working for him in exactly the same post she had under Thomas. "I couldn't believe that she said she didn't know who his replacement was. I was there for a few months before they left," Singleton said in an interview. "I talked to Anita a number of times. You know, we both went to Yale, and it is a small network, so we talked. Clarence had made it clear to me that he was taking Diane Holt with him. I didn't want to be left without any staff, so I asked Anita if she was going to stay. I told her I would like her to stay. But she said, 'Oh no, I'm going with Clarence.' She was lying to the committee."[11]

One of Hill's close co-workers at the time also contradicted her testimony that she was effectively coerced into the move from the EEOC because she feared losing her job. This was an exchange on the matter between Senator Hatch and Diane Holt, Thomas's secretary and one of Hill's friends in the Education Department office:

HATCH: Now she told this committee that she felt like she had to go along with Chairman Thomas over to the EEOC, if I recall this correctly—you correct me, if you saw it—but that she was afraid that she might not have a job. Do you think—

HOLT: To my knowledge, I mean, she never asked me what her options were. I didn't think there was any indecision on her part. We were both enthusiastic about going to EEOC.

HATCH: She was enthusiastic?

HOLT: She was.

HATCH: Well, wasn't that, though, because she wanted to serve in this particularly stronger civil rights area?

HOLT: We discussed that this man was a rising star and we wanted to be there with him.

HATCH: But wasn't that just you feeling that way?

HOLT: No, that was her feeling that way also.[12]

If the statements of Berry-Myers, Fishel, Singleton, and Holt are correct, a portrait of Hill entirely different from the one Hill presented of herself at the hearings emerges from their testimony. With full knowledge of her right to stay on at Education—and in spite of the expressed desire of Thomas's successor that she remain with him—Hill willingly, and even eagerly, accompanied Thomas to the EEOC.

Thomas, of course, could have been sexually harassing Hill at the same time that she elected to follow him. Despite the incredulous statements of Senators Thurmond and Hatch, a woman in Hill's position might have chosen to follow her boss to a more powerful government post despite his history of sexual harassment rather than pass up the opportunity for promotion. Such a woman would have been willing to place career advancement above any concern that the harassment might continue in the new job. This is precisely how Hill's supporters later mythologized her decision. "Prof. Anita F. Hill wouldn't go to bed with Judge Clarence Thomas," Sarah E. Wright wrote in the *Black Scholar*.

As she tells it, she suffered unavoidably through two years of his surreptitious vulgar advances while she was under his supervision. Her humiliation persisted through her work under him in the Department of Education and at the EEOC. But, she was prepared to ignore whatever psychological anguish she had to endure in the privacy of his office or on the infrequent occasions when they met to dine because she was driven by her belief that Thomas could be useful in helping her up the career ladder. . . . He was, after all, a rising star to whom everyone was eager to hitch their careers.[13]

This description, however, was just the reverse of the sworn testimony of Hill that she feared she would have been jobless, did not know she had civil service rank, and did not know who was replacing Thomas. A more truthful explanation—the desire to follow a mentor to a better job, perhaps coupled with uncertainties about being left with a new boss whom she did not know or trust to keep her employed—was foreclosed by the Republican rhetorical attack, which, in its ignorance of sexual harassment, claimed that a victim of harassment would not in any conceivable circumstance follow her victimizer to another post. Hill was therefore forced to objectify herself as the kind of "victim" that the Senate, and the public at large, would easily recognize: A woman who had no choice but to follow Thomas or lose her job. The fact that this was untrue on its face escaped Hill's GOP inquisitors, who left the matter of Hill's truthfulness on this point unresolved.

Another major area of inquiry for the committee was the nature and extent of the contacts that Hill maintained with Thomas after leaving the EEOC in 1983. If the accuser had been harassed by Thomas at Education, and again at the EEOC, why would she have contacted him at all? The Republicans suggested that *no* sexual harassment victim would maintain contact with the man who had harassed her. "Anita Hill continued a personal relationship with Clarence Thomas who she claims degraded and humiliated her. It just doesn't make sense," said Senator Connie Mack of Florida.[14] But this was nothing more than a generalization about sexual harassment victims; though the generalization was accurate as far as it went, it *proved* nothing about the case at hand. The Republicans were so disbelieving that Hill could have had a reason to maintain the contacts that they allowed a key issue of Hill's veracity to slip by virtually unnoticed. When faced with this GOP accusation, Hill did everything she could to understate, diminish or deny the contacts. Yet the testimony of several witnesses showed that Hill told several false and inconsistent stories about her contacts with Thomas in the decade after she left Washington and returned to Oklahoma.

Placing herself in the vulnerable position of a typical victim, Hill at first testified that she kept in touch with Thomas because he still had power to retaliate against her even after she left his employ, "I hoped to continue to maintain a professional relationship for a variety of reasons—one, I could not afford to antagonize a person in such a high position," she told the committee. In other words, Hill was claiming that by *not* calling Thomas she would somehow have incurred his wrath. Specter asked:

> Well, when you say you wanted to maintain a cordial professional relationship, why would you do that, given the comments which you represent Judge Thomas made to you, given the seriousness of the comments, given the fact that they violated the Civil Rights Act? Was it simply a matter that you wanted to derive whatever advantage you could from a cordial professional relationship?
>
> HILL: It was a matter that I did not want to invoke any kind of retaliation against me professionally. It wasn't that I was trying to get any benefit out of it.

But when pressed by Specter in a subsequent round of questioning as to why she would have maintained contact with Thomas, Hill must have realized that her earlier explanation made little sense in light of the fact that she had a tenured post at the University of Oklahoma where Thomas could not harm her. Moreover, she had denied the most plausible motive for the contacts: "It wasn't that I was trying to get any benefit out of it." Hill now told Specter just the opposite of her previous testimony—that she was free to call Thomas because she no longer feared his retaliation.

> Well, the things that occurred after I left the EEOC, occurred during a time—any matter, calling him up from the university—occurred during a time when he was no longer a threat to me of any kind. He could not threaten my job; I already had tenure there.

This answer, of course, still begged the question of *why* Hill had wanted to contact Thomas.

The major evidence on Hill's contacts with Thomas after she left the EEOC was contained in Thomas's old telephone logs, which were presented to the press with much fanfare on the day after Hill's story broke in the media by Senator Danforth. Once again, Thomas's supporters seemed to think that the very existence of the logs—clear evidence that Hill had called Thomas on a number of occasions after leaving his employ—was enough to disprove the harassment charge. "Now, these are the phone messages of the person who has accused Clarence Thomas of harassing her on the job," Danforth said, definitively.[15] The unresolvable debate about whether a victim of harassment *would* or *would not* maintain such contacts obscured the factual issue: Hill's explanations of the Thomas telephone logs were plagued with inconsistencies. The record discredits her sworn testimony.

The logs showed that Hill had left ten telephone messages for Thomas from 1983 to 1991. The notations in the logs read as follows:

Jan. 31, 1984, 11:50 a.m. "Just called to say hello. Sorry she didn't get to see you last week."

May 9, 1984, 11:40 a.m. "Pls. call."

Aug. 29, 1984, 3:59 p.m. "Needs your advice on getting research grants."

Aug. 30, 1984, 11:55 a.m. "Returned your call" (call btwn 1 & 4).

Jan. 3, 1985, 3:40 p.m. "Pls call tonight." [On this message, Hill left the phone for her hotel in Washington, the Embassy Row Hotel, and her room number.]

Feb. 26, 1985, 5:50 p.m. "Pls call."

March 4, 1985, 11:15 a.m. "Pls call re: research project."

July 5, 1985, 1:30 p.m. "Pls. call"

Oct. 8, 1986, 12:25 p.m. "Pls call."

Aug. 4, 1987, 4 p.m. "In town 'til 8/15. Wanted to congratulate on marriage." [Hill left telephone number of friend Keith Henderson's residence.]

Nov. 1, 1990, 11:40 a.m. "Re speaking engagement at University of Oklahoma Law School."[16]

When approached for comment by the *Washington Post*—three days before she was to testify—Hill was quoted by Ruth Marcus as calling the logs "garbage," evidently meaning to imply that they had been falsified. She asserted that she had not telephoned Thomas at all, except to return his calls. "If there are messages to him from me, these are attempts to return telephone calls. I never called him to say hello. I found out about his marriage through a third party. I never called him to congratulate him," Hill told the *Post*.[17]

Apparently unbeknownst to Hill, however, Thomas's secretary Diane Holt always noted in the log whether the contact was an attempt to return a call from Thomas or not. Contrary to Hill's characterization of these phone calls, according to the log only *one* of the ten messages showed that Hill was returning a call from Thomas—one that occurred on August 30, 1984, and followed an unsuccessful attempt by Hill to reach Thomas the previous day, August 29. Thus, contrary to what she told the *Post*, Hill initiated every one of the contacts listed in the log.

By Friday in her testimony, when Senator Specter pressed her about why the logs indicated she had initiated the calls, Hill denied having told the *Post* that she had only been returning Thomas's calls. She now conceded initiating some of them herself but said that they had all been made "in a professional context. . . . None of them were personal in nature." In order to account for those messages that appeared to be more personal than professional, Hill testified that she had been calling her friend Holt, not Thomas, on those occasions.

> I knew his secretary, Diane Holt. We had worked together both at EEOC and Education. There were occasions on which I spoke to her, and on some of these occasions, undoubtedly, I passed on some casual comment to then Chairman Thomas. . . .
> In August of 1987, I was in Washington, D.C., and I did call Diane Holt. In the course of this conversation she asked me how long I was going to be in town, and I told her.

Holt later testified that Hill had called Thomas on those occasions, not her. If any of the calls had been personal ones made to her, and not to Thomas, they would never have gone into the log, Holt said. Furthermore, according to Holt, in August 1987 Hill had given Holt information about the length of her stay specifically so she could pass it on to Thomas.

> HATCH: As I mentioned, Professor Hill spoke of you this last Friday as a friend, and, you know, attempts to diminish the significance of these messages, it seems to me, were made by her . . . by claiming that many were calls placed to you and not to Judge Thomas, or Clarence Thomas at the time; that the messages to Judge Thomas were only accidental developments from her conversations with you. Have you heard that?
>
> HOLT: I heard that, yes.
>
> HATCH: Is that true?
>
> HOLT: That is not true. Had Anita Hill called me and even asked that I pass on a hello to Judge Thomas, I would have done just that, but it would not have been an official message in his phone log.

Holt's testimony not only contradicted Hill's account but also revealed that Hill had called Thomas on at least a half-dozen other occasions not reflected in the log. The only calls logged in were those occasions on which Hill did not reach Thomas on the first try. If the call was put through, it was not logged by Holt.

In addition to the phone logs, there was evidence that Hill had personal contact with Thomas in 1987, when he traveled to Tulsa to give a speech. Thomas stayed at the home of Charles Kothe, the former dean of the Oral Roberts law school, where Hill had taught. On the morning of Thomas's departure, Hill had breakfast at Kothe's home with him, and then drove him to the airport. This incident seemed more incriminating than the telephone contacts, because Hill had willingly placed herself in a vulnerable position vis-a-vis her alleged harasser. There is wide agreement among the experts that victims of sexual harassment, when given a choice, do not characteristically place themselves in situations where the harassers can repeat their unwelcome behavior.

When Specter asked Hill why she would have agreed to drive her victimizer to the airport, Hill—evidently aware that having done so compromised her efforts to make herself appear as a victim—removed the voluntary element from the story. She maintained that she had only driven Thomas to the airport because Kothe had asked her to, implying that she was placed in a rather awkward position by Kothe's request and complied with it only because she did not want to embarrass anyone by objecting. "The dean suggested that I drive him to the airport, and I said I would," Hill testified.

When Kothe testified, however, the Republicans concentrated on drawing out the atmospherics of the meeting rather than any factual evidence. Kothe, therefore, spent most of his time telling of how Thomas and Hill seemed to get along famously, "laughing uproariously," and giving no indication that anything unpleasant had passed between them. This of course was circumstantial evidence that did not necessarily establish anything but Hill's capacity to repress her true feelings. The important test of credibility was whether Hill had told the truth about *being asked* to drive Thomas to the airport. In an interview, Kothe said Hill had *not* been asked, but rather had volunteered:

> She suggested the night before that she drive Thomas to the airport. She was very proud of her new car, and she wanted to show him. That's why she was at our home so early in the morning for breakfast. It wasn't as if it was a formal breakfast where she happened to be invited and then drive him to the airport. It was informal—everybody walking

around, getting ready to go, drinking coffee, talking. She came to take him to the airport.[18]

Hill also denied the sworn statements of other individuals who attested to her having made complimentary remarks about Thomas—that Thomas's nomination to the Supreme Court was "great" and he "deserved it." One such comment had allegedly been made as recently as August 1991, in an encounter at a convention with Carlton Stewart, a former colleague of Hill from the EEOC, and Stewart's friend Stanley Grayson (a Democratic lawyer and former deputy mayor of New York), according to affidavits the two filed with the committee. When confronted, Hill said the statements had been made by *them*, not by her.

SPECTER: . . . I would start, Professor Hill, with one of your more recent statements, at least according to a man by the name of Carlton Stewart, who says [in a sworn affidavit] that he met you in August of this year, ran into you at the American Bar Association convention in Atlanta, where Professor Hill stated to me in the presence of Stanley Grayson, "How great Clarence's nomination was, and how much he deserved it."

We went on to discuss Judge Thomas and our tenure at EEOC for an additional 30 minutes or so. There was no mention of sexual harassment or anything negative about Judge Thomas, he states during that conversation, and there is a [sworn] statement from Stanley Grayson corroborating what Carlton Stewart has said.

My question is, did Mr. Stewart accurately state what happened with you at that meeting?

HILL: As I recall at that meeting, I did see Carlton Stewart and we did discuss the nomination. Carlton Stewart was very excited about the nomination. And said, I believe that those are his words, how great it was that Clarence Thomas had been nominated. I only said that it was a great opportunity for Clarence Thomas. I did not say that it was a good thing, this nomination was a good thing . . . I was very passive in the conversation.

SPECTER: Excuse me?

HILL: I was very passive in the conversation.

SPECTER: So that Mr. Stewart and Mr. Grayson are simply wrong when they say, and this is a quotation [in a sworn affidavit] from

Mr. Stewart that you said, specifically, "How great his nomination was, and how much he deserved it." They are just wrong?

HILL: The latter part is certainly wrong. I did say that it is a great opportunity for Clarence Thomas. I did not say that he deserved it.

Yet Stewart and Grayson both made sworn statements, submitted to the Judiciary Committee, that *Hill* had said Thomas's nomination was "great" and that he "deserved" it.[19] In their Sunday testimony, Stewart and Grayson, subpoenaed to testify about the incident, elaborated:

SIMPSON: And she was very pleased about Clarence Thomas?

STEWART: Yes.

SIMPSON: Or indicated that?

STEWART: Yes, senator.

SIMPSON: Proud of him, was she proud of him?

STEWART: There seems to be—there was such euphoria I would assume she was proud of him.

SIMPSON: You recall that in her voice and her demeanor?

STEWART: Laughing, smiling, warm.

SIMPSON: And saying, isn't it great about Clarence?

STEWART: And how much he deserved it and that, essentially in tones that his hard work was paying off.

GRAYSON: Senator, if I could comment. That particular afternoon was the first, and only time I have met Anita Hill and Mr. Stewart and Ms. Hill really spent a few moments sort of reminiscing, they both worked together. So, sort of as an observer, I clearly walked away from that meeting with the clear sense that Ms. Hill shared the excitement about Judge Thomas' nomination, and was, indeed, very supportive of it.

SIMPSON: Well, I am sure you found her testimony here incredible.

STEWART: Well, I think the reason we are here is incredible. It doesn't surprise me that she would say that after making all of these other allegations.

Rather than flatly deny sworn statements, Hill could have plausibly explained that given Stewart's enthusiasm about the nomination, she had made these comments because she did not want to offend him, or because she did not want to reveal the harassment to him, or because she wanted to conceal her opposition to the nomination on other grounds. But when she was confronted with the comment under oath, Hill denied it rather than open herself up to the accusation that she had misrepresented her true feelings toward Thomas in the conversation with Stewart. The two responses Hill could have given without lying—"I misled Carlton Stewart," or "I changed my mind about the nomination since August"—were not available to her.

There were several other instances where Hill attempted to downplay her continued connections to Thomas after leaving the EEOC. In her press conference at the University of Oklahoma on October 7, the day after the story of her charges against Thomas broke, one reporter pursued the question of Hill's role in the recent speaking invitation extended to Thomas by the OU law school.[20]

Q. Did you invite him [Thomas] to speak at the university?

A. No, I did not invite him. The enrichment committee sent an official letter to him inviting him. The chairman of that committee came to me and said would you follow up and see, make sure he's gotten that letter and that he's going to pay some attention to it.

At that time, I stated very clearly to the chairman of the committee that I did not want him to come here. And I however did make a phone call and spoke mainly to his secretary saying have you got this letter, and they really would like him to come.

The Thomas phone log message in reference to the Hill call about the speaking invitation is dated November 1, 1990:

Re speaking engagement at University of Oklahoma School of Law.

However, the letter inviting Thomas to speak, signed by Associate Professor Kevin Saunders, which Hill said she was "following up," was dated January 31, 1991, three months *after* her phone call, and it began: "I am writing to follow up on your earlier conversation with my colleague, Professor Anita Hill, and invite you to deliver a lecture as part of the Enrichment Program at the University of Oklahoma Law School." Hill misstated the sequence of these contacts, possibly to obscure her own role in inviting Thomas to the campus.[21]

During the same press conference, Hill was asked about Thomas's role in helping her obtain the teaching job at Oral Roberts University, where she had gone after leaving the EEOC in 1983. "I was picked for the job at Oral Roberts University after I made a presentation to a group at a seminar that was being held there," Hill told reporters. Later in the week, in her sworn testimony, Hill said the same thing: "I participated in a seminar, taught an afternoon session in a seminar at Oral Roberts University. The dean of the university *saw me teaching* and inquired as to whether I would be interested in pursuing a career in teaching." [Emphasis added.]

But Hill's account left out the crucial fact that Thomas had brought her into contact with ORU in the first place. In the spring of 1983 Thomas had been invited to speak at an ORU civil rights seminar by Dean Kothe. As he routinely did with his assistants, Thomas asked if he could bring Hill along because she came from a town just south of the ORU campus and the visit would give her a chance to see her family. No suggestion was made by Hill that he had any other motive—and no explanation was offered as to why she would consent to travel with her harasser.

Dean Kothe said in an interview that the question as to whether Hill would consider a teaching post had been put to her at the luncheon where Thomas spoke, which is to say *before* she made her afternoon presentation. This testimony undermines Hill's clear intention to portray the job offer as a reaction to her performance at the seminar—a version that conveniently omitted any role for Clarence Thomas. Kothe specifically denied that he saw Hill teaching before making the offer. He said her connection to Thomas, not her perceived teaching ability, sparked the offer. Kothe testified:

> In fact, the first time I talked with her, I recall, was at a luncheon at which Mr. Thomas was to be the featured speaker. I learned at that time that she was from Oklahoma, and just out of the blue I said, "How would you like to come here and teach?" And she said, "I would like it."

Hill also tried to give reporters the impression that she had not asked Thomas for a letter of recommendation until *after* she had gotten the job at ORU. She told the press conference:

> The dean of the law school contacted me personally and we spoke and I interviewed for that job. And at that time, after the interview took place, after I had been assured that I would get the job, I went to [Thomas] and said would you write a letter of recommendation. And that came only because the process at Oral Roberts University required some kind of letter from a former employer.

In fact, Hill's testimony turned this chain of events on their head, presumably because she did not want to expose how dependent she had been on Thomas as a benefactor. The truth of the matter was that Thomas had been crucial to her securing the job. According to Kothe, the letter of recommendation from Thomas came in as part of the application process, *not* after Hill had been offered the job. The Thomas letter was dated May 31, 1983.[22] Based on the letter, and a subsequent conversation with Thomas, Kothe recommended to the Oral Roberts provost on June 13 that Hill be hired.[23] The offer was extended to Hill in a letter from Kothe dated June 23.[24] The Thomas letter was not, as Hill claimed, an after-the-fact formality.

Why did Hill deny these contacts and connections? She may have been harassed and had perfectly legitimate reasons for staying in touch with Thomas and leading others to believe that nothing was amiss between them. But Hill must have calculated, either on her own or with her advisers and attorneys, that she would make for a more compelling and credible witness if she simply denied the contacts. With the high pitch of their rhetoric, the Republicans had created a climate in which even the most brief and innocent of contacts with Thomas was taken automatically as proof that Hill was not harassed. Therefore, in order to make the harassment charge more believable, Hill found herself backing into a number of false and inconsistent statements about her contacts with Thomas, her true feelings about him and, not least, her professional debt to him.

Thomas's supporters attempted to undermine Hill's credibility further by repeatedly emphasizing the fact that her story grew far more detailed when she told it on national television as compared with what she alleged in her committee statement and her FBI interview.

In her statement and interview, Hill charged that Thomas had repeatedly asked her for dates and spoke to her at the office about the contents of pornographic movies involving bestiality and rape scenes. In her Senate testimony three weeks later, Hill referred to several specific instances of Thomas's behavior that she had not disclosed earlier. Among these were Thomas's alleged references to his own sexual prowess, giving pleasure to women through oral sex, and describing the size of his sexual organ; the reference to Long Dong Silver, the porn star whose name Thomas supposedly brought up in conversation; and the incident in Thomas's office where he allegedly asked, "Who put this pubic hair on my Coke?"

Senator Hatch seemed to regard the fact that Hill's charges were more detailed in her testimony than in her statement or FBI interview as proof that the story was not true. "After having spent nearly seven hours listening to her testimony," Orrin Hatch said, "and comparing her testimony to her earlier statements, I conclude that Professor Hill has not been forthcoming to this committee. Her initial statement to the committee and the FBI did not contain hardly any of the lurid and obscene pornographic details that she brought forth on national television during the hearings."[25] Senator Charles Grassley also found this troubling:

> As I saw it, Professor Hill had three different stories about the harassment she suffered. First there was the harassment she told her friends at the time it occurred . . . she described only a general claim of sexual harassment by her boss. There were no details, no specifics. Second was the harassment Professor Hill told Senate staffers when she requested confidentiality and to the FBI when she decided she wanted the Senate, but still not the public, to know. To them, she said Judge Thomas repeatedly asked her for dates and talked about pornographic movies, but not himself. And the third version of the harassment was the lurid, graphic and offensive stories she told on Friday during her testimony. There can be little doubt that she magnified her allegations for her live testimony on TV.[26]

The palpable anger and incredulity of the Republican senators over the way in which Hill's story became more vivid when she testified, however, concealed yet another factual problem with her testimony. The explanation that Hill gave for why her testimony had more details in it than her FBI interview was that the FBI had not asked for all of the details. The FBI agents, however, directly and powerfully contradicted Hill on this point, insisting that they had in fact asked her for all the details before the interview began.

When Specter asked Hill a question about why some of her more salacious allegations were not made initially to the committee or the FBI, Hill maintained that she had not given the FBI all the details because the agents had told her that she did not need to do so at that time and that they would come back for more specifics if necessary.

> SPECTER: . . . Referring to page five of the statement [the transcript of her testimony] which you provided to the committee, there is a strong allegation in the last sentence. And my question to you is, why did you not tell that to the FBI?

HILL: When the FBI investigation took place I tried to answer their questions as directly as I recall. I was very uncomfortable talking to the agent about that, these incidents, I am very uncomfortable now, but I feel that it is necessary. The FBI agent told me that it was regular procedure to come back and ask for more specifics if it was necessary. And so, at that time, I did not give all the specifics that I could have.

SPECTER: . . . In the last sentence in the first full paragraph, you again make in that statement a very serious allegation as to Judge Thomas, and I would ask you why you didn't tell the FBI about that when they interviewed you.

HILL: I suppose my response would be the same. I did not tell the FBI all of the information. The FBI agent made clear that if I were embarrassed about something, that I could decline to discuss things that were too embarrassing, but that I could provide as much information as I felt comfortable with at that time.

Shortly after watching Hill's televised Senate testimony on Friday morning, the two FBI agents in the Oklahoma City office who interviewed Hill on September 23 each filed written statements with the Bureau that pointed out factual discrepancies in Hill's testimony. According to both agents, they had asked Hill to give them the details of all of the harassment incidents and had told Hill only at the conclusion of the interview that they might come back again. As with all the other witnesses who contradict her statements, it is possible these agents were lying, in this case to cover up a mistake in their report of the interview. But if the agents were telling the truth, the reason Hill supplied for not telling them the details cannot also be true.[27] Special Agent John B. Luton wrote:

> Professor Hill stated that she was advised by the interviewing Agent that she did not have to answer questions if they were too embarrassing as she would possibly be re-interviewed by FBI Agents at a later date. In fact, she was told by Special Agent Luton to provide the specifics of *all* incidents. She was also told that it might be necessary to re-interview her at a later time regarding this matter, but that occurred *at the end of the interview.* [Emphasis added.]

Special Agent Jolene Smith Jameson also signed a statement:

> Professor Hill stated she did not discuss specific incidents in detail because the interviewing Special Agent had advised her that, if the subject was too embarrassing, she did not have to answer. In fact, SA Luton

apologized for the sensitivity of the matter, but advised Professor Hill that she should be as *specific as possible* and *give details.* She was further advised if the questions were too embarrassing, SA Luton would leave the room and she could discuss the matter with SA Jameson.

During the interview with the SAs, Professor Hill stated she could only recall specifics regarding the pornographic incidents involving people in sex acts with each other and with animals. . . .

Professor Hill stated she had been advised early in the interview that SA Luton would re-contact her at a later time to obtain more specific details. In fact, SA Luton advised Professor Hill, *only at the termination of the interview,* that a follow up interview might be necessary if further questions arose. [Emphasis added.]

Hill might have explained that it was only to be expected that more details about the harassment would emerge once the Senate indicated it was interested in hearing her unvarnished story. After all, she was testifying, being closely questioned and cross-examined, for several hours, not writing a four-page statement or doing a short FBI interview. Instead of this reasonable and straightforward explanation, Hill tried to place the responsibility for her incomplete interview on the FBI.

Hill adopted a similar strategy to deflect one other key discrepancy regarding her FBI interview. In her September 23 statement to the Judiciary Committee, Hill wrote:

Finally, he made a comment the content of which I will always remember. He said that if I ever told anyone about his behavior toward me it could ruin his career.

Yet that very evening when Hill was interviewed by the FBI, the content of the conversation that she said she would "always remember" was not the same as what she had written in her statement that very day. According to the report, Hill told the FBI agents that Thomas had said if she ever told anyone of the harassment, "he would ruin *her* career." If the memory was truly so striking it had been held in mind for ten years, how could Hill get it confused in two statements on the same day? The difference in the two stories was that in the earlier version, Hill was the stronger party, in a position to ruin Thomas's career. In the latter version, Thomas was the stronger of the two, threatening to ruin her career. Could it have been that when she told the story to the FBI, she re-told it in a way that portrayed herself as a victim?

When the inconsistency was brought up by Leahy (in a successful move to preempt a Republican attack), Hill maintained that the two trained FBI agents had both gotten it wrong.

LEAHY: Would you read the rest of that sentence [from the FBI report], please?

HILL: "Took her out to eat and told her that if she ever told anyone about their conversation, he would ruin her career."

LEAHY: Now, is that precisely the way it is in your statement?

HILL: That is not precisely the way it is in my statement. That is not what I told the FBI agents.

LEAHY: And what did you tell the FBI agents?

HILL: I told the FBI agents that he said that it would ruin his career.

FBI agents make mistakes, and Hill's contention that they got one word wrong in their initial report was plausible. Yet the FBI was so concerned about this discrepancy in Hill's testimony—when she adhered to the version given in her written statement to the committee—that supervisory agents were sent out on October 11 to interview the two agents who had interviewed Hill. Both agents independently confirmed that Hill had told them a different story from the one she told the Senate under oath that day. The Republicans, however, let the issue fizzle, when they had at their disposal direct testimony from the FBI that Hill was not telling the truth. Having agreed not to publicly reveal the contents of the FBI file, they could not introduce the following passage from the file:

> [Special Agent Jolene Smith] Jameson was asked to recall what statements were made by Professor Hill about comments Clarence Thomas made to her. These comments were alleged to have been made during a dinner Thomas took Hill to as she was leaving the Equal Employment Opportunity Commission. SA Jameson was specifically asked if she could recall whether Professor Hill stated it would ruin his or her career if she talked about things he had said to her. SA Jameson advised Professor Hill stated that Judge Thomas told her, if she mentioned his conversations with her, he would ruin her career. SA Jameson stated she recalled this specific comment because it followed and was in agreement with Professor Hill's statements made earlier in the interview. Professor Hill had stated she did not come forward earlier because she was afraid she would lose her job, Judge Thomas would retaliate against her, or she might not be believed. SA Jameson pointed out she had noted Professor Hill told the Senate Judiciary Committee, during a televised

broadcast on October 11, 1991 that Clarence Thomas had said if she told anyone about his behavior, it would ruin his career.

Special Agent John Luton was also interviewed by FBI supervisors to verify his original FBI report:

> SA Luton was requested to state his recollection of that portion of his interview with Professor Hill. SA Luton advised he recalled the statement made by Professor Hill concerning the alleged incident. SA Luton stated Professor Hill told him and SA Jameson that Judge Thomas had taken her out to eat after she had left EEOC. Hill stated that Thomas told her that if she ever told anyone about their conversations, he would ruin her career. SA Luton was asked if he specifically recalled the statement as being "he would ruin her career." He advised he did have specific recall on that matter.

When first confronted about this problem, Hill had a simple response available to her, namely, that she may have just misspoken in the FBI interview. An honest person testifying under oath would have been likely to admit the possibility of an omission or a mistake—failing to give the FBI details, mixing up her recollection of events, or misstating the threat Thomas had made. Yet whenever Hill was challenged on a matter of fact, her pattern was invariably to blame others in an apparent attempt to shift attention away from any inconsistencies in her account. Hill never even acknowledged the possibility that she—rather than the agents—could have been in error. This adamant stance seems more characteristic of someone who feared being caught in a lie than of someone who simply came forward with a true story. For such a person, the conviction of the story's truth would tend to minimize the significance in her own eyes of any inconsistencies in her testimony.

Another major problem emerged in Hill's account of her contacts with Senate staff. In her testimony Hill emphasized her extreme and continual reluctance when appearing on national television to vent her sexual harassment charge against the nominee. She distanced herself from the public spectacle, thereby successfully creating an impression of integrity and dignified reticence. She did not explain she had been hesitant all along, that she would not have come forward with the charge even in a confidential setting, absent the pressure tactics of the Senate aides. From Hill's testimony, one would never have known the extent of the contacts she had had with Senate staffers and other advisers opposed to Thomas in September, before her charge was registered with the committee.

This omission could not have been an oversight. Hill plainly preferred not to let the committee know about Jim Brudney's "carrot and stick" strategy, by which he alternately pressured and coaxed her into filing the statement. If she had, her acquiescence in a plan to defeat the Thomas nomination in secret would have come into full public view. (The effort to cover up Brudney's role was also greatly aided by Biden's decision not to call any Senate staffer to testify.)

Thus Hill was deceptive when Specter closely questioned her about an account in *USA Today*, in which Hill's friend Keith Henderson had said that she was told by Senate staffers that if she made the charge "quietly and behind the scenes," Thomas might be induced to withdraw.

> SPECTER: But was there any suggestion, however slight, that the statement with these serious charges would result in a withdrawal so that it wouldn't have to be necessary for your identity to be known or for you to come forward under circumstances like these?
>
> HILL: There was—no, not that I recall. I don't recall anything being said about him being pressed to resign.

A few moments later, Hill continued:

> HILL: The only thing that I can think of, and if you will check, there were a lot of phone conversations. We were discussing this matter very carefully, and at some point there might have been a conversation about what might happen.
>
> SPECTER: Might have been?
>
> HILL: There might have been, but that wasn't— I don't remember this specific kind of comment about "quietly and behind the scenes" pressing his withdrawal.
>
> SPECTER: Well, aside from "quietly and behind the scenes" pressing him to withdraw, any suggestion that just the charges themselves, in writing, would result in Judge Thomas withdrawing, going away?
>
> HILL: No, no. Not that I recall.

Apparently, Hill's first instinct—natural enough—was to deny anything that would have cast her in a bad light and raised the question of whether she was attracted by the opportunity the staffers offered her to attack Thomas secretly without revealing herself or facing the potential consequences of coming forward and confronting her victimizer.[28] In the afternoon, however, unprompted by a question, Hill volunteered the following about her first conversation with Brudney in early September:

> HILL: . . . Well, we discussed a number of different issues. We discussed one, what he knew about the law on sexual harassment. We discussed what he knew about the process for bringing information forward to the committee. And in the course of our conversations, Mr. Brudney asked me what were specifics about what it was that I had experienced.
>
> In addition, we talked about the process for going forward. What might happen if I did bring information to the committee. That included that an investigation might take place, that I might be questioned by the committee in closed session. It even included something to the effect that the information might be presented to the candidate or the White House. There was some indication that the candidate or, excuse me, the nominee might not wish to continue the process.
>
> SPECTER: Mr. Brudney said to you that the nominee, Judge Thomas, might not wish to continue the process if you came forward with a statement on the factors which you have testified about?
>
> HILL: Well, I am not sure that that is exactly what he said. I think what he said was, depending on an investigation, a Senate, whether the Senate went into closed session and so forth, it might be that he might not wish to continue the process.
>
> SPECTER: So Mr. Brudney did tell you that Judge Thomas might not wish to continue to go forward with his nomination if you came forward?
>
> HILL: Yes.

Hill's conflicting statements on this question led Specter to charge that had she not changed her testimony, the morning exchange, when she had said there was no suggestion from Brudney that Thomas might withdraw, would have constituted flat-out perjury. In the afternoon, after consulting with attorneys who may have advised her to correct the record precisely to avoid a perjury charge, Hill reversed course and said that Brudney *had* told her Thomas might withdraw. Though it is not clear that Hill would have been convicted of perjury on the basis of her morning testimony, Specter was quite correct in exposing Hill's attempt to mislead the panel about Brudney's calculations.[29]

Hill concealed other facts regarding Brudney under questioning as well. Earlier she had been asked by Senator Leahy about her handling of the statement that she filed with the Judiciary Committee on September 23. During that exchange, Hill omitted crucial information that would have implicated Brudney as the person who had leaked her statement to the media.

LEAHY: When you made that statement, you had it typed up and you signed it, is that correct?

HILL: I typed and I signed it.

LEAHY: You typed and signed it, and kept a copy for yourself?

HILL: I only telefaxed a copy. I did keep a copy, the original.

LEAHY: And you still have that?

HILL: I still have it.

LEAHY: Have you given copies of that to anybody other than the copy you telefaxed, to anybody else?

HILL: Well, I shared the statement with my counsel.

LEAHY: Let's make sure I have this well in mind: You have the original copy, correct?

HILL: Yes.

LEAHY: And you telefaxed a copy, which, in itself, made copies to the committee, is that correct?

HILL: Pardon me?

LEAHY: You faxed a copy to the committee, is that correct?

HILL: Yes.

LEAHY: You gave a copy to your counsel?

HILL: Yes.

LEAHY: Did you give a copy to anybody else?

HILL: No, they told me that they had received a copy from the committee.

LEAHY: Did you give a copy to any member of the press?

HILL: No, I did not.

LEAHY: And so your counsel, the faxed copy and your own copy are the only ones that you had control of, is that correct?

HILL: Yes.

The report of special counsel Peter Fleming, released seven months later, stated that Hill, after an extended discussion of why he needed it, had faxed a copy of her committee statement on September 25 to Jim Brudney, who subsequently appears to have leaked it to the press. Hill withheld this information under oath.[30]

Hill also sought to conceal the reason she initially contacted Brudney. When Specter asked about her knowledge of civil rights law, including the statute of limitations for filing a sexual harassment charge, Hill responded that she considered herself "an expert in contracts and commercial law, not an expert in the field of sexual harassment or EEO law." She added: "I don't even teach in that area any more." Specter bore in:

SPECTER: Well, you did teach civil rights law.

HILL: Yes, at one point.

SPECTER: You taught civil rights law after 1980, right?

HILL: Yes, I have.

The subject came up again later in the day, when Specter continued to question Hill about her contacts with Senate staffers. Hill testified that in the September 9 phone conversation with Kennedy's aide Ricki Seidman, Seidman had suggested that Hill call Brudney, ostensibly because Brudney had worked in the area of sex discrimination and would be able to give her an understanding of the law. Specter asked why she would need someone to advise her on the law, considering her own knowledge of sexual harassment law, her employment as a top attorney at EEOC, and her experience as a civil rights law professor. Hill told Specter:

> I had not practiced in the area. I have never actually practiced in the area. I have taught in the area, but it has been—I haven't taught in the area since 1986, and I understand it is a very fast-developing area of law.

Yet according to the Office of Admissions and Records at the University of Oklahoma Law School, Hill taught a civil rights class in the spring of 1990. While some of the technicalities of sexual harassment law are not covered in law school civil rights classes, Hill would not have needed Brudney to update her on recent developments in this area. That is something anyone with her background could have quickly checked out at the law school library. This fudged testimony seems to have been part of the strategy to hide the real purpose of her discussions with Brudney: To create a behind-the-scenes scenario that might lead Thomas to withdraw his nomination.

Hill obscured the role of other activists in her decision to come forward as well. Grassley asked if anyone other than the three Senate staffers Hill had testified about—Gail Laster, Ricki Seidman, and Jim Brudney—had spoken with her about filing a statement.

> GRASSLEY: This is in regard to your testifying that you were approached by Senate staff members about disclosing these allegations. My question is whether or not any other individuals or any other organizations other than those who you publicly stated today or otherwise, or Senator Specter stated, whether any other individuals or organizations have approached you about disclosing these matters to the Judiciary Committee any time since Judge Thomas was nominated by the president on July 1.
>
> HILL: No. No other individual, no other organizations or individuals have approached me to disclose this to anyone. Do you mean prior to the contact from this or even after that?
>
> GRASSLEY: Or any time during July, August, or September, other than all those names that have already been discussed today?
>
> HILL: No. No one has urged me to do that or even approached me about it.

A few minutes later, Hill realized that she had failed to mention Judge Hoerchner's role:

> Ms. Hoerchner did contact me and reminded me of the situation and we discussed the fact that we had talked about this in earlier years but she did not urge me to come forward at all.

Hill failed to mention a number of other advisers, however. As later disclosed in the Fleming report, during the period in which Hill continued to insist on complete anonymity, and while the Judiciary Committee staff therefore could not proceed to investigate, she spoke at Brudney's urging with the sexual harassment expert Susan Deller Ross of Georgetown University. Hill not only spoke several times with Deller Ross, she gave her explicit permission to discuss the situation with Judith Lichtman, head of the Women's Legal Defense Fund, a key member of the anti-Thomas coalition.

As previously established, after the harassment story broke, Hill sought to cast blame on the Judiciary Committee for failing to act on her charge, while she portrayed herself as completely forthright and unhesitant, a victim of the committee's white male arrogance and chauvinism. The record does not bear out her version of events either.

In her press conference the day after the story broke, Hill explained her contacts with the committee this way: "I spoke with the Judiciary Committee about it early in September, and through a number of discussions it was not until the 20th of September that an FBI investigation was suggested to me. It was at that time I was told that this was the way to get the information before the committee," Hill told reporters in her opening statement. "Now, I spoke and cooperated with the FBI investigation when the concept was provided to me by Sen. Biden's committee, and that was on the 20th."

Hill's rendition of these events seemed designed to suggest that any delay in the committee's consideration of her charges was due to the committee's intransigence and lack of serious interest, rather than her own hesitancy to proceed. As we have seen, however, according to the Biden chronology, when Grant called Hill on September 20 and told her that before the committee members could be informed of the allegation, Thomas and Hill "would both be interviewed by the FBI," Hill refused to involve the FBI at that point. "Grant called Hill at 2:00 P.M. Saturday Sept. 21," Fleming reported. "Hill told Grant she did not want to go through with the FBI investigation." Not until three days after Grant had mentioned the FBI interview, on September 23, did Hill call and say she was finally ready to proceed.

Hill continued to misrepresent what had transpired between her and the committee throughout the press conference:

Q. At what point during your dealings with the Judiciary Committee did you start to feel that the process was not being carried out fully, and did you ever express that idea to any members of the committee staff? Did you make any suggestions as to how the matter ought to be pursued? And did you then suggest that you were willing to testify publicly, if necessary?

A. I suggested to them *throughout* that I wanted to make this information available to every member of the Senate committee for their consideration. . . . I suggested all the time that I did not want to tell anybody how to do their job. But I felt that they had an obligation to hear what I was saying once I had come forward.

Q. Did you at some point offer to make these allegations by name? Did you discuss the removal of your request for confidentiality, and at what point did that occur?

A. The extent of my confidentiality was *never to keep the committee members from knowing my name.* The extent of my confidentiality was making sure that the names [hers and Hoerchner's] were not released to the public—that's what I meant by confidentiality. So *at all times* the Senate knew my name, the committee knew who I was. So that wasn't ever an issue. [Emphasis added.]

The Biden chronology, however, stated that it was not until September 19—a full week after she had first spoken with Grant—that Hill was even willing to *consider* allowing the committee to know her name.

[F]or the first time, she told full committee staff that she wanted all members of the committee to know about her concerns, and if her name needed to be used to achieve that goal, she wanted to know.

In her press conference, Hill left out the entire week in which she had insisted on anonymity *before the committee,* a mischaracterization that projected the false image of a silenced victim of sexual harassment and senatorial chauvinism.

When Hill was interviewed by Katie Couric on the *Today* show the next morning, Tuesday, October 8, she continued along the same lines. In explaining the delay in investigating the charge that was in reality caused by her own reluctance to proceed, Hill sought to shift the onus onto the Senate, suggesting that her charge had not been taken seriously by the committee, and again misrepresenting the chronology of her committee contacts. Couric or someone on her staff had evidently read the record, and she questioned Hill about how the Judiciary Committee had handled her complaint.

COURIC: . . . Do you think your desire to maintain confidentiality impeded the investigation?

HILL: . . . I *never said* that I did not want to give the nominee an opportunity to respond. In fact, when that concern was raised to me, I said that, in fact, that I wanted him to have an opportunity to respond.[31] [Emphasis added.]

Contrary to what Hill told Couric, however, she had been instructed from the beginning—September 12, to be exact—that the accused would have to be told who was making the charge, and this was precisely what Hill had refused to permit for eleven days. When Hill called the committee on September 19 to say that she was willing to abide by the standard procedures and was reminded that this meant the nominee would have to be told her name, she backed off a second time. Not until September 23 did Hill finally agree to this condition.

The committee staffer Harriet Grant's record of her phone conversations with Hill, summarized in the Fleming report, directly contradicts what Hill told Couric: "Hill repeated her desire for confidentiality and, according to Grant's contemporaneous notes, said she *did not want* the nominee to know her name."

When Hill's interview with Couric is compared with Chairman Biden's chronology of committee contacts with Hill, Hill's false statements to Couric about what had transpired become clear.

> [Hill] demanded confidentiality, that Thomas not be informed of her charges, and that the FBI undertake no investigation. . . . Professor Hill specifically stated that she *did not want* the nominee to know that she had stated her concerns to the committee. . . .
>
> [The committee staff] again explained that before committee members could be apprised of her concerns, the nominee must be afforded the opportunity to respond. [Emphasis added.]

By scapegoating the committee in this fashion, Hill lit a bogus political brushfire that masked what happened between September 9 and September 23, when Hill was really contriving to make an anonymous charge and *avoid* an official investigation. Perhaps because she knew her attempt to rewrite the history of her committee contacts would founder under questioning from the Senators, by the time Hill arrived in Washington at the end of the week she no longer voiced any criticism about the way the committee had handled her charge. That was left to the legion of liberal activists and media image makers, who successfully distorted the record along the lines Hill originally suggested in her press conference and *Today* show interview.

In any sexual harassment case, the accuser's recollection of who had or had not been told contemporaneously of the charge, and how much they had been told, would be a key test of the accusation's credibility. Hill's vagrant recollection regarding her witnesses, therefore, was a final troublesome aspect of her account.

Before her story became public knowledge, Hill consistently maintained that she had told only one person—Susan Hoerchner—about the harassment as it was occurring. Moreover, she had made Hoerchner swear an oath that she would not reveal the story to anyone else.

In her original statement to the Judiciary Committee, Hill had stated: "Between 1981 and 1983, I spoke to only one person about these incidents and my feelings about the job. That individual, Susan Hoerchner, was a close friend and law school classmate who did not know Clarence Thomas personally. She, out of personal friendship, has agreed to come forward if necessary. I was too embarrassed to speak to anyone else and feared that if I did Thomas might somehow retaliate." According to the Hoerchner interview with the Senate staff lawyers, Hill also told Hoerchner that she was the only person who knew of the charges:

Q. Did she ever relate to you that you were the only person that knew about these allegations or these problems she was having at work?

A. I think she told me that more recently.

Q. More recently that you were the only person who knew?

A. Yes.

Q. When did she tell you that?

A. It may have been around the time that she wanted to know if I would talk to the FBI.

Q. So we are talking about the last couple of weeks of September?

A. Very recent, yes.

By the time Hill testified, however, she claimed that she had told two more witnesses during 1981 to 1983—her long-distance boyfriend at the time, John Carr, and her friend Ellen Wells. (A third witness, a law professor named Joel Paul, testified that Hill told him of the events several years after they had occurred.)

The FBI, which had also been told specifically by Hill that Hoerchner was the only person she had told, immediately spotted this discrepancy in Hill's sworn testimony. In addition to having told the FBI that Hoerchner was the only person who knew, Hill was specifically asked—and she specifically denied—that she had told her boyfriend Carr. The FBI file reported:

Professor Hill testified she told Ellen Wells and John Carr, her boyfriend at the time, about Thomas's behavior. However, she told SAs Luton and Jameson she never mentioned Thomas's behavior to anyone except Susan Hoerchner. Professor Hill specifically advised she did *not* tell her boyfriend. [Emphasis added.]

Senator Leahy, again acting successfully to foreclose a potential point of vulnerability for Hill, questioned Hill about whether there was a contradiction between what she told the FBI—that she had only told Hoerchner—and the fact that Hill was now producing more witnesses.

> LEAHY: In your statement, you had said that between 1981 and 1983, you spoke to only one person about these incidents—Susan Hoerchner—and you have talked about two others now. Is there a contradiction there?

> HILL: Well, in my statement I do say that I only spoke with one person. That is all that I recalled at the time that I made the statement. I am finding that, I am recalling more about the situation. I really am finding that I repressed a lot of the things that happened during that time, and I am recalling more, in detail.

This would have been a convincing answer had *Hill* identified other potential witnesses as she began to recall events of a decade ago more clearly. While no one on the committee challenged Hill on the matter, each of Hill's witnesses testified that their appearance was not the result of Hill's "recalling more," but rather because each of them contacted her and *reminded her* of what she allegedly had told them. This sequence did not seem to support Hill's claim that more witnesses were located as the result of her overcoming repression. These witnesses came forth on their own initiative, for reasons that will be discussed in a subsequent analysis of their testimony. (Apparently, they were not sworn to secrecy in the manner that Hoerchner was.) This was how each witness described the circumstances:

> JOHN CARR: On Sunday evening, October 6, I saw television reports that Professor Hill had accused Judge Thomas of sexual harassment. I immediately remembered that she had told me of his sexual advances.

> ELLEN WELLS: My call jogged her memory of what she said to me.

> JOEL PAUL: I picked up the *Post,* I read the story, and instantly knew exactly what she was talking about.

Hill went on to tell Leahy, "When I made that statement too, I might add, that I made it rather hurriedly and even though I had been thinking about the situation, I had not perhaps given all of the consideration in terms of who I had told that I should have for the statement." At other points in her testimony, however, Hill asserted the opposite. She told Specter that "it wasn't as though I rushed forward with this information," and she told Biden that she had been "meticulous" with her statement.

There were other inconsistencies regarding Hill's witnesses that escaped notice in the hearing. Hill testified that she confided in three witnesses—Hoerchner, Wells, and Carr—about Thomas's behavior because she wanted their advice on how to handle the situation. But each of the three testified that Hill had *not* asked for advice. Leahy asked Hill to describe the conversation with Hoerchner in which she first told Hoerchner of the harassment:

> LEAHY: What was the nature of your conversation with her?
>
> HILL: Well, I was upset about the behavior. And that's what I was expressing to her as a friend, that it was upsetting and that I wanted it to stop and maybe even *asked for advice* or something to help me out of the situation. [Emphasis added.]

But when Biden asked Hoerchner about this, Hoerchner contradicted Hill:

> BIDEN: Did you advise her to take any action? Did she seek your counsel? Did—
>
> HOERCHNER: She did *not* ask for advice.
>
> BIDEN: Did you say, you should complain? Did you give her any advice?
>
> HOERCHNER: She did *not* ask for advice, and I did not give her advice. [Emphasis added.]

Hill testified that she had asked Ellen Wells and John Carr for advice as well:

> I discussed it, in passing, well, no, not in passing. I discussed it with Ellen Wells, who is another female friend. She and I were close during the time and we had a conversation, in particular, we were talking about what I should do, how I should respond to it, what might make it stop happening.

When Biden asked Wells why she had not given Hill advice, Wells contradicted Hill too:

> BIDEN: Did you give her any advice, and why not, during this period when you knew she was unhappy, you knew this was going on . . . ?

WELLS: No . . . I know Professor Hill was a very private person. And I am a very private person. . . . Now, if you need to talk about it, you need a good ear for that, then I am there for you. And if you want my advice, and you let me know that you want that, then I will give it to you.

Finally, Hill testified in relation to the witness John Carr:

At the time, I was dating someone, John Carr, and we discussed it because I was, I was upset by it. And I wanted to let him know why I was upset and again, just trying to see if there might be some way that he could handle this differently.

But Carr contradicted Hill when asked this question in his interview with the Senate Judiciary Committee lawyers before he testified publicly:

Q. Did Professor Hill ask you for any advice during this conversation?

A. No, she didn't.[32]

Hill's fourth witness was Joel Paul, who met Hill in the summer of 1987 when he was doing legal research at American University. In her opening statement to the committee, Hill testified, "It is only after a great deal of agonizing consideration that I am able to talk of these unpleasant matters to anyone but my closest friends." Yet Hill had apparently told Paul—a man she barely knew—about the sexual harassment in a casual lunchtime conversation. Paul told Grassley:

Senator, as I have testified, I am not a personal friend of Professor Hill's. I am a professional colleague of hers who had always been very impressed by her, and so my recollections are not colored by a personal relationship to her.

Considered separately, each of these glitches involving Hill's witnesses does not seem terribly significant. Taken together, however, they raise more questions about the consistency and credibility of her story. If Hill had repressed the harassment incidents, why didn't she tell the FBI that she was not sure how many people she may have told, instead of insisting that Hoerchner was the only person who knew? Why did she specifically tell the FBI that she had *not* told her boyfriend John Carr, only to have Carr later appear as a witness? Why would each witness deny that Hill had asked for advice if, as she testified, she had asked for it? Why would Hill say she had told only her closest friends of the harassment, when in fact she had told at least one person she barely knew? Why did she swear Susan Hoerchner to silence and neglect to do so in other conversations? Were these contradictions simply the inevitable consequence of reconstructing events ten years past, or were they the inevitable loose threads of a fabricated story?

While that question has no certain answer at this juncture, it is clear that the equal credibility granted to Hill's word in relation to Thomas's by the Senate and the media is undeserved. If the contest did ultimately come down to her word against his, a careful analysis of Hill's testimony provides ample reason for seriously doubting her word. By the time Hill had finished testifying, if one wanted to believe that she had told the truth, the whole truth, and nothing but the truth, one would have to believe that all of the other people who had offered conflicting testimony and evidence were incorrect, or simply lying: Diane Holt, Harry Singleton, John Doggett, Phyllis Berry-Myers, Andrew Fishel, Carlton Stewart, Stanley Grayson, Charles Kothe, Ruth Marcus of the *Washington Post*, Harriet Grant, Joe Biden, the two FBI agents, and all four of Hill's own witnesses—Susan Hoerchner, John Carr, Ellen Wells, and Joel Paul. Alternatively, all of these individuals could have been correct, and Hill could have made more than a dozen false statements under oath.

6

Judge Hoerchner's Amnesia

Anita Hill's case did not rest solely on her word. During her initial discussions with Metzenbaum staffer Jim Brudney in September, Hill stated that she could produce one witness who would corroborate that she had complained about sexual harassment as it was occurring ten years before. That witness was her friend Susan Hoerchner.

When Hill next contacted Harriet Grant of the Senate Judiciary Committee, she again asserted that one witness could corroborate her charge, if necessary. In mid-September, at Hill's suggestion, Hoerchner contacted Grant and, on a condition of confidentiality, said that Hill had made an unspecified complaint of sexual harassment in a telephone call in 1981. Once Hill filed her charges with the committee, she stated in an interview with the FBI that she had told only one person—ever—of the harassment by Thomas: Hoerchner.

In a sexual harassment case, a corroborating witness is a strong indication that the charge has merit and should be investigated, despite the denials of the accused. When she appeared before the committee, Hoerchner testified:

She told me that she was being subjected to sexual harassment from her boss, to whom she referred by name. That boss was Clarence Thomas. . . .

He kept pressing her and repeating things like "I'm your type," and "You know I'm your kind of man, but you refuse to admit it."

Hoerchner was the only witness of the four who appeared for Hill who corroborated both the identity of the harasser and could recount details of the harassment. (The testimony of the other three will be examined in a subsequent chapter.) If Hoerchner's testimony about the call was correct, Anita Hill's complaint about Thomas had to have been ten years old; it could not have been invented to sabotage his Supreme Court appointment. Hoerchner's testimony presented a seemingly insurmountable refutation of this belief, which was widely held in Republican circles—and apparently subscribed to by the nominee himself—during the weekend of the hearings. As Democratic Senator Herb Kohl of Wisconsin put it in questioning Hoerchner, "Yesterday, Judge Thomas said there was a plot afoot in this country to derail his nomination to the Supreme Court. As I hear your comments today, it is obvious to me that if there was a plot afoot, it must have originated ten years ago. So, do you think that Anita Hill plotted for as long as ten years to derail Judge Thomas's nomination to the Supreme Court?"

Kohl's question, of course, was meant to make its answer self-evident. Hill obviously had not plotted against the Thomas nomination for ten years; at the least, Hoerchner's presence proved that Hill had complained in 1981 that Clarence Thomas was sexually harassing her. Yet this left open a question that has never been answered in a satisfying way: If Hill had been complaining about Thomas's harassment ten years back, why did no word of her complaint surface during those ten years, despite strenuous efforts by Thomas's detractors to discover damaging information to use against him in prior Senate confirmations? Why did Hill wait ten years—after Thomas had been confirmed twice as the nation's top sexual harassment law enforcer, and once to a top-level appellate court in Washington—before telling anyone else? On the other hand, if Hoerchner's recollection about the events of 1981 was mistaken, the sole corroborating testimony for Hill's sexual harassment charge would be undermined. The charge itself, therefore, might not have been ten years old after all.

One of the few lasting friendships that Anita Hill formed at Yale was with the woman, Susan Jane Hoerchner, who would later set in motion the most momentous event of her life—her confrontation with Supreme Court nominee Clarence Thomas. Several years older than her classmates, Hoerchner was something of a professional student, having already earned a Ph.D. in American studies from Emory University in Atlanta before arriving in New Haven. She had been born to modest circumstances in Chico, California, and claimed American Indian heritage. The two met in 1978, when Hill became Hoerchner's editor for a Yale Legislative Services project.

Friends from Yale remembered Hoerchner as having a somewhat distracted and confused demeanor, perhaps the result of the tranquilizer Valium, which her friends saw her take on a number of social occasions in the late 1970s, presumably to quell nervousness. "Sue Hoerchner was ditzy," one former classmate said. "It was the same Sue Hoerchner we saw testify years later."[1]

When Hoerchner and Hill graduated from Yale in 1980, they both found themselves headed for careers in the capital. Though she later claimed that she was unaffiliated with "the Alliance for Justice or with any allegedly anti-Thomas group,"[2] in fact Hoerchner went to work for several months in 1980 at the Center for Law and Social Policy, a public interest law organization that was a member of the Alliance for Justice coalition. She then decided to work in the public sector, taking a job as a staff attorney to one of the commissioners at the National Labor Relations Board.

Hill was drawn to a faster track. While still a law student, she had been a summer associate at the Washington law firm of Wald, Harkrader & Ross, one of the hottest law firms in town during the final year of the Carter Administration, and the firm offered her a permanent position in the fall of 1980. Hill left the firm less than a year later, in August 1981, under circumstances that would become one of the enduring mysteries of the Thomas–Hill scandal.

In late August Hill reported for work at the Department of Education, as a special assistant to the new Assistant Secretary for Civil Rights, Clarence Thomas. At the same time Susan Hoerchner went on temporary detail to the San Francisco office of the National Labor Relations Board; her father had had a second stroke, and she wanted to be near him in California.[3] In an interview with Senate lawyers before she testified publicly, Hoerchner said the prospect of transferring permanently with the NLRB had looked bleak, so she set about looking for another job in the Bay area. She soon found one as an associate with the San Francisco law firm of Litler, Mendelsohn, Fastiff & Tische. Once settled in California, Hoerchner recalled, she lost touch with Anita Hill.

In the next several years, Hoerchner faced a series of professional and personal difficulties. She left Litler, Mendelsohn after a year and for the next eighteen months was "self-employed," as she later testified. In March 1984 she worked on a temporary basis for the city auditor in Berkeley. In September of that year she landed a temporary teaching position at Valparaiso University School of Law in Indiana.

The following year Hoerchner got an assignment teaching legal research at Chase Law School of Northern Kentucky University. From there she took a permanent job as a staff attorney for the State of California's compensation insurance fund, which she parlayed into a position as an appeals examiner for workers' compensation claims in August 1990. With the job came the somewhat overblown title "judge."

By the summer of 1991, the forty-seven-year-old Hoerchner was in her third marriage, this time to a fellow workmen's compensation judge in Los Angeles. She was also involved in a sexual harassment controversy at the workers' compensation board that summer. Hoerchner had been on the job in Norwalk, a small working-class city south of Los Angeles, for only six months when, according to an article in the *Los Angeles Times,* she acted as a "key corroborating witness . . . in a California sexual harassment case that resulted in the presiding judge of the Norwalk Workers' Compensation Appeals Board stepping aside." The charge was filed by a probationary workers' compensation judge against Donald Foster, the board's seventy-year-old presiding judge. Hoerchner was the accuser's "supporting witness," according to the *Times,* the same role she would play in the Anita Hill hearings.[4]

"A department affirmative action officer subsequently determined that there was a number of allegations from a series of present and prior subordinates of the judge that seemed to demonstrate a pattern of behavior," the *Times* reported. But in an interview with the *Times,* Judge Foster described the case as a "tempest in a teapot . . . a minor incident." Foster told associates that he had had a spotless public service record for eighteen years, before Susan Hoerchner appeared and incited women to file harassment claims against him.[5]

Whether or not the charges against Foster had merit cannot be determined; the board's home office in San Francisco never reached an official conclusion. In any event, Foster's reaction to the charges may have been the paradigm for what Hoerchner and Hill expected in the Thomas case. Rather than fight the charges, Foster immediately took sick leave once an informal query began, in February 1991.

No formal investigation was ever launched by the state, and Foster retired on July 2. For Hoerchner and her friend in Norwalk, simply lev-
eling the charge, quietly and behind the scenes, had accomplished
their purpose.

All of this occurred during the very same period in which Hoerchner contacted Hill for the first time in seven years to discuss a story
about sexual harassment Hill had told to Hoerchner in a telephone
conversation ten years before. Hearing on July 1 that Clarence
Thomas had been nominated for the Supreme Court, Hoerchner recalled that Hill had complained to her a decade earlier that her boss
had sexually harassed her.

When Hoerchner testified publicly, she stated unequivocally that
the boss Hill had referred to in the early 1980s was Clarence Thomas.
Other parts of the record, however, never released publicly before,
indicate that when Hoerchner called Hill in July she had been unsure about the identity of Hill's harasser. The question, then, is
whether she remembered Clarence Thomas by name, or whether his
name got attached to an old story July 1. In the interview with Senate Judiciary Committee lawyers two days before she stated under
oath that Hill had clearly named Thomas, Hoerchner's recollection
seemed uncertain:

> Q. Getting back to mainly what you talked about, the one tele-
> phone call [in 1981], did Anita Hill mention Clarence Thomas'
> name during that telephone call?
>
> A. I *think* she referred to him as Clarence. [Emphasis added.]

When Hoerchner heard the television news report that Thomas
had been nominated for the Supreme Court, she listened closely to
find out *if* he was the man who she remembered had harassed her
friend. The name itself wasn't enough. In the staff interview, Hoerchner was asked:

> Q. What were your views when Judge Thomas was nominated
> for the court? What were your personal views about that?
>
> A. Shock.
>
> Q. Why was that?
>
> A. I just remember waiting for them to *explain his background* and
> then yelling to my husband, "He's the one!" [Emphasis added.]

It was also made clear in the interview that Hoerchner had not
been holding the idea that Clarence Thomas had harassed Hill in

mind for ten years; rather, on July 1, 1991, Hoerchner thought back to 1981, drew the conclusion that Thomas was "the one," and called her friend for confirmation.

> Q. Now, let me go back to this again. When did the name Judge Thomas or Clarence Thomas have some meaning to you other than— when did you know who he was, I guess is my question?
>
> A. Only when she told me that she was going to go to work for him.
>
> Q. And then the day that he was nominated you called out to your husband and said "That's the one"?
>
> A. Yes.
>
> Q. And the time between—the knowledge you had of him was based on the conversation you had with Professor Hill and then the next time that you realized he was the one was when he was nominated by President Bush?
>
> A. That he was the person that Anita had worked for with whom she had had the devastating experience.

Hoerchner's interrogator, one of the GOP staff lawyers, appeared to grow frustrated at this juncture, prompting Hoerchner to concede that she needed Hill to confirm the harasser's identity. This, too, showed that Hoerchner was not sure whether the harasser was Thomas.

> Q. I found it a little hard to connect this. The fact that a man you had never met that she mentioned in a conversation in 1981 and then you have another conversation with her in 1991, it is a little hard to connect up how when she talked about this happening you would know that the man that President Bush nominated—this was him, this was the man.
>
> A. Well, you know, he had the same name, had the same resume, and Anita, by telephone, verified that he was the one.

Hoerchner's testimony and other parts of the record, however, indicate that Thomas was *not* the one. On hearing that Thomas had been nominated for the Supreme Court, Hoerchner appears to have added two (Hill had complained of harassment) plus two (Hill had worked for Thomas) and gotten five (Hill was harassed by Thomas).

According to the chronology of Judiciary Committee staff contacts with Hill released by Biden, Hoerchner inadvertently revealed to

Biden staffer Harriet Grant that the single telephone call from Hill to Hoerchner in which Hill told of sexual harassment by her boss came at a time when she was not in fact working for Thomas.

> Between September 12 and September 19, full committee staff did not hear from Professor Hill, but received one phone call from Professor Hill's friend—on September 18—who explained that she had one conversation with Professor Hill—*in the spring of 1981.* During that conversation, Professor Hill provided little detail to her friend, but explained that Thomas had acted inappropriately and that it caused Hill to doubt her own professional abilities. [Emphasis added.]

If the call took place in the spring of 1981, as Hoerchner told Harriet Grant, then it occurred six months *before* Hill went to work for Thomas at the Department of Education, and eight to ten months *before* Hill told the Senate she first started being harassed. In her testimony to the Judiciary Committee, Hill stated:

> I began working with Clarence Thomas in the early fall of 1981. . . . Early on, our working relationship was positive. . . . After approximately three months of working together he asked me to go out with him socially.

Hill told Thomas no, according to her testimony, and the first alleged incidents of harassment occurred in "the following few weeks"—i.e., in late December 1981 or January 1982 at the earliest.

Was Hoerchner wrong about the date and right about the identity of the harasser, or was she right about the date and wrong about the identity of the harasser? Enmeshed in a sexual harassment case herself, where she had learned to appreciate the power of such charges, and politically opposed to the Clarence Thomas nomination, Hoerchner may have simply presumed that Thomas was "the one" and phoned Hill without thinking about the timing of Hill's complaint.[6] Hoerchner's testimony that Thomas was the perpetrator was drawn not from her memory of ten years ago but from what Hill verified in July 1991. This hardly constitutes corroborating testimony. Hoerchner's recollection of the date, however, was based not on what Hill confirmed in 1991 but on what she knew to be the facts of her relationship with Hill and where she was living ten years earlier.

Not until Hoerchner spoke with Harriet Grant in September 1991 did she think carefully about the date of the crucial conversation with Hill. In her Senate staff interview, Hoerchner was asked:

Q. . . . At what point did you— what caused you to have to go back and recall that conversation and when it was? When was that?

A. I think it was right at the time that I spoke to Harriet Grant.

Thus, after reflecting on events of ten years ago—for the first time—in preparing to call Grant, Hoerchner placed the date of the call in the spring of 1981. Hoerchner, of course, had no reason to think that Hill *was not* working for Thomas in the spring of 1981, since Hill had confirmed Hoerchner's recollection that Thomas was "the one" on July 1. In the call to Grant, Hoerchner was evidently unfamiliar with the specifics of Hill's employment history and did not realize the implications of what she was saying.

Four weeks after speaking with Grant, Hoerchner was asked several times in the interview with Senate lawyers about the timing of the telephone call. She continued, unwittingly, to provide a time for the call that placed it before Hill went to work for Thomas, and she explained why she believed the call had come before September 1981. Hoerchner said the call was among many weekly telephone contacts the two women shared beginning in the summer of 1980, when they both moved to Washington from New Haven, and ending when Hoerchner went on detail to the NLRB in California in September 1981. According to Hoerchner's statement, after she moved to California in September, the regular telephone contacts with Hill stopped. "I remember mainly one telephone call, and I have only been able to guess at the time—sometime before September 1981. That was at a time when we spoke fairly regularly by telephone," Hoerchner said.

September, of course, was the first month that Hill worked for Thomas, and it was at least *three months* before any harassment was alleged to have started. Later in the interview, one of the GOP staff lawyers apparently realized that the time frame Hoerchner had given for the call—prior to September 1981 and prior to her departure for California—was inconsistent with the period of Hill's employment by Thomas.

Q. And, in an attempt to try to pin down the date a little bit more specifically as to your first phone conversation about the sexual harassment issue in 1981, the year you mentioned, you said the first time you moved out of Washington was September of 1981; is that correct?

A. Right.

Q. Okay. Were you living in Washington at the time you two had this phone conversation?

A. Yes.

Q. So it was prior to September of 1981?

A. Oh, I see what you are saying.

Q. I am just trying for the benefit of everybody to get to the truth, to pin down the—

A. I think I was. Yes. I'm sorry. That isn't something that I can—

Q. Okay.

A. I was living in Washington prior to that time. I'm not sure that was the time of the phone call, but I really think it was.

Q. Okay. You were or were not living in Washington when you think you had this— do you think you were living in Washington or not?

A. I think I was.

Q. So that would make it prior to September of 1981?

A. Yes, if my memory—

At just that moment, one of Anita Hill's attorneys, Janet Napolitano, objected and asked for time to speak to Hoerchner. In either an oversight or an attempt to stack the deck in Hill's favor, Democratic Senate staff permitted Napolitano to monitor the interviews of potential witnesses, even though Hoerchner had her own attorney present and Clarence Thomas had no representation in those interviews. Such a state of affairs would never have been permitted in any serious sexual harassment proceeding. The GOP staff attorneys should have demanded to audit this off-the-record discussion on behalf of Thomas; unfortunately for Thomas, they failed to do so.

Ms. NAPOLITANO: Can I meet with the witness? Can we talk for just a minute?

MR. SCHWARTZ [Senator Biden's aide]: Okay. You want to go off the record?

Ms. NAPOLITANO: Yes.

MR. SCHWARTZ: Sure.

A few minutes later:

MR. WOOTEN [Senator Thurmond's aide]: I would like to say for the record that we took a break so the judge could confer with her lawyers or representatives. Now we are back on the record.

As if cued by Napolitano, a Democratic staff lawyer then asked Hoerchner one final time:

Q. When you had the initial phone conversation with Anita Hill and she spoke for the first time about sexual harassment, do you recall where you were living—what city?

A. I don't know for sure.

Q. Okay. Thank you.

For the remainder of the staff interview, Hoerchner was on alert not to contradict herself about the date of the call, even if it meant giving some rather awkward responses.

Q. Can you give us, maybe, how that came up? Why she talked about Judge Thomas to you?

A. She said she was changing jobs and going to work for him in the Office for Civil Rights, Department of Education, and how excited she was.

Q. Do you remember roughly when you all may have had that conversation when that came up?

A. Have to be that it was before the part where we talked about his behavior.

But what if Hill told Hoerchner she was going to work for Clarence Thomas several weeks *after* Hill had talked about her boss's harassing behavior, and Hoerchner was simply confused about the sequence?[7]

According to Senate staffers, such preinterviewing of subpoenaed witnesses was somewhat unusual for the Judiciary Committee and was primarily used as a damage-control device. This time it seemed to work perfectly. By the time Hoerchner appeared on Sunday in public, she was seemingly struck with amnesia about the date of the call that she was testifying about. Though she had positively stated that it had taken place in the spring of 1981, before her move to California, Hoerchner suddenly no longer remembered what year it was, or where she had been living at the time. Moreover, aware that the date she had given several times for the call—to Harriet Grant, to the FBI, and then to the Senate staff interviewers—placed the call before Hill's tenure with Thomas, Hoerchner went out of her way to state under oath that she was certain the call had taken place at the time when Hill *was* working for Thomas.

> I remember, in particular, one conversation I had with Anita. I should say, before telling you about this conversation, that I cannot pin down its date with certainty. *I am sure that it was after she started working with Clarence Thomas,* because in that conversation she referred to him as her boss, Clarence. [Emphasis added.]

Why would Hoerchner introduce the question of whether or not Hill was working for Thomas at the time, if not to preempt the suspicion that Hill was *not* in fact working for Thomas?

Immediately before she made this statement, however, Hoerchner unwittingly implied that the conversation took place while she had been speaking with Hill on a regular basis. Since that period began in 1980 and ended in September 1981, if Hoerchner was correct about this, the harassment complaint had to have been made before Hill worked for Thomas.

> We were both busy with our new jobs, so we did not get together with great frequency. What we did do, however, was keep in touch by telephone. Those conversations would often last as much as an hour. I remember, in particular, one telephone conversation I had with Anita.

When asked by the Senate interviewers how long the 1981 phone conversation with Hill had lasted, Hoerchner indicated that the call was a local one made while she was still living in Washington. "I'm not sure. She spoke on the telephone usually for a very long time, often an hour." Evidently, in one of these frequent local calls Hill complained of harassment. When Biden asked Hoerchner, "How did you know that the problem continued after first being made aware of it in the conversation that you related to us, here today?" Hoerchner responded, "In telephone conversations I asked and she led me to understand that it was happening, and often would say, she didn't want to talk about it at that time."

Could Hoerchner have been describing a series of events that occurred sometime after September 1981, when Hoerchner was in California and Hill was working for Thomas? This does not seem to have been possible, because Hoerchner told the Senate interviewers that the two women had "less than sporadic" contacts after Hoerchner left Washington in September 1981. According to Hoerchner's own statement, after Hill made her complaint, there were several other calls in which

Hoerchner asked about the harassment and Hill did not want to discuss it. These, too, would have had to be among the series of local calls.

Q. . . . I am trying to get some sense of the kind of relationship with her and the kind of contacts.

A. After that it seemed pretty sporadic, after I left.

Q. After you left where?

A. Washington, D.C.

Hoerchner, in fact, said there had been only one contact between herself and Hill after September 1981, a chance meeting at a professional conference in San Francisco in December 1984, long after Hill had left Thomas's employ. Therefore the call in which Hill alleged harassment by her boss—and the subsequent calls when she declined to discuss it—had to have come before the two lost touch when Hoerchner moved to California in September 1981.

By Sunday, word of this key discrepancy in the Hoerchner account filtered through the top ranks of the pro-Thomas camp. But Thomas's supporters could do little with the information, because they had trouble getting the transcripts of the committee's confidential interviews from Biden's office. The committee Republicans had access to the transcripts, but, contrary to the media portrayal of a well-coordinated strategy to defend Thomas, there was little cooperation between the GOP Senators and Thomas's team in the administration. That held true even among the Senators themselves. Each Senate office acted autonomously, with the political concerns of the individual member taking precedence over getting to the truth about the allegations. Given the time pressures, the raging political firestorm, the media uproar over Specter's charge of "flat-out perjury" the previous day, and the fact that on Sunday afternoon Thomas seemed to have the upper hand, it was hardly surprising that no one wanted to make a victim of Hoerchner by closely examining the discrepancies in her testimony on national television.

Specter got close to the nub of the matter in a series of questions to Hoerchner, but he never quite confronted her directly with the inconsistency of her statements to the committee lawyers versus her testimony during the televised hearings.

SPECTER: Can you, at least, tell us whether you were living in Washington at the time you had the conversation with her?

HOERCHNER: I cannot pin down the date with any further specificity.

Justice Department lawyers punched the air as they watched Specter close in on Hoerchner but miss. Unlike Specter, they were aware that Hoerchner's previous statement that the conversation took place in Washington in the spring of 1981 would negate her corroboration. They had been reluctant to pass the tip on to the Senator, who prided himself on his independence, not to mention his reputation as a prosecutor. In an earlier round of questioning, one of Specter's aides had slipped him a prepared question, and almost got fired on the spot.

Had Specter hit the target, it would have been apparent to all—including a national television audience—that Hill's conversation with Hoerchner, if it had taken place at all, could only have been an allegation about sexual harassment at Wald, Harkrader & Ross, the law firm where she was working prior to September 1981, and before Hill ever met Clarence Thomas.

On Monday morning, a top aide handling the nomination called one of Senator Biden's senior aides and demanded that he begin reading aloud on the phone the committee's confidential transcript of the Hoerchner interview. "You want to talk about hijinks?" the Bush aide shouted into the phone. When the Biden aide came to the exchange where the interviewer asked, "So, it was prior to September 1981?" and Hoerchner answered, "Oh, I see what you are saying," the Biden aide exclaimed, "Oh, shit!" The Judiciary Committee subsequently sealed the transcript of the Hoerchner interview, refusing to make it part of the official record.

At the time of the hearings, Hill's employment history in her first job out of Yale, at the law firm of Wald, Harkrader & Ross, was scarcely mentioned. The question of why Hill departed from the firm was briefly raised by Biden at the opening of the Senate hearing. For no apparent reason, Biden brought up the prospect that Hill might have been asked to leave the firm. ("It was one of those situations where you say exactly what you're *not* supposed to say," one Senate staffer later speculated, referring to a rumor behind the committee's closed doors the day before the hearing began that Hill had been fired from the firm.) Hill gave an answer—the only time she has ever commented on the issue—that was more sweeping than Biden's question required.

BIDEN: Now, did you decide you wanted to leave that law firm, or was it suggested to you?

HILL: It was never—

BIDEN: Did someone approach you and say there's another job you might like, or did you indicate that you would like to leave the law firm to seek another job?

HILL: I was interested in seeking other employment. It was never suggested to me at the firm that I should leave the law firm in any way.

As will be shown, Hill's response to Biden was the most critical misrepresentation she made to the committee in her sworn testimony. The importance of what happened to Hill at the firm extended beyond its potential to impeach the credibility of Hill's testimony. When considered along with Hoerchner's recollection that Hill had complained of harassment before she went to work for Thomas, it placed in question the plausibility of her central charge against Thomas. The evidence suggests that Hill's experience at Wald, Harkrader in 1981, not at the Department of Education or the EEOC, was the basis of Hoerchner's recollection in July 1991 that prompted her call to Hill.

The backstage drama regarding Hill's employment record began a few days before Hill testified, when Judith Richards Hope, an attorney with the Washington office of the Los Angeles-based law firm Paul, Hastings, Janofsky & Walker, perused the morning papers.[8] In a story about the sexual harassment charges leveled against Thomas by Hill, the accuser was identified as a former associate of Wald, Harkrader & Ross. Hope had been a member of the Wald firm's executive committee at the time that Hill worked for the firm, a body that, among other things, handled personnel matters.

Having worked in the Ford White House, Judy Hope brought good Republican connections to the Wald firm when she joined in the mid-1970s. (Also a touch of show business, since she was the daughter-in-law of comedian Bob Hope.) A trial lawyer, she left Wald and joined Paul, Hastings in late 1981. In 1988 she was nominated by President Reagan to the D.C. Circuit Court of Appeals, but the Democrats were hoping to win the presidency, and the nomination was not acted upon. By the time President Bush offered to renominate her in 1989, she had been elected a member of the Harvard Corporation, and she turned the judgeship down. The nomination went instead to Clarence Thomas, whom Hope did not know and had never met.

Yet Hope's curiosity was piqued about the woman who had worked in her firm a decade ago and was now accusing Thomas of sexual harassment. Hope said she remembered that there had been problems with Hill's performance at Wald—problems that precipitated Hill's departure from the firm. And, like any good trial lawyer, she knew that in a case like this, the accuser's employment history might be relevant. Hope therefore made some private inquiries of former Wald partners to see what they remembered about their onetime associate.

She walked down the hallway at Paul, Hastings and approached a younger lawyer who, unlike Hope, had worked directly with Hill at Wald, Harkrader and had later followed Hope to Paul, Hastings. He told Hope that he, too, remembered Hill's performance at Wald as substandard. Hope then called two other former Wald partners, whose names she did not put on the record because the conversations at the time were private. One person Hope called was an old friend now in Chicago who had a thriving environmental practice at the Wald firm and who had occupied the office next to Hope's. She told Hope that Hill did not write well and was not thorough, and added that at a certain point she had refused to work any longer with Hill. Hope called another attorney who had also served on the Wald executive committee. He confirmed that the firm had been dissatisfied with Hill and had eventually helped to find her a job elsewhere.[9]

Hope then called Donald Green, the keeper of the now-defunct Wald firm's employment records and a partner in the Washington office of Pepper, Hamilton & Scheetz. Unbeknownst to Hope, Pepper, Hamilton—an old-line Philadelphia-based firm that subsumed Wald, Harkrader in 1987—was the very place where Anita Hill was being prepared for her Senate testimony against Clarence Thomas. Green had helped arrange a conference room at the firm for use by Hill and her advisers—including Pepper, Hamilton's Robert Skitol, another former Wald partner who was a protégé of the Wald firm's former chairman, Bob Wald, and John Frank, a friend of Wald who had been active in opposing the nominations of Rehnquist and Bork. (Frank had argued the landmark *Miranda* case before the Supreme Court.)[10]

Green told Hope that he remembered Hill as a pleasant person but said he recalled nothing about her performance at the Wald firm. Hope asked him if he had the records of the firm, and Green said he did. She then suggested that Green locate Hill's employment records and review them, to see if anything in the records might be of import to the Senate's investigation of Hill's charges. Green was noncommittal, according to Hope.

Finally, Hope called the Wald firm's former administrator, a non-lawyer now working in New York who had attended the executive committee meetings at the time Hill's future was under discussion.[11]

"He told me she had not worked out, and that we found her another job," Hope said. "We asked Gil Hardy to help her."

In itself, this was not an unusual circumstance. Many young lawyers flunk out—and many more opt out—of life in large law firms, where the day is long and hard and the atmosphere intensely competitive. Gil Hardy, a Wald partner, had been a classmate of Clarence Thomas at Yale. As part of the small network of black Yale law graduates in Washington that included both Thomas and Hill, Hardy was the logical person in the firm to help Hill out of her bind. The Wald firm was known as liberal not only for its political connections to the Carter Administration but also for its easygoing environment, and this extended to the relatively humane way the firm parted company with associates.

Several former Wald attorneys, in fact, said one of the firm's management problems was that it too rarely fired anybody. Though she was not, strictly speaking, fired, some partners apparently felt that if Hill were not encouraged to leave early on, the firm would eventually owe her a partnership for which she would not be qualified or face a discrimination suit. These partners felt that the firm could not afford to carry lawyers like Hill, whose partnership potential was doubtful, any longer. By the time Hill left Wald, the firm's heyday was over. The impact of the Carter recession had set in, as had the new Reagan Administration's effort to ease antitrust enforcement and curb new regulatory actions, the backbone of the firm's business. In 1981, partnership draws were down 10 percent, and the firm was suffering from cash flow problems.[12]

While this might seem a hasty judgment for the firm to reach about Hill's prospects after less than a year on the job, Hill had already acquired a negative track record during her summer 1980 trial run at Wald. Several partners opposed the decision to offer Hill a permanent position, but Bob Wald and other well-intentioned proponents of affirmative action in the firm prevailed in hiring her.[13]

When Hardy was asked by his partners in the spring of 1981 to help Hill find another job, he called Clarence Thomas, who was then expecting a presidential appointment as Assistant Secretary for Civil Rights in the Department of Education. "Clarence later told me Gil Hardy had called and told him there was a woman, a Yale law graduate at his firm, who was in trouble at the firm. And he asked Clarence if he might be able to give her a job," Ricky Silberman, the vice chairman of the EEOC, said, recalling a conversation with Thomas shortly after Hill made the sexual harassment allegation.[14] Harry Singleton, who replaced Thomas at the Education Department in 1982, said that Thomas told him years ago that Hardy had called him and "asked if I could do something because she was having problems at the firm and needed to find another job."[15] "Anita was about to be fired at the law firm and he said he would help her out," Phyllis Berry-Myers, who handled the administrative arrangements for Hill's appointment at Education, recalled. "Gil Hardy, as a favor, asked him to hire her to protect her career."[16]

Thomas explained the situation more gently in his own testimony:

> Anita Hill came to me through one of my dearest, dearest friends—he was the best man at my wedding, we were at Holy Cross College together, we were at Yale Law School together, we were the two slowest guys on the track team, we spent a lot of time together, we lived across the way from each other in law school, we lived together during the summer when my marriage broke up, I slept at his apartment—this was my dearest friend, and when he brought her to my attention, it was a special responsibility that he asked me to take on, and I felt very strongly that I could discharge that in the way that I did, and that was to be careful about her career, to make sure she had opportunities, to be there to offer advice and counsel, and this is something that I continued with my other special assistants. They are family.

That Thomas would hire a young black woman who was having trouble in her career was not unusual for him. Despite his opposition to a federally mandated program of quota-based hiring guidelines, Thomas believed in a kind of voluntary affirmative action in his own staffing, going out of his way to give qualified women and minorities a chance. Singleton commented:

> He always had an odd lot of birds under his wing, and we would compare notes on our charges. That's how I knew she had been in trouble when she came to him. Early on, at Education, he was impressed with her and wanted to give her an opportunity. Thomas used to talk about her as one of his "rising stars," one of the bright young people around him he was giving a helping hand to. Here was somebody he was trying to help. She was having a hard time at one of the Washington law firms, and needed a break.

Hill's "troubles" at Wald may have included sexual harassment—another reason that Thomas, if he was told that she had been harassed, may have readily overlooked any performance problems she had at the firm when he agreed to hire her, and one reason why Hill was not eager to discuss her departure from Wald in her testimony. Thomas's personal sympathies sometimes outweighed his professional judgment. "He wasn't a great personnelist. He would take in every stray dog that came along and put them in positions that were not necessarily good for the agency," Silberman said.

In the first few minutes of her sworn Senate testimony Friday morning, Hill, prompted by Biden, revised this career history. Hill's initial impulse, when thrown a surprise question by Biden, was to deny categorically the unhappy events of 1981 at the Wald firm. Hill had been valedictorian of her high school class. She had done well at the University of Oklahoma and had held her own at Yale. But in her first professional undertaking, hired because she was a black woman from Yale, not because she had been an outstanding summer associate, Hill had not succeeded. This was a major disappointment in her life—her first reversal in a lifetime of positive steps—and she would not wish to relive it on national television.

Nonetheless, some of the former Wald, Harkrader partners who were tuned in were stunned to hear Hill tell Biden: *"It was never suggested to me at the firm that I should leave the law firm in any way."* Judy Hope's inquiry about Hill, undertaken *before* Hill testified, was not particularly significant—she had passed the information to Senator Danforth and the White House for what it was worth—until Hill made this statement under oath, which directly contradicted what Hope had found out. Now Hope had a potential bombshell on her hands, bearing directly on Hill's credibility as a witness.

Throughout the day Friday, Hope tried to reach Don Green at his Washington office with no success. Friday night around 10 P.M., Hope called Green at home. This is her recollection of the call:

"Don, what's going on, Don?" she asked Green. "Where are the records?"

"There aren't any records," Green replied.

"Two days ago there were records," Hope said. "Come on, Don, we've got to tell the truth. I don't want you to be another Alan Fiers" [an Iran–Contra figure who pleaded guilty to withholding information from Congress and was later pardoned by President Bush].

Green told Hope not to call again and hung up the phone.

Gil Hardy, who surely knew the truth, had died in a boating accident in 1989.[17] Having never worked directly with Hill and having no documentary evidence from the old firm, Hope decided she did not have enough firsthand knowledge to challenge Hill's testimony. The three people Hope had spoken with about Hill also chose to remain silent. But the story of how Hill had been asked to leave the firm in 1981 surfaced anyway.

That morning another former Wald, Harkrader partner had been listening to Hill's account of her experience there. While Hope's curiosity about Hill may have been spurred by her political affiliations, John Burke, managing partner of the Washington office of the Boston-based law firm Foley, Hoag & Eliot, was a liberal Democrat, a civil rights activist, and a close friend of Bob Wald. He was even Wald's personal lawyer for a time. Burke had been one of several Wald partners who supervised Anita Hill's assignments in 1980 and 1981. He had firsthand knowledge about Hill that deeply troubled him, but he was also worried that he might lose his job if he told what he knew.[18]

Nevertheless, by Sunday evening Burke found himself in the offices of Senator Danforth, who grilled Burke with detailed questions to make sure he was absolutely certain of what he was about to swear to. Danforth was satisfied, and Burke swore to an affidavit that directly contradicted Hill's statement that "it was never suggested to me at the firm that I leave the firm in any way." The document said in part:

> It was the practice of that law firm to evaluate the work performance of its associates approximately every six months. I recall a time, which I believe to be in the late winter or early spring of 1981, when I met with Anita Hill in my office at the law firm to discuss her work performance with her. At that time, I was the partner in charge of coordinating work assignments for the tax, general business and real estate section of that law firm. Anita Hill had performed work assignments for the lawyers practicing in that section, including several assignments for me.
>
> To the best of my recollection, that performance evaluation lasted between 30 minutes and one hour. During the course of that performance evaluation, the specific details of which I am unable to reconstruct, I expressed my concerns and those of some of my partners, that her work was not at the level of her peers nor at the level we would expect from a lawyer with her credentials, even considering the fact that she was a first-year associate.
>
> During the course of that performance evaluation, I suggested to Anita Hill that it would be in her best interests to consider seeking employment elsewhere because, based on the evaluations, her prospects at the firm were limited. I also discussed with Anita Hill the fact that Wald, Harkrader & Ross was not a firm which treated its lawyers harshly and would assist her, as it would any of its associates, in finding an appropriate legal position and that she should avail herself of that assistance.[19]

Burke's affidavit was corroborated in later interviews with attorneys from the old firm. One attorney who worked closely with Burke and asked not to be quoted by name said, "I can confirm this much: She was not succeeding. Sometimes I would ask her to do something, and get no response at all. Just a blank look. [Burke] eventually explained to her that things just weren't working out." Other lawyers in the firm knew of the situation too. Former Wald partner David Berz said, "She was new and had a lot to learn. What was going on was getting her to be more an advocate, get more confidence in her analytical effort. John [Burke] was a tax lawyer, and they had an unhappy experience with her. She needed a lot of work. Her analytical work was okay, but the advocacy was not there, and her writing was unclear."[20]

When the Burke affidavit was delivered to the Judiciary Committee late Sunday, a move was made by the Republican members in closed session to subpoena the Wald, Harkrader records. That would have settled the question of fact one way or the other, but the Democrats, either unconcerned with discovering the truth or simply trying to hide it, blocked the request on a party-line vote. "In a sexual harassment law suit," Larry Thompson, one of Thomas's legal advisers, said, "the defendant would have been able to discover the plaintiff's previous employment history. The Democrats fought like hell to keep us from getting those records."[21]

"I pushed hard to get the employment records," Orrin Hatch recalled. "This man [Burke] was an honest liberal who couldn't sit by and watch her lie."

On Sunday night the Burke affidavit was released to the press by Danforth, and word of it reached Donald Green. A former reserve colonel in the Marines and a staunch Wald, Harkrader loyalist who had been responsible for the firm's associates at the time, Green swore out his own affidavit. "Certainly, the Associate Development Committee, which I chaired, did not ask or press her to leave," Green wrote of Hill. That assertion, so far as it went, could well have been true. But it was also irrelevant to the fact that Gil Hardy and John Burke had told Hill she was going to have to seek employment elsewhere, and then helped find her another job. Green also wrote that Hill's "performance was not held to be unsatisfactory by the Wald firm."[22] To anyone familiar with law firm terminology, this construction meant only that Hill had not been summarily fired from the firm.

Furthermore, Green had told Judy Hope only the prior week, before the issue erupted into a controversy, that he did not recall anything about Anita Hill's performance one way or the other. And if

Green had *not* been sure of his recollection, he would have had to check the records of the firm—records he told Hope he did not have.

When press reports briefly mentioned the Burke and Green affidavits in stories on Monday and Tuesday before the confirmation vote, they were presented as though they were completely contradictory, though in fact they were not.[23] None of the reporters focused on the real issue, which the Green affidavit merely served to confuse: Did John Burke suggest to Hill in any way that she leave the firm?

On this point, Green's affidavit did not contradict Burke's. In an interview with the *Houston Chronicle,* Green himself acknowledged that his affidavit did not address the issue to which Burke had sworn. If Burke had suggested that Hill leave the firm, Green said, "he took it upon himself—although he had no authority and was not speaking for the firm—to tell Anita that he did not think she had a future, which I think is a terrible thing to do to a young lawyer." But regardless of what Green did or did not know or do, and regardless of whether or not the communications to Hill were official and proper, if Burke's affidavit was correct, it is hard to avoid the conclusion that Hill had flatly lied under oath. Given the subsequent corroboration from former Wald attorneys and the information that Judy Hope gleaned *prior* to the controversy, there is no reason to think that Burke was in error.

Although the "conflicting" testimony of Green and Burke was presented as yet another impenetrable mystery by the media—to the very limited extent that this crucial matter bearing on Hill's credibility was covered at all—at bottom the Wald episode was not much of a mystery after all. Bob Wald, who eventually left Pepper, Hamilton to start his own very small firm, and his friend Don Green had cast their lot with Anita Hill, their former associate, early in the week, before she testified publicly.[24] Both Wald's current firm, Nussbaum & Wald, and Green's firm, Pepper, Hamilton, were financial supporters of the Women's Legal Defense Fund, whose director played a vital role in getting Hill to make the charge and was a leader in the anti-Thomas campaign.[25] With Green's assistance, Pepper, Hamilton was serving as the base camp for the Hill forces.

Bob Wald had brought in friends to help prepare Hill's testimony. Together with his wife, Patricia, a circuit judge on the U.S. Court of Appeals for the District of Columbia appointed by President Carter to the same court where Clarence Thomas sat before his Supreme Court confirmation, he was a savvy member of the capital's liberal legal network. Pat Wald was close to Senators Kennedy and Simon, to whom she had reportedly whispered criticisms of her colleagues Bob Bork and Douglas Ginsburg when they were nominated to the Supreme Court. Furthermore, in the months before Thomas was nominated for the high court, Wald implied to White House counsel C. Boyden Gray, the President's point man on judicial nominations, that Thomas was not qualified for a higher appointment. The Walds also knew how to work the press. While Wald's firm suffered massive partner defections for several years before it finally collapsed, Wald continued to get admiring press notices. This skill may have helped Wald and Green escape a serious media inquiry into their roles in the Hill affair.

But a fly landed in the ointment when, on Friday morning, Hill misrepresented the circumstances of her departure from the firm. Wald, who as a member of the firm's executive committee and a former name partner presumably would have been in a position to know more about Hill's status than Green, did not come forward officially. Green was chosen for the job instead, perhaps because, as he told Judy Hope, he knew so little. One top Bush Administration official who handled the Thomas nomination and researched Hill's employment history at the time of the hearings charged, "It was a liberal law firm, and they covered it up."

Considering Hill's experience with John Burke at Wald, the details that Susan Hoerchner provided about the 1981 phone call in which Hill complained of sexual harassment seemed to apply to the firm, not to Hill's experience at the Department of Education. According to Hoerchner, the sexual harassment complaint was voiced during one of the regular discussions the two women had about how they were faring at work, and at the time Hill was clearly in professional trouble. Hoerchner testified:

> It was clear when we started this conversation that something was badly wrong. Anita sounded depressed and spoke in a dull monotone. I asked Anita how things were going at work. Instead of a cheery, "Oh, just busy," her usual response, this time she led me to understand that there was a serious problem. . . . She told me that she was very humiliated and demoralized by Mr. Thomas's behavior and that it had shaken her faith in her professional ability.

Earlier Hoerchner had told the Senate lawyers that Hill had been complaining generally about her job just before she mentioned sexual harassment.

Q. At any time during this conversation, and then I will ask the broader question later, did Anita Hill express to you either happiness or unhappiness about her job?

A. About— other than his behavior about her job?

Q. That includes everything.

A. Oh, yes. Yes, she did earlier, I think. I am not quite sure but I think the conversation started with how are things at work, kind of thing, and due to the very depressed sounding response I kept asking questions.

In the same interview Hoerchner explained, "When we had that major telephone call that I can— at least the major one in my memory, she said that she was going to give herself some time and she was going to leave because of that, whether or not she had another job." Hoerchner also said, "She used the term, more of a term like demoralized. She talked a lot about the loss of confidence in herself as a professional."

Hoerchner was then asked:

Q. Now, the conversation that you had in 1981. I believe you said it was before September, I believe, of '81 [before Hill had gone to work for Thomas], you said that Ms. Hill, or Professor Hill, sounded depressed when she talked to you. What caused you to characterize the conversation that way?

A. Flat tone, short answers, and her saying that she wasn't happy.

In the spring of 1981—the time Hoerchner originally gave for the call—Hill had ample reason to be demoralized, to be doubting her professional abilities, to be depressed and unhappy, and to be planning to leave her job with or without another offer. She was on the verge of being let go from her first job at Wald, Harkrader & Ross. On the other hand, she had no known professional troubles at the Department of Education, and by her own account had never planned to leave the department under any circumstances—until Thomas offered to take her to the EEOC in May 1982, whither she eagerly followed.

If this conversation occurred in the spring of 1981, Anita Hill either was being sexually harassed at the Wald firm at the same time that John Burke was advising her that she was going to have to leave the firm, or she told her friend Sue Hoerchner that she was being sexually harassed as a way of explaining away her professional problems. Hill may have been a victim of harassment at Wald during the period that she was also having performance problems and only chose to tell Hoerchner half the story about why she was leaving Wald—the harassment half, not the poor performance half. Hill may have also floated a false story about being harassed at work to cover what could have been an embarrassing exit from her first job out of law school.

A cover story of either racial or sexual discrimination would have been an effective means of cutting off any uncomfortable discussion of her professional inadequacies. But because the Wald firm was known for its aggressive recruitment of women and minorities, sexual harassment would have been a more plausible choice. In 1981, when sexual harassment laws were very new to the books, and many people did not appreciate the serious of such charges, telling a friend on the telephone that she was leaving her job because her boss was a "pig" would not attract nearly the attention that such a statement would today. In failing to tell Hoerchner that she had gotten a negative personnel review from John Burke, Hill was not, of course, doing something unheard of. Lying to protect oneself is one of the most common forms of dishonesty. Many people do not advertise their professional difficulties, even to close friends, and if they do, they invariably explain such difficulties so as to cast themselves in a sympathetic light.

There is no physical evidence that Hill was sexually harassed at Wald, Harkrader. Since no formal complaint was made, only Gil Hardy other than Hill would know if any such charge was involved in Hill's departure, and Hardy is dead. However, there is testimony that Hill may have told not only Hoerchner but several other people, including Clarence Thomas, that she had left the Wald firm because she was being sexually harassed. According to Senator Danforth, during one of their many heart-to-heart talks after the Hill revelations were made public, Thomas said that either Gil Hardy or Anita Hill herself had told him in 1981 that she had left the Wald firm because she had been sexually harassed there.[26] Diane Holt, Thomas's personal secretary at the Department of Education and the EEOC, also recalled being aware in 1981 that Hill had been sexually harassed at Wald, Harkrader. "I can't be sure if Judge Thomas told me that he had brought her over because she was being sexually harassed, or if Anita told me herself in one of our conversations toward the end of the work day that she was harassed," Holt said in an interview, "but I clearly do remember being told by one of them that she was sexually harassed at the law firm."[27]

Carlton Stewart, a former special assistant to Thomas at the EEOC who worked closely with Anita Hill at the agency, also remembered hearing that Hill had been sexually harassed at the law firm. "I remember asking around about why she left the firm, because it seemed to me to be a drastic move. The usual way to do it is to work in the government, and get your experience, and then move from firm to firm. It is very difficult to do it the other way. Here she had left a big firm to go to the Department of Education, which wasn't a place like the Justice Department, or even the EEOC, where a promising young lawyer might go. It didn't make sense to me. And I was told that she left the firm because she was sexually harassed. Of course, I didn't attach any particular significance to it back then," Stewart said.[28]

During the October hearings Hill's sexual harassment story from Wald, Harkrader did not seem relevant to anyone who remembered it, because none of them knew of the Hoerchner discrepancy. Even if Hill *had* been harassed at Wald, as Thomas, Holt, and Stewart recalled, the issue at hand was her claim to have been harassed by Thomas as well. If Thomas's supporters had known not only that Hill had complained that she had been sexually harassed at Wald, but also that the call from Hill to Hoerchner had come before September 1981, when Hill worked at Wald, Harkrader, they would have been able to conclude that Hoerchner had the wrong man in mind when she called Hill ten years later and asked if she was going to say anything to keep that "pig" Thomas off the court.

But how could Hoerchner make such a fateful error? As to the elusive state of Hoerchner's memory, there was this exchange between Hoerchner and the Senate interviewers:

Q. Just moving ahead in the time frame, did you ever discuss with Anita Hill her reasons for leaving her job at the EEOC?

A. Yes, I did. When we had that major telephone call that I can— at least the major one in my memory, she said that she was going to leave because of that, whether or not she had another job.

Hoerchner was plainly confused. There was no way Hill could have been working at the EEOC at the time of this call. If she had been working for Thomas at all, it would have been where Hill first worked for him, at Education. Hill had made this plain in her own testimony:

LEAHY: Let's talk about Ms. Hoerchner. Was that when you were at EEOC or the Department of Education?

HILL: That was at Education, I believe.

After another series of questions from the Senate lawyers, Hoerchner was prompted to concede her mistake:

Q. Is it possible, Judge Hoerchner, that she was referring to— again, I understand the comments you made about your recollection—is it possible that she was referring to the same time period in which she worked at EEOC?

A. Well, I was trying to remember all this at first. At one point, I thought it was EEOC, but I was drawing conclusions based on other parts of my memory.

When Specter quizzed Hoerchner about this suggestive comment, she gave another ambiguous answer, again putting in question whether or not she knew at the time Hill complained of harassment that it was Thomas whom she was complaining about.

SPECTER: I was concerned, when I saw this reference that you said that "I was drawing conclusions based on other parts of my memory" and my question to you is what did you mean by that?

HOERCHNER: Well I did know that Clarence Thomas became the chair for the EEOC. Now, whether I knew that at the time I spoke to Anita and we had the most memorable conversation or not, I can't really say.

Did Hoerchner, after all, learn only later that Thomas had become "chair" of the EEOC, or was it only later that she learned Thomas was the harasser of whom Hill had complained? Once she realized that Hill could not have been talking about Thomas in any call before September 1981—"Oh, I see what you are saying," Hoerchner had said in the Senate interview—it appears that, having brought her friend Anita down this path in the first place, Hoerchner pressed ahead. To support Hill, she may have perjured herself by unequivocally naming Thomas as the perpetrator of the harassment.

The identity of Hill's harasser was not the only matter that seemed to confuse Hoerchner. After the hearings, when she embarked on a speaking tour on the subject "What It's Really Like to Testify Before a Senate Committee," Hoerchner claimed that the Republican Senators during the hearings had stripped away Hill's stature and dignity by referring to her simply as "Anita." "Certainly addressing her as Anita was improper," Hoerchner said. However, no such thing had happened in the course of the hearings.[29]

Judging by the other inconsistencies, calculated vagueness, and contradictions in Hoerchner's sworn testimony, she was hardly a credible witness. For example, under questioning from Simpson she made the statement, "To be frank, I don't remember ever giving Anita advice about anything in my life." A few minutes later Hoerchner told Biden:

> Well, as I testified just a moment ago, I have never given her advice, and the reason is that she is so independent and that I respect her judgment so much that I would not presume to advise her. I cannot imagine a force that could take her and use her as a malleable object.

Yet Hoerchner had been doing nothing *but* giving Hill advice throughout the month of September 1991. According to the FBI interview of Hill:

> She [Hill] advised the interviewing agents that she made the decision to prepare the statement after several telephone conversations with her personal friend, Susan Hoerchner. The last conversation between her and Hoerchner was on a Sunday night prior to her preparation of her statement.

Hoerchner, in fact, had advised Hill to file the statement as a way of postponing or averting the FBI interview. Hoerchner told the Senate interviewers that Hill "was told [by Senate staff] her only option was to be investigated by the FBI, and we both thought it was odd, and I thought there should have been some alternative where she could make a statement with her name being used, as some sort of an intermediate measure."

Hoerchner was also caught misleading Senator Simpson about her role in bringing charges against Judge Foster, the presiding judge of the workmen's compensation board on which Hoerchner sat. This was yet another example of how the Republicans continually missed opportunities to hammer Hill and her witnesses on legitimate issues of fact. The elements of Hoerchner's undoing—her sudden amnesia, and her role in the Foster case—came briefly into view during the hearings, only to be left unpursued.

> SIMPSON: Judge Hoerchner, I asked you if you had ever filed a charge of sexual harassment. I don't think you indicated to me that you had.
>
> HOERCHNER: That's correct.
>
> SIMPSON: I have a record from California, in Norwalk County or Norfolk County, California, that you did file a claim against a fellow judge, a man named Judge Foster. Is that correct?

HOERCHNER: I was not sure how far in the proceedings that went. It was my understanding that he had negotiated a settlement. I was told that my statement was never taken up to the home office or our board, so—

SIMPSON: But you did file a claim of sexual harassment against a fellow judge within your system?

HOERCHNER: I cannot say that I didn't.

It appears from this exchange that in addition to playing a supporting role in the charge against Foster, as the *Los Angeles Times* reported, Hoerchner may have eventually filed her own charge as well. Hoerchner apparently thought no one would find out what she had done in the Foster case, and thus chose not to divulge it to Simpson. But why not? Did she fear that her efforts to bring charges against Foster would seem to have a bearing on her role in the Thomas case?

Hoerchner was cornered again over the question of how she knew that she was Hill's only witness. When first questioned, Hoerchner said that Hill had told her she was the only witness for the harassment charge. During the Senate staff interview, Hoerchner was asked:

Q. Did she [Hill] ever relay to you that you were the only person that knew about these allegations or these problems she was having at work?

A. I think she told me that more recently.

Q. More recently that you were the only person who knew?

A. Yes.

Later in the interview this subject came up again:

Q. I should have asked you this earlier, and I apologize. You said, going back to the you were the only person– Anita Hill told you you were the only person who knew about the allegations of sexual harassment, and you said that she reiterated that recently to you. Was this in one of those phone conversations?

A. No. She never told me until recently.

Q. That you were the only person that knew.

A. Right.

Q. When did she tell you that?

A. It may have been around the time that she wanted to know if I would talk to the FBI.

Q. So we're talking the last couple of weeks of September?

A. Very recent. Yes.

Yet after Hill's charges were broadcast in the media, three other witnesses for Hill materialized. If Hoerchner had stood by her first answer, that *Hill* told her she was the only witness, she would have raised an intriguing question about the accuracy and consistency of Hill's story: Why would Hill insist in September that Hoerchner was the only one who knew, when in her Senate testimony Hill claimed she told two other witnesses—Ellen Wells and John Carr—of the incidents contemporaneously? Perhaps to protect Hill, Hoerchner later changed her story to make it *the FBI* who told her she was the only witness. Therefore, the FBI would have been unaware of the other witnesses.

During the infamous Napolitano gap—when Hill's attorney Janet Napolitano asked to go off the record, and Hoerchner came back suddenly struck with amnesia about the timing of the call—Napolitano seems to have coached Hoerchner to say that Hill had never told her she was the sole witness. When the interview went back on the record, Hoerchner, unprompted by a question, reversed her story:

> Okay. I recently came to the conclusion that I was the only one that she had told at the time. And I believe that the basis for the conclusion was that I was told by the FBI agent who interviewed me that there were only three names on— either in the affidavit or stemming from her FBI interview. I am not sure which, I think the affidavit, and that my name was the only one she listed as a corroborating witness.
>
> Now the three names are, of course, herself, Thomas, and myself. I don't know whether what he said to me was accurate or not.

Another serious inconsistency came in Hoerchner's Sunday testimony. Hoerchner repeatedly emphasized that she was testifying only about one conversation with Hill. "I have said that I remember mainly one conversation. I believe there were other conversations in which she led me to understand that the problem was continuing, but I do not have any detailed recollection," she told the panel. When Hoerchner called Harriet Grant of the Biden staff in mid-September, she told Grant that she had no specifics on this one "major" call in which Hill supposedly identified Thomas as her sexual harasser. According to the Biden chronology, the staff "received one phone call from Professor Hill's friend—on September 18—who explained that she had one conversation with Professor Hill—in the spring of 1981. During that conversation, Professor Hill provided little details to her friend, but explained that Thomas had acted inappropriately and that it caused Hill to doubt her professional abilities."

But in her public testimony three weeks later, Hoerchner produced a number of specifics about what Thomas had allegedly said to Hill that neither Hoerchner *nor even Hill* had ever provided to the committee, the FBI, or indeed anyone ever before:

> He kept pressing her and repeating things like "I'm your type," and "You know I'm your kind of man, but you refuse to admit it."

If Thomas had made these specific comments, why would they have been absent from Hill's own account? The statements that Hoerchner recalled did not appear in Hill's committee statement, in her FBI interview, or in her public testimony. Nor did they appear in the notes of Hoerchner's initial conversation with Grant or in Hoerchner's FBI interview. Where did the details suddenly come from, if not from Hoerchner's imagination, activated by her need to testify persuasively as Hill's key corroborating witness?

There was one other significant detail that Hoerchner recalled from the one telephone conversation with Hill:

> One thing Anita told me that struck me particularly and that I remember almost verbatim was that Mr. Thomas had said to her, "You know, if you had witnesses, you'd have a perfect case against me."

Under questioning from Leahy, Hoerchner elaborated:

> LEAHY: Now, back to you, Judge Hoerchner, you have come here and you have testified under oath about a conversation some years ago. The conversation, because of its nature, apparently stands out strongly in your mind, is that correct?
>
> HOERCHNER: There are certain aspects of the conversation that stand out in my mind. They are the fact that her boss' name was Clarence. He repeatedly asserted to her that he was her kind of man, she would not admit it, he said, and that if she had any witnesses she would have a great case against him.

According to Hill's testimony, Thomas had made this comment—that if she had any witnesses, she would have a great case against him—at dinner on her last night of work at the EEOC in July 1983. Yet according to the FBI interview of Hill: "Hill did not discuss the sex conversations with Hoerchner *after the winter of 1981*, until the announcement of Thomas's nomination for the Supreme Court." How then could Hoerchner have possibly corroborated a statement that Hill said Thomas made *in 1983*? Could it be that

Hoerchner was "corroborating" on Sunday something she had heard Hill testify to only two days before? The anecdote about the "great case" did not appear in Hoerchner's interview with the Senate lawyers, which was given *before* Hill testified.

Moreover, contrary to Hoerchner's sworn testimony, Hill could not have told her of the "great case" comment and also referred to her boss as "Clarence" in the same conversation. According to Hill, the "great case" comment was made on her last night of work at the EEOC—thus, if she told Hoerchner about it afterward, Thomas would no longer have been her boss. He would have been her *former* boss. Nor would Hill have had any reason to be "depressed" about her job and "doubting her professional abilities," as Hoerchner described the call. Hill would have been on her way to a new life in Oklahoma. Therefore one or the other, or both, of these details cited by Hoerchner—either the great case anecdote, or the fact that "Clarence" was her boss—was a blatant embellishment by Hoerchner of the fateful conversation. The most plausible explanation of this inconsistency is that Hoerchner appended the "boss Clarence" remark to her testimony so that no one would figure out that the call actually predated Hill's employment by Thomas.

If Hoerchner was wrong about the date of Hill's call, there was no longer *any* evidence that Hill had complained about being sexually harassed by Thomas contemporaneously with the alleged event. Thus, if Hoerchner had the wrong man, Hill's sexual harassment story would not have to be ten years old.

Indeed, if Hoerchner in fact had the wrong man, Hill's story did not have to be any older than ten weeks—dating back to July 1, 1991, when Hoerchner called Hill and may have literally *created* the sexual harassment charge against Thomas right there on the telephone:

Q. Let me go back to one thing. You said you asked her, "Are you going to say anything?" Two questions. The first one is, is that as close as you can recall or paraphrase? Did you provide any more detail?

A. You know, she knew I knew. I knew she knew I knew.

Q. And what was it that you were referring to when you said, "Are you going to say anything?"

A. The sexual harassment that she had told me about 10 years ago.

I knew she knew I knew. What if Hill "knew" no such thing, but simply confirmed Hoerchner's intimations that Thomas was the one? Perhaps Hill had told her friend Hoerchner a half-truth or a white lie about why she had to leave Wald, Harkrader in 1981. When Hoerchner called out of the blue ten years later and suggested that the conservative black who had just been nominated to the Supreme Court that day was the "pig" Hill had been talking about ten years before, Hill would have been caught quite off balance. In the split second in which she had to respond, she may have chosen to go along with Hoerchner's misimpression rather than explain that it had been at the law firm where she was harassed, in which case she would have had to come up with another name from the distant past, and embellish an old story so that it remained convincing. Alternatively, Hill could have told Hoerchner that the harassment never happened, and that she was really let go from the Wald firm on grounds of performance. Either way, Hill would have been quite embarrassed. So there was really nothing else for Hill to do *but* go along, to let it seem as if she knew what Hoerchner thought she knew. Hill would have taken the path of least resistance.

At the same time, in this call to Hill, the two may have discussed Hoerchner's recent experience with a sexual harassment charge in the Judge Foster case. If Hoerchner told Hill that an informal charge had forced Foster's resignation, this may also have inclined Hill to silence at the very moment Hoerchner mistakenly identified Thomas as the harasser. If, that is, Hill had a motive to stop Thomas's Supreme Court nomination.

Hill's own testimony suggests that this is exactly how it happened. In her staff interview, Hoerchner described the call to Hill on the day Thomas was nominated as it began:

> I believe, I am not sure, I believe I was able to call and have her answer, rather than call and leave a message. I pretty much said, "Well, you've heard the news," and she told me she had heard the news.

When Hoerchner called, Hill already knew that Thomas had been nominated to the court. Yet Hill testified:

> Ms. Hoerchner did contact me, and reminded me of the situation, and we discussed the fact that we had talked about this in earlier years but she did not urge me to come forward at all.

If Thomas had sexually harassed her, why did Hill have to be *reminded* about it by Hoerchner soon after hearing that Thomas had been nominated to the court? Hill's suggestive comment could be simply the result of imprecise language. But what if Hoerchner's "reminder" to Hill was actually the first time anyone had linked Thomas to a sexual harassment charge? Then the explanation for why Hill had stayed silent for ten years, and why no sexual harassment charge, either Hill's or anybody else's, had ever surfaced anywhere—not in Thomas's five FBI background checks, not in four prior Senate confirmations, not even in the rumor mill at the EEOC—would be that the charge never existed prior to Hoerchner's call to Hill in July 1991. The charge went from Hoerchner to Hill, to Gary Phillips, to the Alliance for Justice, to Howard Metzenbaum's staff, and finally to the media.

"It never made sense to me," said Dick Leon, who acted as Thomas's counsel during the Hill–Thomas hearings and had also been his counsel for the appeals court nomination in 1989. "People have been fanning the nation for years looking for things on him, and nothing even remotely like this ever came up. When I heard about it, I thought 'There is something wrong.' The first reaction of disbelief was personal. But the second reaction of disbelief was rational: How could this have not come out before? It allegedly happened ten years ago. They looked under every rock for his appellate court nomination [in 1989] because they knew he was going to the Supreme Court if they couldn't stop him then."[30]

Assuming that the charge was false, Hoerchner's unwitting invention of it also explained its least credible aspect: Why would Hill leave a permanent job at the Education Department to follow her abuser to the EEOC? If Hill wished to invent a story, it would have appeared far more convincing if she had said the harassment had begun at the EEOC. But Hill was stuck with the story that the harassment began at Education because the author of the charge, who later became her sole corroborating witness, remembered a telephone call from 1981—when Hill had been at Wald, Harkrader, and at Education—not from 1982 or 1983, when she was at the EEOC.

7

The Myth of the Typical Case

The unquestioned credence granted Susan Hoerchner as a corroborating witness was of a piece with the virtually unchallenged effort by Anita Hill's supporters to characterize her charges against Thomas as a "typical case" of sexual harassment. The moment Hill's allegations broke on National Public Radio and in *Newsday* on Sunday, October 6, a legion of women's activists rushed forward with this message—before Hill had testified about the specifics of her case or produced any evidence for the charge.

On October 8, two days after the disclosure, the *New York Times* carried a piece headlined, "Professor's Description of Events Called Typical."[1] The law professor Catharine MacKinnon, whose arguments have been instrumental in determining how the courts have come to define sexual harassment, was quoted as saying that Hill's story was "the very most common kind of case." Judith Resnik, a law professor at the University of Southern California Law Center, told *Time* that Hill's testimony was a "paradigm of a sexual harassment case."[2] The *Time* article did not disclose that Resnik was advising Hill, and therefore had a direct interest in characterizing her as a "typical" victim of sexual harassment, thereby creating a prejudice

239

on behalf of Hill in the public mind and also shifting the burden of proof onto Thomas.

This judgment was a subjective, emotional, and political reaction to the event of a woman's charge of sexual harassment against a man, not an objective, reasoned assessment of the facts and evidence of the case at hand. The unspoken premise was that all women charging men with harassment must be *automatically* believed simply on the basis of their word, and the advocates strongly implied that a failure to do so was in itself evidence of sexism.

Unfortunately, the Judiciary Committee accepted the slogans of the women's groups and declined to hear testimony from nonpartisan experts knowledgeable in the field of sexual harassment law. Had such experts testified objectively, their appearance might have gone a long way toward dispelling the "myth of the typical case" that was constructed by the relentless public relations effort waged on Hill's behalf by activists like MacKinnon and Resnik.

The core of this myth is that sexual harassment cases rarely rest on anything but the accuser's word that the harassment occurred. This is demonstrably false. Even a cursory consideration of the literature on harassment shows that several key elements are normally present as valid evidence of harassment *beyond* the accuser's word: witnesses who can corroborate that the accuser complained contemporaneously of harassment or exhibited behavior that would indicate that the woman was victimized; a pattern of harassment by the accused with other women; and other evidence regarding the accused, such as a penchant to subject women to unwelcome talk about sex or pornography. An effort has been made by Hill's supporters both during and—perhaps even more so—after the hearings to apply each of those attributes to Thomas. But, as will be shown, each imputation was without merit.

How would a professional sexual harassment investigator approach an accusation like Hill's? The EEOC's policy guidance on sexual harassment—adopted, ironically enough, in 1988 by Thomas's commission after extensive consultations with advocates for victims of sexual harassment, all of whom hailed the guidance as an enlightened step forward in eradicating harassment from the nation's workplaces—is a widely accepted standard for defining sexual harassment and establishing employer liability. The most persuasive evidence that an accuser can provide in a harassment case is a contemporaneous complaint or protest, according to the guidance. Did the accuser make a complaint about the unwelcome conduct at the time or shortly after it was occurring, either to an appropriate authority, in a written record, or to a third party, such as someone in the workplace or a friend on the outside?[3]

The Commission's policy guidelines acknowledge that firsthand witnesses to sexual harassment are difficult to produce, since harassment is most often committed in private. Hill's lack of eyewitnesses was thus indeed typical. But Hill's lack of *any* corroborative evidence was unusual. The "Commission may make a finding of harassment based solely on the credibility of the victim's allegation. As with any other charge of discrimination, a victim's account must be sufficiently detailed and internally consistent so as to be plausible, and lack of corroborative evidence that logically should exist would undermine the allegation," the guidance states. What sort of corroborative evidence should exist? In the absence of eyewitnesses, such corroboration could consist of "testimony . . . obtained from persons who observed the charging party's demeanor immediately after an alleged incident of harassment. . . . Other employees should be asked if they noticed changes in charging party's behavior at work, or in the alleged harasser's treatment of charging party." Was the accuser, for example, ever observed to be upset or unhappy after being in the accused's presence, or did she try to avoid being in the presence of the accused?

Even in cases where there is no evidence whatsoever for an allegation other than the accuser's word, an uncorroborated charge can be sustained if there is evidence that the accused had harassed others before or since. "Evidence that other employees were sexually harassed by the same person" would be accepted as persuasive corroboration of the allegation, according to the Commission's guidance. "The investigator should determine whether the employer was aware of any other instances of harassment and if so what was the response."

Applying these legal standards to Hill's ten-year-old charge, of course, would begin with its dismissal, since such allegations are only actionable within 180 days. Leaving that aside, it is worth noting that plaintiffs do not normally win their cases if they have no evidence other than their own word to back up their charges. In *Sardigal* v. *St. Louis National Stockyards Co.*, for example, a waitress charged she was harassed over a period of nine months in a restaurant during the lunch hour, when a "constant flow of witnesses or customers" were present. Her allegations were rejected by a district court because she could produce no testimony from any witness to support the charge. An appeals court, affirming an important lower court decision in *Hart*

v. *D. H. Holmes Co.,* rejected a plaintiff's account of sexual harassment because "there is not a scintilla of evidence to corroborate" the plaintiff's version.

Similarly, Hill's case met not one evidentiary test. She had little or no contemporaneous corroboration; she had no witnesses who said that she had exhibited the demeanor of a harassment victim at the time the conduct was supposed to have been happening (in fact no co-worker of Hill has ever come forth on her behalf); and she could not show that Thomas had ever been accused of sexual harassment by anyone else, much less that he had ever engaged in a pattern of abusive or lascivious behavior. Hill's partisans, nonetheless, continued to inflate the merits of her case in the months following the hearings. Helen Winternitz, a co-author of Tim Phelps, asserted at a symposium on the hearings that the "balance of evidence" had been on Hill's side—"her witnesses were highly credible and she passed a lie detector test"—but the evidence was discounted because a "black woman's credibility" is always less than a "white woman's or a black man's."

Yet notwithstanding her analysis, this sexual harassment case really did rest *solely* on Hill's word, a highly unusual state of affairs. In an article in the *Chronicle of Higher Education* that appeared shortly after the Thomas–Hill hearings concluded, Billie Wright Dziech, a professor at the University of Cincinnati and the author of *The Lecherous Professor: Sexual Harassment on Campus,* took her fellow sexual harassment experts to task for exhibiting professional irresponsibility by unequivocally embracing Hill's case as paradigmatic, despite the lack of any corroborative evidence or any pattern of harassment by the accused.

> The "experts" also did a grave disservice by suggesting to prime-time television audiences that this was a typical case. It was not. This was a "worst possible scenario," one of those extraordinarily difficult allegations in which there were no witnesses, no compelling evidence, no verifiable pattern of previous harassment by the accused. There was only "his word against hers," which is not, in my experience, the situation in most sex-harassment cases. What the public and academicians must never lose sight of is that while sexual harassment may be a one-time experience for victims, most perpetrators have multiple patterns, identifiable patterns, and extensive "track records" of abuse that may continue for years before a victim or colleague protests. . . . Given all our expertise in problem solving and conducting research, surely we

are intelligent enough to increase understanding of "his word against hers" cases by engaging in more systematic investigation and analysis.[4]

The first and most important criterion in weighing a harassment charge is corroboration by other witnesses. During the public hearings, the appearance of Hill's panel of witnesses Sunday afternoon seemed to present irrefutable evidence that Hill had complained of sexual harassment by Thomas as early as 1981. Perhaps more than anything else, these witnesses created the presumption that Hill had a good case against Thomas. "4 Testify Hill Spoke Years Ago of Harassment," was the *Washington Post*'s dramatic banner headline.[5] In the only moment when he found his voice during the entire weekend, Senator Kennedy claimed that the Hill panel had shown that her testimony was credible, and that her story could not possibly have been a recent politically motivated invention:

> But I hope, Mr. Chairman, that after this panel we are not going to hear any more comments, unworthy, unsubstantiated comments, unjustified comments about Professor Hill and perjury, as we heard in this room yesterday. I hope we are not going to hear any more comments about Professor Hill being a tool of the various advocacy groups, after we have heard from Ellen Wells and John Carr and Joel Paul, all of whom have volunteered to come forward after they heard about this in the newspapers—comments about individual groups and staffers trying to persuade her. . . .
>
> I hope we are not going to hear a lot more comments about fantasy stories picked out of books and law cases, after we have heard from this distinguished panel, or how there have been attempts in the eleventh hour to derail this nomination.

"Four witnesses—two men and two women, two black and two white distinguished Americans, including a Federal judge and a professor of law—testified, under oath, that Anita Hill had told each of them about these sordid carryings on by Thomas at the time of their occurrence or in the years that followed," June Jordan wrote in the *Black Scholar*.[6] In an analysis of the case in the *ABA Journal*, an Illinois lawyer named Stuart Lefstein made the point most vividly. "Of course, no partisan of Judge Thomas could comfortably claim, and none did, that those four witnesses—among them a workers' compensation judge, a law professor, and a Wall Street corporate lawyer—had all committed perjury," Lefstein wrote. "Therefore, the case was not the word of one woman against one man. It was five against one, with the basic core of Hill's testimony having been massively corroborated."[7]

As was shown in the previous chapter, it is likely that Hill's star witness, Susan Hoerchner, "corroborated" a sexual harassment complaint made by Hill in a telephone conversation in 1981, months before Hill had gone to work for Clarence Thomas. More than that, Hoerchner may have literally created the charge against Thomas by leaping to a mistaken conclusion before calling Hill on July 1, 1991. Hoerchner's unwitting role in creating the allegation would explain why Hill had been so sure when she later told Hoerchner, the Senate staff, and the FBI that Hoerchner was her sole witness.

But what of Hill's three other witnesses? In light of Hill's insistence that Hoerchner was her only witness, Hill may have been more surprised than anyone when three other witnesses approached her—not vice versa—on the eve of her testimony, offering to corroborate aspects of her story. As she herself maintained, she may have forgotten (or "repressed") the fact that she had shared the information with other people, though no one has explained why she did not also swear these witnesses to silence at the time, as she supposedly had with Hoerchner. A simpler explanation may be that Hill's initial statement to the FBI that no one but Hoerchner knew about the charge was in fact correct. Hill may not have identified witnesses other than Hoerchner, or attempted to contact any of them, because she had never told any of them that she had been sexually harassed by Thomas.

In fact, a close examination of the testimony of these three witnesses shows that none of the three could corroborate that Hill had told them Clarence Thomas had sexually harassed her. John Carr, the New York corporate attorney and long-distance boyfriend of Hill from the early 1980s, and Joel Paul, the American University professor of law who met Hill in the summer of 1987, testified that Hill said she had been sexually harassed at the EEOC. But neither could testify that she had named Thomas as the harasser. Like Susan Hoerchner, both Carr and Paul added two (Hill had complained to them that she was sexually harassed by an unnamed boss) plus two (Hill now was charging former boss Clarence Thomas with harassment) and got five (Hill had been referring to Thomas when she mentioned being sexually harassed by her boss years ago).

Wearing steel-framed glasses and a conservative suit, John Carr said in his opening statement:

> During the final semester of the 1982–83 academic year, I developed a social relationship with Anita Hill.

I lived in Cambridge, Massachusetts, and she lived in Washington, D.C., which made seeing one another very difficult. However, during this particular period, we spoke several times at length on the telephone.

During one of these telephone conversations, Anita Hill revealed to me that her supervisor was sexually harassing her. I recall that she did not initially volunteer this information. Rather, during the telephone conversation, it quickly became clear to me that she was troubled and upset. In response to my expressions of concern about her feelings, Anita Hill told me that she was upset because her boss was making sexual advances towards her. I recall that she was clearly disturbed by these advances and that she cried during the telephone call.

I knew that Anita Hill worked for Clarence Thomas at the EEOC. In this telephone conversation, it was immediately clear to me that she was referring to Judge Thomas.

But when Specter asked Carr how he knew Hill was referring to Thomas, Carr could not say whether Hill had referred to him by name:

SPECTER: Well, aside from what is clear in your mind, my question to you is did she say it was Clarence Thomas?

CARR: I don't recall.

In his opening statement to the committee, Carr explained how he was moved to offer to corroborate Hill's story. "On Sunday evening, October 6, I saw television reports that Professor Hill had accused Judge Thomas of sexual harassment. I immediately remembered that she had told me of his sexual advances."[8] But the evidence—including Hill's own statement to the FBI that she had never told her boyfriend of the harassment—suggests that Hill did *not* tell Carr that Thomas had harassed her.

Furthermore, if Carr knew Thomas had harassed Anita Hill, why did he stay silent when the Association of the Bar of the City of New York was considering its rating of Clarence Thomas for the Supreme Court? Carr never told the chairman of the association, Conrad Harper—coincidentally an important partner at his own New York law firm—about the sexual harassment incident involving Thomas. Nor did Carr fulfill his duty by recording the incident when the association sent all members of the bar written notice of a request for comments on the fitness of the nominee to serve. According to the *Wall Street Journal,* officials from Harper's organization at the time were calling federal judges in New York, canvassing for dirt on Clarence Thomas.[9] So why did Carr fail to say anything if, as he testified under oath, it had been "immediately clear to me that she was referring to Judge Thomas" *in 1983?* Carr may simply have forgotten this tearful call from Hill about Thomas, to be reminded of it only when Hill's story was broadcast. But from the evidence it seems more plausible that Carr concluded Thomas was the man who had harassed Hill only *after* Hill's story broke in October 1991.

Though he attempted to portray his decision to testify as a risk to his career ("I do not believe any client I have represented would be pleased to know that their lawyer was before you or before the cameras"), Carr may have had a hidden motive for concluding that Hill had been referring to Thomas in 1983 once the publication of Hill's charges afforded him the opportunity—namely the approval of one of the senior partners in his firm, Conrad Harper. Under Harper's leadership, the New York bar withheld its "approved" rating from Thomas, citing concerns about his view of the U.S. Constitution. In a statement, the executive committee pointed not to Thomas's judicial record but to some politically incorrect "public statements," without citing any of them. The committee said the statements raised questions as to whether Thomas had a "sympathetic understanding of the court's role under the Constitution in the protection of the personal rights of individuals."[10] In addition, during Harper's tenure the bar association issued a policy statement endorsing goals and timetables for hiring in New York law firms and corporate legal departments—exactly the kind of policy Thomas had opposed throughout his career.[11] "To achieve the goal of hiring, during the period 1992 through 1997, a substantial number of minority lawyers, subject to the availability of minority applicants meeting the hiring criteria of such firm or corporate legal department. A desirable goal (not a quota) to be achieved would be equal to 10 percent for the total number of all lawyers hired by such firm or corporate legal department during the period 1992–1997," the statement said.

The witness Joel Paul's process of recollection mirrored Carr's; Paul also seemed not to know that Thomas was Hill's harasser until after her charges became public. Paul, a slight man with short black hair who was a professor at American University, where Hill worked on a research project in 1987, testified:

> I arranged for Professor Hill to come to our school during July of 1987, where she was given an office, secretarial support and use of our library facilities for the summer. At that point, a number of faculty were very interested in encouraging Professor Hill to apply for a visiting professorship at the American University. During the course of her research at our school, we had a number of occasions to talk about her interest in the American University and our interest in having her join the faculty.
>
> During one such occasion, over lunch in the university cafeteria, I asked Professor Hill why she had left the EEOC. This was a logical question to ask in the course of discussing her employment history. Professor Hill responded, reluctantly and with obvious emotion and embarrassment, that she had been sexually harassed by her supervisor at the EEOC.
>
> I was shocked and astonished by her statement, which is why I remember the incident so vividly. I do not recall whether she went on to say the name Clarence Thomas, but if she had said it, the name would not have meant anything to me at that time.

Under questioning from Biden, Paul disclosed that Hill had not specifically identified Thomas:

> BIDEN: What was the term that she used to you when you asked her why she left the EEOC?
>
> PAUL: Senator, the specific terms that I recall were, that she said that she was sexually harassed by her supervisor at the EEOC.

In his staff interview with the Senate Judiciary Committee, Paul further revealed that he had not linked Hill's story about sexual harassment to Clarence Thomas until October 1991. "I picked up the [Washington] *Post*, I read the story, and instantly I knew exactly what she was talking about."[12]

If Paul had known since 1987 that Thomas had harassed Hill, why did he fail to express opposition to Thomas's nomination before the story of her allegations broke, when he was presented with the opportunity to render judgment? Trying to establish that he had no political motive to testify against Thomas, Paul said in his opening statement that he had "not taken any position with regard to Judge

Thomas's nomination prior to these allegations. Indeed, a national petition of law professors opposing his nomination was circulated at my law school several weeks ago. I was asked to sign it and I refused, despite the fact that eighteen of my colleagues signed that petition, as well as many others from other law schools." But if Hill had told Paul that Thomas was a sex harasser in 1987, why *didn't* he sign it?

Furthermore, Paul was disingenuous in presenting himself on national television as a professor of business law totally disengaged from the judge's wars. Like Carr, Paul had a political motive for reaching a retrospective judgment on the eve of the second hearing that Thomas was the harasser Hill had spoken of in 1987. This became clear in December 1991, just a few weeks after he testified, when Paul appeared at a Washington symposium on the judiciary in which he criticized the nominations of both Bork and Thomas, and delivered a defense of an enhanced role for the Democrat-controlled Senate in advice and consent on judicial nominations.

Leaving aside any question of motive, however, Carr and Paul corroborated only that Hill had said she was being harassed by a supervisor at the EEOC. As everyone in the federal government knows, "supervisor" was an exceedingly unusual way for a special assistant like Hill to refer to the chairman of a federal agency. What if Carr and Paul were wrong in their assumption, years afterward, that the "supervisor" to whom Hill had referred was Clarence Thomas?

In subsequent testimony Phyllis Berry-Myers suggested that Hill had a supervisor other than Thomas at the EEOC to whom she could have been referring in her tearful conversation in 1983 with John Carr, and in 1987, when she told Paul that she had left the EEOC because she was sexually harassed. During the testimony late Sunday night, Berry-Myers, the former head of the Congressional Relations Department at the EEOC under Chairman Thomas, said:

> A point I would like to make, I was listening some to Mr. Carr's testimony this morning or today, and he had indicated that Anita said to him that "I was harassed by my supervisor." Clarence Thomas was not the only supervisor that Anita had, and Mr. Carr seemed to make this gigantic leap, because he knew that she was on Clarence Thomas's personal staff, that the supervisor that she must have been referring to was Clarence Thomas.
>
> SPECTER: Who were others who could be classified as a supervisor?

BERRY: Mr. [Chris] Roggerson was her supervisor in Congressional Affairs, and when I succeeded him to Congressional Affairs, he became the Executive Assistant, and so he was also her supervisor. How can I say this? Mr. Roggerson doesn't have such an impeccable reputation.

SPECTER: So, you think, in the case of one of the witnesses this morning, Professor Paul might just have the wrong man?

BERRY: I am saying that's possible. He seemed to make that— he didn't identify. He said, "Anita Hill said to me she was being harassed by her supervisor," and he said "I dominated the conversation and, because she worked for Clarence Thomas, it must have been Clarence Thomas."

Chris Roggerson, a senior career civil servant, was the director of Congressional Affairs when Hill first arrived at the agency in May 1982. One of Hill's primary tasks as Thomas's special assistant was to act as a liaison between the chairman's office and the Congressional Affairs director on legislative matters. Roggerson worked closely with Hill in that capacity. In late 1982, Roggerson was named executive assistant to Thomas, which gave him certain supervisory responsibilities in the chairman's office and placed him above Hill, one of the staff assistants in that office. Later in 1983, Allyson Duncan, a lawyer from the agency's office of general counsel, became Thomas's chief legal adviser, and she assumed supervisory responsibility over the lawyers in the chairman's office, including Hill. Though Hill was not required to report through Roggerson to Thomas in either of his posts, during much of her time at the agency she worked in a position junior to Roggerson's and he was, as Berry-Myers testified, considered to be one of her "supervisors."

Roggerson did not work long as Thomas's executive assistant, in part because his reputation was, as Berry-Myers put it, not so impeccable. As Berry-Myers later explained the reference in an interview, when she succeeded Roggerson in the Congressional Affairs job, one female staffer in the department told her that she was being harassed by Roggerson and asked for advice on how to handle the situation. Another special assistant to Thomas, who also worked closely with Hill, said that she had been sexually harassed by Roggerson in 1982. "He took me to lunch one day and insisted on driving his car," the woman said in an interview. "After we finished lunch, he said he had to go by his townhouse to pick something up. I was thinking 'Sure,' since Chris had a reputation. Well, when we got there he insisted I come in and see what a great place he had. When I walked in I couldn't believe it. There were pornographic pictures covering all the walls. There was an inflatable doll on a couch. I mean this guy was a pervert. And if he did it to me, there is no reason to think he didn't try it with Anita." Roggerson later accosted this woman in an EEOC elevator. (She never officially complained about the behavior.)[13]

Other EEOC special assistants said they heard Roggerson talk about his personal collection of pornography in the EEOC office. "Chris was a womanizer. He couldn't keep his hands to himself," Armstrong Williams, a former aide to the chairman, said. "His office was right next door to Anita's. Eventually, Thomas fired him from his staff because he heard about this stuff."[14]

Interestingly, when Hill described the management structure at the EEOC in her Senate testimony, she never mentioned Roggerson, the one EEOC supervisor with whom she worked who had a reputation for sexual harassment.

BIDEN: Who was your immediate supervisor at EEOC?

HILL: At the EEOC, initially, Clarence Thomas was my immediate supervisor. After a period, Allyson Duncan was appointed to be the director of the staff.

Why would Roggerson slip so completely out of her memory? Had Hill simply forgotten about him? Was she answering the question in narrow technical terms? Or did she neglect to mention him because she was trying to hide the fact that she had actually been complaining about Roggerson, not Thomas, in her conversations with Carr and Paul? If so, of course, this would explain why Hill did not originally identify Carr and Paul as witnesses against Thomas.

The testimony of the last witness for Hill, Ellen Wells, is somewhat stronger than Carr's and Paul's, and therefore more problematic. Wells testified that she had a firm memory that Hill had referred to "inappropriate" comments and behavior "of a sexual nature" by Thomas. Unlike the other three witnesses, however, Wells could not even supply one detail about Thomas's alleged behavior. Wells, therefore, was not able to corroborate Hill's charge of "sexual harassment."

In Wells's opening statement to the committee, she said, "In the fall of 1982, Professor Hill shared with me, in confidence, the fact that she considered Judge Thomas's behavior in the office to be inappropriate. Professor Hill did not at that time nor in subsequent conversations provide exact details about the actions she found to be inappropriate conduct. She did tell me they were of a sexual nature."[15] In her confidential interview with Senate staff lawyers four days prior, however, Wells had seemed less sure about the sexual part:

Q. . . . All right. She said to you at that time, as I understand your testimony—and correct me, if I am mischaracterizing it—that Judge Thomas had made "inappropriate comments" to Ms. Hill at the office. Now, can you—

A. And conduct.

Q. Did she elaborate in any way beyond her term "inappropriate comments and conduct"? Did she describe in any way what the nature of the inappropriate comments and conduct was?

A. As I indicated earlier, I think she led me to understand that inappropriate conduct was sexual in nature.

Q. Did she go beyond that and describe or quote verbatim or approximately verbatim what Judge Thomas told her?

A. She did not provide me with exact details of that nature.

Q. Did you ask for such details?

A. No, I did not.

Wells *thought* that Hill *led her to understand* that the comments were sexual in nature. In other words, Hill appears not to have told Wells that the comments were sexual. How, then, could Wells testify that they were, and not be able to provide even a clue about what might have led her to draw this conclusion?

Wells's testimony might be interpreted in this way: In the fall of 1982, unhappy in her job, appearing "deeply troubled and very depressed," Hill complained about Thomas's "inappropriate" behavior—which could have covered just about anything, including critical comments about Hill's work, failing to give her good assignments, or passing her over for promotion. On Sunday, in response to a question from Senator Dennis DeConcini of Arizona as to why she had given Hill no advice on how to handle the situation, especially since she had been sexually harassed herself, Wells said she would have done so had she known "the actual nature of the charge." But apparently she did not.

The clear implication is that only after hearing of Hill's sexual harassment charge in the media nine years later did Wells pull a conversation from 1982 out of its context and place it into a completely different one, concluding that in 1982 Hill had *led her to understand* that Thomas made comments of a sexual nature. "I called the law school and left a message of support and willingness to be of assistance, if needed," Wells told the committee. "My call jogged her memory of what she said to me."

Like Carr and Paul, Wells had ideological sympathies that may have caused her to draw unfounded conclusions. Wells worked at the American Welfare Association, a major Washington lobby representing state welfare departments. In an interview, she declined to comment on her views of the Thomas nomination. But according to Ronald Langston, a close friend of Wells, she opposed the nomination on ideological grounds. Wells and Langston met in the late 1970s, when they were both members of an organization for black Republican Congressional staffers on Capitol Hill. Wells worked for a liberal Republican Congressman, John Anderson, and Langston worked for the conservative Iowa Senator Roger Jepson. Wells was also introduced at the time to Clarence Thomas, who worked for Senator Danforth.

Langston called Wells a few days after the Thomas nomination was announced in July. "I said isn't this wonderful about Clarence," Langston recalled. "And she said she had reservations about his stand on abortion. She said she didn't like where he was coming from, the things he was saying, his views were too conservative. Of course, she never said anything about sexual harassment or Anita Hill, and I think that's the kind of thing you'd tell a friend. I never knew she even knew Anita until I heard Ellen was going to testify."[16] Langston's account implies that Wells knew nothing about the sexual harassment allegations until *after* the story of Hill's charges broke.

What, then, can be concluded about the corroboration offered by these witnesses? Hill had made no formal complaint about the harassment at the time it was occurring, which is indeed quite typical of harassment victims. What was so unusual about Hill's case is that she told no one, not even family members or close friends, any of the details of the harassment—neither who was doing it, nor what exactly they were doing. Hill evidently complained to both Carr and Paul that she had been harassed by an EEOC "supervisor," but she told neither one of them that the harasser was Clarence Thomas. This is a conclusion they reached on their own. Another man who was a supervisor of Hill's was a known sex harasser, and quite conceivably could have been the supervisor to whom Hill had referred. Thus the testimony of both Carr and Paul could have been completely truthful, and also irrelevant to the case against Thomas.

If Thomas was innocent, however, Wells, under oath, would have to have embroidered her recollection of a 1982 conversation. Wells testified that Hill had complained about inappropriate comments of a sexual nature made by Thomas. The absence of any detail whatsoever about these alleged comments, however, raises the possibility that Hill had been complaining in 1982 about Thomas the way that anyone might complain about a demanding boss they were unhappy with, and further suggests that only after Hill's sexual harassment accusations became public did Wells—a political opponent of the nomination—convince herself that she had been "led to understand" that those vague comments from nine years back were sexual in nature. On the other hand, the possibility that Hill really had told Wells about sexual behavior by Thomas in 1982 cannot be definitively discounted.

Hill's inability to show a pattern of harassing behavior by Thomas was another atypical aspect of her case. If Hill was telling the truth, Thomas had chosen to harass her sexually—and only her—among the dozens of women who had worked for him over the years. The columnist Stephen Chapman wrote in the *Chicago Tribune* at the time of the hearings that "to believe Hill, we have to believe that someone who had been the soul of probity suddenly, on her arrival, became a sexual thug—and then, the moment she left, wholly reverted to his saintly self, never to transgress again."[17]

The heightened awareness of sexual harassment that was a valued legacy of the Thomas–Hill scandal set the stage for harassment accusations to be lodged against three U.S. Senators—Democrats Brock Adams and Daniel Inouye and Republican Bob Packwood—in 1992. Though they did not attract the same level of attention, each of those cases was far stronger—and more typical—than Hill's, principally because in each instance more than a half-dozen women came forward, some under a veil of anonymity, and made allegations that, if true, constituted an undeniable pattern of abusive behavior by the Senators. Eight women made allegations against Adams; nine against Inouye; and almost two dozen against Packwood. Anita Hill, however, remains Thomas's lone accuser.

That was a significant factor in the Senate's decision to confirm Thomas. As Democratic Senator Sam Nunn of Georgia put it in a speech on the Senate floor announcing his support for the nominee, "A responsible, credible citizen presents information about a nominee on a matter of personal behavior, on which there are no direct witnesses and little direct corroborating evidence. . . . In such a case, I look closely at the individual's background and the FBI files to determine whether there are patterns or habits of behavior that would make it more or less likely that the individual behaved in the offending manner."[18] In Thomas's case, the evidence showed no such pattern.

Hill herself, who has taught in the area of civil rights law, stated at a press conference after her charges were leaked to the media: "One of the things that I will say about sexual harassment generally, and I suspect that it's true in this case too, in fact I've heard rumors to that effect, but I cannot substantiate any of those. I will say, however, that harassment usually isn't an individual issue. It's not an issue with one person. It is behavior that people engage in. So I don't think that this was something that was directed at me personally." When asked about the absence of a pattern by NBC's Tom Brokaw, Catharine MacKinnon also acknowledged that sexual harassers tend to be repeat offenders, and that Hill's case was therefore anomalous. But despite the fact that Thomas had no other accusers from his thirteen years in Washington, she asserted that his case should not be closed— Thomas should be regarded as guilty until proven innocent. As she said to Brokaw: "Well, I hate to put it this way, but he's not dead yet."[19]

More than anything else, then, "another woman" with a credible charge would have so enhanced the plausibility of Hill's case that the Thomas nomination would probably have been defeated. Shortly after Hill's allegations made the papers, headlines announced that another woman might come forward with sexual harassment allegations against Clarence Thomas. On the morning Hill was to testify, a lead story in the *New York Times* reported: "Conflict Emerges Over a 2nd Witness: Thomas Panel to Hear Woman—White House Protests."[20] The reports of a second witness sent a shudder through the pro-Thomas camp, which feared that now that Hill's charge was in the public domain, it would be open season on Thomas for anyone with a motive to seek revenge against him.[21] Like any chief executive of a large organization, Thomas had taken a number of adverse personnel actions over the years.

Amazingly enough, only one such person—Angela Wright—surfaced before the committee. Wright never testified, but in a late-night deal struck with the phantom witness, her interview with Senate Judiciary Committee lawyers was entered into the official record (unlike the other staff interviews), and made publicly available. Even scandal-hungry reporters, however, would not touch Wright's statement at that point. Within a few days after her name first surfaced in the press her credibility collapsed in both Democratic and Republican circles, for reasons that will soon become evident.

At the time of the hearings, therefore, little was known publicly about the Wright story after the initial flurry of headlines. Yet in a demonstration of how the history of the Thomas–Hill hearings was rewritten after Thomas was confirmed, the Wright statement began to take on a second life when it was discovered belatedly by the satirical magazine *Spy* in the spring of 1992.[22] If Hill's case was not typical when presented, it would be strengthened later in the annals of history. *Spy* reprinted sections of Wright's committee statement in an effort to show that the testimony of this "other woman" was suppressed by the Judiciary Committee. Soon thereafter, the cartoonist Garry Trudeau picked up portions of the transcript too, uncritically accepting the suggestion that the Thomas forces blocked her testimony. Doonesbury's fictional Representative Lacey Davenport "readmitted the testimony" of Wright: "Ms. Wright, whose experience with Thomas was remarkably similar to Ms. Hill's, was blocked from publicly testifying. Instead, her statement was quietly slipped into the record. Few people have seen it . . . until now, dear hearts."[23]

Other Anitaphiles began invoking Wright's name throughout the spring and summer of 1992. In a May speech at Stanford University, NPR's Nina Totenberg said:

> Now there are some things that happened during those hearings that nobody knows about, and maybe in the next few months or years we will find out about the deals and counter-deals that were made behind the scenes as those hearings ground on for twelve, fourteen, sixteen, twenty hours sometimes at a clip, but we do know a few things. And one of the things that we do know is, I think, somewhat indicative. And that is the story of Angela Wright. Angela Wright was the so-called "other woman" who made allegations of sexual harassment against Clarence Thomas. . . . Angela Wright, in a sworn deposition, said that Clarence Thomas had sexually harassed her.[24]

Yet Totenberg was wrong on two counts: The Wright statement was not sworn, and—one good reason why it warranted little attention during the hearings—it did *not* charge Thomas with sexual harassment.

The campaign to rehabilitate and publicize the unsubstantiated comments of a woman who never came forward and never charged

Thomas with sexual harassment continued in Tim Phelps's *Capitol Games:*

> The decision about Wright's testifying was probably the most important of the whole hearings. The question of whether more than one alleged victim of Thomas' sexual harassment existed was absolutely critical in many senators' minds . . . the result would be that Wright was no longer a factor in the outcome of the hearings. Written testimony was far less dramatic, or convincing, than live testimony. The Democrats had allowed themselves to be intimidated [by the Thomas camp], sidelined at a crucial point in the game.[25]

The revisionist tilt in favor of Hill's case and against Thomas's was completed on the first anniversary of the hearings, when Angela Wright's story was transformed from a subject of deep skepticism, even among Democrats on the committee, to a subject for political satire, to suppressed evidence that would have reversed the outcome of the Thomas confirmation vote. An October 1992 cover story in *U.S. News and World Report* quoted Paul Simon as saying that if Senators had known more about Wright and an alleged corroborating witness for her, it "could have toppled Thomas."[26]

Ordinarily, one would not credit such unsworn statements as Wright's by publicizing them further. But because they have been continually cited by defenders of Hill like Simon, who quoted extensively (and credulously) from the Wright statement in his book *Advice and Consent,* her story has taken on a disproportionate significance.[27] Wright's story is also interesting for its several parallels with Hill's—casting further light on the operations of anti-Thomas Senate staffers.

The parallels begin with the way each prospective witness first came to the attention of the Senate Judiciary Committee. In both cases, Senate staffers sought out the alleged victims as part of anti-Thomas dirt-digging expeditions and solicited the stories. Neither Hill nor Wright had contacted the committee of their own volition, and neither evinced any enthusiasm for talking when first approached. But the staffers would not take "no" for an answer.

Now an assistant metropolitan editor at the *Charlotte Observer* in North Carolina, Wright wrote a draft column about Hill's allegations—not her own experiences—after they became public. Someone at the newspaper apparently tipped off Senator Biden's Judiciary Committee staff about the unpublished column as soon as it became a subject of discussion within the paper. Wright had hopes of becoming a columnist for the *Observer* and had been casting around for something compelling to write a sample column about. Since she had worked for Thomas at the EEOC, Hill's charges seemed a tailor-made topic. What Wright wrote in the unpublished column is not known; she refused to release it to the Judiciary Committee, saying that it was a draft not intended for publication. Presumably, she took the position that Hill's charges were credible based on her own impressions with or experiences of Thomas.

Wright was asked about the circumstances of her "coming forward" in an interview with Senate lawyers. Her hostile responses and pointed refusal to make any charge against Thomas underscored the fact that Wright was at best an ambivalent participant in the proceedings.

Q. . . . Can you tell us why you chose to wait until now to come forward?

A. Well, I think a more appropriate explanation of what is going on here is I'm answering questions that are just now being asked. But I must say that I was perfectly willing to keep my opinions to myself, except, of course, when asked about the Clarence Thomas nomination. I did not feel that it was a good thing, until I saw Anita Hill on television Monday night and my conscience started bothering me because I knew I felt from my experience with Clarence Thomas that he was quite capable of doing what she said. And it became a very moral struggle with me at that point.

I was struggling with trying to determine, trying to decide whether to say something, when I got a call from the Senate Judiciary Committee and that question became no longer a question.

Q. All right, now you say that you got a call from the committee when you decided you were going to come forward, did you call somebody or did somebody first call you?

A. Somebody first called me.

Q. Can you tell us who that was?

A. It was Mark Schwartz [a Biden staffer].

Q. And so he first called you?

A. Yes.

Q. Do you have any idea as to how he got your name?

A. He said that he had gotten information that I worked for Clarence Thomas. He knew of a column that I had written that was going to be published detailing my opinion of this, of Hill's allegations.[28]

Q. I'm sorry, your opinion of what?

A. Of Hill's allegations.

Q. I see, could you make that available to us?

A. No.

Q. Can you give us some general description of what you said?

A. No, I'd rather not. Because the column was not written in, with the intent of publishing it. It was written in the context of a discussion that I was having with my, with my supervising editor about becoming a columnist.[29]

At another point in the interview, addressing Senator Thurmond's staffer Terry Wooten, Wright said, "I am sorry, Terry, but I cannot answer, I cannot answer the questions if you are going to insist that I decided to come forward. Obviously, I did not come forward with anything."

Despite suggestions to the contrary in virtually every account of the Thomas hearings, Wright did not charge Thomas with sexual harassment. "You know, Clarence Thomas I think felt very comfortable around me, and I want you to understand that I am *not* sitting here saying to you that I was sexually harassed by Clarence Thomas," Wright told the interviewers.

Q. Did you take them [Thomas's alleged comments] as a joke or did you take them as something that maybe, you know, you had been harassed? You said you had not been harassed. I mean did you take them as a—

A. Not sexual harassment, no.

Though she did not charge harassment, Wright did say in the interview with the Senate lawyers that Thomas had asked her for dates and had made comments about parts of her anatomy.

Q. Were there comments that he made to you that maybe you considered inappropriate?

A. Yes. . . . There were several comments he made. Clarence Thomas did constantly pressure me to date him. At one point,

Clarence Thomas made comments about my anatomy. Clarence Thomas made comments about women's anatomy quite often. At one point, Clarence Thomas came by my apartment at night, unannounced and uninvited, and talked about the prospect of my dating him.

Wright also claimed that at an EEOC banquet Thomas said to her, "You look good, and you are going to be dating me, too." But like Hill's initial recollection of her experience with Thomas to the Judiciary Committee and the FBI, Wright could give few specifics of what Thomas allegedly had said to her and generally refrained from quoting Thomas verbatim. What, for example, had Thomas said about women's anatomy?

Q. Do you remember specifically—now I understand that you told us that there was this general environment of this, but do you remember any specific comments that Clarence Thomas made to you along these lines prior to this banquet?

A. Prior to this banquet?

Q. Correct.

A. No, I cannot give specific comments.

Q. And what about after this banquet, you remember any specific comments where he talked to you about dating him?

A. No, I can only remember them in general.

Q. Okay. Why don't you tell us what you remember, in general.

A. In general, given the opportunity, Clarence Thomas is the type of person—well, let me back up a minute. In general, given the opportunity, Clarence Thomas would say to me you know, "You need to be dating me, I think I'm going to date you, you're one of the finest women I have on my staff," you know, "we're going to be going out eventually."

Even if she did not charge "harassment," if Thomas did in fact say these things, Hill's portrait of Thomas as someone who preyed on subordinates for dates and spoke in a lewd fashion would be more plausible. Thus the question turns to Wright's credibility as a witness.

An attractive woman with long, braided hair, Wright arrived in Washington in the late 1970s from her native North Carolina and took a job as an aide to Democratic Representative Charles Rose of North Carolina. Wright was soon fired from her job on Capitol Hill for intemperate and erratic behavior in the office, and she went to work for the Republican National Committee. She had drifted to the Republican side of the aisle not out of an intense ideological commitment or conversion but rather as the result of personal connections made at an association of black Republican Congressional staffers, where she was first introduced to Clarence Thomas.

At the RNC, Wright's reputation did not improve. Former office mates remember having to restrain Wright from pouring boiling hot water from a coffeemaker out a window onto a crowd of pro-choice demonstrators outside the committee's offices. Wright frequently made suggestive comments like "I'm freezing my tits off" and told male co-workers that she liked to walk around her house in the nude.[30]

Wright next took a job in the Reagan Administration as a political appointee at the Agency for International Development, where she worked from the spring of 1983 to January 1984. There she repeatedly clashed with Kate Semerad, AID's Assistant Administrator for External Affairs, who had hired Wright to coordinate the agency's media relations. These clashes would end in a vindictive maneuver by Wright to stop Semerad's Senate confirmation with unfounded eleventh-hour allegations.

According to Semerad, Wright's staff "complained that she did not give clear direction and was sometimes verbally abusive. Her immediate supervisor told me that on several occasions she reversed his specific direction for action and that she was often argumentative, uncooperative and unresponsive." Semerad held regular counseling sessions with Wright, trying to work out the problem, to no avail. Wright's behavior became "more and more belligerent," Semerad said in a letter to the Senate Judiciary Committee, until an order was signed for Wright's dismissal.[31]

On her way out the door, Wright suddenly charged Semerad with racism, an incendiary tactic apparently meant to satisfy a vengeful impulse. By all accounts, the racism charge was baseless. The FBI file on the Thomas nomination recounted the following from an interview with Semerad:

> Semerad advised that she received reports from coworkers that Wright was delinquent in the performance of her job. She related that Wright was having problems with adequately performing her job responsibilities. She related she confronted Wright concerning major problem areas that needed to be improved: a) Wright's confrontational attitude b) Wright's showing up to work on time.

Semerad advised that Wright's immediate supervisor at AID was Thomas Blank, deputy assistant of external affairs. She related that Blank was head of the news department and Wright reported directly through him. Semerad stated she received information from Blank stating that Wright's management and writing skills were not satisfactory. Semerad stated she received additional complaints from Blank and from around the AID office that Wright was not putting in a full day's work. She stated that Wright would leave work early and take long lunch hours. She advised that this was creating a morale problem in the office.

Semerad advised she attempted to counsel Wright about her behavior in an attempt to correct the problem. Semerad stated that Wright advised her she felt she was being unfairly treated. Wright informed Semerad she would not be Semerad's lackey and would no longer be treated as a subservient subordinate.

Semerad advised Wright that she would have to fire her if her job performance did not improve. She advised before she could fire Wright she received a letter of resignation from Wright claiming race discrimination on the part of Semerad. Semerad also stated she denied any type of bias or prejudice concerning Wright. She stated she treated Wright fairly and waited until she had no choice but to confront Wright concerning her unsatisfactory job performance. Semerad advised that if Wright had not resigned she would have been left no choice but to fire her.

[Semerad] did characterize Wright as being overly sensitive about being a young, attractive black woman. She stated that Wright felt she was not being treated fairly and people were judging her on her appearance instead of her accomplishments. . . .

Semerad stated she was aware of the applicant having difficulties on past employments she had held. She stated that Wright worked for [Representative] Charles Rose of North Carolina before she worked for AID. She stated she did not know of Wright's dates of employment or title, but did state Wright was fired from her position.

Semerad characterized Wright's personality as being vengeful, angry, and immature. She advised that after Wright resigned from AID she took a letter of resignation claiming unfounded racial discrimination claims to Capitol Hill seeking revenge on Semerad.

Wright was not content to file the charge with the appropriate party upon leaving the agency. When Semerad was later nominated for a higher agency post that required Senate confirmation, Wright followed her with the racism allegation, taking it to Senate staffers working for GOP Senator Jesse Helms of North Carolina, who were looking for damaging material on the nominee. Ultimately, the Senate found the charge to have no merit, though the story does suggest Wright's *modus operandi*. According to a public statement issued by Jay Morris, the former deputy administrator of AID:

> Mrs. Semerad came to me and said Ms. Wright's performance was abysmal. She often failed to come to work or came in late. She was difficult to work with in the opinion of her peers and supervisors. Moreover, her work was unprofessional—that is, late, incomplete, and ungrammatical. . . . Based on [Semerad's] advice and my own observations I agreed that she should be dismissed and issued the appropriate order.
>
> Subsequent to Ms. Wright's dismissal, Mrs. Semerad was nominated by President Reagan to the post of Assistant Administrator for External Affairs. Upon her departure, Ms. Wright had written a letter to AID accusing Mrs. Semerad of racism and incompetence and threatening retaliation. The accusations were ridiculous on their face. Mrs. Semerad is one of the most fair-minded people I know. She is also one of the most competent public affairs specialists I have ever met.[32]

Morris submitted the statement to the Judiciary Committee because of his belief that Wright might try to do to Thomas what she had done to Semerad:

> The reason I am offering this statement is that I am struck by the startling parallels between what Ms. Wright did then and what she is doing now. She vowed vengeance on a former supervisor for dismissal on the basis of competence. She seemed incapable of accepting responsibility for her own shortcomings and blamed the episode on external factors. She delayed in making her charges until after the confirmation hearings were concluded. When she made her charges she did so at the 11th hour to a staff member who would be sympathetic because he was "looking for dirt." The entire process suggested a last ditch attempt to stop the advancement of someone she resented. I see the same pattern of behavior today in the case of Judge Thomas.

Wright went from AID to a political appointment at the EEOC under Thomas, arranged by Phyllis Berry-Myers, a friend from Republican political circles. Her performance there, in a similar position to the one she held at AID, was also problematic, to put it mildly. "Angela had a foul mouth. She would curse the press out on the phone," Diane Holt, Thomas's secretary, recalled.

In his testimony, Clarence Thomas was asked about the circumstances of Wright's quick departure from the agency:

SIMPSON: . . . Angela Wright will soon be with us, we think, but now we are told that Angela Wright has what we used to call in the legal trade, cold feet. Now if Angela Wright doesn't show up to tell her tale of your horrors, what are we to determine about Angela Wright? Did you fire her, and if so what for?

THOMAS: As I indicated, Senator, I summarily dismissed her, and this is my recollection. She was hired to reinvigorate the public affairs operation at EEOC. I felt her performance was ineffective, and the office was ineffective. And the straw that broke the camel's back was a report to me from one of the members of my staff that she referred to another male member of my staff as a faggot.

SIMPSON: As a faggot?

THOMAS: And that is inappropriate conduct, and that is a slur, and I was not going to have it.

SIMPSON And so you just summarily discharged her?

THOMAS: That is right.

SIMPSON: That was enough for you?

THOMAS: That was more than enough for me. That was my recollection.

SIMPSON: That is kind of the way you are, isn't it?

THOMAS: That is the way I am with conduct like that, whether it is sex harassment or slurs or anything else. I don't play games.

SIMPSON: And so that was the end of Ms. Wright, who is now going to come and tell us perhaps about more parts of the anatomy. I am sure of that. And a totally discredited and, we had just as well get to the nub of things here, a totally discredited witness who does have cold feet.

According to several EEOC staffers, Thomas was already thoroughly dissatisfied with Wright's general performance at the time she made this comment. "The faggot remark was just the precipitating event," said Pamela Talkin, Thomas's former chief of staff.[33]

Years later, Wright would be offered the chance to settle this score when contacted by the Judiciary Committee staff about the column she had written on Thomas. She gave a statement to Senate staffers. Once she did, and it was evident that Wright had not charged Thomas with sexual harassment, the testimony that had whetted the appetites of Thomas's opponents and unnerved the Thomas camp was judged to be fairly tepid after all. Wright had, nonetheless, recounted conversations with Thomas that lent an air of authenticity to Hill's account.

Wright refused to be interviewed by the FBI. The FBI, however, was dispatched to the field to interview friends and former employers of Wright to assess her credibility. The result only added to the sense among supporters of both Thomas and Hill that Wright's testimony would not damage Thomas—and might even damage Hill by association. Thelma Duggin, a mutual friend of Wright and Thomas, told the FBI that she doubted the veracity of Wright's story:

> Duggin stated that she has known Wright since about 1978 or 1979 adding that they met as co-workers at the Republican National Committee. . . . She described Wright as a friend who is high strung to a certain extent. She said Wright would react without thinking. In her opinion, Wright is "a little shaky on the integrity side. . . ."
>
> Duggin stated that Wright is not one who would be intimidated by the sexual advances of a man. She said Wright is very attractive and if one tried to "hit on her and make a pass" she would "cuss like a sailor" and probably hit them. She said Wright isn't the type who would make a sexual harassment charge, she would "deck a person." Duggin advised that Wright could be described as a "seductive-type person." She has known Wright to enjoy a few beers and then dance on the table at the clubs. Duggin said Wright is a person who likes to party. Duggin said that to some extent, Wright would invite the sexual advances of a man and then brag about having guys hit on her. Duggin said Wright enjoyed the attention of men. . . .

Duggin was not joking about Wright's proclivity to "deck" people. One legendary story from Wright's days at the EEOC concerned an altercation with one of her male staff members at an EEOC conference. Wright and the man exchanged cross words about the conference arrangements he had made, which Wright found inadequate. Wright socked him in the jaw. He landed flat on his back and slid under a table in front of several stunned EEOC staffers.

Duggin went on to describe the history of Wright's relations with Thomas and how she had threatened to get even with Thomas as recently as two months before she made her statement. Duggin also revealed that Wright lied to her about the circumstances of her dismissal from the agency.

> Duggin stated that Wright was always very critical of her supervisors. She said Wright always complained about her supervisors and had a problem working within a structure and keeping a job. . . .

Duggin related that she does not know if Wright ever filed any complaints claiming sexual harassment. She said she can recall Wright speaking about racist employers and the possibility of filing a complaint but she does not know whether or not she actually made a complaint.

Duggin said Wright called her about one to two weeks after Thomas fired her. Duggin stated that Wright was very upset. Duggin said that to the best of her recollection, Wright told her she was fired because Wright had not made the proper preparations for a meeting that was to be attended by various commissioners. Duggin said that Thomas was making a bigger deal out of the situation than was necessary.

Duggin advised she last spoke to and saw Wright in August 1991 in Charlotte, North Carolina, when Duggin was in town. She said that at this time Clarence Thomas had already been nominated and since both of them knew him they had some conversation about Thomas. In particular, Duggin recalled Wright stating "I want to get him back." She said Wright also said that she "was pissed that he had fired her." Duggin advised that she was surprised to see that Wright wanted revenge on Thomas so many years later. Duggin went on to say that Wright told her the *Charlotte Observer* was pressuring her to do something about Thomas. She said Wright stated that "she didn't know if she was going to write anything about Thomas but she was looking for a way to get him back."

A former EEOC aide, Armstrong Williams, had a similar experience with Wright when he visited her in North Carolina in 1989. According to Williams, Wright told him over dinner, "If it's the last thing I do, I'll get him [Thomas]." When Williams spoke with Wright in the summer of 1991, after Thomas was nominated to the court, Wright told him, "You know I'm still pissed at him for firing me, but I'm not going to do anything."

Wright may have decided *not* to do anything because filing a baseless charge against Kate Semerad showed that such tactics do not work. Once Hill's charges broke in the press, Wright may have been satisfying her search for revenge by writing the sample column. After the column was leaked to the Senate staff—further evidence of the media's tilt in the Thomas affair generally—Wright was drawn into the controversy in a manner similar to the way Hill was drawn in. She had said (or written) something incriminating about Thomas, and the Senate staff wanted to know more.

After the interview with Senate staffers, Wright flew to Washington in anticipation of testifying before the Judiciary Committee on Sunday. Why she never appeared has been the subject of speculation and widely diverging accounts. In *Capitol Games,* Phelps reported that in addition to Republican efforts to keep Wright from testifying, Anita Hill's camp had effectively blocked Wright's appearance, fearing that Wright would undermine Hill's credibility. However, in an interview Charles Ogletree of Harvard University, one of Hill's attorneys during the hearings, said that this was false. He said that Hill's advisers strongly favored calling Wright to testify and charged instead that the Republicans and some unnamed Democrats had colluded to keep Wright off the stand to protect Thomas.[34]

Why any of the Democrats would have wanted to protect Thomas is not readily apparent. They may simply have wanted to protect themselves from public embarrassment if Wright testified. As the FBI report indicated, they certainly had cause for concern. As for Ogletree's suggestion that the Republicans conspired to keep Wright from appearing—a suggestion that has become a tenet of liberal orthodoxy from *Spy* to Garry Trudeau to Paul Simon—the Republicans insisted they were all for hearing Wright's testimony—probably for the same reason the Democrats wanted it hushed up. "I was laying in the weeds waiting for Angela Wright to testify, just laying there," Alan Simpson recalled. "I said, 'Oh, Joe, this is the woman who was fired for calling someone a faggot. Oh, Joe, bring her out. I'd like to examine her.' "[35]

Contrary to the conspiratorial views of Trudeau, who implied that her statement was "slipped into the record" as the result of a corrupt political deal—or possibly by a courageous Senate staffer who would not sit by while damning testimony was covered up—the disposition of the interview was agreed to by Wright herself after negotiations with the committee. Late Sunday night Biden's staff reached an agreement with Wright. She would not testify, but her statement would be placed in the record with no opportunity for the pro-Thomas side to rebut it. Biden interrupted the hearing to announce that Wright had decided not to testify. He read from a letter he had written Wright, "It is my preference that you testify. If you want to testify at the hearing in person, I will honor that request." In a subsequent interview with *U.S. News,* Wright claimed that Biden's staffers were "lying" and that they had kept her from testifying.[36]

The coverup charge, however, is implausible. After the loud media criticism of the way the committee had mishandled Anita Hill's allegation—and the uproar among women's groups—Biden could not have afforded to keep Wright off the stand, even if he had wanted to. Only Wright herself could have done that. Perhaps fearing that her testimony would be easily impeached, in the end Wright decided not to appear.

A final criterion that is often an aspect of sexual harassment cases is a pattern of interest in pornography or a propensity toward locker room talk in the workplace. Despite Republican efforts to cast Hill's testimony as unbelievable because the details were simply too horrible for anyone but a "psychopath" to have uttered, as Senator Hatch put it, Hill's account of talk about pornography and sexual prowess was not unfamiliar to experts who deal with sexual harassment cases. Such cases are filled with allegations of men discussing pornography or displaying pornographic photos in the office, asking their female employees what kind of sex they have with their husbands or boyfriends, and describing their own sexual adventures in graphic and offensive ways. Where Hill's case faltered was in failing to establish any independent corroboration that Thomas had ever behaved in the manner that she alleged. If Hill's testimony was true, a man who made a point of very visible commitment to proper conduct in this area—and who was further highly conscious that his political enemies would seize on any misconduct by him or his staff to use against him—had thrown caution to the winds in order to harass and intimidate one woman out of the dozens who worked for him.

To be sure, Thomas's joking references to pornography during his days at Yale proved to be an Achilles' heel in this case. Even a year after the hearings, a *Newsday* headline touting Tim Phelps's book *Capitol Games* read: "X-Rated Justice?"[37] There it was again, a black man and his unbridled appetite for sex, a stereotype that Thomas would never shake, despite the fact that even Phelps could come up with nothing more than warmed-over anecdotes about Thomas at Yale.

Even if Thomas had looked at pornography, of course, this would not mean that he was a sex harasser, as his critics implied. A couple of movie viewings that by all accounts began and ended twenty years before when Thomas was a student had little if any bearing on the Anita Hill charge two decades later, much less on his fitness to serve on the Supreme Court. Certainly there was no evidence that Thomas had ever brought such discussions into the workplace. Writing about the pornography rumors in *Advice and Consent*, even the Thomas critic Paul Simon conceded, "Even if we found them to be completely true, and we did not investigate them, I am not sure there is a direct tie-in between watching pornographic films and sexual harassment, at least I have not seen evidence of that."[38]

The first story ever linking Thomas to pornography was published in *U.S. News and World Report* on September 16, 1991, a week before Hill's allegation was filed with the Judiciary Committee. Buried deep in the text was the following seemingly innocuous paragraph:

> The son of a woman who works 18-hour days is no stranger to long hours. He was at the dining hall when it opened for breakfast at 7, sometimes regaling other early risers with hilarious descriptions of the x-rated movies he liked to watch for relaxation. He never came to a party before 10, when the library closed. Even sports were played flat-out, full tilt, as classmate Lovida Coleman Jr. remembers. "I've never seen anybody who could overthrow his receiver by 30 or 40 yards the way Clarence could. I would not say he was a finesse player," says Coleman.[39]

Although Coleman was the source of the pornography story, she had never meant it to be publicized, she said. She had told the story to Steven Roberts off the record, as an example of Thomas's famously hearty laugh. "I specified that it not be used in print because I knew the American people would hear pornography and might misunderstand the context," Coleman later said. "It was nothing unusual. They were showing films like *Behind the Green Door* all the time on campus. And there were people who competed with Clarence to make it funny." She was astonished to find that Roberts broke the rules of journalism and used the story anyway.[40] Thomas's Yale classmate Harry Singleton confirmed Lovida Coleman's recollection. "There was a group at the law school, sort of a film society, that would show underground movies. I think they went through a period where they were showing *Behind the Green Door, Deep Throat, The Devil in Miss Jones.* The movies were shown on campus, and a lot of people went to see them."[41]

White House officials suspected that Lovida's father Bill had alerted Steven Roberts to Thomas's discussions of pornography at Yale with his daughter, as part of the elder Coleman's quiet efforts to sabotage the nomination. By this juncture, in mid-September, father and daughter were at war. Lovida, a Yale classmate of Thomas, had written a letter to Senator Leahy after his famous exchange with Thomas on *Roe,* in which Thomas stated that he had never debated the contents of the decision. In her letter to Leahy, Coleman wrote that Thomas's statement was totally consistent with her own recollection of Yale in the early 1970s: She didn't recall any conversations in law school about the decision either.[42] Lovida's father was furious, accusing her of breaking their agreement not to take sides on the nomination. One evening he threw her out of his Virginia home in a rage. During the Anita Hill hearings, while the elder Coleman was quietly promoting the porn story as something the committee should consider, Lovida had openly abandoned her own neutrality, as her father had slyly done the month before. She was roaming the corridors of the Capitol, buttonholing senators for Thomas. "I felt that the Anita Hill issue should not have been responsible for his defeat," she later said.

Nothing came of Lovida Coleman's seemingly harmless reference to pornography in *U.S. News* until after the Hill story broke in October, igniting media interest in the anecdote, since only in that context did it seem significant. By October 13 the *New York Times* had dug up the month-old *U.S. News* anecdote and interviewed Coleman: "Earlier this week, in an interview, a friend of Judge Thomas, Lovida H. Coleman, Jr., said that in his Yale Law School days Judge Thomas 'at least once humorously described an x-rated film to me and other colleagues.' On elaboration, she acknowledged that this had occurred more than once."[43] After the *Times* story ran, Coleman issued a statement clarifying that Thomas described the pornographic films he had seen in a humorous way, and she did not consider the discussion offensive. "Indeed we would have been hypocrites to have been offended since very few of us failed to attend one or more similar films that were shown on the Yale University campus while we were in school," Coleman said.[44] The *Times* never reported these comments.

In the hearing, Leahy attempted to question Thomas about the matter, but Thomas drew the line, refusing to answer questions about his personal life. He stated clearly that he had never discussed pornography with anyone in the office and had never discussed pornography with Hill at any time. Unfortunately, taking the high road may have smacked to an ill-informed public of coverup rather than what it really was—a principled refusal to permit an irrelevant fishing expedition. If Thomas had been trying to cover something up he could have simply lied rather than declined to answer.

LEAHY: . . . Let me ask you—she has been asked whether this happened—let me ask you: Did you ever have a discussion of pornographic films with Professor Hill?

THOMAS: Absolutely not.

LEAHY: Have you ever had such discussions with any women?

THOMAS: Senator, I will not get into any discussions that I might have had about my personal life or my sex life with any person outside of the workplace.

LEAHY: I'm not asking—

THOMAS: I will categorically say that I have not had any such discussions with Professor Hill.

Leahy quickly backed off the personal question:

LEAHY: Please don't misunderstand my question, Judge. I am confining it to the workplace. I have no interest in what may be your personal life in this. That's yours. What I'm asking is within—she alleges within the workplace. Make sure I fully understand—I'm asking you this question, so that you can give the answer. Am I correct in understanding your answer, within the workplace with Professor Hill, you never had such a discussion?

THOMAS: Right.

LEAHY: You never had such discussions within the workplace with any other women?

THOMAS: That's right.

LEAHY: Or with anyone for that matter?

THOMAS: That's right.

There was no evidence linking Thomas and pornography after his days at Yale law school, though a rumor to that effect circulated fairly widely in the Washington press corps before and during the Anita Hill hearings. Nina Totenberg, in her Stanford speech, described the rumor and her own fruitless attempts to hunt it down. That Totenberg of all people had given up on the story should surely lay it to rest.

Let me take first the primary rumor that I've heard about Justice Thomas. And that is he was a regular renter of pornographic movies including "Long Dong Silver" movies, and that various news organizations have a list of the movies that he rented from a Washington video store and have suppressed it. As far as I know, that isn't true. There is an individual who called first me and then I think other news organizations telling us that Judge Thomas had rented pornographic videos at a particular store in Washington, that the owner of the store would corroborate that, and that they liked to talk about the details of the movies, and that they had, that the owner of the store, I talked to the owner, he denied remembering renting any particular pornographic videos to Judge Thomas who he did remember as a customer of the store, Thomas with his son, and in addition to that the owner of the store told me, and I corroborated this elsewhere, that the store routinely destroys its computer records of rentals every thirty days. So none exist. So that story evaporated like the morning mist.

Hill's testimony about Thomas, therefore, was the only source of evidence that Thomas had made references to pornography subsequent to his days at Yale. Remarkably enough, in a little-noticed television interview, that testimony was undermined by the statements of one of Hill's own supporters.

According to Hill, Thomas had told her about films depicting "women with large breasts having sex with animals." He allegedly also told her, "You should see these materials." Feminist law professor Catharine MacKinnon, an expert on harassment and a leading activist in the feminist crusade against pornography, appeared on the Phil Donahue show the Monday after Hill testified. In explaining for the benefit of a no-doubt incredulous studio audience that hard-core films of this nature really existed, she revealed that such films were not widely available for home viewing at the time that, according to Hill, Clarence Thomas had invited her to view them:

MACKINNON: Video rentals did not have animals in them ten years ago. That's partly why most of you who have seen these things on video have not seen sex with animals and wouldn't find it back then . . .

DONAHUE: Let's understand your point here. In 1981, bestiality, as we've come to refer to this, would be available where?

MACKINNON: In the loops. What the loops are—at peep shows where men go to put money in and watch live women in boxes, all right? And the loops are short pieces of pornography that you play over and over.[45]

In order to credit Hill's story, then, it was necessary to believe that the high-profile chairman of a federal agency—a man who knew that he was being closely watched by political enemies in both parties— was so addicted to hard-core pornography that he was willing to abandon all caution and principle in order to sneak into peep shows in the Washington vice district, despite the risk to his career if he were

discovered doing so. Not only that, he imprudently revealed this incriminating taste for graphic and degrading sexual sideshows to a female employee. There is the further problem that if Thomas had
seriously intended for Hill to see these sex shows too, she would have
had to see them, like Thomas, in seamy vice-district establishments.
Was she supposed to sneak into peep shows, whose clientele was uniformly male? But that is what Hill contended in her testimony:

> BIDEN: Why do you think, what was your reaction, why do you
> think he was saying these things to you?
>
> HILL: . . . I took that to mean, we ought to have sex or we ought
> to look at these pornographic movies together.

As MacKinnon herself has established, this was simply not a credible scenario in 1981. Not only were such hard-core films generally un-
available for private viewing at the time, but the video casette recorder
itself, which made it easy for consumers to view pornography in the
privacy of their own homes, had not as yet been widely marketed.

Hill's story about a man inviting a woman to watch such "materials" with him as a sexual overture was thus more likely to have been
a story from *1991* than from ten years earlier—a story told by someone who was perhaps knowledgeable about the types of hard-core
films that are more readily available for home consumption today
than a decade ago.[46]

The idea to link Thomas with pornography may have sprung from
the September 16, 1991, *U.S. News* article that—for the first time anywhere—reported Thomas's joking remarks about soft-core pornographic movies when he was a student at Yale. If Hill, or one of her
friends in Norman, or one of her interlocutors in Washington, had
seen that article, they would have understood that raising the pornography issue a week later in her September 23 committee statement
would stick to a black man accused of a sex crime, as it surely did. Hill
would only have had to be sufficiently familiar with pornography herself to add a few compelling details to her statement.

Regardless of what movies Thomas did or did not watch in his private life, however, those who knew him professionally found it inconceivable that Thomas would have discussed pornography, or any
other sexual matters, with anyone in the workplace. Thomas aide
Armstrong Williams recalled one occasion when he had bought a
copy of *Playboy* on his lunch hour. The issue had featured photos of
Vanessa Williams, the former Miss America who was afterwards forced
to give up her crown. "I remember once when we'd had lunch over

at the Plaza. I had gone in the store. There had been all this publicity about Vanessa Williams posing for *Playboy*. We were in this store. I bought the magazine. When I was walking out he saw the magazine and he said. 'What is that?' I said, 'Oh, man, this is Vanessa Williams.' He said, 'Are you crazy? They exploited this girl. They used her. How can you buy that trash and take it up to the agency and show it to people?' He said, 'You're beyond that. You're above that. You must learn to do better.' He said, 'And plus, it reflects on me and the agency. Throw that in the trash can.' "

Thomas's comments about *Playboy* were an indication of his upright demeanor, according to Williams, and of his acute consciousness of how his own conduct and that of his staff might be viewed by his many political enemies. "He was always tight-necked, professional, tough. It was a rigid environment. I wondered 'Does he ever loosen up?' I traveled with him every week and we could never meet in his room. He always felt you had to set a professional example. We would meet in the lobby."[47]

Thomas explained why he conducted himself in this formal manner to the committee: "[I]n this country when it comes to sexual conduct we still have underlying racial attitudes about black men and their views of sex. And once you pin that one on me, I can't get it off. That is why I am so adamant in this committee about what has been done to me. I made it a point at the EEOC and at Education not to play into those stereotypes, at all. I made it a point to have the people at those agencies, the black men, the black women, to conduct themselves in a way that is not consistent with those stereotypes, and I did the same thing myself."

In answering a question posed by Biden, Thomas also testified:

Senator, my attitude was, in my work environment, my staffs were almost invariably predominantly women. The senior person on my staff was a woman. I could not tolerate individuals making that environment uncomfortable or hostile. I could not tolerate individuals who had to segregate their language or conduct in order to get along. The conduct had to be purged of offensive attitudes and I made that a constant effort, and that was something that I was proud of and it was something I am sure the people who worked for me felt comfortable with and understood.

At another point Thomas said, "If I used that kind of grotesque language with one person, it would seem to me that there would be traces of it throughout the employees who worked closely with me; there would be other individuals who heard it, or bits and pieces of it, or various levels of it."

Thomas's testimony was powerfully corroborated by a panel of women Sunday night. Yet the public was deprived of an opportunity to reach an informed judgment about Thomas's conduct when this panel—consisting of nine women who had worked closely with Thomas over the years—did not testify until after midnight Sunday evening. In an unlucky break for Thomas, most of the viewing audience already had gone off to bed. The witnesses were also limited to two-minute statements each, a rule that reflected the attitude toward the panel on the part of some of the Senators. "We already know what they're going to say," Senator Metzenbaum said with derision.

Pamela Talkin, a liberal Democrat who was Thomas's former chief of staff at the EEOC, described Thomas as a man who is keenly attuned to the way in which even the most subtle forms of sexual harassment demean women. As did many other former employees of Thomas, she depicted someone who was almost prudish in his workplace demeanor:

> I have been in the work force for over 30 years. During that time I have endured varying degrees of sexual harassment, sometimes serious, sometimes subtle. I view myself as very alert to this; some of my men friends say, overly sensitive. It is in that context that I tell you that I have never met a man as sensitive. He has a feminist's understanding of sexual politics. He is a man who loathes locker room talk. This is a man who, when I had momentary lapses of language, looked discomfited and never responded in kind. This is a man who looked at his shoes when other men were craning their necks to look at a woman. This is a man who spent countless hours talking to me about his efforts to raise his adolescent son to be a decent, dignified, reverent man with women, and urging his son to treat his teenage female companions with dignity and respect despite his raging hormones.
>
> This is a man who understood the inherent imbalance of power in the workplace between men and women, and frowned upon even consensual romantic relationships because he did not want one woman in the agency to even mistakenly believe that her dignity had been compromised.
>
> I have spent over 18 years enforcing laws against employment discrimination, and I can tell you that I have never worked in a work environment where any individual, man or woman, was more committed to establishing a workplace free from discrimination and harassment.

It is the saddest of ironies to me that the behavior that Judge Thomas found most abhorrent is the behavior that he is now being accused of.

Constance Newman, a former EEOC official and Bush's director of the Office of Personnel Management, told the committee that in a large government agency like the EEOC, where the gossip mill churns constantly, abusive behavior by a controversial chairman would not remain secret for ten years.

> I have known him for 10 years. That does not mean that we have not disagreed. We have. We have argued. Through the years he has changed his mind some; I have changed mine a little. But I have not changed my view about the basic decency and integrity of this man. I know him and have worked with him. I have walked the halls of EEOC. Not once did I hear a hint of improper conduct. I would have heard. I heard of disagreements, but not improper conduct.

Significantly, no one who had worked with both Thomas and Hill, and who therefore had seen the two interact on a daily basis, came forward to say they believed her account. No one recognized any behavior either on her part or on his that would have indicated that something untoward was going on. Anna Jenkins, a former secretary in the chairman's office, told the committee:

> I had daily contact with Anita Hill and Judge Thomas. We shared a suite of offices consisting of a reception area, conference room, kitchen, and five offices. Judge Thomas's conduct around me, Anita Hill, and other staffers was always proper and professional. I have never witnessed Judge Thomas say or do anything that could be construed as sexual harassment. I never witnessed him making sexual advances toward any female, nor have I witnessed him engaging in sexually oriented conversations with women.

Nancy Altman, who worked with Thomas at the Education Department, testified to the utter lack of evidence of any kind for Hill's charge. A victim of sexual harassment herself, Altman said that in most cases close co-workers will observe some type of unusual behavior on the part of the victim to indicate that harassment is occurring.

> I have myself been the victim of an improper, unwanted sexual advance by a supervisor. Gentlemen, when sexual harassment occurs, other women in the workplace know about it. The members of the commit-

tee seem to believe that when offensive behavior occurs in a private room, there can be no witnesses. This is wrong.

Sexual harassment occurs in an office in the middle of the workday. The victim is in a public place. The first person she sees immediately after the incident is usually her harasser's secretary. Co-workers, especially women, will notice an upset expression, a jittery manner, a teary eye or a distracted air, especially if the abusive behavior is occurring over and over and over again.

Further, the women I know who have been victimized always shared the experience with a female co-worker they could trust. They do this to validate their own experience, to obtain advice about options that they may pursue, to find out if others have been similarly abused, and to receive comfort. Friends outside the workplace make good comforters, but cannot meet the other needs.

It is not credible that Clarence Thomas could have engaged in the kinds of behavior that Anita Hill alleges, without any of the women who he worked closest with—dozens of us, we would spend days having women come up, his secretaries, his chief of staff, his other assistants, his colleagues—without any of us having sensed, seen or heard something.

An EEOC social science research analyst, Linda Jackson, told the Senators of her relationship with Thomas—both professional and personal. Like Talkin, Jackson said that Thomas was more sensitive to the concerns of women than most men. She found him easy to confide in when her own abusive marriage came apart.

After meeting Clarence Thomas through my job, I ran into him in the hallway of my apartment building and found we lived in the same place. We began to have numerous conversations about work, politics and personal issues. We became very good friends in the process.

I believe I know the basic nature of this man better than most people in this room. I believe, unequivocally, Clarence Thomas's denial of these allegations. This is a very honorable man who has the highest respect for women. He always treated me with utmost respect and was more sensitive to women than most men I know. He never engaged me in discussions of any kind that could be considered demeaning to women.

He was often troubled by those women he knew, both professionally and women who were having difficulties with personal problems, particularly treatment by male friends, co-workers or spouses. He and I had numerous conversations about abuse of women, physically, emotionally and verbally. You see, Senators, he helped me pick up the pieces of my own crushed spirit, after I left an abusive marriage.

His sensitivity and honor, his respect for women, his helping attitude toward all people in need, makes these allegations even more ludicrous.

Finally, Janet Brown, who had worked with Thomas on Senator Danforth's staff and was another sexual harassment victim, testified that she turned to Thomas to help her through the devastating experience. Brown also took issue with the "men just don't get it" slogan. Gender, she said, does not determine one's ability to understand the ill effects of sexual harassment.

> A number of years ago, I was sexually harassed in the workplace. It was a demeaning, humiliating, sad and revolting experience. There was an intensive and lengthy internal investigation of this case, which is the route that I chose to pursue. Let me assure you that the last thing I would ever have done is follow the man who did this to a new job, call him on the phone or voluntarily share the same air space ever again.
>
> Other than my immediate family, the one person who was the most outraged, compassionate, caring and sensitive to me was Clarence Thomas. He helped me through the pain and talked me through the options. No one who has been through it can talk about sexual harassment dispassionately. No one who takes it seriously would do it.
>
> I don't subscribe to the belief that men, because they are men, don't understand sexual harassment. My husband, my father and my brother understand it. Clarence Thomas understands it. And because he understands it, he wouldn't do it.

The testimony of these women, drafted in their own hand with no coaching from the Thomas camp, was ignored or dismissed by the professional women's activists. There were scores of similar—yet totally unreported—accounts from those who had known or worked with Thomas over the years, both women and men. Many came from men who understood what kind of negative stereotypes and intense scrutiny Thomas, as a black conservative, had faced in his Washington career. Dick Leon remembered moving to Washington in 1984 and meeting his old friend for lunch. "He told me he was trying to change an institution [the EEOC]. As a result, he was under a microscope. He had to be above reproach. He knew he was being watched. Those were his words."[48]

"I never even swore in front of Clarence because I knew he wouldn't like it," Clint Bolick, a former EEOC aide, said.[49] Thomas's aide Armstrong Williams specifically remembers Thomas telling him: "You don't date anyone at EEOC." And Carlton Stewart, a former special assistant to the chairman, quoted Thomas as saying: "Look guys, we're in a fishbowl here. We have to be on our best behavior. Anything we do will be looked at negatively. If you guys do anything to embarrass the agency, I'll fire you."[50]

Ricky Silberman, the EEOC's vice chairman, said Thomas admonished the black men on his staff that they must be superior role models for young black men, doing nothing to contribute to vicious stereotypes about blacks and sex. "He called it zipper disease, and he disdained it," said Silberman. "Of course, I realize that we are at the point now that it will be said he was overcompensating for and repressing his own guilt. But that's the nature of a public trial like this. The truth about Clarence doesn't matter any more."

Silberman also pointed to Thomas's distinguished public record on sexual harassment. The sexual harassment case of GOP Senator Bob Packwood, a close political ally of Kate Michelman, the NARAL director, and a strong supporter of the women's rights agenda, showed that a commitment to such principles in public life does not necessarily translate into private behavior that is respectful of women.[51] Thomas, however, would have to be an even more accomplished hypocrite than Packwood if he too was a sex harasser. Thomas put the EEOC on the front lines of the battle to win more legal protections for women against such behavior. When the first sexual harassment case reached the Supreme Court in 1985, *Meritor Savings Bank* v. *Vinson,* Thomas personally intervened to persuade the Reagan Justice Department to back the EEOC's guidelines on sexual harassment, which advocated a legal standard that would have prohibited by law all forms of sexual harassment, including maintaining a hostile environment in the workplace. Some in the Justice Department believed that the EEOC guidelines went too far, that such a so-called hostile environment should not be illegal. In another example of his search for a reasonable and moderate approach, Thomas prevailed within the Administration, which filed an *amicus* brief in the case. The Supreme Court eventually upheld EEOC guidelines, voting 9–0 to outlaw hostile environment harassment.[52]

Thomas understood that sexual harassment is a particularly insidious form of discrimination against women. He admonished EEOC managers in one policy memo to "take the strongest disciplinary measures" against employees guilty of harassment. "He used to say sexual harassment is a power thing more than a sex thing," John Marini, another former aide to Thomas, said. "And Clarence Thomas had a lot of respect, particularly for people who had less power than he did.

He would never try to take advantage of a subordinate. Whenever you went with him, he knew the names of the women mopping the floors, the security guards, and he always treated them with great respect."[53]

This respect for others and, as pro-Thomas witness Nancy Fitch described it, inherent "decency" were things that everyone working around Clarence Thomas felt. The Judge, Fitch said, "was a role model and mentor who would, by his life and work, show the possibilities in America for all citizens given opportunity. A person such as this would never ever make a parallel career in harassment, ask that it not be revealed, and expect to have and keep his real career."

The enormous goodwill that Thomas had fostered over the years among his co-workers, especially women, carried him through the darkest days of his life. It was hard to imagine any political figure in contemporary Washington commanding such loyal and loving support. Thomas spoke about this accumulation of moral capital, evinced by the outpouring of support from his female co-workers, with one friend during the Anita Hill ordeal: "I guess I'm getting my reward now for having lived the life I have."

On one of Thomas's first days at the Supreme Court, some of the cleaning women there approached him, told him how much they had supported him, and wished him well on the court. They also told Thomas they could never have approached Thurgood Marshall that way.

Considering the many inconsistencies and even falsehoods in Hill's testimony, the lack of firm corroboration from her witnesses, and the massive support *for* Thomas, the sole remaining testament to the credibility of her case consists in the fact that she passed a polygraph examination on Sunday afternoon as the hearings drew to a close. The lie detector test "may not be admissible in a court of law but it is certainly going to weigh heavily on the minds of a lot of senators," Senator Patrick Leahy said after the results were announced. The result "goes further to the question of credibility, favorably for her."[54]

The polygraph was an attempt by the Hill camp to regain the momentum they had lost on Friday evening, when Thomas described the hearings as a "high-tech lynching," and all day Saturday during his testimony. While he struck some of Thomas's supporters as patronizing in his tone, Senator Hatch drew on his keen ability to play to human emotion in eliciting from Thomas perhaps the most memorable and effective testimony of the weekend:

Senator, as I have indicated before and I will continue to say this and believe this, I have been harmed. I have been harmed. My family has been harmed. I have been harmed in my life. I wasn't harmed by the Klan, I wasn't harmed by the Knights of Camelia, I wasn't harmed by the Aryan race, I wasn't harmed by a racist group, I was harmed by this process, this process which accommodated these attacks on me. If someone wanted to block me from the Supreme Court of the United States because of my views on the Constitution, that is fine. If someone wanted to block me because they don't like the composition of the court, that is fine. But to destroy me, Senator, I would have preferred an assassin's bullet to this kind of living hell that they have put me and my family through. . . .

When I appeared before this committee for my real confirmation hearing, it was hard. I would have preferred it to be better. I would have preferred for more members to vote for me. But I had a faith that, at least this system was working in some fashion, though imperfectly.

I don't think this is right. I think it's wrong. I think it's wrong for the country. I think it's hurt me and I think it's hurt the country. I have never been accused of sex harassment. And anybody who knows me knows I am adamantly opposed to that, adamant, and yet, I sit here accused. I will never be able to get my name back, I know it.

On Saturday evening, Hatch and his wife invited Thomas and his wife, Ginni, and Jack and Sally Danforth to have dinner at Morton's Steak House in the Virginia suburbs. The fight was by no means over, but the group felt the day had gone extraordinarily well for Thomas. What they did not fully realize was that the nation had been riveted to their television sets all day long. The waitresses and busboys commented on various aspects of the testimony. When the Hatch party rose to leave, Thomas was given a standing ovation by the restaurant patrons.[55]

Early Sunday morning, Ken Duberstein, the former Reagan chief of staff who had been brought in by the Bush Administration to handle the nomination, told Danforth things were going so well that they ought to anticipate a last-minute polygraph surprise from Hill. Expecting a call for Thomas to take a polygraph as well, they decided in advance they would reject any such call as inappropriate and undignified for a Supreme Court nominee, whether Hill passed it or not. (The feminist leader Eleanor Smeal did demand that Thomas also take a test.)[56]

Just as Duberstein suspected, Hill's attorney Charles Ogletree announced at a late afternoon press conference Sunday that she had passed a polygraph test, thereby vindicating Hill in the battle for public credibility. Ogletree said he wanted to be "able to settle once and for all for our satisfaction whether or not Ms. Hill—whether or not Professor Hill was truthful when she related the incident about sexual harassment. We're not seeking to introduce this into evidence. Our concern has always been . . . to be able to show that she's telling the truth. . . . I think, from our point of view, it puts the issue to rest."

The polygraph machine does not actually detect lies. It measures physiological responses, such as increased blood pressure, pulse rate, breathing rate, and sweating, to a series of questions. Shortly after the test results were released, a number of polygraph experts were quoted in the press on the general issue of what the tests demonstrated. Their comments suggested that this test was of little importance to the issue of Hill's truthfulness.[57] David T. Lykken of the University of Minnesota, one of the country's foremost polygraph experts, told the *Washington Post:*

> Collectively, if you're disturbed by a question, you'll show a disturbance in one of these channels. But nobody knows why you're disturbed, whether the question made you scared. . . . It tends to corroborate a little bit the idea that she believes what she's said. But if she's pathological or if she's one of these people who can hallucinate a romantic relationship . . . then she might pass the test because she believes she's telling the truth even though she might not be. The amount of probative value that this test has in this situation is minuscule—it's in her favor, but it doesn't solve the problem by any means.

Ray Bull, a professor of psychology at Portsmouth Polytechnic, told the *Financial Times* that "focusing on erotic thoughts or placing a drawing pin [a thumbtack] in one's shoe" could fool the polygraph machine by leading to a false reading on the so-called control questions that are interspersed with the relevant questions (affecting the case at hand) as a benchmark. This would throw the result.[58] Other experts said the polygraph could be defeated if the subject pressed her toe against the floor, bit her tongue—or performed any physical activity over and over—to produce a fixed response on the machine when a question was asked. The lie detector subject could also have invalidated the result by "desensitizing" herself through a lack of sleep or taking tranquilizers, according to the quoted experts.

The easily fooled polygraph machine itself is not the main source of the problem with the test, however. The most common difficulty is incorrect administration and interpretation of the test. Bill Roemer, a former FBI polygrapher, told the *Washington Times:* "It's not the machine that gives the results, it's the operator. All he does is

make a recommendation. There's no science to it."[59] Hatch, who with
Ted Kennedy had cosponsored the Polygraph Protection Act to protect employees from being forced to take polygraphs in the workplace, said during the hearings Sunday afternoon:

> I can tell you right now, you can find a polygraph operator for any-
> thing you want to find them for. There are some very good ones and
> there are some lousy ones, and a whole raft in between. And to do that
> and interject that in the middle of this is pathetic, as if it has any rele-
> vance whatsoever. It wouldn't even be admissible in a court of law . . .
> there is no question that polygraphs should only be given under cer-
> tain circumstances, with the approval of both sides, and unilaterally by
> one side that may be very biased. You can find a polygraph operator
> to do anything you want them to do, just like you can find a pollster.
> Some pollsters in this country, not many, but some will do anything.
> They will find any conclusions you want, just by changing the ques-
> tions. . . . So to throw that right in the middle of a Supreme Court nom-
> ination as though it is real, legitimate evidence is highly offensive, that
> is my only point, and highly political, and again, too pat, too slick, ex-
> actly what a two-bit slick lawyer would try to do in the middle of some-
> thing as important as this.

Biden seemed to agree with Hatch. When Metzenbaum tried to insert the polygraph result into the official record of the hearing, Biden
said, "If we get to the point in this country where lie detector tests are
the basis upon which we make judgments . . . we have reached a sad
day for civil liberties in this country."

There were several unusual aspects of the Anita Hill test that made
it even less reliable than a typical polygraph. According to the information released by her handlers, the Hill polygraph took two hours.[60]
Typically, the examiner has a pretest conversation with the subject
covering the ground that he or she will be examined on. When the
examination begins, the relevant questions are mixed with control
questions—such as the subject's date of birth—that can be readily verified. If the physiological responses of the subject change when the
relevant questions are asked, this indicates that the subject is lying.

For one thing, Hill's result could have been skewed because it was
administered in a friendly environment by an examiner chosen by
Hill's attorney, rather than a neutral party like the Senate Judiciary
Committee or the FBI. Unlike most polygraph subjects, Hill had no
reason to fear that if she failed the test, the result would be released.
In a legitimate test, an announcement is made *beforehand* that the subject has decided to undergo a polygraph to show he or she is telling

the truth. In the Hill case, no one knew the polygraph had been given until *after* she had passed it. If she had failed, it is unlikely that the test result would have been acknowledged publicly.

According to the report released by the examiner, Paul K. Minor, a former chief polygrapher for the FBI now in private business in Virginia, Hill was asked the following "relevant" questions during the interview:

A. Have you deliberately lied to me about Clarence Thomas? (No).

B. Are you fabricating the allegation that Clarence Thomas discussed pornographic material with you? (No).

C. Are you lying to me about the various topics that Clarence Thomas mentioned to you regarding specific sexual acts? (No).

D. Are you lying to me about Clarence Thomas making references to you about the size of his penis? (No).

"Deception was not shown in a relevant question," Minor said at the news conference. "Nothing like that. . . . It's my opinion that Anita Hill is truthful when she answered the questions."[61] Yet without knowing what Hill had told the examiner before the interview, it was impossible to judge whether or not her responses to the questions were meaningful. For example, if Hill told Minor *nothing* in the pretest about Thomas's mentioning specific sex acts, there would have been an indication of "no deception" on the polygraph machine.

In a deviation from standard practice, Ogletree and Minor refused to release the control questions and the actual readout from the polygraph machine. "There are other questions having to do with irrelevant issues, control questions, and so forth. But those were the meaningful issue questions, and that's a complete listing of them, none are left out," Minor said.

There was also an unexplained delay in releasing the results of the polygraph. During his press conference, polygrapher Minor said, "We started at 11 A.M. this morning, and completed the test at 1:15 this afternoon." The examination report also stipulated those times. However, according to an account in the *American Lawyer* (an account that Ogletree later said in an interview was accurate): "Ogletree was told that Hill had passed the lie detector test late Sunday afternoon, at about the same time that Hill's first panel of corroborating witnesses disbanded" after 5 P.M. Why the four-hour gap?[62] Did Hill keep taking the test until she passed it?

Finally, the credibility of the test was completely undermined when the examiner himself, Paul Minor, told an outright lie at his news conference:

Q. Have you had cases where you later found out that the polygraph did not accurately report?

A. I've heard of such cases, but I don't know that I have ever had one. I don't think so.

It turned out that Minor *had* been involved in two celebrated cases where his results were shown to have been wrong. The *Los Angeles Times* reported the following about Minor:

In July of 1980, Minor, who was then with the FBI, administered two polygraph tests to Herman Sillas, then the U.S. attorney in Sacramento, to determine the veracity of allegations that he had taken a $7,500 bribe from a prison inmate several years earlier. Sillas resigned after failing both polygraph tests.

At the request of his attorneys, the results were later examined by other experts who concluded that the tests had been improperly administered and the results "seriously flawed," according to Dr. Chris Gugas, chairman of the National Polygraph Assn.

Another expert, Lynn Marcy, who was then president of the American Polygraph Assn., was called in to administer the test for a third time and the results of that test indicated that Sillas was telling the truth.

"We filed complaints against Minor with the FBI and asked the American Polygraph Assn. to investigate him," said Richard Hickman, a San Francisco-based polygraph expert who along with Gugas reviewed the results of Minor's test.

Hickman said that the way in which Minor phrased the questions he put to Sillas, along with what he remembers as being "serious" shortcomings in the methodology Minor used, raised troubling questions about his competence at the time.[63]

Gugas told the *Washington Times* that Minor admitted his mistakes and apologized, so the complaint was dropped. "I don't think he's run that many tests. He was an analyst more than someone who administered the tests frequently," Gugas said. The *Times* continued:

Mr. Minor also administered a polygraph test in August 1989 to male prostitute Stephen L. Gobie for the *Washington Times* to determine whether Gobie's allegations about this relationship with Rep. Barney

Frank were true. Mr. Minor told the *Times* that Gobie was lying about everything in regard to the Massachusetts Democrat.

But subsequent reporting by the *Times* and Mr. Frank's own admission proved that much of what Gobie was saying was true. Mr. Frank was reprimanded last summer by the House of Representatives for using office perquisites on Gobie's behalf.

Another polygraph specialist, Billy Franklin of Virginia Beach, was skeptical of Mr. Minor's technique at the time. He told the *Times*, "He asked too many questions. He asked no control questions. He had nothing to compare [the answers he elicited] with. I would say the fault lies with the technique the examiner used."[64]

The final word on the polygraph should be given to three Judiciary Committee members who have long been skeptical about its utility. "The American Medical Association, testifying before the Labor Committee, stated that polygraph tests 'measure nervousness and excitability, not truth. . . .' We cannot have careers and reputations depending on the results of such a frightening, unscientific test," Howard Metzenbaum said in March 1988. In December 1987, Paul Simon said, "Honest people are more likely to fail polygraph tests than dishonest people." And in March 1988, Ted Kennedy stated: "Who fails it? If you are an altar boy, you will probably fail it. You would have a sense of conscience and potential guilt. But who passes it? The psychopaths, the deceptive ones."[65]

At this juncture, each pillar of the "case for Hill" has crumbled. Hill did not come forward voluntarily after suppressing an experience of sexual harassment for ten years; rather, she was induced to file a complaint by Senate staffers and interest group partisans who wanted to defeat the nomination regardless of the charge's truth or falsehood, and then "outed" Hill when the plan did not work. Hill's sworn testimony was filled with evasions, suppressions, and falsehoods. None of her four witnesses was able to corroborate the charge. Angela Wright, the so-called "other woman" who failed to testify, never charged Thomas with harassment and had major credibility problems. Thomas's alleged penchant for pornography was nothing more than a typical collegiate experience and had no bearing on the sexual harassment charge. Hill's polygraph test was conducted in secret, with the result announced only *after* it had been administered; moreover, the examiner had previously produced inaccurate results and lied to the press when asked about them.

However, deconstructing Hill's case in this fashion is admittedly inadequate, since it does not explain how Hill could have been so persuasive to millions of viewers if she knew she was telling a lie. The creation of a false or misleading image of Hill by her supporters and the media cannot entirely account for the impression of veracity she made. Rather it was the power of her palpable assurance and her sense of moral rectitude that persuaded many people—even if they did not believe her—that she at least believed what she was saying. What other source of confidence and strength could she have had, if not a profound conviction of the truth of her own story? The answer to this question can only emerge from the reconstruction that now follows of "the real Anita Hill." As we will see when the question of motive is opened, Hill's strongly held political beliefs and her sense of herself as engaged in a moral struggle for the future may have led her to believe that deception in the service of a higher cause was justified.

8

The Search for a Motive

After an entire weekend of testimony, no one was able to establish a convincing motive for Anita Hill to have come forward and perjured herself by bringing a false charge of sexual harassment against Clarence Thomas. Hill as she appeared before the public—the reticent woman who quietly suffered the sexual overtures of her boss until she was forced to leave her job and was now candidly and self-assuredly recounting her experience for the sake of the nation's highest court; the Republican Reagan appointee who had supported the nomination of Judge Bork; the prim and proper Southern Baptist flanked by a dozen members of her family from rural Oklahoma—could not, it seemed, have a plausible reason to lie.

Hill's assertions that she had "nothing to gain" from testifying were accepted at face value. "There is no motivation that would show that I would make something like this up," she said. Her supporters, quoted credulously in the media, did everything possible to reinforce this contention. Joel Paul, one of Hill's witnesses, told *Time,* "She doesn't have the motivation or desire to attack a judicial nominee." An analysis in the *Atlanta Constitution,* spelling out the "case for Hill," reported, "Ms. Hill's cross examiners could not show that she was driven by an evil motive."[1] Several months after the hearings, two

287

books repeated this refrain. Senator Paul Simon, in *Advice and Consent*, composed a ledger of reasons for believing Thomas, and reasons for believing Hill. The strongest factor in Hill's favor, Simon wrote, was that "it is difficult to find any motivation for her other than a sense of public duty."[2] In *Capitol Games*, Timothy Phelps concluded, "The one point that the Democrats were successful in making, the only one, was that Hill seemed to have no plausible motive for fabricating her story."[3]

In the wave of commentary that followed the hearings, any suggestion that Hill may have had a motive was indignantly dismissed as a racist or sexist trope, which had the effect of discouraging serious consideration of the issue. Writing in the Toni Morrison collection, for example, Wahneema Lubiano of Princeton University charged that "demonic narratives" had been created by the Senate and the media to explain Hill's reasons for testifying. In her analysis, no adequate conceptual category existed to contain and account for Hill's character and actions. Her image was therefore refracted through existing racist and sexist stereotypes to produce a misleading conception of Hill as "the embodiment of black female betrayal, or 'white' feminist cat's paw"; she was either a "lunatic," a "lesbian," or an "indication of the pathology of African American culture . . . the welfare queen."[4] Though her analysis reflects the radical assumptions of current academic cultural criticism, Lubiano did have a point. The search for a motive by Thomas partisans produced a number of highly conjectural and defamatory portraits of Hill ranging from that of a conniving, vengeful female bent on punishing Thomas for some unstated reason—"Watch out for this woman!" Senator Simpson had exclaimed at one point—to the deluded victim of a "fatal attraction" who had turned on Thomas when he remarried in the late 1980s.

The only direct testimony on motive during the hearings came during an exchange between Senator Howell Heflin and Hill that was immediately dismissed as comic relief. Drawing muffled chuckles from the audience, Heflin asked a series of ironic questions that were, despite his cornball delivery, mostly on target.

HEFLIN: Are you a scorned woman?

HILL: No.

HEFLIN: Do you have a militant attitude relative to the area of civil rights?

HILL: No, I don't have a militant attitude.

HEFLIN: Do you have a martyr complex?

HILL (laughing): No, I don't.

HEFLIN: Well, do you see that coming out of this, you can be a hero in the civil rights movement?

HILL: I do not have that kind of complex. I don't like all of the attention that I am getting, I don't—even if I liked the attention, I would not lie to get attention.

HEFLIN: There may be other motivations. I just listed some that you usually look to relative to these. Are you interested in writing a book?

HILL: No, I'm not interested in writing a book.

In this exchange, Heflin touched on a range of potential motives, from frustrated professional or personal desires, to political ideology, to a quest for fame and fortune as a leader in the women's movement. Hill was able plausibly to deny each suggestion because neither the Judiciary Committee Democrats nor the press made any effort to develop more than a perfunctory profile of the accuser, so as not to seem to victimize her further, while the Republicans were unable to get beyond name-calling and innuendo with no factual basis.

Even Thomas, who knew more about his relationship with Hill than anyone but Hill herself, refused to speculate about her motives, allowing her case to rest with no attempt to explain why she might have come forward with a false story.

Senator Leahy asked Thomas:

You have Anita Hill, a woman who has gone to Yale Law School, certainly one of the finest law schools in this country, and I'm sure as its graduate, you accept that. She's obviously quite bright. You have certainly stated in the past a high regard for her. You've hired her in two positions of significant trust and responsibility, gone through all the things—going through the bar exam and all that, not easy tasks for anyone. She held those two positions of high trust and responsibility, both in the Department of Education and at the EEOC. She then went to a university where she is a law professor and has done well enough to become tenured. Holding that—not only the degree, but the license to practice law—something that she has worked extremely hard for for years, protected and nurtured all this way through, added to her experience and all, why should she come here and perjure herself, throw away all of that, for what? I mean, what would she possibly get out of throwing all that away?

"Senator, I don't know. I know the Anita Hill who worked for me, and the relationship that I've had with her from time to time on the intermittent calls or the few visits over the years," Thomas testified. "I don't know what's happened since 1983. All I know is that the allegations are false and I don't have a clue as to why she would do this."

Other nominees facing a similar confrontation might have funneled ammunition to their allies on the Senate committee to use against their accuser. But Thomas was so flabbergasted by the charges that the most he would say, testifying at another point, was, "I don't know what goes on in her mind." Thomas took this position to a stubborn extreme in refusing even to watch Hill's televised testimony. By thus shielding or refusing to describe their real relationship, for whatever reasons, Thomas denied his supporters the tools to open up the motive question in a meaningful way and inadvertently ensured that the myth of Anita Hill as a courageous lone dissenter who had come forward only out of a sense of public duty would go completely unchallenged. In the absence of probative testimony, Hill's portrayal of their relationship and her categorical denial of any motive to harm Thomas would therefore be accepted as the truth.

Yet the real Anita Hill would have been more correct to answer "yes" than "no" to Heflin's questions, for each of these possible motives may have come into play—though not necessarily in the way suggested by Heflin—in her decision to testify.

Nobody, of course, can know what went on in Hill's mind as she testified. But it is not really necessary to know what went on in her mind at this stage. All that needs to be determined now is whether she had any plausible motives for testifying against Thomas other than the high-minded civic ones that were supposedly established at the time. Establishing such motives first requires that one of the major questions left open by the hearings be resolved: What was the true nature of the relationship between Clarence Thomas and Anita Hill in the early 1980s? "One year after the showdown," a cover story in *U.S. News* reported, "a host of educated guesses substitutes for real knowledge about what happened between Clarence Thomas and Anita Hill."[5] Virginia I. Postrel, writing in the *Los Angeles Times* on the first anniversary of the hearings, made the same point: "Whatever transpired between Thomas and Hill remains as great a mystery today as it was a year ago."[6]

Despite Thomas's blanket denials, many viewers of the hearings seem to have concluded that the answer to the mystery lay somewhere in between their two accounts. While many thought Hill's claims of sexual harassment may have been a distortion or misrepresentation of actual events, something did appear to have transpired between these two people years before that Thomas, and perhaps even Hill, was trying to conceal from the committee. What was it? Did Thomas ask Hill for dates? Was Hill a "scorned woman"? Did they have an affair? The answers to these questions lie in a closer examination of the nature and dynamics of the relationship between Thomas and Hill, beginning at the Department of Education and continuing at the EEOC. Established facts and the testimony of several friends and former colleagues must be contrasted with Anita Hill's uncorroborated version of events.

Anita Hill joined Thomas at the Department of Education's office for civil rights in the fall of 1981 as his sole legal assistant, on the recommendation of Thomas's friend Gil Hardy. Hardy had called Thomas in mid-1981 and asked him if he could help Hill, a promising young Yale law school graduate who was nevertheless having trouble in her first job at the Wald, Harkrader law firm. Thomas was sympathetic and agreed to hire her.[7] Hill's account of this event, however, omitted her urgent need to leave the firm. This omission helped create the false impression that Anita Hill was, like Thomas, a conservative Republican who specifically sought a position in the Reagan Administration, when in reality Hill simply accepted the first job that Gil Hardy could procure for her. Significantly, Hill portrayed herself as being less in need of help, hence less beholden to Thomas, than she actually was.

Assistant Secretary Thomas, then thirty-two, supervised an office of several dozen education bureaucrats and support personnel. But his personal staff was small, comprising Hill, who at the time was twenty-five years old, Diane Holt, his secretary, who later testified on Thomas's behalf in the hearings, and two other administrative aides. According to Harry Singleton, who replaced Thomas at the department in May 1982 when he was appointed EEOC chairman, Thomas saw himself as Hill's mentor, a role he relished playing with the younger associates whom he brought in as his special assistants over the years.[8]

Thomas's penchant for playing the role of a mentor was no doubt gratifying to most of his protégés. Indeed, Thomas was widely praised by those who knew him for his active interest in the progress of other talented young blacks in Washington, and much of the indignation expressed on Thomas's behalf by his supporters seems to have been motivated by Hill's manifest ingratitude to Thomas after all he had done to help her. However, it bears noting that Anita Hill, while clearly Thomas's dependent at this stage, and therefore understandably reluctant to express such sentiments, may well have viewed this paternalistic habit in a different light.

However that may be, Thomas and Hill did have the opportunity to become well acquainted personally during this period, no doubt largely due to the fact that they had quite a lot in common. Both were raised in humble circumstances in the rural South, both graduated from Yale Law School, and both went on to pursue careers in Washington. Hence, just as many observers suspected, there was a friendly, easygoing dimension to their relationship and a special bond that extended beyond their formal roles as employer and employee. In her initial written statement to the Judiciary Committee, Hill described their early relationship, noting how she came to view herself as Thomas's principal adviser on policy matters, and voicing her assumption that their common life experiences had also given them a common philosophical outlook.

> From the beginning, our working relationship was relaxed and open. He spoke often about his childhood experiences and how they shaped his perspectives on issues of race, civil rights, and politics. I had grown up under similar conditions, on a farm in a remote part of Oklahoma, in poverty, the youngest of thirteen children but with very strong disciplinarian parents. I, initially, believed that our common experiences in terms of background and legal education were the reason he hired me. Early on, our working relationship was positive. He gave me a good deal of responsibility for and independence on assignments. I considered that he trusted my judgment though we often entered into long discussions in which I would have to justify my position.

Thomas and Hill were also closer ideologically during this period than they would be later on at the EEOC. Thomas earned significant attention during his short tenure at the Department of Education when he openly criticized the Reagan Justice Department's efforts to defend a tax exemption for Bob Jones University, which discriminated against blacks. Moreover, the scope of his responsibilities at Education, which involved civil rights enforcement only in schools, was much narrower than the full panoply of discrimination issues that Thomas and his advisers, including Hill, would later face at the EEOC. As a consequence, he and Hill would later find many more occasions on which to disagree, sometimes vehemently. Hill would also have grounds to believe that Thomas's growing conservatism as EEOC chairman represented a significant departure from his personal and political "roots" as a black man from the rural South.

In her Senate testimony, Hill omitted this description of the pleasant and tranquil early days of their relationship at Education, beginning instead with the first alleged incident of harassment. Hill testified that three months or so after her arrival at the department, Thomas asked her several times to go out with him. When she rebuffed these alleged overtures, Thomas began to talk about pornography with her, and described his own sexual prowess, while continuing to press for dates. The incidents occurred either in Thomas's office—where he once allegedly asked her who had put a pubic hair on his Coke—in her office, and in the employee cafeteria, according to her testimony. The behavior stopped, she said, shortly before Thomas was named EEOC chairman. She followed him to the agency because she feared that she would be jobless if she did not.[9]

There is no evidence other than Hill's testimony that Thomas asked Hill for dates. Confusion surrounded this issue at the time of the hearings due to an error in Nina Totenberg's original report on Hill's allegations. "Thomas, according to Senate sources, told the FBI he had asked Hill to go out with him, but when she declined, he said, he dropped the matter," Totenberg reported.[10] Never having had access to the FBI report, Totenberg simply got this wrong and never corrected the record. Thomas never told the FBI he had asked Hill out; he categorically denied Hill's allegations to the FBI. Unfortunately, the *New York Times* and other publications repeated Totenberg's erroneous report that Thomas had asked Hill out. On October 7, the *Times* reported, "Judge Thomas told the FBI's investigators that he had asked Ms. Hill out a few times and, after she declined, eventually dropped all advances."[11] This created an apparent discrepancy in Thomas's account—the *only* discrepancy in his story that has been identified either during or after the hearings.

In describing her relationship with Thomas, Hill said nothing about any contacts with him *outside* the office. According to her account, their relationship was strictly professional and had been confined to the workplace. When Thomas later testified, however, he disclosed that when Hill worked at Education, he occasionally offered her rides home from the office to her Capitol Hill duplex, since they lived near one another in the Southwest section of the city. This revelation raises the question of what transpired on these occasions—which overlapped with the period in which the worst harassment had supposedly occurred—and why Hill omitted them from her testimony.

According to Thomas, Hill accepted the rides and sometimes invited him into her apartment, where the two engaged in lengthy discussions about their backgrounds, life in Washington, politics and policy. "What I said was, when we were at the Department of Education, there were, as I recall, a number of instances in which I gave her a ride home, and she asked me just to drop in to continue discussion, and I would have a Coke or a beer or something and leave. That was, again, nothing, I thought nothing of it. It was purely innocent on my part and nothing occurred with respect to that, other than those conversations," Thomas testified. On one such occasion, Thomas said, Hill asked him to help hook up new stereo equipment, hardly something that an employee would request of her boss unless the two were on good terms and had a relationship outside the office.

In an exchange with Biden, Thomas revealed that he had informed the FBI of these encounters with Hill several days before her allegations became public. Thomas, therefore, was forthcoming at the outset about the contacts; Hill, however, neither mentioned them in her committee statement nor in her FBI interview. If Thomas was harassing her during these visits, surely she would have said so.

> BIDEN: . . . Let me ask you another question. Did you inform the FBI that you had, on occasion, driven—I assume the way you describe it, as a favor—Professor Hill home or that you had, on occasion—a single occasion or more than one, I will let you describe it—gone in for a coke or a beer after work, did you tell the FBI that?
>
> THOMAS: I think I did, Senator, again these events have unfurled very rapidly. And I don't think that was a particular issue. Their response was, or their questioning went to specific allegations . . .
>
> BIDEN: Can you give us any sense of how often it happened that you would go in and have a coke or a beer after work?
>
> THOMAS: Oh, it couldn't have happened any more than maybe twice or three times. Nothing, there was no, it was nothing ma-

jor. It was just a matter of, you know, we may have been arguing about something, debating something, a policy or something.

Thomas had also told his friend Laurence Silberman about the contacts before the story of Hill's charges broke in the press. "I asked him 'Was there any social connection with this woman at all?,' " Silberman said, reprising a private conversation he had had with Thomas after Hill made her charges to the Judiciary Committee and the FBI had begun to investigate. "He said 'All I remember is driving her home a few times. She offered me a wine or a Coke. I have a memory of a roommate [Sonia Jarvis] being there in sweats, walking to and fro.' We thought it would have been inculpatory," said Silberman, meaning that Thomas's presence in Hill's apartment might be used by Hill to show that he had been interested in her socially, bolstering the claim that he had asked her out. "I took his telling me this as an indication of his total candor," Silberman said. "But it turned out to be exculpatory, because Hill never mentioned it, and he was in her apartment by her invitation."[12]

Indeed, as Silberman's comments suggested, Thomas's Friday evening testimony about the visits to Hill's home troubled the Hill camp. Sonia Jarvis, Hill's roommate at the time, swore out an affidavit apparently designed to contain the damage done to Hill's case by the testimony. Jarvis stated that she recalled the time that Thomas hooked up the stereo in their home, but she expressly contradicted his suggestion that he had been in the house more than once. "I never saw or heard of Judge Thomas being at the house at any other time. I never saw or heard of his driving Anita Hill home," Jarvis stated.[13] Jarvis, of course, had no way of knowing whether Thomas had been in the house on occasions when she was not at home. Thus the importance of her affidavit was that it corroborated Thomas's testimony that he was indeed in their home at least once by Hill's own invitation. After the Jarvis affidavit was released, Hill filed her own affidavit, stipulating to the visit from Thomas involving the stereo, but denying other aspects of his account. "This is the only time Judge Thomas was ever in my home. He never drove me home, he never came in to visit and talk politics or any other thing; he simply was never there again."[14]

If Hill was telling the truth, and Thomas had been in her home only once, the incident in question may well have occurred before the harassment began. It could even be believed that Thomas mistook this invitation for a sign of Hill's personal interest in him, which he might then have pursued, possibly to an inappropriate degree. But this plausible suggestion was not made. And if this was the case, the question of why Hill never mentioned inviting Thomas into her house until he mentioned it himself still seems puzzling. Why would Hill stay silent until compelled to reveal it, somewhat awkwardly, after she had testified and her former roommate had corroborated Thomas's testimony? Was she concerned that even one such invitation would have shown Thomas as a mentor and friend, rather than in the light that she was trying to portray him, as a menacing sex harasser? The only reasonable interpretation is that she, not Thomas, was the one who had some interest in concealing this aspect of their relationship, possibly because it would tend to undermine her credibility.

Contradicting Hill's affidavit, Armstrong Williams, a special assistant at the EEOC who was close to both Thomas and Hill, said that Hill had told him in 1983 of more than one occasion on which she accepted rides home from Thomas and invited him into her home when the two worked together at Education. Hill also told Williams that she had wanted to establish a more personal relationship with Thomas, a desire he apparently did not share. Along with Diane Holt, Williams was one of the very few people on the EEOC staff who was on friendly terms with Hill. Now a public relations executive in Washington and a regular columnist for *USA Today*, Williams—like everyone else at the EEOC who observed Thomas and Hill interact—was a vocal supporter of Thomas during the hearings. He bore her no ill will, he said, and considered her "a good person." But he believed that Hill's behavior toward Thomas at the EEOC was not consistent with that of a sexual harassment victim.[15]

Williams specifically remembered Hill's description of one occasion on which Thomas had driven her home from the Department of Education. "She said she was on her way home early because the government had run out of money and they went on furlough," Williams recalled. "Thomas offered her a ride. She told me she tried to get him to loosen up, but he was uncomfortable. She invited him into her apartment and offered him wine, but he refused. They ended up talking for two hours. But she told me all he wanted to talk about was ideas, education, Reagan, his grandfather. She said she started to think 'Obviously he doesn't notice me, he doesn't let his hair down.' "[16]

Those who remain partial to Hill will undoubtedly be tempted to dismiss this account and to question Williams's motives for saying so.

However, if Hill had indeed been interested in getting to know Thomas better, this would hardly have been shocking or unusual. She was a young woman with few friends, who had little experience in dating relationships with men, and who may have been a bit taken with her boss, a man with whom she had so much in common, who was acting as her mentor, and who had saved her from the indignity of being fired at Wald, Harkrader. Hill and Thomas may have seen their relationship somewhat differently, with Hill viewing the chats over a drink in her apartment as potentially romantic or at least intimately friendly situations, while Thomas had no such intentions. The truth of this, of course, cannot be known. However, at the very least, Hill's stated wish to get Thomas to "let his hair down" with her seems to show that their early relationship held an ambiguous promise for Hill that she later omitted from her testimony.

During this period, Thomas was going through the painful process of divorcing his first wife, Kathy, and it might therefore be expected that he would manifest an interest in other women. Yet according to those who knew him well, he displayed no such interest in Hill. In fact, at the time he was dating a woman named Lillian McEwen, who worked for Senator Biden on Capitol Hill. "He was involved with her seriously during the entire time Anita worked for him," Holt said.[17] When they became aware of Hill's allegations a decade later, Thomas's friends found it implausible that he would have been asking Hill—or anyone else—for dates during this particular period. "He was very involved with someone at the time," said Harry Singleton, who knew both Thomas and Hill. "There is no way he was asking her for dates. There was no amorous interest there on his part, and I think that was part of the problem."[18]

Hill, for her part, had lamented her desultory social life for years in conversations with close friends. "She talked about how the people who she wanted to date never wanted to date her," said one of Hill's friends from Yale, a man who was in a twenty-student seminar with Hill during their first year and who maintained a friendship with her throughout the years in Washington. "She would say there must be something wrong with them, they were immature or arrogant if they didn't want to date her. She would get slightly pissed off when her interests weren't reciprocated. I believe she was engaged to someone from Oklahoma when she first came to Yale, but that was broken off. After that, and in the years in Washington, I don't think she ever had a successful dating relationship with anybody. She had a series of failed relationships."[19]

In time, Hill would indeed become angry with Thomas when he

failed to accord her the sort of attention she wanted. Though possibly not "scorned" in the romantic sense, it appears that Hill did eventually have reason to feel abandoned and even betrayed by her "mentor" at the EEOC.

After eighteen months at the Department of Education, Thomas, Hill, and Diane Holt went over to the EEOC. Many of Hill's colleagues there, including two former special assistants who testified for Thomas in the hearings, J.C. Alvarez and Phyllis Berry-Myers, seemed to dislike her intensely.

"She was very strong-willed, she liked to do things her way, and that was always the way she—that was the way she gave the impression, that she kind of had her own agenda, her own way of doing things," Alvarez testified. "So, no matter what the rest of the team was doing, she was going to do it Anita's way. . . . She was opinionated, arrogant, and a relentless debater. She was the kind of woman who always made you feel like she was not going to be messed with, like she was not going to take anything from anyone. She was aloof. She always acted as if she was superior to everyone else, holier-than-thou."

"Anita was the kind of person where if you disagreed on a point, weeks later if she was given the slightest opportunity, she would bring it up again. Then she would give you that shit-eating grin. She always had to be right," said Carlton Stewart, who briefly supervised Hill's work at the agency. Another EEOC staffer recalled Hill as "nobody's victim," certainly not a male chauvinist's. "A powerful guy from another agency came in for a meeting, and he referred to her as 'Anita.' And she shot back, 'Call me Ms. Hill!' She chilled the entire room. This was a woman who took no crap from anybody, no matter how powerful they were."[20]

Alvarez testified that she was dumbfounded by the Anita Hill who appeared before the Judiciary Committee, cloaked in the victim status conferred by her allegations of sexual harassment.

SIMPSON [quoting Alvarez's prior testimony]: "I don't know how else to say it, but it blew my mind to see Anita Hill testifying Friday. Honest to goodness, it was like schizophrenia. That was not the Anita Hill I knew and worked with at the EEOC. On Friday, she played the role of a meek, innocent shy Baptist girl from the South who was a victim of this big bad man." That is quite a powerful statement. Why did you say this reference to schizophrenia?

ALVAREZ: Because there were two different personalities. When I worked with Anita Hill and I knew her, as I said, she was not a victim. She was a very tough woman. She stood her ground. She didn't take a lot of anything from anyone, and she made sure you knew it.

And the person who was here Friday was somebody who played a totally different role. Who was "I am meek, I am shy, I am overwhelmed, I am victimized." And that was not the Anita Hill I knew. It was two different personalities.

Thomas echoed Alvarez on this point: "If you asked me to describe the Anita Hill who worked for me meek would not be the word," he said. "She was very bright. And she would argue for, particularly with the other special assistants, argue for her position and, sometimes to a fault. And by that, I simply mean she would become entrenched in her own point of view and not understand the other point of view. And she was certainly capable of storming off and going to her office, and that happened on any number of occasions."

Oddly enough, the clear dislike of Hill evinced by some of these witnesses rebounded against them, raising the suspicion in some quarters that they may have been moved to condemn her by an ugly ulterior motive. Wahneema Lubiano, for example, suggested that the witnesses had come forward to attack Hill simply in order to enhance their status with Thomas, their powerful patron. In her essay on the hearings, she excoriated "women who were supporters of a very powerful man (who will become even more powerful) [and who] came forward to do battle on behalf of the continued operation of uncritiqued power. Women like J.C. Alvarez who defined 'real' womanhood and told us what a 'real' victim of sexual harassment would do, seized the category 'woman' in order to make it impossible for other women, or at least one woman in particular, to be heard."[21]

No one who wrote about the hearings seemed to be aware that some of the witnesses—and others who came forward to defend Thomas, including Phyllis Berry-Myers—had been asked to leave Thomas's staff years ago following professional disagreements with him. They therefore had no discernible motive for backing him, especially in such a hostile public arena. (Diane Holt, for her part, had been Thomas's loyal secretary at both agencies, but had not worked for him for three years when she testified.)

But while it seems necessary to defend these witnesses against the personal and ideological attacks of Hill's partisans, it is also important to stress that these and other supporters of Thomas appear to have misjudged the real source of Hill's objectionable conduct. They seem not to have considered that the brash and overbearing demeanor that had made her so unpopular in the office might have sprung not from unwarranted egotism and pugnacious self-confidence, but rather from deep-seated insecurity, uncertainty, and a need to find and defend her place in a chaotic professional environment. In addition, many of the aides who now had Thomas's ear, such as Berry-Myers, were committed Republicans, which may have exacerbated Hill's sense of being embattled at the agency.

What Thomas, Alvarez, and others failed to see was that Hill really was a victim in a sense, though not perhaps of sexual harassment. Hill had been highly successful in high school and at Oklahoma State University; but once admitted to Yale Law School, and then to the Wald, Harkrader firm, by preferential admissions and hiring policies, her professional troubles began. The earlier reconstruction of the circumstances surrounding Hill's departure from Wald suggests that her Yale credentials may have set a standard of achievement that she was unable to meet in her first job in a major Washington law firm. Her negative experiences at Wald appear to have affected her self-image, leaving her with a permanent chip on her shoulder. Evidently she enjoyed a certain closeness with Thomas at the Department of Education; but her next job at the EEOC placed her in an environment where she was not at home politically and where her poor work habits and increasingly defensive attitude made her more and more dependent upon special consideration from Thomas in order to thrive. When she did not receive the support that she expected from him, and thus began to falter again, it visibly affected her behavior. She became easily upset, short-tempered, vulnerable, and began to employ every strategy available to her in the hope of avoiding another failure. In the end, the evidence will show, Hill left the agency, smarting from her failure to obtain a desired promotion and feeling angry and resentful of Thomas, who in her eyes had coldly rebuffed her, but unwilling to let go of her connection to an influential man who still considered himself to be her friend and patron.

More telling than what Hill's co-workers saw as her attitude of superiority and her indiscriminate need to be always "right" was the way she behaved toward her alleged victimizer. In the Senate hearings,

Hill's critics, arguing that a victim of sexual harassment would not be likely willingly to continue an association with her harasser, made a major issue of Hill's having stayed in touch with Thomas after leaving his employ.[22] But far more revealing was the way Hill behaved toward Thomas at the office *while* she was allegedly being harassed. This was probably why no one from either Education or the EEOC who saw the two working together on a daily basis testified for her, and why all of the sources who had first-hand information about their relationship believed Thomas rather than Hill. Her behavior did not seem to indicate that she was being harassed in any way; indeed, it suggested something else entirely.

Writing in the *Chronicle of Higher Education,* Billie Wright Dziech, a sexual harassment expert, noted that while Hill's case was not unusual in that most victims do not confront their harasser or ever file formal grievances, most choose to deal with the situation informally by avoiding the harasser to the extent possible. In the literature on sexual harassment, this response is known as "avoidance," and it is almost always perceptible to those nearby, who are often later called on to corroborate the sexual harassment claims. But Hill had no such witnesses, leading Dziech to voice a reluctant skepticism about her claims. "The point is that advocates for this issue cannot pick and choose their facts," Dziech wrote. "If avoidance is often part of victims' complex response to sexual harassment, and Anita Hill did not avoid Clarence Thomas, those who truly care about sexual harassment must be honest."[23]

Hill testified that by the time she went to the EEOC, she had already suffered the most horrendous episodes of sexual harassment by Thomas that she would endure and was hoping it had stopped for good. She portrayed her decision to follow Thomas to the EEOC as the lesser of two evils, a circumstance in which she felt she had no choice. Yet according to Diane Holt, Hill was "enthusiastic" about the new job and had said she was following Thomas because she wanted to work with a "rising star" in the Washington firmament.

At the new agency, however, Hill became one of several legal and administrative assistants to the chairman; she consequently had far less personal contact with Thomas at the EEOC than she had at Education.[24] Thomas explained the new arrangements in his testimony. "The relationship, as I indicated in my opening statement, Mr. Chairman, changed primarily because my job changed, and the staff went from those two professionals to maybe 10, 12, 15 professionals with a chief-of-staff, office directors of 14 individuals, and a chief-of-staff being in charge of my personal staff, as opposed to the staff having direct access. So even the special assistants could not see me on an 'as available' basis. The chief-of-staff could see me on that basis but she [Hill] could not."

If Hill's were a "typical case" of harassment, one would have reasonably expected her to manifest relief that she no longer had to work so closely with her former boss. Instead, by all accounts, Hill's new distance from Thomas severely disappointed and frustrated her. She worried that he no longer regarded her as his number one assistant and felt uncomfortable at having to compete for his attention. Thus Hill not only failed to avoid Clarence Thomas; she made strenuous efforts to maintain her old status.

In an exchange with Leahy, Hill revealed that she had not expected their relationship to change when she made the move, and implied that she had not wanted it to:

LEAHY: Now walk me through again, please what was the nature of the job that would be available to you at EEOC, how did you hear about it, what did you do to apply for it and so forth?

HILL: I did not apply for it. I heard about it from Judge Thomas. He indicated to me that I could go with him to the EEOC and I would have *the same type of position* that I had at the Department of Education.

LEAHY: And that was?

HILL: That of a special assistant who would be *working directly under him,* advising him on a number of projects and issues that came up. [Emphasis added.]

On arriving at the EEOC, however, Hill found that she would be reporting to Thomas through various supervisors and gatekeepers. She was no longer "working directly under him," as she believed she had been promised (and as she later tried to make it appear in her testimony). According to EEOC colleagues, Hill did not want to report to anyone but "Clarence," as Hill pointedly referred to him, despite Thomas's preference that everyone on his staff address him as "chairman." If Hill was being harassed, her reaction was hard to explain, unless she was so ambitious that she would place herself directly in the line of fire by tempting her harasser to renew his unwanted attention.

One strategy Hill pursued when jockeying for position with coworkers was simply to deny that any change had taken place, and to fall back on her prior connection to Thomas. This proclivity to flaunt her "special relationship" with Thomas was one evident cause of her colleagues' dislike. "She tried to give the impression that she was closer to him than she was," said Phyllis Berry-Myers.

Hatch questioned J.C. Alvarez on this same point:

HATCH: From your experience of working with Professor Hill and Judge Thomas at the EEOC, did Professor Hill think that she had some sort of a special relationship with Judge Thomas?

ALVAREZ: Yes, she used to give that impression. She used to like to tout the fact that she had worked with him before. You know, when we would get into debates on how we were going to handle the issue, she would say, 'Well, I know how he thinks, I know how he likes his papers written or I know the position he wants to take,' or something like that. That was something she always sort of held out in front of everyone on the staff, that she had this sort of inside track to him.

Alvarez told Simpson the same thing:

SIMPSON: Well, based upon the years that you have known her, all of you, and worked with Anita Hill, have any of you ever known her to exaggerate small slights that you might have seen, make a big deal out of something that didn't warrant it?

ALVAREZ: Well, the exaggeration that I saw in her probably most often was about her relationship with the chairman. You know, she knew how he thought, she had some sort of special insight into him, that sort of thing. That was the exaggeration I saw.

Even John Doggett, the Yale Law School friend of Thomas who knew Hill glancingly and whose testimony was otherwise unpersuasive, noticed this. In his Judiciary Committee affidavit, Doggett wrote, "She also made it very clear that she was very proud to know Clarence Thomas and to have worked with him. In fact, she gave me the impression that she was a more important member of his staff than was justified by my observations and conversations with Clarence Thomas."[25]

Hill's diminished stature relative to Thomas at the agency did not, however, lead her to fade into the background. In fact, it seemed to drive her in the opposite direction. Now she would do everything in her power to close the growing gap between herself and Thomas. "The demands on his time grew, and she [Hill] wanted a bigger piece of the pie," said Janet Dorsey, another former EEOC official. "She didn't adjust very well to the new situation. I always thought of it as if she was one of his children, the baby, who demanded a lot of attention. As she saw it, her time with him was more important than others'."[26] (Hill was, in fact, the youngest of 13 children in her family.)

Former EEOC official Andrew Fishel, a civil servant who, unlike the special assistants in the agency, did not owe his job to Thomas, took an interest in Hill's career because he had known her at the Education Department when he was a personnel administrator there. At the EEOC, Fishel said, "Hill made a habit when we were waiting for a meeting to start of making sure she got a seat directly next to Clarence Thomas. She certainly never tried to physically distance herself from him." Fishel said Hill also "insisted on meeting with Thomas in cases where it didn't warrant it."[27]

Hill's experience with Thomas was not unique. Everyone else at the EEOC was distanced from him by the bureaucratic layers that intervened between the chairman and his staff. "For the first month or two, people went in and plopped down in the chairman's office," said Carlton Stewart, who acted as an unofficial staff chief for Thomas in his early months at the agency. "We soon regulated it for everybody. The rule was that Diane [Holt] would put you on a list. You had to say why you needed the appointment. She [Hill] needed Diane's approval to see him for some matters, and mine for others. Anita would try various ruses to get around that. Whenever I went anywhere, to the hill, or out to lunch, she would try to get in. When Diane left to run an errand or something, the same thing would happen.

"You can tell when somebody really wants to be in somebody's presence," Stewart continued. "She would say she had something really important to talk to Clarence about. The chairman would invite me to the meeting, too. Well, whatever it was could always have been resolved in five minutes on her own if she had thought about it. She'd spend the meeting sitting there smiling, and batting her eyes, and talking about the good old days at Education. I thought it was a girlish crush. She always wanted to be in the vicinity of where he was. Diane and I used to joke about it," he added—a memory that Holt confirmed.

Phyllis Berry-Myers also believed from her observations at the time that Hill may have been sweet on the chairman. "She talked about him in such glowing terms, and she always wanted to be where he was," she said. "I thought it was a crush, that she wanted to date him."[28] Barbara Lawrence, who had worked for Senator Biden before joining

Thomas's staff, said: "Women sense this more than men do. I think she liked him. There are different kinds of like and I think hers went beyond the way the rest of us liked him. She thought she was hot stuff. And she liked his attention."[29]

Hill's evident interest in Thomas was not confined to the office; one friend believed she was unusually curious about Thomas's social life as well. This co-worker of Hill's lived in the same apartment complex as Thomas, and the woman happened to become friendly with both Hill and Thomas. "Anita started asking me a lot of questions about Clarence. What did Clarence do last night? What's Clarence doing this weekend? That's all she would talk about. It was obsessive. I started to think she was using me to get information about him, it made me very uncomfortable. I gradually had to end our friendship over it. It was the only way I could get her to stop."

The conclusion drawn by Berry-Myers and others that such comments and behavior must have been the signs of a romantic crush, however, seems an overly simplistic view of Hill, and must be especially suspect as an *ex post facto* explanation for her harassment charge. Most of Hill's colleagues were unaware of the adverse circumstances that had led to her being employed by Thomas in the first place. They therefore would have failed to appreciate the special sense of dependency Hill may have felt regarding Thomas, and thus misjudged how hard she would fight to preserve her close relationship with him. A more complete understanding of Hill's position and background might indicate, instead, that her behavior was nothing more than a strategy to ingratiate herself with Thomas. Even her earlier effort at Education to get to know him outside the office, and to encourage him to "let his hair down," may have been a way of more securely hitching herself to Thomas's "rising star" after a brush with professional disaster at Wald. That unsettling experience would most likely have intensified Hill's need for his approval and attention in her next job.

Whatever Hill's reasons may have been for her evident desire to get closer to Thomas, however, the relevant point is that she was thwarted on *two* counts once they moved to the EEOC: The fact that the chairman was less accessible in the office was only compounded by the fact that he was no longer available after hours as he had been at Education. The times that Thomas drove Hill home from the office, was invited in for a drink, and was asked to help fix her stereo occurred while the two were at the Department of Education and lived near to one another. All such social contact stopped during the

EEOC years, when the busy chairman was driven home in a government car and had less time for social activities.

Hill testified that Thomas began harassing her again once they arrived at the EEOC, and she ascribed her increasing unhappiness, fears of dismissal, and eventual decision to leave the agency in 1983 to this unwelcome and abusive behavior. But according to her former colleagues, from almost the moment she arrived at the EEOC Hill was unhappy that she had become only one of a dozen special assistants. Now that unhappiness would deepen as she encountered difficulties in meeting the demands of her new job, while Thomas, taking note of her disappointing performance, which he apparently ascribed to inexperience, downgraded her role on the staff. This phase of their relationship is crucial to understanding how their views of what occurred at the EEOC could have diverged to the point where they became irreconcilable, and yet could be presented at the hearings with equal conviction. While Thomas seemed to see the change in their relationship as stemming from Hill's limitations as a lawyer, Hill apparently believed that she was being pushed aside by Thomas as he grew more and more conservative, abandoning his roots and thereby, it seems possible to think, transforming Hill herself into a symbol of his earlier, authentic self which he had now rejected.

Harry Singleton spoke often with Thomas throughout this period, and the two occasionally discussed how Hill was faring at the EEOC. According to Singleton, Thomas and Hill had not worked together long enough for him to have fully assessed her performance. "They barely had time to turn on the lights at Education," he explained. "There is a learning curve in any new job for six months or so, and during that time he was high on her and her abilities."[30] From what Thomas told him, Singleton concluded that Hill was out of her depth at the EEOC, and growing increasingly irritable.

> Things seemed fine at Education. But at the EEOC it was a different game entirely, dealing with Title VII. It was an entirely new body of law, different case law that she had not had at Education. It was employment discrimination law, not just civil rights in the schools.
>
> Anita was his attorney adviser at Education. And he went over to EEOC, and the case load for her was six times what it was. There were new precedents, new regulations to learn. Well, he got up to speed, and she couldn't help him anymore. She had problems mastering the law. He had to rely on other experts, and she did not adjust to that

well. That began to have an effect on her. She wasn't happy, and didn't get along with other people in the office.

Andrew Fishel had a similar impression of Hill's problems, drawn from conversations with her in which she indicated she was both overwhelmed by the volume of work confronting her, and at the same time disappointed with a position that she saw as less important than the one that she had held at Education. Hill's idealized expectations had not been met in the transfer to the EEOC. What was happening?, Hill must have wondered. She had had a rewarding relationship with Thomas at Education, she had worked for him longer than anyone, she understood him best. Why didn't he recognize this any longer?

"Thomas always looked for women and minorities to give opportunities that they would not ordinarily get," Fishel said. "At Education, she was young and inexperienced but it wasn't so much of a problem. At the EEOC, she lacked the kind of background you would normally have, and that the other lawyers on the staff had. The position itself also seemed less important to her. What a legal adviser at EEOC would do wasn't so important for policy as her position at Education was. At the same time, the job was too challenging. There was a lot of pressure. She did not work well under pressure." Fishel recalled that Hill's in-box would "get higher and higher and her temper would get shorter and shorter, she would snap and say 'Look at all this work I have to do,' and 'I'm too busy.' She was also upset that she wasn't doing well in terms of jockeying for good assignments."

In fact, according to Berry-Myers, in her first several months at the EEOC Hill had a relatively important assignment in the chairman's office which she lost in late 1982, in a move that appeared as a demotion. One of Hill's initial responsibilities was to be the liaison on key legislative matters between the chairman and the director of the Office of Congressional Affairs, EEOC veteran Chris Roggerson. When Roggerson was moved out of that post and replaced by Berry-Myers, who had a close working relationship with Thomas, Hill's liaison's duties were eliminated.

"At that point, I think she became confused about her role," Berry-Myers said. "It was a very confusing situation. Remember that we had inherited an agency in disarray. And in those first several months we were constantly changing jobs, lines of authority, responsibilities. Things were in flux constantly. And I think she could never find her niche and so she kind of got left behind. At the same time she saw people who had come into the agency with her as special assistants who were doing very well, getting promoted and finding out what they were good at doing. And, you know, a lot of these people, like myself, hadn't come from Yale."

It was at this time, in the fall of 1982, that Ellen Wells would later testify that Hill had complained to her of "inappropriate conduct and comments" from Thomas; since Wells could not recall a single detail from this conversation that could have led her to conclude that these comments were sexual in nature, Hill could well have been referring, however obliquely, to her demotion, not to sexual harassment. It is also possible that she was referring to harassment by Chris Roggerson, rather than Thomas.

Thomas himself testified that Hill had been relegated to tasks that were considered "grunt work" because she was not as able as her colleagues.

> BIDEN: When you saw her though, was it essentially the same professional woman in terms of her professional attitude? Did she seem more confident, less calm? Was there any difference in the Anita Hill, not necessarily in terms of access, but the professional lawyer, Anita Hill who worked for Clarence Thomas? Was there any, was she the same woman in terms of when you were with her?
>
> THOMAS: Senator, I can't—all I can say is this, that I can't tell you that there was a specific change. What I can say is that she was having more of a difficulty, I thought, from my perspective, she was having more difficulty in the role at EEOC because there were so many more staffers. And there were so many different levels of communications. For example, on—or responsibilities—for example, I would rely on individuals with more experience to work on projects that were of great significance to me. There were routine assignments that would be, what I would call grunt work, much more than we had at Education. There was sort of a pecking order and I don't think that she, in that role, at EEOC was very high on the pecking order because of experience.

In the opinion of other EEOC officials, Hill fell farther in the pecking order not because she was sexually harassed by her boss, but due to a perceived compulsive ambition, coupled with an attitude of entitlement. In their view, Hill wanted status conferred on her without having to earn it. "Did I see ambition? Yes. Did I see energy and drive? No," said Janet Dorsey. "She cut corners to get ahead. If she could cut a corner, she would."[31]

"Later on, Hill's work wasn't good enough," said Barbara Lawrence. "She spent less time on her stuff than any of us did. My clearest recollection is of her sitting on a couch outside [Thomas's] office, very nicely dressed, flipping through magazines."[32]

Stewart, who, with Roggerson, had some supervisory authority over Hill during her early months at the EEOC when he was acting as chief of staff, echoed this assessment. He said that Hill had essentially wanted a nine-to-five job but still thought she could be his top aide. "She tried to avoid those things that were anything more than rote," Stewart recalled. "The most important thing we did was prepare the chairman's agenda for the Tuesday morning commission meetings, helping to decide what position he would take on various things that came before the commission. Assignments would be given out the prior Thursday, and he liked to have everything in hand by Monday noon so that he could study the material, make up his mind on various things, ask questions or for more information. She didn't want to do it because it meant three days of very hard work, and maybe the weekend. You couldn't just look up two or three cases. You had to find out and coordinate with the positions of various other agencies. For example, on the Age Act, you had to talk to the IRS, the Social Security Administration, OMB [the Office of Management and Budget]. I think she could have done it, but she simply thought it was too involved."

But Hill's colleagues may have judged her too harshly in this respect. What they interpreted as laziness and an irritating sense of entitlement, based on her prior closeness to Thomas and on her Ivy League credentials, was more likely a basic inability on Hill's part to do the challenging legal work that this fast-paced position required. Thomas, meanwhile, did not relax his demanding standards on Hill's account, a fact that was gradually, and ominously, settling on her. In short, Thomas seems to have brought Hill into a much more difficult professional environment at the EEOC without taking any special measures to help her adjust—proof that his egalitarian, merit-based approach to professional performance could be harsh. "She was not getting her stuff done in a timely way. She was not analyzing an issue, just responding to it. I spoke to her about her poor performance," Stewart said. "When I complained about her to Thomas, he said, 'If Anita's not doing her work, you know what to do.'"

Hill's testimony sought to suggest that her concern about her future at the agency was due to her fear of retribution by Thomas for spurning his advances. Hill testified that she was concerned that

"Judge Thomas might take it out on me by down-grading me, or by not giving me important assignments. I also thought that he might find an excuse for dismissing me." A fairly generic statement in a sexual harassment case, this explanation omits the entire context of Hill's experience at the EEOC. Did Hill really fear retaliation by Thomas, as she testified? Or did she fear downgraded assignments and dismissal because she was not performing well and could not find her niche?

In her testimony, Hill did not acknowledge her diminishing status at the EEOC. But she did allude, perhaps unintentionally, to her performance problems there and to the reasonable fears that they engendered. Hill testified that after refusing to submit to Thomas's alleged sexual demands, she had made a careful record of her work performance in order to protect herself from possible retaliation. But if Hill had taken the trouble to protect herself in this manner, why did she not also record his sexual comments and document his other obnoxious behavior? Arlen Specter inadvertently exposed the real source of Hill's problems at the EEOC when he asked her about the matter:

HILL: One of the things that I did do at that time was to document my work. I went through very meticulously with every assignment that I was given. This was, this really was in response to the concerns that I had about being fired. I went through, I logged in every work assignment that I received, the action that was requested, the action that I took on it, the date that it went out, so I did do that in order to protect myself, but I did not write down any of the comments or conversations.

SPECTER: Well, when you comment about documenting your work to protect yourself because of concern of being fired, wouldn't the same precise thought about documentation have led you to document Judge Thomas's statements to you?

HILL: Well, I was documenting my work so that I could show to a new employer that I had in fact done these things. I was not documenting my work so that I could defend myself or to present a claim against him.

SPECTER: Well, why would you need to document with precision the time the assignment came in and the time you completed the work for a new employer? Wouldn't that kind of documentation *really relate to the adequacy and speed of your work* at EEOC, contrasted with a finished product which you could show to a new prospective employer?

HILL: I'm sorry. I don't quite understand your question. Are you saying that the new employer would not be interested in knowing whether or not I turned my work around quickly?

SPECTER: What is the relevancy as to when you got the assignment and how fast you made it, for a new employer?

HILL: Because it goes to whether or not I was slow in turning around the work product in a very fast-paced job situation. [Emphasis added.]

Specter pursued the same point in a later question to Thomas, who indicated that Hill's behavior was more consistent with that of an employee who was worried that the quality of their work might be challenged, as opposed to someone who might be expecting to defend themselves against retaliation from a boss for resisting sexual overtures.

SPECTER: My question to you is this, Judge Thomas: Where she says she is concerned about being fired and she says that she is taking precautions and writes down the details of work assignments, if she is looking for retaliation from you, is it credible that, statements having been made, that she would not make a written note of those statements in the context where she writes down notes on all of these other matters?

THOMAS: Senator, it does not seem credible to me, but I think there is a further point. Often times, when individuals are concerned about their ratings, they will document their work product, the quality of their work product or copies of their work product and the speed with which they turn around the work product, so that they can then argue during the rating period that they should receive a higher rating. That is not unusual, particularly if there have been some complaints that the work was not being done in a timely fashion.

The complaints voiced about Hill at the EEOC—poor analytical and writing skills, an inability to respond quickly to assignments— were of the same kind that had led to her abrupt exit from the Wald, Harkrader law firm in 1981. Hill's unpleasant experience at Wald must have compounded her fears and insecurities when the same problems cropped up again at the EEOC. Though she was bright and

articulate, leading her EEOC colleagues to attribute her poor performance to a bad attitude on her part, Hill was in fact not a very
good lawyer, a handicap she bore throughout her career, as further
evidence will show; nor was she a particularly adept bureaucratic in-
fighter. Ironically, she appeared to be far less assertive and ambitious
than either J.C. Alvarez or Phyllis Berry-Myers.

To make matters worse, Thomas's usual pattern in dealing with employees who did not meet his standards would certainly have heightened Hill's discomfort. While initially enthusiastic about Hill during
their days at Education, Thomas apparently came to conclude that she
was not the "rising star" he had hoped she would be. While he was
eager to give people from all walks of life the chance to succeed by
bringing them onto his staff and mentoring them, he was also a demanding and very formal boss; he would take affirmative action only
so far. When people disappointed him, he could be distant and insensitive, leaving bruised feelings and a sense of abandonment in his wake.

In their eagerness to portray him in the best possible light,
Thomas's supporters did not seem to allow for the possibility that his
sometimes brusque and formalistic manner, combined with his demanding expectations, might have produced in Hill feelings of rejection and worthlessness. Moreover, the image promoted of Hill by
Stewart and other supervisors—as someone who was not applying her
talents and yet expected to get special consideration and attention—
was just the sort of entitlement mentality that Thomas scorned. As
one EEOC staffer explained, describing Thomas's flaws as a manager,
"Thomas had a way of turning you off if he was disappointed in your
abilities. He often didn't confront you directly, but he would subtly
let you know that you were not up to his standards and he would go
on to others who did. You were dropped and treated like you no
longer mattered."[33]

Thus there probably *was* some basis in Thomas's conduct toward
Hill that sowed the seeds of her decision to leave the agency feeling
as though Thomas had severed and betrayed their bond. Moreover,
Hill's emerging view of this "rejection" as evidence of Thomas's moral
and political corruption would eventually bear fruit in her recep-
tiveness to suggestions from her friends Susan Hoerchner and James
Brudney that she ought to do something to stop his Supreme Court
nomination.

Though Thomas may well have "dropped" Hill and treated her as
though she "no longer mattered," Hill's abrupt and emotional deci-

sion to leave the EEOC came only after an unambiguous and hurtful signal from her erstwhile patron. Hill's effort to deny that her star had fallen, and her view of her relationship with Thomas as a special one, were exposed in one humiliating moment as fanciful, not only to her colleagues, but—more devastatingly, perhaps—to Hill herself.

Throughout 1982 and into early 1983, Hill had dealings with two people in supervisory and administrative positions in the chairman's office: Carlton Stewart, and then Chris Roggerson, who was moved out of Congressional Affairs and made Thomas's executive assistant in late 1982. Hill never mentioned her dealings with Roggerson (nor for that matter with Stewart) in her Senate testimony, creating the false impression that she reported to no one but Thomas at the agency. If the committee had known that Hill had supervisors other than Thomas, one of whom was said to be a sexual harasser, the testimony of her corroborating witnesses that she had complained about harassment from an unnamed "supervisor" at the EEOC would have been seriously undermined.[34]

In early 1983, Thomas decided to appoint a chief legal adviser to supervise the work of the lawyers on his staff. This meant that Hill would have yet another new boss to contend with and through whom she would formally report to the chairman. The fluid arrangements that had prevailed under Stewart and Roggerson would thus become rigid, and she would lose any direct access to Thomas. She would also for the first time have a boss other than Thomas who would be officially evaluating her performance—unless, of course, she got the job herself.

According to her co-workers, Hill did set her sights on getting this job, apparently hoping at last to find her niche at the agency and regain her status with Thomas. She also may have hoped to reverse his conservative drift. "She never fully gave up the idea that she was his favored protégé," said Armstrong Williams, "until she didn't get the job she wanted."

Hill lost out to another young woman named Allyson Duncan, a well-respected career lawyer brought to the chairman's staff from the office of legal counsel. A graduate of Duke Law School, and the daughter of upper-middle-class educators, Duncan was everything that Hill was not: sophisticated, a light-skinned black woman, the object of fawning male attention in the office, and a highly competent attorney as well.[35] "Allyson worked hard at it, and she deserved the job," said Barbara Lawrence. Hill, by contrast, never overcame the perception among her peers that she was essentially "a hayseed from

Oklahoma," as Singleton unkindly put it. This promotion of a member of the black "elite" may have made it all the harder to accept, confirming the suspicion in her mind that Thomas was betraying the authentic racial outlook they had shared at Education.

After former EEOC staffers issued statements to the committee saying that Hill had left the agency embittered after failing to get the promotion, Howell Heflin asked Hill about the episode. Hill denied that she had specifically applied for the job, but she did not categorically disavow her interest in it.

HEFLIN: Now, was there an occasion when you were at the EEOC that you wanted a different job or a promotion or a higher job?

HILL: I never sought a promotion with Clarence Thomas while at the EEOC. I never sought a promotion with anyone while at the EEOC.

However, two of her co-workers later painted a picture of Hill as having actively campaigned for the job.

HATCH: Now let me just ask this last question. There has been some indication that part of the problem here was she was ambitious and desired a position in the department, and if I have it correctly, Allyson Duncan was promoted above her. Am I correct? . . .

ALVAREZ: It was common knowledge. I can't recall exactly who said what, but there were several times that people made reference to [Hill] wanting the job . . .

BERRY: She didn't indicate to me specifically, but I heard from other members from the Commission, throughout the Commission, that yes, she [Hill] desired that position.

Specter also asked Thomas about the matter:

SPECTER: Did Professor Hill not get a position that she was working for within your staff?

THOMAS: Again, I can't remember the exact details of it but I think she wanted to have that position, the executive assistant position. But that's again, Senator, that is speculation as to what the motivation would be, and I hesitate to even mention it.

In January 1983, when Armstrong Williams joined the Thomas staff, Hill apparently tried to enlist him in her effort to win the position. New to the staff, Williams was presumably the only interlocutor to whom Hill could turn, since by this time Thomas's other aides had either formed a negative impression of her work or had concluded they did not care for her personally (or in most cases, both). Hill's effort was indirect, not the sort of arrogant and pushy display that would have seemed in character for the woman described by some of her colleagues. It mainly took the form of a campaign of flattery evidently intended to reach Thomas's ears and thus win back his favor more subtly.

According to her testimony, in early 1983 Hill had suffered renewed harassment by Thomas for more than six months. Yet at this time she was telling Williams how much she admired Thomas and what a bright future she thought he had ahead of him. More than once in early 1983, Hill complained to Williams that Thomas—her alleged victimizer—"didn't even notice me," Williams said. Since Williams traveled with the chairman, Hill often asked him whether Thomas had said anything about her. If he had, Williams said, "she would be elated. She would even suggest to me statements that I could make in her favor to Thomas when I was with him. She wanted him to know that she was on his team."

In the irony of ironies, Hill told Williams that "it was great to be working for Thomas, because he was fair, he had so much integrity, he hired women, he was the ideal boss." Assuming Williams's memory is accurate, if this statement did not constitute evidence that Hill had not been harassed by Thomas, then it represents an amazing capacity on her part to swallow her indignities and baldly lie for personal advantage. To underscore her point, Hill confided to Williams that she knew what it was like to work around men who had less integrity and respect for women than Thomas did. "She then told me how she was sexually harassed at Education, and that she had dealt with it," said Williams, who, given the context of the discussion, never for a moment thought that Hill could have been referring to Thomas. His recollection is yet more evidence that Hill had complained casually and vaguely of "sexual harassment" several times in the early 1980s, in situations that did not appear to implicate Thomas.

Given her difficulties in fulfilling the demands of her current position, Hill had no reasonable chance to get this job, nor was she ever seriously considered for it, according to Williams. But she pressed ahead regardless, evidently suppressing or denying her own shortcomings. While most of her colleagues saw Hill's desire as a manifestation of unseemly ambition, the more likely interpretation was that Hill saw the job as a chance to set herself on firmer footing at the

EEOC and renew the close relationship she had had with Thomas at Education.

According to Williams, Thomas had a conversation with Hill sometime in February 1983 in which he told her, in so many words, that any hopes she had of getting the legal adviser's job were misplaced. "I walked right into this situation," Williams recalled. "It was becoming clear to her that she was not going to get the job in February. Then Thomas told her that she was not going to get it. He told her that she was just too young and inexperienced to expect that. She would have to put in several years before she could ever be considered for such a position. He blew her off."

There is no way to know exactly what Thomas said to Hill in this conversation, or the tone he used in saying it. But if Williams's description was accurate, this rather blunt and, one would have to add, unfeeling way of telling her would certainly have had a major impact. Clearly, Hill reacted strongly to the news. She may even have been emotionally traumatized. Hill testified that in February she was hospitalized for acute stomach pain, an ailment that her doctors could diagnose only as "stress." Though in her testimony she attributed this stress to Thomas's harassment, she also seemed to link it with the Duncan promotion. "Though the cause of the pain was not determined by my physicians, I am convinced that the illness was in reaction to the stress I felt at work. Once out of the hospital, I became committed to finding other employment and further to minimize my contact with Thomas. This became easier when Allyson Duncan was assigned as office director." Since the hospitalization occurred in precisely the same month that she learned about Duncan's promotion, Hill's "stress" may well have been due to her severe disillusionment over this turn of events (perhaps compounded by harassment from Chris Roggerson, who had recently become Thomas's executive assistant).

In any case, Duncan's promotion was by all accounts a turning point for Hill. She must certainly have felt publicly embarrassed and betrayed by Thomas's decision. She may also have feared not only that she would never find a niche at the agency, but that Duncan would now be in a position to evaluate her work and even fire her. She may therefore have concluded that the time had come to seek employment elsewhere. Clearly, her attitude underwent an abrupt shift at this time, culminating in her decision to depart from the agency only two months later. "When Allyson got it, all of a sudden Anita refused to attend meetings," Holt said. "She would say things like, 'I'm as smart as her' and 'If you've got her, why do you need me?' She didn't want to take Allyson's direction. It was very childish behavior. Her [Hill's] papers went in to Allyson, and she would be told by Allyson, 'This is totally useless.' Anita didn't like it."

"She pouted and withdrew once Duncan got the job," Phyllis Berry-Myers remembered.

In a letter to Senator Strom Thurmond at the time of the Thomas–Hill hearings, Williams stated an even stronger recollection:

> I found her [Hill] to be untrustworthy, selfish, and extremely bitter following a colleague's appointment to head Office of Legal Counsel at EEOC. . . . After she was passed over for promotion, she was adamant in her desire to leave the agency and discussed this with me privately.[36]

"She did not want to work with Allyson because Allyson was tough," Williams continued. Moreover, according to Williams, Hill's attitude toward Thomas "turned bitter overnight." Williams was so concerned about Hill's reaction that he went to Thomas and warned him that Hill was now his "enemy" and "emotionally unstable," though Thomas seemed not to believe it. This was a point that Specter began to draw out in Thomas's testimony, though he stopped short of getting the all-important details.

> SPECTER: And finally, you mentioned that there had not been any detailing given to the comment about an associate of yours who classified Professor Hill as your enemy which you had disregarded because of your view of the generalized loyalty of your staff. Can you amplify what happened in that regard?
>
> THOMAS: Well, there were some members of my—at least one member of my staff who felt that she did not have my best interests at heart and he would continue to, as I remember it, articulate that point of view, and I would, again, dismiss it.
>
> SPECTER: Well, did he tell you why he felt that way?
>
> THOMAS: It must have been based on specific things at that time. I can't recollect the bases of his conclusion nor his statements, but he would say it repeatedly when he saw evidence of it.

In conversations with Williams, Hill began to invoke a self-serving interpretation of these events, portraying her perceived rejection as a political decision rather than simply a desire by Thomas to rely on the best talent available to him. The choice was evidently not political, since Hill had no realistic prospects of getting the job, and Allyson Duncan was not a conservative in any event.

Repeating the Wald pattern, Hill's need to salvage her self-esteem led her to blame a professional reversal on something other than her own inadequate capabilities. At Wald, the problem had been "sexual harassment," as she told Susan Hoerchner at the time, and as both Clarence Thomas and Diane Holt were later told as well. Within the EEOC, where no one who knew both Thomas and Hill would have believed that she was being sexually harassed by Thomas, Hill's rationalization was an appeal to "political differences."

Politics was an obvious and fitting choice, because Hill and Thomas had openly disagreed on matters ranging from affirmative action to busing to comparable worth throughout their time working together. In fact, at the time of the Duncan promotion, Hill had been recently assigned to write a brief on comparable worth which touched off a round of heated arguments with Thomas. In a letter of recommendation Thomas wrote for Hill as she prepared to leave the agency, he alluded to these differences: "While we have disagreed on the positions to be taken in particular matters . . . we are able to resolve the disagreements professionally." While her colleagues may have seen these disputes as signs of her obtuseness and arrogance, a deeper understanding would suggest that Hill was really working hard to win Thomas back to a more liberal position on various issues, though she had already come to believe that her prospects for success were diminishing. Not until she was passed over for promotion, however, did her long-standing political disagreements with Thomas finally seem serious enough to warrant leaving the chairman's staff.

"Anita was one of the most liberal people I've ever met. She always said she hated Ronald Reagan, she always disagreed with Thomas on everything, but now, she was acting on it," Williams recalled. "All of a sudden, she would argue harshly with Thomas over policy, over anything, affirmative action, voting rights. She would storm around, banging things. I finally asked him, 'How can you have such a liberal here?' " Williams recalled. Hill told Williams that Thomas had "turned against his own people" because of his views on affirmative action, she characterized Thomas as a "dangerous thinker" and said his views were "warped and frightening."

"Over time she thought he had grown more conservative and it wasn't good for blacks or women," Williams said. "She thought her influence diluted until it evaporated. She told me he was a dangerous thinker, and told me I had to talk to him. 'I've been with him since Education and I should know,' she told me. She said she had no future with him. She felt he had become set in his views, and her ability to influence him had declined to the point where she might as well leave," Williams said, adding, "She had lost some kind of struggle."

In the two years Hill worked for him, Thomas did in fact become more conservative. As viewed by his critics, this development resulted not from a careful critique of liberal positions and policies, but from a cynical ambition to gain power in Washington. Manning Marable expressed this view in *Race-ing Justice*, adding hypocrisy, opportunism, and treachery to the indictment:

> Clarence Thomas's climb to power is directly related to his abandon-
> ment of the principles of the black-freedom struggle. A quarter cen-
> tury ago, as a college student in the late 1960s, Thomas proclaimed
> himself a devoted disciple of Malcolm X. Thomas wore the black beret
> of the Black Panther Party and signed his letters "Power to the Peo-
> ple." . . . Yet less than a decade later Thomas would condemn affir-
> mative action as being destructive to blacks' interests. When initially
> appointed head of the Equal Employment Opportunity Commission,
> Thomas embraced for a time the use of numerical hiring goals and
> timetables as a means to increase the employment of blacks. Yet fol-
> lowing Reagan's landslide electoral victory of 1984, he reversed him-
> self and strongly attacked goals and timetables . . . during these years
> Thomas attempted to "transcend" his blackness and condemned those
> who argued that his race necessarily imposed an obligation to conform
> to certain progressive political attitudes or policies.[37]

The evolution of Thomas's conservatism is crucial to understanding Hill's motives in coming forward ten years later to testify against
him. Thus it should be recalled that when Thomas assumed the chairmanship of the EEOC, he was in his early thirties; his intellectual and
political moorings would not be firmly fixed for another decade. Confronting many issues of civil rights policy for the first time, in his early
days at the EEOC he tried to forge a middle ground between the positions of the Justice Department and those of the civil rights establishment. Thus while his objections to the idea of affirmative action
had been brewing for some time, his actions as a policy-maker were
more often affected by the shifting positions of both the Reagan Administration and the federal courts. In one case, Thomas would support an affirmative action plan, perhaps because it was already in
place; in another case he would oppose one. Nor did his opposition
to quotas prevent him from applying them as a remedy in cases where
a company had a proven record of discrimination.

The subsequent development of Thomas's views at the EEOC was
more uniformly conservative. This is partly due to the fact that his re-

sponsibilities increasingly involved him less with existing or inherited plans and policies and more with developing new approaches to law enforcement. The conservative direction of the Reagan-appointed judiciary no doubt facilitated this as well.

Years before the view of Thomas as a traitor to the cause of civil rights and a racially alienated, self-hating black became current among his enemies, Anita Hill had privately developed the same view. Working with him closely in his early phase at the EEOC, she may have viewed his prudent flexibility as a sign of a wavering character. This would have allowed Hill to see herself as waging an important struggle, fighting to persuade him to adopt positions that would advance the civil rights cause. She blamed their failed relationship on Thomas's growing conservatism, thus rationalizing her diminishing role in his professional life. As the episode with Duncan eventually made clear, she could not hold her own against the other, more able staff members (many of whom were also more conservative) in competing for assignments or for influence with Thomas. But Hill could not see it that way.

By early 1983, Hill seemed to have elevated the "struggle" with Duncan for the chief legal adviser's job into a moral struggle for Thomas's conscience or soul. When she lost, her view of Thomas changed irrevocably. The "good" Thomas who had relied upon her for advice and was open to liberal views was no more; the "bad" Thomas who had allowed his "true philosophy" to be corrupted by ambition and who shunted her aside—thereby severing his link with his black roots—emerged triumphant.

Hill's newly negative view of Thomas was not confined to the political realm. Just a few weeks before Duncan's promotion Hill had told Williams of her frustrated attempts to draw Thomas into social conversation at her home, and to get him to "let down his hair"; she now expressed a different view of Thomas. Apparently unaware that Thomas was dating Lillian McEwen, Hill told Williams she could "see why he isn't dating anyone. He would make a great father and all that, but he's boring. There's nothing exciting about him." Hill's comment that Thomas was "boring"—and would make a "great father"—occurred long after he supposedly regaled her with vivid tales of his own sexual exploits and descriptions of scenes from pornographic movies.[38] Rather than suppose that Hill was lying to Williams at this point, for no apparent reason, it is easier to see these comments as another way for Hill to distance herself from Thomas and prepare to break their bond.

Hill's pained reaction to Duncan's ascension injects a poignant note into the story, because Thomas had not actually rejected her. His actions toward Hill in both the professional and personal spheres—though they may well have been neglectful and insensitive—could constitute rejection only if measured by Anita Hill's exaggerated hopes. That Hill perceived Duncan's promotion as a personal rejection would be consistent with her general defensiveness and lack of real self-confidence. But Thomas did not view Hill as a failure, merely a disappointment. In fact, he continued to see her as a very bright and promising young woman, which she manifestly was. When Thomas recommended her for her next job, or when he gave her professional advice in subsequent years, he remained in his role as a mentor, even if Hill did not see it that way.

Hill testified that she left the EEOC because she could no longer tolerate Thomas's harassment. But the timing of her decision, following as it did only a few weeks after her blunt conversation with Thomas, suggests that disappointment at being passed over, combined with fear of a future in which Thomas might no longer protect her and frustration over her inability to find a secure role at the EEOC, were the real factors weighing on Hill's mind.

In April 1983 Thomas asked Hill if she would like to accompany him to a civil rights seminar at the law school at Oral Roberts University in Tulsa, a highly religious institution founded and run by conservative evangelist Oral Roberts. Thomas thought the trip might be a way for Hill to combine business with a visit to her family, most of whom lived in the Tulsa area. Hill accepted the invitation from her alleged harasser, and accompanied him unchaperoned.

During a chat over lunch, the dean of the law school, a vigorous white-haired man named Charles Kothe, who also testified in the Thomas hearings, asked Hill if she would be interested in coming to ORU to teach. Kothe made the approach because he thought the presence of a black female might help burnish the school's image in its accreditation battles with the American Bar Association. The law school had opened in 1980 under the 72-year-old Kothe's direction, but did not win accreditation until 1981, after suing the ABA. ORU claimed that it was being denied accreditation because of the school's religious bent. "To have a Yale graduate, a woman, a black, on my faculty at the time we were being accused of lack of diversity was something," said Kothe. "We were the first law school in the Southwest to have a black woman on the faculty."

Hill expressed interest in the offer. Kothe then consulted with

Thomas, who, perhaps thinking that the more relaxed pace of academia would better suit her talents, said that Hill would make a fine teacher. In June, a firm offer was extended to Hill, which she accepted.

As she prepared to leave Washington, Hill never told anyone at the EEOC that she had been sexually harassed. Though Hill's stated reason for going was political, most of her co-workers believed that she was leaving because she did not want to work for Duncan, was generally unhappy with the "grunt" work she had been compelled to do, could not compete with them on an equal footing and, not least, wished to escape their patent hostility towards her. "I remember on her last day, nobody had mentioned to me a going away party, which is what usually happened," said Holt. "So I asked her about it, and she snapped, 'I don't care. They don't like me, and I don't like them.' " Holt took Hill to see a Cicely Tyson matinee at the Kennedy Center, the two had drinks, and Hill left for Oklahoma the following week.[39]

Many of Hill's friends outside the agency would later believe her accusation when they heard it in 1991 because they had taken note of her disenchantment with Thomas and the EEOC in the spring of 1983. In his interview with Senate lawyers, Hill's friend Gary Liman Phillips recalled, "I just remember—I'm one of those people where if a friend of mine is unhappy and I'm around I almost like feel guilty, and I feel a little bit helpless. I couldn't like—I didn't know why Anita was unhappy . . . sometimes I would ask her, you know, what's going on or she would just sort of not seem happy, and she was very ambiguous about why . . . the only thing I would say is Anita—Anita's enthusiasm for the job and for Judge Thomas seemed to diminish, and she was never specific about it." Mark DelBianco, another friend of Hill's from Yale who was an attorney in Washington, told *Newsday,* "Let's just say that when this issue broke, I wasn't completely surprised. It's been clear to me for years that something happened."[40]

But Phillips and DelBianco can have had no idea of the real circumstances behind this state of affairs. They had likely been impressed when Hill became Thomas's top assistant at Education, and she may not have told them of her troubles at the EEOC, any more than she could bring herself to tell Susan Hoerchner, or anyone else, why she had really left Wald, Harkrader. Of course, compounding Hill's unhappiness at the EEOC, there could well have been sexual overtures from the unnamed "supervisor" referred to in her tearful conversation in early 1983 with John Carr.

Aside from Williams's warnings, which he did not take seriously (to his detriment afterwards), Thomas had no idea of Hill's feelings as she prepared to leave. This is undoubtedly why years later, Thomas was unable to suggest a plausible motive for Hill in coming forward to oppose him. Apparently, Hill's pride did not allow her to let her patron know that he had wounded her and let her down. According to Thomas's phone log, Hill's roommate Sonia Jarvis called him on July 20, two days before Hill's last day at the agency. Jarvis evidently did not know that anything was amiss in Hill's relations with Thomas, either.[41] "Called to invite you to a party for Anita Saturday eve," the log said.

Given that judicial nominations have become so politicized in recent times, it is hard to understand the Senate's failure to consider as a possible motive the political differences between Thomas and Hill which dated back to 1983, and which Hill told co-workers had been serious enough to warrant her departure from the agency. The only thing that might explain it is the power of the image of Anita Hill that somehow got established at that time. The false presumption on the committee and in the press was that, because she served in a Republican administration, Hill herself was a political conservative who had supported Ronald Reagan's civil rights policies. As a result, Hill's supporters were able to assert with great effect that she did not have political differences with Thomas, thus denying the Thomas camp its most obvious line of defense.

Since the press did not report on the circumstances of Hill's departure from the Wald firm before joining the Reagan Administration, the fact that Hill went to work for Thomas because she quickly had to find another job, and therefore may have given little thought to political questions, was not considered. Nor was any note taken of the fact that, according to Phyllis Berry-Myers, Hill was appointed to a career civil service slot only because she could not get clearance from the White House on a political appointment. But the most egregious oversight was the failure of the press to examine Hill's relationship with Thomas in a serious way, which would have plainly revealed their political differences.

Another item from Hill's resumé that tended to suggest she was a conservative was her stint at Oral Roberts University. But on this subject as well, the press tended to accept Hill's intimation that she had long planned to leave the EEOC because she was being sexually harassed by Thomas, and eventually chose to take a position at Oral Roberts. What really happened was that Hill made a frustrated and emotional decision to go to a school whose political outlook did not jibe with her own because it was the first job that came up and was close to her hometown.

The strongest evidence that Hill had conservative politics came from the testimony of her witnesses. Howell Heflin asked Susan Hoerchner if Hill was "a zealous cause person, whether it be in civil rights, the feminist movement, or whatever? Did she ever indicate to you that she was a zealous cause person, who was willing to do great things, move forward and take drastic steps in order to advance whatever her cause would be?" Hoerchner replied:

> Most definitely not, Senator. I know that she worked under the Reagan administration. To this day, I have no idea how she votes. I have very little sense of where she would fit on the political spectrum. Further, due to the quiet and gentle strength of her nature, she is not someone who seeks a public forum.

But Hoerchner, despite her confident assertions, may really have known little of Hill's politics, since she lost touch with Hill at precisely the moment that she went to work for Thomas. During the period when they were in regular contact in Washington, Hill had been working at Wald. There would have been little reason for political discussions at that time, since Hill was quite at home in Wald's liberal climate. Hoerchner, therefore, even if sincere in her assessment, was not only in no position to corroborate Hill's sexual harassment charge; she was also in no position to present an accurate view of Hill's attitude towards her period of service in the Reagan Administration.

More striking was the testimony of law professor Joel Paul, who said that Hill had defended Robert Bork in discussions at American University in the summer of 1987. In his opening statement, Paul told the committee: "I cannot believe she could be politically motivated. I know from numerous conversations with her that she served faithfully in the Reagan Administration, that she was generally in sync with the goals of that administration, and that she did not disagree with the overall policies of the administration. Indeed, when Judge Robert Bork was nominated to the Supreme Court in the summer of 1987, I remember vividly that Professor Hill supported his nomination and told me that she held him in extremely high esteem, as a former teacher of hers at Yale. Her strong support of Judge Bork led to a number of loud lunch table disagreements between Professor Hill and other colleagues of mine. Thus, I cannot accept the conclusion that her statements have been motivated by political ideology."

Under questioning, Paul amplified this account. "The summer that she was visiting at our school was the summer of Judge Bork's nomination to the Supreme Court. If you recall, that was a controversial nomination. . . . Members of my faculty were, I would say, mostly opposed to the nomination, and in defending Judge Bork as she did at that time, she could not have thought she was advancing her opportunities to return to our school. She did so. She did so eloquently. She did so with tremendous force and conviction."

The press seemed content to accept this testimony without further investigation. Three major profiles of Hill appeared at the time of the hearings. *Time* reported that Hill "gives no signs of having a political ax to grind." The magazine quoted Joel Paul: "I suspect she's a card-carrying Republican. She is cut from the same political cloth as Clarence Thomas." OU Professor Harry Tepker echoed this assessment. "She's a scholar in commercial law. That's not exactly the sort of field that firebrands go into."[42]

A *New York Times* profile portrayed Hill not as a conservative, but as essentially apolitical. "Some of her closest friends here at the University of Oklahoma have trouble remembering any of her political beliefs beyond a deep commitment to the welfare of minority students on campus . . . she seems to have little interest in politics . . . several of her friends were stumped when asked about her private interests and beliefs," the *Times* reported. OU law professor Leisha Self, who was identified as a "close friend" of Hill's, said: "She's really not a political person. I would never think of her that way in the sense that she's not interested in getting up on a soapbox to tell you about her views and convincing you that her positions are right. . . . She's the kind of person who constantly deflects conversation away from herself and towards the person she is talking to."[43]

"Public records indicate she is not a registered voter here," the *Times* continued. The only hint of Hill's views was the presence of a "fanciful postcard of 'the Supremes Court' that shows three black women in judicial robes sitting behind a courtroom bench."

A four-column front-page profile of Anita Hill in the *Washington Post* did not once broach the subject of her political views.[44]

Whether these omissions were the consequence of lean reporting in the teeth of strict deadlines, reportorial disinterest or laziness, or a conscious effort to avoid exploring any subject that might impinge on Hill's credibility, cannot be determined. But the record suggests that at least one reporter, NPR's Totenberg, deliberately concealed the truthful answer to the question of Hill's politics. In a January 1992 *Vanity Fair* profile, Totenberg claimed she had "checked Anita Hill's credentials up the wazoo and everybody said she was a saint, that her integrity was the highest, that she was a Bork supporter, a conservative, and an Evangelical."[45] Yet a few weeks later in an off the cuff question-and-answer session following a speech at Stanford University—where Totenberg may have had her guard down, as opposed to the more formal circumstance of being interviewed by a national magazine—she was asked:

> Q. I know you don't want to say what your personal opinion is, I believe anyway, but I was wondering do you think there's any chance in my lifetime—I'm 31—that we could see somebody like Anita Hill nominated to the Supreme Court?

> A. If you want somebody even remotely her political/judicial persuasion, you're going to have to elect a Democratic president.[46]

In the absence of independent reportage, Hill's defenders were able to take the testimony of witnesses like Susan Hoerchner, who had not spoken with Hill for seven years before 1991, and Joel Paul, who barely knew her, as proof that she had no political motive for trying to stop the Thomas nomination. "Professor Hill has simply no motive to lie," the Women's Legal Defense Fund asserted in a press release. Apparently drawing on Paul's testimony, the statement continued: "Professor Hill was an active participant in the Reagan Administration's civil rights program, told a prospective employer that she had no basic quarrel with those policies, and publicly expressed support for the Supreme Court nomination of Judge Robert Bork. Nothing in the record suggests she is a 'closet liberal' or part of a conspiracy to deny Judge Thomas the nomination on ideological grounds."[47] "I hope we are not going to hear more about politics," Ted Kennedy said in his Sunday afternoon statement. "You can imagine what Professor Hill would have gone through if she had been a Democrat, and we hear this afternoon she was a Bork supporter; worked in a Republican administration. I hope we are not going to hear a lot more comments about politics."

This line of interpretation was constantly invoked by Hill's supporters in the year following the hearings. "Why would she lie? What did she actually gain from her actions? Politically a conservative and identified with her tenure in the Reagan Administration, she clearly was not a liberal," Manning Marable confidently wrote in *Race-ing Justice, En-gendering Power*.[48] Marable went on to attack columnist William Raspberry, who had written that Hill's allegations smacked of "eleventh hour . . . character assassination." Yet Marable conceded that Raspberry's "stuffy rhetoric" *would* make sense "if Hill's politics had been identified with feminism or the left." In the same volume of essays, novelist Michael Thelwell made the ludicrous assertion, unsupported by any evidence whatsoever, that Bork was Hill's "mentor and friend." Therefore, he concluded, it was impossible to think she was a "willing agent" in a political campaign to defeat the like-minded Thomas.[49]

But one essay in the Morrison book did more than any other to stand the truth about Anita Hill on its head, and illustrates the extent to which even quite sensible and discerning observers could be drastically misled by false appearances. The distinguished Princeton philosopher Cornel West was frankly unsympathetic to Thomas, on the familiar grounds that "his claim to black authenticity is for the purpose of self-promotion, to gain power and prestige." West viewed Thomas through the lens of Marxist cultural analysis, as the victim of "market moralities." West saw Thomas as "the exemplary hedonist, addicted to pornography and captive to the stereotypical image of the powerful black man who reveals his sexual prowess in a racist society."

Though he excoriated Thomas's opponents for indulging in the kind of "racial reasoning" that raised mendacious questions as to whether the nominee was "really black," West uncritically accepted every myth about Hill *and* Thomas that was echoed in the press. It is a tribute to his moral and intellectual consistency, then, that West was scarcely kinder to Anita Hill, whom he characterized as a female Clarence Thomas. "Anita Hill," he wrote, "appears as the exemplary careerist addicted to job promotion and captive to the stereotypical self-image of the sacrificial black woman who suffers silently and alone." From this perspective, Hill's only praiseworthy act in a lifetime of equivocation and compromise was finally to have overcome her opportunism in order to come forward against Thomas.

> There was also little doubt that Anita Hill's truthtelling was a break from her careerist ambitions. On the one hand, she strikes me as a person of integrity and honesty. On the other hand, she indeed put a premium on job advancement—even at painful personal cost. Yet her speaking out disrupted this pattern of behavior and she found herself supported only by people who opposed the very conservative politics she otherwise championed, namely progressive feminists, liberals, and some black folk. How strange it must have felt being a hero to her former foes. One wonders whether Judge Bork supported her as fervently as she did him several years ago.[50]

This passage illustrates what skillful and compelling flights of fantasy are possible on the basis of small errors compounded by repetition and an absence of rational scrutiny. As we will see, West's view of Hill as being uncomfortable and out of place in feminist and liberal circles is a fiction whose genesis not even Hill herself seems to have understood.

Writing in the *Seattle Weekly* ten months after the hearings, Kathryn Robinson observed,

> In part because of [Hill's] zealously guarded privacy, shockingly little has been uncovered about womanhood's new hero. She has become the Ross Perot of feminism, revered more for what she represents than who she is. Her politics, murkily sketched as Reaganesque and Borkian during the hearings, remain vague and undocumented. . . . [Yet] a more liberal picture of Hill's ideology . . . allows for the possibility of something her fans regard as unthinkable: that perhaps there was more to her allegations than met the eye.

Anita Hill herself, it must be said, did not mislead the Senate committee or the press about her political views, nor has she subsequently tried to conceal or apologize for them. Hill was simply never pressed on the point, with the exception of Heflin's question about whether she was a "zealous cause person"—a characterization that anyone, ideologue or otherwise, might reasonably reject out of hand. Indeed, at several moments in the hearings, Hill seemed to indicate that she did have political differences with Thomas. But this fruitful avenue was generally neglected by the Senators and, at one crucial moment, actively blocked by Senator Biden.

> THURMOND: . . . Professor Hill, I understand you told the FBI that you had concerns about the political philosophy of Judge Thomas and that he may no longer be open-minded. Is that accurate?
>
> HILL: I told them that I did not quite understand, but as they had been represented, yes, that I did have some concerns.
>
> THURMOND: I have the FBI report here, and I just wondered if you remember telling them that.
>
> HILL: I remember discussion about political philosophy and I remember specifically saying that I'm not quite sure that we un-

derstand his political philosophies. But based on what I understand, yes, there is some discomfort.

Thurmond was referring to a key section of the FBI report on Hill's interview, in which, in the midst of a description of Thomas's sexual harassment, Hill began to discuss her philosophical disagreements with the nominee. This open discussion by Hill was perhaps the strongest sign that she did not want to hide her political objections to the Thomas nomination, and may have even been a hint that these objections were the real compelling reasons for her testimony. Orrin Hatch, who claimed he was out of the room when the committee caucused privately and agreed not to disclose the contents of the FBI file during the public hearing, read this section of the FBI report into the record:

> HATCH: . . . Judge Thomas, yesterday, Senator Heflin repeatedly asked you to ascribe some motivation to Professor Hill's allegations, and I think, from the way I look at this record, there are some profound differences in political philosophy between you and her.
>
> I am about to read an excerpt of one of her statements that I think is worth putting in the record:
>
> "Hill said that her initial impression of Thomas was very favorable and she respected him for his accomplishments and concern for others. She said that she also came from a poor family, so she related closely to his circumstances. She said that when she started working for Thomas, he supported quotas for minorities in employment and federal sanctions against employers who did not comply with the quotas, and then went on." That is the relevant part.
>
> "Later, Hill said that she has also seen Thomas change his political philosophy since 1981 to the present, from supporting quotas for minorities in employment with sanctions for noncompliance to no quotas. She is concerned that these may be changed for personal political expediency and may not represent his true philosophy. If that is the case, he may no longer be open-minded, which is essential for an Associate Justice of the United States Supreme Court."

Hill's concerns about Thomas's philosophy voiced to the FBI recall her explanation for Allyson Duncan's promotion and her subsequent decision to leave the EEOC. Hill had told Armstrong Williams that Thomas was reasonable and flexible at the Department of Education when she was his sole attorney-adviser, but later became a "dangerous thinker" as Hill's role was eclipsed. Thus while Hill's *expressed* problem with the Thomas nomination was that Thomas had "changed his political philosophy since 1981," this problem was fused in her memory with Thomas's "rejection" of her at the EEOC.

A few minutes later, Hatch continued to question Thomas about Hill's disagreements with him at the agency.

HATCH: . . . Judge Thomas, I take it she disagrees with you on your stand on quotas?

THOMAS: She disagreed with me when she was on my personal staff on that issue, Senator.

HATCH: Was that a matter of some contention between you?

THOMAS: I think in the instances she would get a bit irate on that particular issue, as I remember it.

HATCH: Because she took the opposite position?

THOMAS: That's right.

HATCH: She was for quotas?

THOMAS: She was adamant about that position.

Senator Hank Brown, a pro-choice Republican, was able to establish that Hill believed she and Thomas did not see eye to eye on the abortion issue either, just before being cut off by the chairman.

BROWN: With regard to the judge himself, you clearly, in working with him as you had, were familiar with a portion of his philosophy. Do you find you were in agreement with his philosophy on most issues proposed? What can you share with us on that?

HILL: Well, I am not really sure what his philosophy on many issues is. And so I can't say that I am in agreement or disagreement. I can say during the times that we were there, worked together, there were matters that we agreed on and some that we did not agree on and we had discussions about those matters. But I am not really sure what his philosophies are at this point.

BROWN: Would that be the case with regard to say, abortion or *Roe* v. *Wade?*

HILL: That I am not sure of his philosophies?

BROWN: Sure of his philosophy or do you perceive a significant difference between the two of you in that area?

HILL: Yes.

BROWN: Can you tell us what that might be? I don't mean to pressure you here. If you would prefer not to, please don't. But if there is something that you could share with us in that area, I think the committee would like to hear it.

BIDEN: Senator, I don't, on behalf of—from Judge Thomas's position this was supposed to relate to harassment not an investigation of Judge Thomas's views on abortion.

BROWN: Mr. Chairman, you are perfectly correct. If there were something that wished to be offered there I thought it would be helpful. I see the red light is on so I will conclude.

But Biden was perfectly incorrect to characterize Brown's line of questioning as he did. The issue at hand was not Thomas's views on abortion but whether Hill's disagreements with Thomas on this and other matters were strong enough to constitute a motive. According to Brown, "Biden later told me he wished he had allowed me to continue."[51]

At the point that Brown was interrupted, Hill seemed poised to reveal that she was a supporter of the *Roe* decision, and believed that Thomas was not. In one of the very few exceptions to the persistent media myth of Hill's conservatism, a *Wall Street Journal* column by Lally Weymouth on Hill's politics, published a month after the hearings concluded, reported, "At the Oklahoma Law School, Ms. Hill is an adviser to a feminist group, the Organization for the Advancement of Women. One former member, Susan Stallings, who likes Ms. Hill personally, says that 'Anita Hill is a liberal . . . she was for such things as comparable worth. At our meetings, if it wasn't Reagan bashing, it was Bush bashing. They were terrified of *Roe* v. *Wade* being overturned.' "[52]

Though *Newsday*'s Tim Phelps followed the journalistic pack in depicting Hill as a conservative at the time of the hearings—"Number one, Anita Hill argued, according to the testimony, very strongly in favor of Judge Bork," he told C-SPAN interviewer Brian Lamb[53]—he developed a more accurate picture of Hill's politics in the reporting for his book. In *Capitol Games,* he acknowledged, albeit with coy understatement, that Hill had "credentials as a mild-mannered feminist" and "did endorse women's rights in a soft, nonideological fashion."[54] Phelps went on to observe, quite correctly, "In fact, Anita Hill's political beliefs were vastly different from Thomas's but no one seemed then to have a clear concept about her quietly held convictions favoring rights for women and minorities. Other than the point made by Orrin Hatch about quotas, the Republicans failed to exploit Hill's politics as an issue."[55]

Irrefutable evidence about Hill's politics came from her own words in interviews after the hearings concluded—words that most of her defenders are either unaware of or have simply ignored. These comments bespoke an attempt by Hill to correct the misimpressions publicized by her supporters. They do not, as Cornel West mistakenly assumed, reflect Hill's discomfort in the role of a liberal hero, but rather her discomfort in being associated with the Republican Party, Ronald Reagan, and Judge Bork. Appearing on *60 Minutes* in February 1992, Hill rejected the label "conservative" and told Ed Bradley that—Ted Kennedy and the *New York Times* notwithstanding—she was in fact a Democrat. Bradley was speechless for several moments, then changed the subject without any followup question. (*Newsday* was the only newspaper at the time of the hearings to report correctly that "County records show she is a registered Democrat."[56] The story was not written by Tim Phelps.)

If Hill had been asked further questions about her politics in the hearings or by the press, there is no reason to believe she would have hid them. Her witnesses and her supporters found it useful to portray her as a conservative, but in a revealing March 1992 question-and-answer interview with *Essence* magazine, Hill was quite forthcoming in setting the record straight. Though she had served in the Reagan Administration, she said, she was not sympathetic with its position on civil rights matters. On issues of policy, she sided with the EEOC's career bureaucracy against the political elements of the administration. As for the Bork nomination, Hill explained that her supportive words on Bork's behalf had evidently been misinterpreted by Joel Paul and others. While she was uncomfortable with the attacks on her former professor's character during his nomination, she did not support Bork's originalist judicial philosophy.

Q. Have you changed politically as a result of what's happened?

A. There is this sense that I was an absolute staunch conservative, that I was opposed to affirmative action, that I supported Robert Bork. A lot of that has been misunderstood. First of all, I have never been against affirmative action, and while I was extremely uncomfortable with the way the hearings were conducted, *I did not support Robert Bork on the issues.* My position is that the man should not be judged on his personality. We decided we didn't like him as a person, that he was strident, arrogant, and therefore he was not a good person for the Supreme Court position. My position was that he should fall or stand on issues.

Q. Was it difficult at the EEOC, with the lack of support for affirmative action during the Reagan Administration?

A: I didn't work directly with the legal counsel's office on cases. I reviewed EEOC policy, and I consistently pursued an approach consistent with the longstanding policy of the commission, which was often *antagonistic to the position of the Reagan Administration.*[57] [Emphasis added.]

To return to Senator Heflin's much-derided inquiry, then, Hill did see herself as scorned by Thomas, though she was not the jilted lover or the fantasizing spinster that the term implied. The unhappy circumstances of her departure from the EEOC raise the question of whether a desire to avenge Thomas's "rejection" might have played some part in assuaging her conscience as she was moved deeper and deeper by persistent Senate staffers, women's activists, and her friend Susan Hoerchner into implicating Thomas with a sexual harassment allegation.

By her own admission, Hill was not the conservative Bork-supporter she was said to be at the time of the hearings. Her comments suggesting that Thomas had betrayed both himself and his race by adopting conservative positions would seem to indicate that she was, in fact, a zealot for the cause of civil rights. More suggestive still is the way these two potential motives, personal and political, seemed joined in Hill's view of her disappointing relationship with Thomas and her failure to succeed at the EEOC.

But even this seems insufficient cause or explanation for the events of 1991. Questions remain about what happened to Hill after she left the EEOC; the meaning of her continued complaints of "sexual harassment" in those years; why she stayed in touch with Thomas during this period; what she had to gain from coming forward; and how her deepening ideological commitments made her vulnerable to subornation, while a firmer sense of self may have enabled her to act on those commitments in a very public way.

9

The Real Anita Hill

The refusal of the Democrats on the Senate Judiciary Committee to permit questions about Anita Hill's political differences with Clarence Thomas—differences which extended back a decade and ostensibly brought an end to her Washington career—foreclosed whatever chance there may have been of discovering the motive for Hill's appearance. Seeing Hill as she really was—deeply disillusioned by Thomas both politically and personally, hostile to Robert Bork and the judicial philosophy he shared with Thomas, and an active proponent of civil rights policies to which Thomas and the Reagan Administration were opposed—plainly suggest that political considerations may have been central factors in Hill's ultimate decision to testify.

But it remains to be shown just how and why Hill may have acted on these possible motives. Only a deeper understanding of the person she became after leaving Washington can account for her belief that Clarence Thomas had to be prevented from ascending to the nation's highest court, and explain how she could have come to see herself as having an important role to play in the struggle to stop him.

The single most important factor in explaining the growth of the Anita Hill myth was the misleading *New York Times* article which re-

335

ported that Hill's "closest friends" on the OU campus could think of
nothing to say about her political beliefs one way or the other. Hill
was further portrayed by the national press as a particularly straightlaced Baptist girl from small-town Oklahoma, of the sort who would
have been profoundly shocked by such offensive language as Thomas
purportedly used, and deeply scandalized by any suggestion that she
might tell a bald-faced lie on national television in order to revenge
herself on Thomas or stop his nomination for political reasons.

If anyone in the national press had bothered to follow these stories up, it would have quickly become apparent that the "real Anita
Hill" was very different from the way her friends portrayed her. However, the press was notably uninterested in the question of Hill's character. While reporters broke into Thomas's garage and sifted through
his garbage looking for incriminating evidence, the image of Anita
Hill was taken at face value. Therefore aspects of the following depiction of the real Anita Hill may strike some readers as surprising
and even bizarre—in some respects as hard to credit as anything Hill
said about Thomas. Nonetheless, this reconstruction of her subsequent career in academia will provide crucial clues that may help to
explain many of the anomalies and mysteries that have so far remained unresolved.

Both Hill's Washington friends as well as her new acquaintances in
Tulsa must have wondered why a Yale graduate who had been special
assistant to the chairman of a powerful federal agency, an extremely
desirable commodity in the job market, would want to teach at Oral
Roberts law school.

For one thing, the school seemed far too conservative for a woman
who had told her colleagues that she was leaving the EEOC because
of political differences with Clarence Thomas. It was a highly religious,
arch-conservative, and barely-accredited school in a cultural backwa-
ter, controlled with an iron hand by the evangelist Oral Roberts. For
another, the position itself was not very attractive. Though she had
been involved exclusively in civil rights law for two years in Washington, the bulk of her new teaching assignments would be taken up with
teaching commercial law, a legal research and writing course, and re-
medial classes. Hill also taught a class in constitutional and civil rights,
but she would not be permitted to specialize in that field.

Perhaps the most unattractive aspect of the job was that Oral
Roberts did not believe in tenure and so Hill's post would never be

secure. Appointments to the faculty were made for three years and then were subject to renewal.

In the fall of 1983, Hill joined a law faculty of six white men. Not only was she, as a black woman, something of an oddity on campus; at the time she was only 27 years old, younger than most of her students, many of whom came to the school later in life or after failing to gain admission to more mainstream institutions. Others enrolled because they were attracted to its conservative, religious orientation.

Thus Hill may well have felt a bit isolated and uncomfortable on the campus, not least because of this evangelistic emphasis. The school required the faculty to pledge a code of honor. Prayer was offered each morning before classes began, and a dress code required coat and tie for men, and "modest dress" for women. Dean Charles Kothe gave speeches like one titled "Stir It Up and Pour It Out," in which he exhorted the students to "stir up the gift of God within you, pour it out." According to Kothe, Hill did not actively participate in these religious rites, though she did belong to a Baptist church off campus.

Hill's career up to that moment suggested that she, like Clarence Thomas, had wanted to rise as far from her humble beginnings as possible. Born on a cotton farm in Lone Tree, Oklahoma, she had been valedictorian at her high school and an honors graduate in psychology from Oklahoma State University. From there she had been able to catapult herself into Yale Law School, and thence to the nation's capital. But now, her dream of a Washington career would not be fulfilled. "She basically realized she couldn't hack it in Washington," said Harry Singleton.

The main attraction of the Oral Roberts job for Hill, then, may simply have been its location about an hour and a half outside Lone Tree. The move was not only a major shift in career path but a return to the environs where she was raised, and it seemed to represent an acknowledgment that her days as an up-and-coming Washington civil rights attorney were over. Perhaps after the stresses and disappointments of Washington, the idea of returning home was a comfort.

Once back in Oklahoma, Hill chose not to tell anyone that following the Allyson Duncan episode she had made an abrupt and emotional decision to leave the corridors of power when the first opportunity to do so was offered by Kothe. Instead, when pressed, she vaguely spoke of sexual harassment. Here a pattern of behavior on her part may be discernible. On leaving Wald, Harkrader, she had told Susan Hoerchner that she was being sexually harassed in order to explain why she was "quitting" an associate's position at a high-powered liberal firm to become an aide to Clarence Thomas—then a fairly obscure figure—in one of the least prestigious or promising government agencies for an aspiring lawyer. This being so, it seems possible to think that sexual harassment by an unnamed boss could have simply become Hill's standard explanation for why she had stepped off the fast track and ended up at Oral Roberts. Several accounts, both sworn and unsworn, lend credence to this view.

Helen Jones was president of the Tulsa Equal Opportunity Compliance Association in 1984–1985, and Hill had acted as an intermediary for the group in extending a speaking invitation to Thomas in the spring of 1985. Impressed with Hill's professional background, Jones once asked her, " 'Anita, why are you wasting your time in Tulsa?' And you know, she told me she had to leave Washington because she was having problems with her supervisor harassing her," Jones said. Jones did not consider at the time that the unnamed supervisor might have been Thomas, mainly because Hill had volunteered to act as the Tulsa group's contact with Thomas in arranging the engagement, and spoke highly of her former boss.[1]

In the summer of 1987, after a year at the University of Oklahoma, where she would go after leaving ORU in 1986, Hill was doing research at American University in Washington, and was interested in obtaining a full-time teaching post there. Hill was asked by Joel Paul, a member of the faculty who was also impressed with her and was encouraging her to apply, why she had left her job at the EEOC to go to Oral Roberts University. Hill told Paul, as she had Helen Jones, that she left Washington because she had been sexually harassed by an unnamed "supervisor."

Indeed, the "pattern" in the Thomas–Hill story seemed not to be a pattern of sexual harassment by Thomas, but of sexual harassment or racial discrimination claims by Hill. "Anita's whole life revolved around racial or sexual discrimination," a law professor and former visiting faculty member at OU recalled. "Everything was sexism or sexual harassment, she was obsessed with it," said the professor, who got to know Hill well during his stint at the school in the late 1980s. "I called them her 'atrocity stories.' Every time she walked through a crowd someone was trying to grab her breasts. When she really got going, every guy she ever worked with sexually harassed her. The sheer numerosity of it struck me. Six or eight people, she'd name a bunch of male lawyers who were superiors or co-workers. She would ramble on in obsessive soliloquies. I would think, someday she is going to get sued for false light defamation. Every failure in her life was due to discrimination. She would say she left Washington because she was sexually harassed. And she would say she was racially discriminated against at Oral Roberts." All the while, Hill never mentioned Clarence Thomas in connection with harassment, according to this professor. "They were names I didn't recognize, and I knew who he was. I would have recognized him," he said.[2]

Hill spent three academic years at ORU. As with any professor, opinions varied on the quality of Hill's teaching and scholarship. But the preponderant view among those who knew and worked with her was that Hill was distinguished in neither respect. Hill had never taught before, and she found the requirements of the job to be in some ways even more onerous than those of her staff job at the EEOC. John Eidsmoe, a law professor on the ORU faculty, recalled, "On her student evaluations, the general feedback was she was not regarded as a competent professor. She didn't know where she was going; she was hard to follow and unprepared."[3]

Just as preferential hiring practices placed Hill in a position that she could not quite handle at Wald, Harkrader, that system—employed more cynically at ORU, where Hill was hired, as Kothe said, mainly to help the school's image with the ABA—once again thrust her into a situation for which she was ill-prepared. Roger Tuttle was a member of the faculty recruitment committee that hired Hill, and was later Hill's supervising dean upon Kothe's retirement from that position in 1984. In a somewhat condescending fashion, Tuttle said he was concerned from the outset that Hill was not qualified to teach. "I personally had a degree of worry. This girl might be fine, but she had virtually no practical experience, nor much administrative experience in D.C. She was not knowledgeable enough to teach any particular field. If she were a white male, you'd be laughing. I thought we should send her back to D.C. after the interview. But Kothe said we couldn't afford to offend Clarence Thomas, and we had a need.

"When I assumed the deanship, I had a line of students outside my office complaining every time she taught," Tuttle explained further. "It got worse when she was put into a common law course out of need—creditor's rights, bills and notes, the uniform commercial code. She didn't know much about the course. She didn't burn the midnight oil to familiarize herself with the material. She stayed ahead of the students by one week."

Tuttle said he would have fired Hill, but "there was little point cutting her adrift when the money was running out anyway." In 1986,

Oral Roberts, his ministry in financial straits, pulled the plug on the law school, selling it off to televangelist Pat Robertson, who moved the library and other facilities to Virginia.

In the fall of 1987, Hill moved to a position at the University of Oklahoma in Norman, outside Oklahoma City, where she taught contracts, commercial law, and civil rights, and was promoted at a record rate, achieving tenure in four years rather than the usual six. It was at OU—a typically sprawling public institution in a more cosmopolitan setting, with a more liberal faculty and a more open-minded and ethnically diverse student body than she had encountered at ORU—that Hill was able to achieve both a stable professional footing and a sense of self-fulfillment in her work. In short, Hill finally seems to have met with success at OU after a series of missteps, awkward career moves, and outright reversals.

Hill sat on the ABA's Committee on the Uniform Commercial Code and an ABA working group on international law. Though she was not published often, she occasionally wrote scholarly articles for publications like *Banking Anthology Today*. But Hill's energies were directed less toward scholarship and the law and more toward campus affairs. Hill became fast friends with a group of mostly female—and very liberal—law school colleagues who had a disproportionate influence on the policies of the law school, which is ranked in the lower half of law schools nationwide. She was elected to the faculty senate; sat on the university president's advisory committee on minority affairs and the dean's advisory committee on Afro-American studies; she was a member of the Center for Research in Minority Education's Board of Directors, faculty adviser to the Black Law Student Association and adviser to the Organization for the Advancement of Women. She was also an administrative fellow in the office of the dean.

Off-campus, Hill sat on the board of directors of the Norman Women's Resource Center, a counseling center for victims of domestic violence, sexual assault, and sexual harassment that is considered a feminist beacon in the Oklahoma City area. Hill had a heightened awareness of sexual and racial discrimination and harassment, and a familiarity with its special language, long before she complained about Thomas's behavior in 1991. During the Thomas–Hill hearings, Judy Robinson, the center's former director, told the *Atlanta Journal and Constitution* that Hill had recently been involved in several sexual harassment issues at the center, though she never mentioned being harassed by Thomas.[4]

Though she was more popular with the faculty and students at OU than she had been at ORU, the reviews of her teaching, and of her generally defensive demeanor, did not greatly improve. One recent graduate of the Oklahoma law school, a young woman working for a major Tulsa law firm, said she respected and admired Hill for coming forward with her charges against Thomas, but acknowledged, "I always avoided her classes because of her reputation. If anyone else was teaching the class, you would take it from them." Keith Lapayude, another OU law graduate, said, "She was unable to take you to the logical point in an argument. She never took you through the thought process."[5]

In a letter to the Senate Judiciary Committee during the hearings, Dennis Olson, the associate dean of the Dallas–Fort Worth School of Law, wrote:

> Prior to coming here, I was on the faculty at the University of Oklahoma College of Law. Anita Hill was a colleague of mine in Oklahoma.
>
> My personal impression of Anita Hill was that she is a detailed, cold, and calculating person. Students commented to me that she was particularly ineffective in class and was not concerned about improving her performance. She appeared to recognize her protected position as a black woman in an era of affirmative action and to use that protected position for all it was worth—accelerated promotions, specially arranged teaching schedules, etc.

"She came out of Yale with huge gaps in her basic understanding of the law," said William Michael Roberts, a former visiting colleague on the OU faculty. "She's fluent in public policy but she doesn't know how you put on proof, or the law of torts. I taught contracts too, and her students would come to me panicked that she wasn't teaching them anything. One time, I looked at some of their notes to see what the problem was. It was politics, not law."[6]

Indeed, politics began to infuse everything Hill did at OU. While there were mixed reviews of Hill's abilities as a professor, her admirers and her detractors on the faculty and in the student body all agreed that she had a strong and uncompromising political outlook. While Hill had tried to sway the Reagan EEOC in a more liberal direction by working quietly on the inside, and subsequently avoided political discussions with her more conservative colleagues and students at Oral Roberts, she was free to become quite openly political at OU.

Despite the inability of the *New York Times* and other publications to characterize Hill's political views during the hearings, calls made virtually at random to the OU law school yielded the universal opinion that she is a committed liberal. "Well, she is a liberal Democrat, no doubt about that," said Professor Osborne Reynolds, a colleague of Hill's on the law faculty who knows her well. Professor Leo Whinery, like Reynolds an older, mainstream faculty liberal, said, "On issues pertaining to race and gender she would be an extreme liberal."[7] How Hill's "closest friends" could have told the *New York Times* otherwise is hard to imagine, unless they were trying to shield the "real Anita Hill" from the public eye.

Hill is described by students as the sort of professor who routinely brought her politics and her prejudices into the classroom. A statement prepared for the Senate Judiciary Committee by Todd Cone, a third year law student at OU who was not a student of Hill's, echoes in most respects what many current and former OU students said in interviews about Hill conducted for this book. (Most of them declined to be identified for fear of retaliation by Hill and her supporters on the faculty.)

What emerged from these interviews is a portrait of Hill as holding many of the prevalent campus attitudes on racial and sexual victimization and multiculturalism, including the intellectual intolerance and reverse discrimination that often accompanies such ideas. What also emerged is a portrait of OU law school as an institution struggling with an ideological movement in its midst that pitted more traditional faculty liberals and a few conservatives against a group of younger (so-called "politically correct") radicals, for whom the politics of race, gender—and in the law school, the politics of the law, and of the federal judiciary—is all-consuming. As it turns out, Hill is very much a part of this self-described radical vanguard.

OU student Todd Cone drew on multiple accounts of Hill's classroom behavior to provide a portrait of Hill as militantly anti-male and obsessively concerned with race and gender issues. Many such statements regarding Hill—sworn to by lawyers in some cases—were received by the Judiciary Committee, but the time pressures of the hearings did not permit an investigation of her background, and even the Republican Senators, seeking to avoid the wrath of women's activists who believed that the accuser should not herself be the subject of scrutiny, were reluctant to confront Hill on national television with the material. Cone wrote:

Before coming to the University of Oklahoma Law School, I was fore-warned to stay away from classes taught by Prof. Hill because she was very liberal and did not take kindly to males. . . . On Oct. 9, I spoke to many of my fellow students . . . many of those I spoke to have her currently as a professor and are still in school. They fear repercussions from the professors and resentment from other students. . . .

A third year female law student said Prof. Hill had a "really poor attitude." She believed that the black students received favorable treatment both in class and in grades. Her impression was that Prof. Hill felt that the black students had come from rougher backgrounds and that this was Prof. Hill's way of "evening things out."

A third year male law student found her "racist in class." His class had one black female in it. He found that this one black female received special treatment in class. . . .

Another third year female law student said . . . black students tended to receive favorable treatment in her class. White males, she said, who previously had received high grades received their lowest grades in her class, while black females fared rather well. . . .

A third year student, who did not support the Clarence Thomas nomination for political reasons, stated that he did not think Prof. Hill treated students unfairly but that she did have a "major chip on her shoulder." He said that Prof. Hill's view of society was "white males on top and black females on the bottom." Black females, according to Prof. Hill, were in constant battle to try and fight their way up and stay up. Further, his impression was that Prof. Hill had a civil rights agenda and she felt women were stepped on and blacks put down. Finally, he found Prof. Hill extremely sensitive to gender issues. From his experience in class, he found that she "blew gender issues out of proportion."

Another third year student found her extremely sensitive to gender-related issues. He conveyed three such examples: First, during class, when a student would use the pronoun "he," Prof. Hill would jump all over the student and question how they knew it was a man.

Second, several male students recounted that they were so concerned about her obvious discriminatory treatment of men, that they attempted to write their tests in a fashion that made the writing appear to be written by a woman. They also used only the pronoun "she" in their tests.

Third, at the beginning of every school year, the faculty has a get-together for each of the first year sections. The purpose is for the students and professors to mingle and get to know each other. The student, a white male and a friend of mine, walked up to Prof. Hill during the mingling and lightly put his hand on her shoulder. He intended nothing. Prof. Hill became irate. She yelled at him to get his hand off her shoulder and proceeded to let him have a piece of her mind. A second year law student, who highly respected Prof. Hill as a teacher and who thought she was extremely professional, found it obvious that "she had a feminist agenda." He described her as very active with feminist issues. He found that when even a minor feminist or gender issue arose, Prof. Hill would "jump all over it."

Finally, all of the students said she was subject to wild mood swings.[8]

This statement and others of a similar kind quoted here were the subject of Alan Simpson's statement in the hearings that he was "getting stuff over the transom about Professor Hill. I've got letters hanging out of my pocket. I've got faxes. I've got statements from her former law professors, statements from people who know her, statements from Tulsa, Oklahoma, saying 'Watch out for this woman!' "[9] The statement was widely characterized as McCarthyite, and Simpson's critics had a point. The information contained in the letters presented a radically different view of Anita Hill from the one that appeared on television, and if Simpson believed that the authors were credible, he had the responsibility either to introduce the material into the hearing in a serious way or else leave it unmentioned.

Nothing in Cone's somewhat overwrought account, of course, amounts to much more than standard feminist consciousness-raising and racial victimization theorizing. The response of Cone and the other students who described Hill in essentially the same terms, particularly the more conservative white men, was in all likelihood just the kind of angry response that Hill and like-minded feminists seek to provoke as a tool of "enlightenment." Another OU law student, Christopher Wilson, also wrote to the Senate Judiciary Committee. Though he acted independently, his account, which was more balanced in tone, nonetheless confirmed Cone's general view of Hill:

> I am a first year law student at the University of Oklahoma. During the past few days I have had the unique opportunity of hearing the comments, both favorable and unfavorable, made by fellow students. . . . On September 14 [three weeks before the Hill charges became known], when speaking of Thomas's nomination to an OU graduate, he stated to me his opinion that if Anita Hill could do anything to stop Thomas's nomination, she would. He went on to later say Hill was liked as a professor, but not respected. She would evoke liberalism at any chance when she taught. She would always take the liberal version of the law. . . . He remembers Ms. Hill as being very political, she was in politics and aware of it. As he put it there was no way she could not know what she was doing and it is absurd to think this is not political.

I also spoke to a third year female who called her class a "bastion of liberalism." She suggested that since I am a white male I should stay away from her classes. . . .

Another graduate of OU law school told me of an instance in contracts class where he had a discussion with Ms. Hill. It was a case in which a woman sued a man she had slept with for child support when there was no proof he was the father. The woman was awarded child support. When asked how this judgment was fair Ms. Hill responded *women should be supported regardless of proof.* [Emphasis added.]

Other students said that to the extent they could discern it, Hill's legal philosophy was firmly on the Left side of the spectrum. An October 12, 1991, article in the *Daily Oklahoman,* Oklahoma City's major daily, quoted one student's analysis of Hill's legal theories:

"When she was prepared for class, Professor Hill would often advocate legal theories premised upon judicial intervention and liberal social policy. Such theories can have application in contract law, although judicial intervention primarily occurs in constitutional, labor and employment areas. The theories she advocated generally had the effect of nullifying or altering contractual agreements entered into between private individuals. In essence, she advocated a system wherein a judge, under the guise of considering the 'equities' of an agreement, could insert his or her personal preferences into the contract.

This had the effect of not interpreting private contracts pursuant to the agreement of the parties but pursuant to what the judge personally felt was fair. Such jurisprudence, if prevalent, would enable an activist judiciary to engage in economic regulation. Professor Hill consistently advocated these theories in place of principled contractual interpretation. However, due to her ineffectiveness as a teacher, the theories were not always well articulated."[10]

When challenged by students on such arguable interpretations, Hill would often lose her composure and invoke racism or sexism rather than defend the substance of her position on its merits. "If the students questioned whether she might be wrong, she would throw a tantrum," said former Oral Roberts dean Roger Tuttle, adding, "Her performance did not improve over time."[11] Elaborating in a letter to the Senate Judiciary Committee, Tuttle seemed to describe the same Anita Hill that her EEOC colleagues remembered—temperamental, willful, a woman who always had to have the last word:[12]

As a full professor on the faculty, I observed her performance, and later as Dean I was her supervisor. She was not, at that time, a competent teacher, lacking in experience of handling students in the classroom and in her ability to adequately convey knowledge to the students. Unfortunately, when called upon later to teach more substantive courses she would take a dogmatic posture in the classroom and frequently, when challenged by students with respect to her assertions, and proven demonstrably wrong in conveying information, she would react in anger with the students and remonstrate with them, both publicly and privately. She attempted to use her position as a teacher to intimidate and harass students, which was unacceptable to me as Dean. Her general posture was far from being "meek and mild" but rather a person who would not be disagreed with under any circumstances.

But Dean Tuttle and the students seemed to understand Hill no better than her colleagues at the EEOC, who mistook her insecurity for arrogance. Hill's uneven temper and rigidity were most likely defensive reactions to what she perceived as a hostile environment, rather than a desire to abuse her authority. Hill acted from weakness, not strength, as Thomas alone seemed to recognize. He testified that Hill would sometimes throw tantrums at the EEOC, storming into her office when she was unable to defend her position in a policy dispute, and suggested this was due to her closed-minded inability to entertain a different point of view.

Anita Hill was a black woman who knew perfectly well that she had been admitted to Yale Law School under a program of affirmative action. In high school and college, she had no reason to doubt her abilities; whatever honors and distinction she attained, she had certainly earned. But as authors Shelby Steele and Stephen Carter—the latter a professor at Yale Law School—have recently argued, the beneficiaries of affirmative action are often plagued by doubts about whether they really "belong" at the institutions that have accepted them on the basis of their color. These doubts invariably dissipate for those whose abilities are equal to a challenging environment. But for those who do *not* measure up, the doubts intensify, and may become a psychological obstacle, a presence in the mind—a ghost or demon—that demands to be explained, denied, or exorcised.

Given the unflattering assessments of her skills as a lawyer and teacher, it may not be completely surprising if, when she grappled with an issue or material that she did not completely comprehend, Hill (as many people do) became defensive, feeling as though she personally were under attack. Faced with a choice between acknowledging her failings or explaining them, she understandably attributed these "attacks" to an environment that was hostile to her on the grounds of her race and her gender (or, in the case of Thomas's

EEOC, on the grounds of political difference). This may explain why Hill frequently saw evidence of sexist and racist hostility and prejudice where often none existed. On one memorable occasion at OU in the fall of 1986, Hill accused her entire commercial law class of "racism," when, in frustration with her teaching, they stopped preparing for class. "Either she didn't know or understand the material or she just wasn't communicating it," recalled Jim Wagoner, a student in the class. "Well, everybody in the class got so frustrated they stopped reading. One day she came in and started calling on people and everybody said 'I'm not prepared,' or they passed. She slammed her book shut and said, 'You have stopped reading because I'm black.' And she stormed out. 'We all thought it was crazy. We weren't reading because we weren't getting the material, not because she was black.' "[13] Of course, if the profile sketched above is valid, Hill's extreme sensitivity to race may have really made her feel as though *she* were the one being harassed.

Cone, Wilson, Tuttle, and Wagoner may well have had their own political or personal reasons for volunteering testimony intended to undermine Hill's credibility. But Hill's radical views and inflamed sensitivities, expressed in her own words, are on the record as well. In her Georgetown speech on the first anniversary of the hearings, for example, she claimed that the institution of marriage often fails because it is based on "gender subordination," and likened marriage to slavery. Reporting on the event, the *New York Times* reporter—evidently puzzled at this performance, compared with that of the Anita Hill who testified in the Senate—noted that Hill spoke "in the arcane language of the academic doctrines currently fashionable in legal and literary criticism."[14]

Further evidence that Hill was in the forefront of the radical critique of the existing social order came in a 1992 interview with the newspaper *Metro Norman,* in which she argued that schools should teach students the following view of what constitutes racism: "I think you have to explain to them that there are two different kinds of racism," she said. "There's one that says 'I don't like black people.' That's one type of racism. There's another kind of racism that says 'I think urban cities are just the worst situation imaginable. I would never live in Detroit.' " In the same interview, she propounded the view that "cultural diversity" in the curriculum is necessary because people of different racial heritages think differently. "You can have your kaffee klatsch with a group of people that look like you and think like you and do the same things as you . . . if that's what you want," Hill said.[15] And in a campus seminar in 1988 on "The Constitution and Minorities," Hill spoke of how to "truly come to grips with cultural diversity," a subject much in vogue among the Left in the academy, though controversial for its quota approach to curriculum content.

But more than anything, Hill's activities as the head of an effort to ban so-called "hate speech" on the OU campus clearly identified her ideological sympathies and marked her coming of age as a full-fledged campus radical. In the 1990 school year, Hill spearheaded a campaign to institute a code governing speech and behavior on campus. This attempt to ban offensive and insensitive speech is perhaps the most extreme project of the "politically correct" movement on campuses across the country. Hill drafted a policy for the university that went beyond banning racial discrimination to prohibit "invidious racial intolerance." Hill and her supporters wanted to ban "racial hostility," with the goal of "making all students feel comfortable," she said in a speech to the faculty senate.

Such racial harassment and hate speech policies have been struck down by the courts on the basis that they violate free speech guarantees. They have also been criticized because their vagueness about what constitutes harassment tends to place the judgment in the hands of self-described victims rather than on any objective evidentiary basis. According to an account in the campus newspaper, the *Oklahoma Daily*, when the OU administration declined to endorse Hill's draft as too far-reaching, she said, "I would like to see individuals punished for engaging in abusive behavior. I think this would send a clear message that this type of behavior is intolerable." It is likely that Hill and her friends viewed this rebuff as a political defeat, which probably increased their sense of being an embattled "progressive" minority fighting an entrenched and powerful conservative enemy on all fronts in a cultural war.

As the hate speech episode showed, Hill was deeply involved in issues of university governance and could not possibly have been mistaken for an apolitical business law professor. Hill and her fellow liberals also voted as a block when it came time to make faculty appointments and set institutional policy. Hill herself sat on "Committee A" of the law school, which controlled faculty hiring and tenure decisions. "They were the liberals, or the ultraliberals," said Bob Friedlander. a visiting professor at OU in 1988. Former visiting professor Olson said, "There was an inner council, including Shirley Wiegand, Judy Maute, Teree Foster, Anita, and Rick Tepker. It was the controlling cabal, and they would get another dozen or so to go along with them on anything."[16]

Two members of this group particularly close to Hill are her best friend, Shirley Wiegand—regarded as the most radical member of the OU law faculty and an outspoken critic of Supreme Court decisions dealing with privacy rights claims by women and gays—and Harry "Rick" Tepker, who had served as a professor-in-residence at the EEOC in 1988–89. Hill apparently had said nothing at the time or since then to Tepker about Thomas and harassment. Tepker is an abortion-rights supporter, a death penalty opponent, and had criticized the jurisprudential views of Judge Bork and former Attorney General Edwin Meese in print on a number of occasions.[17] During his stint in Washington, Tepker denounced Justice Scalia as "the most evil man in America," according to one EEOC staffer. "He also disagreed with the ways Thomas was running the agency."[18]

"Anita and her friends turned the school into a politically correct sleaze-pit," said William Michael Roberts, perhaps overstating the case somewhat. An OU law graduate in the mid-1970s who returned to the school as a visiting professor in 1988, Roberts was shocked to see that hiring decisions were now being made solely on the grounds of politics, sex, and race. "It was well known that if you were a white male you would have trouble there, and if you weren't a liberal, forget it." Several current OU faculty members also said that Hill's group worked hard to relax academic standards at the school, and to ensure that the school's hiring policy, even for visitors, was keyed to racial and gender preferences. "Anita is devoted to the proposition that black people are owed something, whether it is a difference in requirements or whatever. She has a flaming commitment to affirmative action," one of Hill's tenured law school colleagues said.

Roberts, Olson, and other white men who did not obtain full-time positions at OU following their temporary appointments may have been victims of these preferential policies themselves, and their criticism should be viewed with that in mind. Neither Roberts nor Olson, however, seemed to dislike Hill personally, and their testimony about such considerations of "diversity," mixed with run-of-the-mill academic politics, is nothing very unusual for a contemporary campus.

What does seem significant is that it was in this environment that Anita Hill finally found her "niche." The liberal views that she had tried to put forward at the EEOC, where a conservative philosophy then reigned, were not only accepted at OU but rewarded. In contrast to Wald, Harkrader, where her status as a black woman had not been enough to protect her, and to Thomas's EEOC, where other, more able black women were passing her by, being black and a woman were highly valued attributes at a liberal academic institution like OU.

Under the tutelage of her new friends, Hill also seems to have mastered the kinds of bureaucratic skills that she lacked at the EEOC, when she was often frustrated in her efforts to compete with other staffers. Unlike the passive way in which she had campaigned for the job that Allyson Duncan got—with sugar-coated comments about the boss that she hoped he would notice—she learned at OU how to operate quietly and behind-the-scenes to produce a desired result. In one case, Hill apparently deployed these skills to enhance her own chances of gaining tenure. A letter filed with the Senate Judiciary Committee by Mary Constance Matthies, a Tulsa attorney, described the following situation:

> On the afternoon of Oct. 11, 1991, I went to the conference room of another law firm in my office building to watch a portion of the hearings during which Ms. Hill was being questioned. Also present were two or three young women lawyers who had recently graduated from the University of Oklahoma Law School, and who had Ms. Hill as an instructor during the time that they attended law school.
>
> These young women stated that Ms. Hill was very outspoken with respect to her views. This trait was reportedly present in Ms. Hill to such excess that these women lawyers characterized her as a "bitch". . . .
>
> Ms. Hill also reportedly was considered to be overly ambitious and a vicious in-fighter by these women. They described an incident where there had been a very popular visiting professor (male) who was teaching Contracts. Ms. Hill reportedly wanted to teach that course very much, and reportedly did her best to insure that this teacher was not invited to become a part of the permanent law school staff by attacking him both personally and professionally. As a result of Ms. Hill's attacks, this male professor left the University of Oklahoma Law School, and Ms. Hill then took over the teaching of the Contracts course which she had wanted to teach.
>
> I am now in the process of trying to contact these women to ascertain if they would be willing to repeat to the committee what they told me privately yesterday. I swear under penalty of perjury that I have accurately reported their statements, to the best of my knowledge and belief.[19]

The students in question never came forward.[20] But one of the students who spoke with Matthies and other sources familiar with the situation on the OU campus said in interviews that the male professor "attacked" by Hill was a man named Alvin Harrell, who had been a visiting professor at OU for two full years in the late 1980s before finding out that he would not be offered a tenure-track position. According to faculty members, Hill trafficked in rumors about Harrell to undermine his position. What her students regarded as the behavior of a "bitch," however, was merely a strategy of running down bureaucratic opponents that is commonly deployed in workplaces by insecure people every day. Now teaching at Oklahoma City University's law school, Alvin Harrell could not confirm the story and had nothing disparaging to say of Hill. "It's quite possible that she could have done it, it wouldn't surprise me, but if she did I wouldn't have known about it," Harrell said, adding, "I was teaching those courses at the time."[21]

OU faculty members speculated that Hill may have felt threatened by Harrell because he was a friend of OU Law Professor Fred Miller. Miller and Hill both taught commercial law. A well-respected scholar, Miller was on the Permanent Editorial Board of the Uniform Commercial Code, and most students preferred to take commercial law classes from him, rather than from Hill. Perhaps Hill—untenured at the time and therefore vulnerable—seized the opportunity to rid herself of other competitors in this area. In any event, after Harrell left, she began to teach his contracts classes.

The most efficacious element of the Anita Hill myth presented to the public in the Senate hearings was that of a prim and proper young woman, a "Real Straight Arrow," as *Time* magazine put it in a profile. The *Time* piece described Hill as "sober," "reserved," and "polite," and reported that when Hill graduated from Yale, she "had reservations about living in Washington, which seemed too loose and unbuckled a place." Hill's academic specialty, commercial law, is a "buttoned-down field," the magazine noted.[22]

But the question must be asked whether this image of Hill was founded on any better evidence than the reportage on Hill's political beliefs, her relations with Clarence Thomas when they worked together, the circumstances of her "coming forward," or the characterization of her case as "typical." The *New York Times* profile of Hill—the very same that could find no evidence of Hill's politics—had this to report on the subject of her demeanor: "Indeed, in the yearbook and in a display of senior class pictures in the front hall of the high school, almost half the girls in the class of 1973 are posed in faux feathered V-necked drapes like toned-down showgirls while Anita Hill is seen smiling broadly beneath black-rimmed glasses in a white dress with puffy sleeves and wearing a gold chain with a cross."

This passage merely substituted an anachronistic cultural stereotype for serious reporting on Hill's character, and apparently did much to establish her pristine image for the television audience. "Like Thomas, Hill was aware that a symbolic dimension to her accusations and even to her presence did exist," Gayle Pemberton wrote in *Race-ing Justice, En-gendering Power.* "She was dressed very conservatively—her habit, we were told. At her side were members of her very large family, all hardworking, pious Christians who had pulled themselves up from rural poverty in Oklahoma. . . . She was the vision of decorum."[23]

In the same volume, Nellie Y. McKay wrote, "She was impressive; and in appearance and demeanor she confirmed the words of others who knew her well and later spoke on her behalf. Politically conservative, deeply religious, by temperament repelled by the nature of the allegations she made, but a woman of strength and integrity willing to stand behind those allegations, however painful that stance was for her, she would have needed years of drama lessons to perfect her act that day had she been other than what she appeared to be."[24]

In the Georgetown speech in October 1992, Hill also acknowledged that her symbolic appropriation of traditional demeanor during the hearing conferred upon her a certain "power and credibility." With a touch of sarcasm in her voice, she said, "Many people who believed me did so because of my association with traditional values and religion, the powerful image of my family filling the Senate hearing room." In the next sentence, Hill distanced herself from the impression created in the hearing, saying, "But I am not a stereotype or a monolithic being."

Faced with this powerful image, and working from the premise that the story was a lie or a fantasy, the Republicans clearly needed to explain where the details in this straightlaced Southern Baptist woman's story could have come from if not from the burly black man who sat behind the witness table. The question became all the more pressing when Hill appeared for her televised testimony, when her story went well beyond the references to dating, bestiality, and group sex in her written committee statement. Her testimony included a startling account of Thomas as having spoken of his sexual prowess and the size of his penis; of his having given women pleasure with oral sex; as well as the Long Dong Silver and "pubic hair" remarks.

This challenge to their nominee's veracity led the committee Republicans on a fevered search for the possible source of these details. The only public effort to provide an answer came on Saturday morning in a series of questions to Thomas from Utah's Orrin Hatch. Hatch's theory was that Hill, a seemingly demure professor of law, had gone to the library and photocopied the details of her testimony from various texts.

Denouncing the "slick lawyers" surrounding Hill, Hatch held up a copy of the *Exorcist* and began reading, "Oh Burk, sighed Sharon. In a guarded tone, she described an encounter between the Senator and the director. Dennings had remarked to him, in passing, said Sharon, that there appeared to be 'an alien pubic hair floating around in my gin.' " Hatch then asked the nominee:

> HATCH: Do you think this was spoken by happenstance? She would have us believe that you were saying these things, because you wanted to date her? What do you think about that Judge?
>
> THOMAS: I think this whole affair is sick.
>
> HATCH: I think it's sick, too.

Hill also testified that Thomas had discussed with her a film "depicting an individual with a large penis," whom she identified as Long Dong Silver. After one of his squeamish aides tried to talk the Senator out of using the word "penis" on national television, Hatch then evoked a parallel between Hill's testimony and a sexual harassment case from Kansas. The case was called to Hatch's attention after attorneys in the office of current EEOC chairman Evan Kemp discovered it in a computerized data-base search for the term "Long Dong Silver" on Friday, during Hill's appearance.

> HATCH: There is an interesting case that I found called *Carter* v. *Sedgwick County, Kansas,* a 1988 case, dated September 30. It is a tenth Circuit Court of Appeals case. It is a District Court case. . . . I apologize in advance for some of the language, I really do. It is a civil rights case, an interesting civil rights case. . . . "Plaintiff further testified that on one occasion Defendant Brand presented her with a picture of Long Dong Silver—a photo of a black male with an elongated penis." I apologize again. Well, it goes on, it gets worse, maybe not worse, but it goes on. That is the public opinion that's available in any law library. I have to tell you I am sure it is available there at the law school in Oklahoma and it is a sexual harassment case. . . .

Though it may have been a reach, Hatch's theory was not an attack on Hill's moral character and in fact it reinforced her pristine image. Hatch presumed that as a law professor with an interest in sexual harassment and sexual discrimination, Hill could have easily come across this case from the judicial circuit that included Oklahoma, where she taught. But the availability of the case in a library hardly constituted proof that Hill had ever seen it before.

Senator Hatch was not the only one, however, who found the details of Hill's testimony eerily reminiscent of the case. On October 15, two days before the hearing ended, the *Kansas City Star* published a story under the headline "Hill's Story Sounded Familiar to Wichita Woman." The article revealed something about the case that Hatch did not know, since the computerized search for "Long Dong Silver" focused only on that term, and no one had read the entire case:

> The Senate inquiry into sexual harassment allegations against Supreme Court nominee Clarence Thomas held several big surprises for Jean Carter of Wichita.
>
> The first came when Hill testified about a particular porn star and about an incident *with a pop can.* . . . In Carter's case, which claimed sexual and racial harassment, supervisors harassed her by, among other things, pinning up a photo of the porn star [Long Dong Silver] and *placing a plastic phallus on her pop can.* Carter said she was surprised by the similarities when Hill started building her case.
>
> "The more I heard, the more I thought her case was similar to mine," she said. . . .[25] [Emphasis added.]

Carter's case was tried, successfully, in 1988. She had been fired from her job in Sedgwick County Community Corrections Department in 1985, and she filed the harassment complaint shortly thereafter.

While Hatch's suggestion cannot be dismissed out of hand, particularly in light of the pop can similarity, the notion that Hill must have consulted case law in a library to discover such salacious details may have been based more on his own prudish view of pornography than on any hard evidence. At one point in an exchange with Thomas, Hatch had claimed that anyone who would say the things that Hill was alleging "would not be a normal person. That person, it seems to me, would be a psychopathic sex fiend or pervert." Hatch's presumption that discussions about pornography and sexual acts were strange and unnatural, intended to make the point that *Thomas* would not have said such horrible things, may have actually reinforced the image of Hill as so wholesome that she *must* have heard them from her boss, widely rumored to have an interest in pornography.

While Hatch was striving to rehabilitate Thomas for the television audience, Republican Senate staffers were busy canvassing students and former students of Hill's looking for dirt on the professor, about whom almost nothing was known. The staffers did not have to look very far before they came upon the story of a former ORU student of Hill's who claimed that she had put pubic hair in one of his law school exams. Some of the Republicans believed that the story, if true, might indicate that Hill had a neurotic fetish that would explain the strange "pubic hair on my Coke" remark that she attributed to Thomas. While the story was never publicized during the hearing (or afterwards), it created a behind-the-scenes sensation among the few top Republicans who knew about it during the weekend.

When the story was relayed to Senator Danforth, he immediately called the Justice Department and asked that government lawyers be sent out to obtain an affidavit from the former student, Lawrence Shiles, now a Tulsa attorney. Top department officials resisted strenuously, arguing that the charge could never be substantiated and would backfire on the Thomas camp in any event. According to one former Justice official, the Shiles story was regarded within the department as "akin to an Elvis sighting." "Here was a United States Senator, a minister, a man known as St. Jack, demanding that we produce a pubic hair affidavit."[26]

As it happened, Shiles took it upon himself to swear out an affidavit on Sunday, which he filed with the Judiciary Committee under no pressure from the divided Thomas camp in Washington. Shiles recounted the alleged episode from the 1983–84 school year at Oral Roberts:

> At that time for both the first and second semesters, Affiant was a student in the class being taught by Anita Hill. The following events are true and accurate recollection as they occurred.
>
> Shortly after the class had begun, Professor Hill gave us a written assignment which I completed and duly turned in. When this assignment was passed out to the class after having been marked by [the] professor, sitting next to me were fellow students Jeffrey Londoff and Mark Stewart. Upon opening the assignments and reviewing our grades and comments made by Anita Hill, I found ten to twelve short black pubic hairs in the pages of my assignment. I glanced over at Jeff Londoff's assignment and saw similar pubic hairs in his work. At that time I made

the statement to Londoff that either she had a low opinion of our work or she graded our assignments in the bathroom. Mark Stewart overheard the conversation and said that he has similar pubic hairs in his assignment also. This became the standing joke among many students for the remainder of the year in her classes.[27]

Why did the students think the hair was pubic? In a later interview, Shiles said, "There was no question in my mind that it was pubic hair. It was short, curly, and kinky. The assignments had plastic covers on them. And scattered through the pages of each paper were several pubic hairs."[28] While he said he could not be sure of their source, Jeff Londoff, now an attorney in St. Louis, corroborated the affidavit and said virtually the same thing about the hairs in an interview: "They were short, coarse, and curly."[29]

But by Sunday, the momentum had shifted so solidly in their direction that Senator Danforth and others in the Thomas camp felt it was too risky to surface the pubic hair affidavit. Of course, it could never be proven that the hairs were pubic. One of the students had traveled to his parents' home to search for the ten-year-old term paper in an attic, but when he located the paper, the hairs were gone. In an interview, Charles Ogletree, representing Hill, shrugged off the suggestion that there were pubic hairs in the papers. "Those could have come from her armpit," Ogletree said.[30]

A more credible and disturbing recollection reached the committee from one of Hill's former students at Oral Roberts University during the weekend. This male student of Hill's said that he had been sexually taunted by her in 1983. The information came to the committee's attention when the father of the former ORU student contacted Alan Simpson's staff during the weekend of the Thomas–Hill hearings. The student's father had been a law partner of Simpson's in Wyoming. On Saturday afternoon, the Senator spoke to the student, who is now a prominent attorney in his thirties in a Western state as well as an amateur pilot. Handsome, and roughly the same age as Hill, the student told Simpson that Hill had approached him in the law school at ORU as he checked his telephone messages one afternoon and said, in a suggestive manner, "I know your favorite flavor is chocolate." On another occasion, Hill allegedly asked the student, teasingly, "Who do you think you are, Long Dong Silver?"[31]

Hill's former student, who had no apparent motive to offer disparaging testimony about Hill, confirmed this account independently in an interview, averring that at the time he thought of Hill as "the world's kinkiest law professor." He also spoke with other GOP committee staffers during the weekend of the hearings, and told them precisely what he had told Simpson, according to their contemporaneous records of the conversations. "This is a serious young man. He doesn't pull pranks," Simpson said in an interview, responding to a skeptical question. "The question of an affidavit was raised, but his father didn't want him to do it, thought it would hurt his career, and I respect that." Simpson said that when he referred to the "proclivities" of Hill, who has never married, during the hearing late Saturday afternoon—widely taken to be a coded reference to lesbianism—he was actually thinking of Hill's alleged reference to "Long Dong Silver" in the conversation with the student. "It was to this reference, this particular descriptive term," Simpson said.[32]

Given the image of Anita Hill as a moralistic Baptist girl from rural Oklahoma, such testimony, if offered at the time, would have struck most viewers as incredible. But what if she was simply not as prudish and straightlaced as she was thought to be? There is, in fact, some further evidence that the image of Hill as naïve about sexual matters may also be misleading.

Hill's friend Diane Holt, for one, was especially incredulous that Hill claimed to have been offended by the off-color remarks she attributed to Thomas. Holt and Hill talked candidly all the time about "men and sex" at lunch in the early 1980s, Holt said, and recalled, "she always bragged that all the men in the office were coming on to her."[33] Holt emphasized that there was nothing particularly unusual about such conversations. "It was 'nasty girl' stuff." At the least, Holt's recollections show that Hill was more comfortable with sexual banter, albeit among her girlfriends at lunch, than later seemed to be the case during her Senate testimony.

Another man who became well acquainted with Hill while he was a visiting professor at the University of Oklahoma agreed with this assessment.[34] He said that Hill was quite familiar with pornography and often casually talked about sex in explicit terms. During the first semester of his visit to OU, the visiting professor was a member of the so-called Bar Review, a group of eight to ten young law professors, including Hill, who went out socially most Friday nights. He also regularly lunched with Hill, and one or two of her women friends on the OU faculty.[35] "Anita would not act out in the larger group, but she did with her close friends. They talked about sex a lot," the professor said. "One of them had tried a sodomy case, and they would talk about that in detail. They would talk about heterosexual anal sex, different positions for it, and rape fantasies. They talked about bestiality. Anita talked about movies as though she watched them at her house. They all watched movies and would sit around at lunch talking about them. Anita would describe the size of men's penises, and talk about firm butts. She was obsessed with oral sex. They also had magazines, and they had sexual devices, and they talked about them. I was invited to go watch movies with them, at a barbecue at one of their houses, not Anita's. And they put a movie on, an old porn movie."[36]

Although the foregoing account may be difficult for some readers to credit, this may be simply due to the contrast it presents with the powerful but misleading image of Hill that was presented by the media at the time. The next question is whether Hill was, as she testified, simply coming forward with information on the nomination for the Senate's consideration while harboring neither personal nor political motives to stop Thomas. At the time she left the EEOC, Hill was angry and resentful of Thomas for his perceived betrayal and abandonment. But what was Hill's relationship with Thomas, and what were her true feelings about him, in the years leading up to his Supreme Court nomination?

The main evidence of continued contacts between the two consisted of ten telephone calls placed to Thomas by Hill in an eight year period (there may have been as many as a half dozen other calls made by Hill which were not recorded in the phone log, as Diane Holt explained, because they were put directly through to Thomas). Ironically, Republican attempts to use the logs to show that Hill's feelings about Thomas during this time were warm and friendly distracted attention from the disputes between Hill and Thomas at the EEOC that may have been the foundation for her motive. "Why is she calling Judge Thomas—then Chairman of the Equal Employment Opportunity Commission—if she was so upset at him?" Senator Hatch asked on the Senate floor. "If this really had happened, why would she call him, of all people?. . . . Here is a woman who was so offended that she is willing to accuse this person, who everybody else knows to be a reasonable, wonderful, upstanding person of integrity and honesty, and she is continually calling him. . . . Does this sound like a victim of sexual harassment? It does not to me."

The fact of the matter is that Hill *was* upset with Thomas, dating back to her departure from the EEOC, and yet she called him anyway. The question is why she would do so. A close examination of the phone log shows that eight of the ten calls were placed while Hill was teaching at Oral Roberts University. Most of these calls appeared to be solicitations for Thomas's help in obtaining research grants, compiling statistical information for various projects, or acting as an intermediary for local groups extending speaking invitations to Thomas. Only one call was placed in 1987, after the ORU law school had closed and Hill had gone to the University of Oklahoma. And a final one came in 1991, when Hill extended a speaking invitation to Thomas at the behest of an OU colleague, according to Hill's testimony.

The distribution of the calls—which no one seems to have parsed during the hearings—suggests that Hill felt a far greater need or desire to be in touch with Thomas while she was at ORU than afterwards. This would have been natural enough, since Thomas had recommended her for the job at ORU, and he subsequently forged a close relationship with Dean Kothe. Since Hill's performance would be evaluated by Kothe and others, who (in the absence of tenure arrangements) would be deciding every few years whether or not to renew her appointment, Hill's connections to Thomas were obviously valuable. She may have been at odds with him politically, but the fact that she had been his special assistant in the Reagan Administration helped anchor her in ORU's conservative culture, where she was not otherwise very secure.

Hill was able to enhance her status at ORU by acting as the contact for civil rights groups in Tulsa seeking access to Thomas. And when in 1985 Kothe retired from the deanship but remained a powerful fixture on campus, Hill, perhaps trying to cement her position further, encouraged Kothe to become a consultant to Thomas at the EEOC. "She never let you forget that she was a big wig to a big wig," said former ORU student Keith Lapayude.

During her first year at OU, however, Hill had contact with Thomas only twice, so far as the record shows. The first occasion was at Charles Kothe's house in April 1987, following a conference that Thomas, Hill and Kothe had attended in Tulsa. Kothe later testified that he recalled the meeting as a "joyous occasion," with the two "laughing uproariously." Hill had volunteered to drive Thomas to the airport, Kothe said, because she wanted to show off her new car.

In 1987, of course, Hill was new to OU, she was untenured, and she had no reason to discontinue her association with Thomas or raise Kothe's suspicions about their real relationship. Unless she had been sexually harassed by Thomas, it should have been no surprise that on the evening before Thomas was to depart Tulsa, Hill would have called Kothe and volunteered to drive her former boss and mentor to the airport. In the interview with Senate lawyers, Hill's friend Gary Phillips said, "I think Anita did not want to burn her bridges and I know—I will say something else too. I know Anita was very concerned about making tenure at Oklahoma. And my assumption is that Anita had occasional contact with Judge Thomas to keep up the networking, to make sure she wasn't burning her bridges."[37]

The pace of Hill's networking was far more intensive at ORU than at OU, however. During her first year at OU, no telephone calls were logged from Hill to Thomas. The first telephone call after Hill had gone to OU came in the late summer of 1987 when Hill was in Washington doing research at American University and thinking about applying for a job there. Hill left her telephone number on this message, as she had on another occasion in 1985, which if nothing else suggested that she did not view Thomas as a sex harasser likely to abuse this information. Some Republicans tried to impute to this fact the suggestion that Hill was open to a sexual liaison, but the truth was probably far more innocent. Hill may have been simply trying to rekindle her relationship with Thomas because she might need him for a job reference at American University.

The other controversial aspect of this log entry was the fact that Hill left the message "wanted to congratulate on marriage." Because this was the last message in the log for four years, until 1991, the Republicans interpreted the break in sequence to suggest that Hill was angry and jealous that Thomas had remarried. After reading that particular message into the record, Senator Hatch demanded to know, "What is going on here?"

From Hill's own statements, there is some reason to think that she disapproved of the marriage to Ginni Thomas, who is white. But there is no evidence that this disapproval was in any way linked to her own romantic interest in Thomas. Armstrong Williams remembered a conversation with Hill in 1983, after Hill discovered that Thomas had been seriously involved with Lillian McEwen, who was racially mixed. Hill made a disapproving comment about Thomas's preference for lighter-complected women. "Anita talked about who he was dating and she said, 'Well at least he's not dating a white woman.' Interracial dating was a big sticking point with her," Williams said.

In an exchange with Senator Specter, Thomas also alluded to Hill's sensitivity regarding the skin tone of both Lillian McEwen and Allyson Duncan. In a meeting with Specter prior to the leaking of Hill's charges, but after she had filed them in written form with the committee, Thomas told Specter that he recalled Hill voicing such concerns. In the hearing, understating the case as he often did when speaking of Hill's possible motives, Thomas said:

> And the point that I was making to you is that there seemed to be some tension between, as a result of the complexion of the woman I dated and the woman I chose to be my chief of staff, or my executive assistant and some reaction, as I recall it, to my preferring individuals of the lighter complexion.

Hill's attitude on this issue, however, hardly seems enough to explain the abrupt termination of her attempts to contact Thomas, especially since most of the contacts were professional in nature. At the most, Thomas's remarriage may simply have confirmed the view that Hill already held of Thomas, as she expressed it to Williams when she left the EEOC, as a self-hating black and racial traitor. This would have been doubly true for Hill because Ginni was not only white, she was also a conservative Republican activist, a lobbyist for the U.S. Chamber of Commerce, and the person responsible for Thomas's involvement in the conservative Episcopalian church whose anti-abortion activities Senator Simon had found so objectionable.

The calls probably came to a halt in 1987 for a more obvious reason: namely, that as she became more securely established at OU, Thomas was less and less useful in a professional sense to her. No longer was she trying to survive at the conservative ORU law school where the dean was close to Thomas. Now, Hill was settling into a comfortable left-wing academic milieu where disparaging Thomas— the controversial black conservative—would have won her more plaudits than claiming him as a mentor. Hill no longer had to keep the conservative door open. She was free publicly to adopt the view of Thomas that she had privately expressed years earlier when Allyson Duncan was promoted over her: Thomas was a "dangerous thinker." In 1988, for example, one professor recalls Hill arguing against extending an invitation to Thomas to speak on campus because he "could have done more at the EEOC on civil rights than he had, and she didn't like his conservative philosophy. There was a moral tone in her judgment," the professor remarked.

The final piece of evidence that seemed to indicate Hill's "true" feelings about Thomas during the hearings was the testimony of Carlton Stewart and Stanley Grayson, who told the committee that in August 1991, just two months before her Senate testimony, Hill had praised the Thomas nomination in a discussion at an American Bar Association convention. According to the two men, Hill had told them "how great Clarence's nomination was and how much he deserved it." In an interview, Stewart explained that when he came upon Hill at the conference, she was conferring about the Thomas nomination with a woman from the NAACP Legal Defense and Education Fund, an anti-Thomas group. "She's the one you have to worry about," Hill told Stewart, with a nervous laugh.

The Republican interpretation of this episode was that in August the "real Anita Hill" evidently had no political or personal objection to the Thomas nomination, but that she had radically—and inexplicably—altered her view in the short time since the ABA convention. "Something that bothers me is this woman is so upset at Judge Thomas, suddenly, after ten years and after all these opportunities to tell her story, all of these positions being important positions, all confirmable positions," Senator Hatch said. From this perspective, Hill's comments to Stewart must have either represented her true feelings about Thomas, or perhaps gave evidence that she was not in possession of her faculties. If the former, Hill's "sudden conversion" over the summer could only be ascribed to a conspiracy of liberal activists who had somehow persuaded Hill to perjure herself in a desperate attempt to defeat the nomination.

However, the view that Hill was either mentally unbalanced or had been suborned seems overblown. The Republicans simply did not know enough about the real Anita Hill to have seen that Hill's comments to Stewart cannot possibly have represented her true feelings. A much more likely explanation is that when Stewart left the EEOC in early 1983, he did not know that Hill's relations with Thomas had become strained over disagreements on a variety of policy issues; nor did he know that Hill had justified her decision to leave the agency on political grounds after failing to attain the promotion she desired. Assuming that Hill did make these complimentary comments about Thomas, despite her sworn denials, her intention may have simply been to conceal her reservations about the nomination. By acceding to Stewart's view, Hill thus implicitly acknowledged that the real Anita Hill was very different from the woman he expected her to be, based on their experience together at the EEOC.

While she never mentioned sexual harassment, Hill was quite open in expressing her political opposition to the Thomas nomination in conversations with at least three law school colleagues during July and August. Hill's comments at this time, before she knew that anyone other than Hoerchner was aware of the sexual harassment charge, and long before she was forced by the leak of her allegations to assume a public role in the nomination process, were probably her genuine views about the nomination. "She indicated when he was nominated that she didn't support his ideas when we were all sitting around having coffee one day," said one OU law professor. "I had a conversation with her right after Clarence Thomas was nominated. She indicated she didn't like his political agenda," said another.

In an interview in the *Los Angeles Times,* Rick Tepker, one of Hill's closer friends, revealed that Hill shared his antipathy not only to Thomas but to Republican judicial nominees in general. As the *Times* reported on October 15, the day of the confirmation vote: "Tepker said that Hill had mentioned to him casually some weeks ago that she believed Thomas's selection for the court was 'political' and that Thomas was not as qualified as some others who could have been chosen. 'But she was not particularly intense about it,' Tepker said. 'She had said much the same thing about [Supreme Court Justice David H.] Souter.' "[38]

When reporters called Hill during the summer to inquire about Thomas, she was also willing to reveal her political reservations about the nominee. At this point, she had spoken of harassment only to Hoerchner and Gary Phillips, one of whom was responsible for the story reaching Nan Aron of the Alliance for Justice and then Tim Phelps of *Newsday.* According to *Capitol Games,* Phelps telephoned Hill almost immediately on first hearing rumors about the sexual harassment charge in late July. Phelps had promised his source not to ask Hill about the rumor, so Phelps asked about Thomas's political background instead.

At the time, Phelps was evidently fishing for information linking Thomas to Jay Parker, head of the controversial Washington think-tank, the Lincoln Institute. Parker was a long-time black conservative who had supported Barry Goldwater for president in 1964, and a friend of Thomas's. Parker had also been a lobbyist for South Africa in the 1980's, and Phelps had been trying to use Parker's South Africa connection to incriminate Thomas. Phelps's Parker stories became one of the main lines of attack against Thomas during the first round of hearings, when they were picked up by Paul Simon. Simon used them as the basis for hostile questioning of the nominee, which suggested that he condoned apartheid.

Hill, a former Washington insider, undoubtedly understood that linking Thomas to Parker could damage his nomination. It is therefore significant that when Phelps asked Hill about the Parker–Thomas connection, she seemed eager to oblige in helping Phelps make his tendentious case that Parker, who could easily be smeared as a cynic, opportunist, and race-traitor, was Thomas's "secret mentor." Thus three months before she would testify about Thomas's alleged harassment, claiming that she had no motive to do so, Hill had already been complicit in an attempted "borking" maneuver. As Phelps wrote, "When I telephoned Hill, I interviewed her about Jay Parker, the lobbyist for South Africa who was Thomas's secret mentor. Having worked for several years as an aide to Thomas, she was familiar with his political life." Hill then told Phelps:

> My impression was he really looked up to him and he looked to him for political advice and used him as his political connection to the Reagan Administration. They were very close. He was practically an adviser to Thomas.[39]

Phelps used this information from Hill in subsequent stories, but he protected her identity, and indeed never revealed her as a source of this material until he published *Capitol Games*. But while the incident showed that Hill was willing to cooperate in a veiled journalistic attack on Thomas, it showed something more as well. Phelps knew that a sexual harassment rumor had already been tied to Hill at the time of this interview, and the main purpose of his call had been to establish contact with Hill in the hopes of developing the sexual harassment story later in the summer. Thus he may have hoped to forge a tacit understanding with Hill that he was the Washington reporter who was interested in nailing Clarence Thomas. This may explain why an anonymity deal was struck on the Parker–Thomas story.

Hill, however, did not know at the time Phelps called her that he knew about the brewing sexual harassment charge. She seemed not to realize that the rumor had gotten around Washington so quickly after she spoke to Hoerchner and Gary Phillips. While Hill may have felt she could control the relationship with Phelps, just as she later tried to control the harassment story itself, she was actually being positioned by Phelps for something well beyond her capacity to manage.

A few weeks later, on August 17, Hill was interviewed by a reporter for the *Kansas City Star.* In this interview, Hill contended that when Thomas was at the Department of Education he would have made a better Supreme Court nominee than the Clarence Thomas of 1991. Since according to Hill's Senate testimony she had suffered the worst harassment from Thomas at Education, it seems odd that she would think of him in any sense as being *more* qualified for the court at this time. Hill told the newspaper:

> Judicial experience aside, the Clarence Thomas of that period [at the Department of Education in 1982] would have made a better judge on the Supreme Court because he was more open-minded. I think he honestly believes self-help is best for all disadvantaged people. He doesn't realize there are so many things that will keep them disadvantaged.[40]

This quote seemed to establish that Hill's reason for opposing the nominee was not that he was a sexual harasser but that he had become more conservative in the years since he served at Education. It was also during this period that Hill had concluded that her influence with Thomas had diminished as he relied less and less on her counsel. As Hill stated her view, Thomas "honestly believes" in his conservative philosophy because he "doesn't realize" its effects. He does not realize this, she seemed to be saying, not because his views had matured but because he had lost his political and social bearings in the time since the two worked together at Education.

By late summer, in an indication that she was closely following the progress of the nomination fight, Hill's on-the-record comments began to display a certain lack of spontaneity, echoing the charges against Thomas made by the opposition groups in Washington which had been repeated in the national press and were now filtering through the nation's law schools. In early September, just before she was first contacted by Kennedy aide Ricki Seidman and then Metzenbaum aide Jim Brudney—and presumably before she knew that the sexual harassment story had reached Washington—Hill told a reporter from the *Washington Post* that she considered Thomas to be self-centered, insensitive, and hypocritical, subtly shifting the grounds of her criticism from questions of ideology to concerns about his character. The *Post* reported on September 9:

> Anita Hill, a former special assistant to Thomas at the Education Department and the EEOC, was particularly disturbed by Thomas's repeated, public criticism of his sister and her children for living on

welfare. "It takes a lot of detachment to publicize a person's experience that way" and "a certain kind of self-centeredness not to recognize some of the programs that benefited you," said Hill, now an Oklahoma law professor. "I think he doesn't understand people, he doesn't relate to people who don't make it on their own."[41]

Though Hill had adopted these general views of Thomas long ago, the speech in which Thomas criticized his sister had been extensively circulated by the NAACP and the Alliance for Justice throughout the summer, and the charge that Thomas was a hypocrite for criticizing affirmative action was a constant theme of the civil rights groups.

If Hill was seriously contemplating "coming forward" and filing an official harassment charge with the Senate, it seems unlikely that she would have compromised her chances of being viewed as an unbiased witness by openly disparaging Thomas's politics and character to colleagues and reporters during the summer. But as we have already seen, Hill *never* intended to come forward. At the most, she may have been wondering how to circulate an anonymous sexual harassment charge, and was therefore free to speak her mind—until the Senate staffers called in early September.

It is now possible to reconstruct the genesis of the sexual harassment charge, and to see what concerns may have been weighing on Hill's mind when she took the first tentative steps to put this rumor into circulation in July.

Susan Hoerchner remembered that in 1981, Hill had complained of sexual harassment by her boss, and she remembered that Hill had worked for Clarence Thomas. After watching a television report on the Thomas nomination on July 1, Hoerchner jumped to the conclusion that he must have been the one Hill had complained about.

Hoerchner then called Hill, to whom she had not spoken for seven years. Alluding to Hill's 1981 sexual harassment story, she suggested that Thomas was the "pig" who had harassed her in 1981 and asked Hill if she was going to "say anything."

Hill should have realized at this point that when she originally complained to Hoerchner in 1981, she had not yet been working for Thomas. However, given the ten-year interval, she may herself have been confused about the timing of that prior conversation, and only discovered that it was a hole in her story later on during Hoerchner's testimony, when Hoerchner discovered it herself. Given her proclivity to use harassment, or political differences, or both as an excuse for her personal and professional problems, it would have been hard for her to keep her stories straight in her own mind. Thus for all she knew, she may indeed have complained to Hoerchner about harassment at the time she was working for Thomas at Education, rather than previously when she was working at Wald, Harkrader. To the extent that Hill was confused about this sequence, Hoerchner's certainty may have convinced her that this conversation really had occurred as Hoerchner thought, thereby in effect supplying Hill with a memory that did not exist. To believe this, one need only allow for the possibility that Hill recalled no better than Hoerchner the date of their last conversation.

Alternatively, Hill may have realized immediately that Hoerchner's recollection was mistaken. But as someone who was reasonably familiar with sexual harassment law, Hill would also have known that the strongest evidence for such a charge would be contemporaneous corroboration from a third party. She may thus have concluded that Hoerchner's fortuitous error would be useful in grounding a charge, and allowed it to go uncorrected. Either way, however—unless she was not of sound mind—she must have known that Clarence Thomas was not the guilty party in this case.

What could possibly have tempted Hill to exploit Hoerchner's error by bringing a false charge of sexual harassment against Thomas, knowing that she risked exposure as a perjurer? She must have believed that an anonymous charge of sexual harassment might be used to real effect in harming the nomination. The evidence suggests that this idea was also put into her mind by Susan Hoerchner. During the course of their July 1 conversation, Hoerchner almost certainly referred to her own recent experience as a corroborating witness in a sexual harassment case at the workmen's compensation board in Norwalk, California. In that case, once the charges were made, and before any formal investigation had been undertaken, the board's presiding judge retired. This occurred at precisely the time of their phone conversation. Thus Hoerchner was probably the first to suggest that an anonymous harassment charge might have the desirable effect of quietly derailing the nomination—a suggestion that would later be made more firmly by Metzenbaum staffer Jim Brudney.

When Hoerchner asked if Hill was going to say anything at that point, Hill said that she would not. However, she did release Hoerchner from an oath that she had allegedly sworn years before never to discuss the matter with anyone else. Hill took this step in full knowl-

edge that Hoerchner was a committed opponent of the Thomas nomination and that she had worked for a public interest law group in
Washington, and thus presumably retained connections to the activist
community there. Indeed, Hoerchner's brother was a close friend of
Brudney, whom Hill also knew. This makes it possible to think that
Hill intended for the story to reach the committee staff itself by an
indirect route early on in the process.[42]

Having established that she had the opportunity to harm the nomination, it still must be asked why Anita Hill would have knowingly
brought a false charge of harassment against Thomas. In previous
chapters we have seen that, unbeknownst to Thomas, Hill had come
to view her former patron as a dangerous thinker, a traitor to his race,
a hypocrite who had profited from affirmative action and then tried
to eliminate these preferences for others; she saw him as closed-
minded, uncompassionate, and insensitive, a man who had turned
his back on his own disadvantaged roots and knowingly undermined
the cause of civil rights at the EEOC. He had even publicly attacked
his own sister as an example of welfare dependency. In addition to
these political considerations, Hill had a personal motive as well,
based on her perception that Thomas had betrayed and abandoned
her to her fate at the EEOC, all the while thinking of himself in flat-
tering terms as her "mentor." Thus Hoerchner's insulting characterization of Thomas as a "pig" may not have been too far off the mark
from Hill's perspective.

It remains to be explained how Hill could have made such a strong
impression on the Senate committee and the public during the hearings and afterwards, when her evident poise and conviction made it
seem that she really believed her own story. For those who are inclined to believe her, the positive results of the polygraph test would
only further strengthen that impression of veracity. However, it also
seems plausible to think that Hill, over the course of three months,
under considerable pressure from all sides to come forward, may
have persuaded herself that the memory supplied by Hoerchner was
true. What Hill portrayed as a protracted struggle with her conscience should perhaps be understood as an internal psychological
struggle to square the circle in her mind between her hatred of
Thomas and the specific charge of sexual harassment. Here, the figure of Chris Roggerson, mysteriously missing from her testimony,
may have played a crucial role. Based on corroborating testimony
from Hill's former colleagues at the EEOC, Roggerson was perfectly

capable of having said and done the things that Hill ascribed to Thomas. It may thus not be too much to suggest that Hill conflated Roggerson and Thomas in her mind—all the easier since Thomas had appointed Roggerson to a position of authority over Hill, and thus was complicit in Roggerson's presumed mistreatment of her. Hill may even have concluded that Thomas intended to punish her for their political disagreements by proxy, via Roggerson's harassment.

After speaking with Hoerchner, Hill tried the story out for the first time ever on Shirley Wiegand, her closest friend on the law school faculty. In a letter to the Senate Judiciary Committee after the hearings concluded, Wiegand wrote, "When Anita and I first began to discuss her obligation to tell the truth about Clarence Thomas, we knew there would be repercussions. We knew her life would be disrupted and that some would not take her concerns seriously. In fact, my concern as early as August was that you senators would not care about whether she had been sexually harassed."[43] However, this comment seems more like an ex post facto adaptation of the anti-Thomas sloganeering that occurred during the hearings than a reasonable anticipation of difficulty in getting the "white male" Senate committee to take the harassment charge seriously; Hill and Wiegand may indeed have been discussing whether or not the charge would be "taken seriously," but what they were more likely wondering was whether an anonymous charge of sexual harassment would be enough to stop the nomination.

By late July, three weeks had passed with no repercussions from the Hoerchner call. At this juncture, Hill called her friend Gary Phillips and told him that she had left the EEOC because Thomas had harassed her. Was this simply idle conversation that Hill had intended should go no further? Possibly so, but given the seriousness of the charge it seems unlikely. Was she perhaps seeking his advice on how the Senate might view the allegation? Phillips was an experienced Washington lawyer and had friends who had worked on the Judiciary Committee; presumably he therefore had some insight into its operations and perhaps some direct personal contact with its staff. In fact, it seems likely that she chose to tell Phillips for this reason. If so, then Thomas's opponents, hearing the story third-hand, would then have to approach her with the request that she testify, thus enabling her to claim, as she later did, that she would never have made the charge at all if she had not been approached by the Senate committee. This also meant, however, that she would not have any knowledge about the progress of the rumor one way or the other until she heard back from the committee.

Only Hill can say what her precise intentions were. But clearly at the time she was speaking to Wiegand and then Phillips in late July about "sexual harassment," she was not staying out of the struggle over the nomination. Hill told her colleagues and friends and even reporters that she opposed Thomas on political grounds. As the *Post* story indicated, Hill was watching the progress of the nomination from the sidelines, and was anxious to charge Thomas with insensitivity to women. She also knew that she could play a role in its defeat, as shown by her willingness to participate in a borking scheme in which she provided Tim Phelps with a damaging anonymous quote on Thomas and Parker.

Clarence Thomas, meanwhile, plainly had no idea how Hill felt about him when she left the EEOC. From everything he might have gathered in following years, their relations remained as friendly as ever. Hill called from time to time, asking for assistance on various projects. She had stopped by the EEOC once for a reference. When Charles Kothe was assigned to write a history of the agency in his capacity as Thomas's consultant, Thomas told him to "ask Anita" to help appraise his tenure, despite what he knew to be their political differences. She had come to Kothe's house early one morning in 1987 to drive him to the airport. He had worked with both Kothe and Hill on one of Hill's research projects, "developing a model EEO program"— on sexual harassment!

But perhaps the surest sign that Thomas never imagined he had anything to fear from Hill came during the weekend before this story ran September 9 in the *Post.* In early September, a Justice Department official mulling over potential pro-Thomas witnesses for the first round of Senate confirmation hearings suggested to Thomas that Anita Hill be asked to testify for him. Thomas encouraged the suggestion, and said she could be contacted at the University of Oklahoma. Certainly Thomas would have easily deflected any overture to Hill by the Justice Department if he had known that he was guilty of sexual harassment. But the idea of Hill testifying for the nominee was quietly shelved a couple of days later when the *Post* story appeared and Thomas, for the first time, began to wonder if Hill might not be the friend he had thought she was. Armstrong Williams read the article and telephoned Thomas to remind him of his warning about Hill a decade ago: "That's just what I told you. She's been on a mission since 1983."

Nowhere were Hill's true views about the Thomas nomination better captured than in a little-noticed front-page story headlined: "Prof Says Thomas Not Best Choice," which appeared in mid-September in the *Oklahoma Daily*, the student newspaper on the OU campus. Hill was clearly expressing a long-held and deeply felt view of Thomas in this article, not a new view emerging in response to the confirmation controversy. The lead paragraph of the story stated: "A former assistant to Supreme Court nominee Clarence Thomas said Wednesday that *based on her experiences with him*, 'there were a lot better (possible) nominations.' " [Emphasis added.]

As Hill explained it to the student reporter, the Clarence Thomas of the Education Department period, when she was his top assistant, was the "good Thomas," a flexible and sympathetic person less firmly committed to conservative positions on civil rights. "My experience with him was that at Education, he was a very open-minded person," Hill said. "He was able to see all different sides of an issue much more readily than I think he can now." She went on to say, as the reporter paraphrased her view, that "part of what makes a good Supreme Court justice, is the ability to look at a case from all different perspectives and angles."

But the later Thomas, the "bad Thomas," lost the ability to be open-minded and objective and began to adhere to a rigid ideology. Thus he would not make a good justice, in Hill's view—a view shared by many other critics of the Thomas nomination. But Hill believed that she had special insight into Thomas, having seen this ideological view encroaching on him as early as 1982. "I think he is locked into position," she said. "He thinks that he has found the solutions to any number of issues, and he thinks that other solutions are unmerited. I think his mind is made up on a lot of cases, and I think that's *bad*," Hill said. Again paraphrasing Hill, the reporter wrote, "She said the country needs a justice who will look at each case and determine where it should fall on its own merits."

Hill went on to question Thomas's ability to empathize with the disadvantaged, condemning his criticism of an affirmative action system that had helped him succeed and his advocacy of self-help strategies rather than government-mandated quotas for overcoming discrimination. "The other thing that bothers me about him, almost at the same level, is that he shows very little ability to empathize with people who are unfortunate," Hill said. "He had, in many ways, a disadvantaged background, but in many other ways, he had an advantaged background. I think he is now thinking that most people who are disadvantaged aren't making it because they don't have the will to make it, not because the odds are stacked against them," she said. "Granted, he's a person who has defied the odds, but he would say that those other people should defy the odds too, and I would say, let's prevent the odds from being stacked against them. Let's try and even the odds."

Hill ended by enjoining OU students to pay attention to the Supreme Court confirmation process. "Hill emphasized that people should not brush off the nomination as some distant happening in Washington," the paper reported. "This whole process is very interesting, and I think people ought to be aware of it," Hill said. "You don't have to be a legal scholar to have a position on this, and you shouldn't have to be one. It's an important time and an important nomination, as every one is. It's something you should care about."[44]

Hill herself did care about the nomination, and what it might mean for the future of the Supreme Court. By this time she had acted on those concerns by speaking with Biden staffer Harriet Grant. However, Hill had insisted on anonymity to protect herself from an FBI investigation and confrontation with the nominee. When Hill gave the campus paper interview several days earlier, she was still under the mistaken impression that her anonymous allegation to the committee might suffice to induce Thomas to withdraw his nomination. Hill never intended to give up her anonymity, and therefore had no reason to conceal her opposition to Thomas in this interview—or any other—during the summer.

As has been shown, the anonymous charge had been made earlier in September, after Ricki Seidman of Senator Kennedy's office and Jim Brudney pressured Hill to acknowledge the harassment rumor brought to them by the Alliance for Justice. Hill had no reason to know that what she had "confirmed" to Susan Hoerchner and then told to Gary Phillips would be quickly intercepted by Nan Aron at a Washington dinner party, and then reported to Seidman and Brudney. But it is possible to think that while she had no firm idea of how the rumor would be transmitted, Hill had wanted to reach Brudney all along—either through Hoerchner, whose brother was a friend of his at Yale, or through Phillips, who, like Brudney, had been part of Hill's circle of friends from law school in the early 1980s.

Thus it can never be known exactly who was manipulating whom at any given moment as the sexual harassment charge moved forward. Hill should have known Brudney was working hard to defeat the Clarence Thomas nomination, and would therefore be in a position to assess whether the strategy that had been employed by Hoerchner against Judge Foster might be used to the same effect against Thomas. Brudney, for his part, in addition to using the threat of unwanted publicity to perhaps frighten Hill into moving ahead behind-the-scenes, would have known that Hill had a motive to do so, because he surely knew of her political disillusionment with Thomas when she left the EEOC. This was why their friendship during the time that Hill worked for Thomas in 1983 was so significant for the events of September 1991.

"She turned Brudney against Thomas years ago," Armstrong Williams speculated. Williams recalled that the two were in regular contact during Hill's most trying period at the EEOC in early 1983, when she lost the chief legal adviser's job to Allyson Duncan, was hospitalized for stress, and then decided to leave Washington. As Williams stated his opinion, "That's why Brudney was Thomas's enemy all those years."

Brudney, therefore, knew too much about Hill to be the first staffer to call her when the sexual harassment rumor first surfaced. He must have thought it would be far less risky if either Gail Laster or Ricki Seidman was able to get Hill to come forward. But when Hill seemed reluctant, with time running out and the borking effort failing—except in raising a character question about the nominee—Brudney intervened directly.

The full contents of the Brudney–Hill telephone call on September 13 also will likely never be known. Hill's recollection of the call is the only one in the record, and hers may not be a completely candid account. While Brudney clearly used all of his powers of persuasion to get Hill to contact the Judiciary Committee, it seems reasonable to conclude that the desire to stop Thomas by floating the sexual harassment story was one that Hill shared mutually with Brudney.

The sticking point was the issue of whether or not Hill would have to identify herself. Brudney may have misled Hill during this call into thinking that she could remain anonymous in the hope of pushing her further later on, since he must certainly have known that a condition of total anonymity would have prevented consideration of the charge by the committee. But since by Hill's own account Brudney told her to expect an FBI investigation, Hill probably misinterpreted Brudney's promise of confidentiality to mean a guarantee of anonymity.

When the committee refused to consider the anonymous charge, Hill got caught in the churning gears of the Shadow Senate. When

Brudney discovered that Hill had misinterpreted his promise and had expected total anonymity, rather than respect Hill's wishes, he convinced Susan Deller Ross and Judith Lichtman to push her into signing a statement to be filed with the Judiciary Committee.

After doing so, Hill seemed concerned for the first time that she had gone on the record opposing the nomination, a sign that she sensed she may have gone too far in signing the statement. A few days after the story containing her criticism of Thomas appeared in the *Oklahoma Daily*—and just *after* she had been persuaded to surrender her anonymity and file her confidential September 23 statement— Hill telephoned Margot Habiby, the student reporter who had written it. Hill asked whether she had written anything from the interview she had done with her, and Habiby told her that a story had been published. When the student offered to send Hill a copy through the campus mail, Hill asked that it be faxed to her immediately.

Little did Hill know that Habiby was the least of her worries, however. Once the written statement was filed, Hill's fate was in the hands of the Thomas opposition in Washington. When Thomas declined to withdraw, as a guilty person might have been expected to, and no Senator on the Judiciary Committee was willing to place Hill's confidentiality at risk by calling for further investigation, the opposition knowingly subverted the constitutional process of the Senate, sacrificing both Thomas and Hill for its political ends.

The confidential charges were leaked to the media by Senator Simon and Jim Brudney, the true villains of the piece. Brudney was particularly irresponsible since he must have known that Hill was politically and personally motivated against Thomas, and he surely knew how concerned Hill had been all along to assure that her name would never be publicized. By ensuring the trial by leak, the leakers were directly responsible for ruining the reputations of both Clarence Thomas and Anita Hill.

If the Thomas–Hill scandal proved nothing else, it showed that a Senate hearing—particularly a televised one conducted in great haste— is not a reliable way to discover the truth. Both Thomas and Hill were defamed in the course of the hearings, Thomas by having to defend himself in a public forum against an unsubstantiated charge, and Hill by the attempts of Thomas's defenders to explain how and why she would have come forward with a story they were certain was false. In short, the Judiciary Committee Senators behaved like politicians, not judges or trained investigators. The leakers, and the feminist groups that demanded a public inquiry on the basis of no evidence, must ultimately be held accountable for the political excesses of this episode.

When the hearings gaveled to a close, Thomas appeared to have won. Two days later, he was confirmed to the Supreme Court. Anita Hill's defenders have yet to offer a persuasive explanation for the outcome; Margaret Burnham, writing in Toni Morrison's collection, called the public's strong backing of Thomas "a peculiar case of cognitive dissonance." Others have argued that black opinion was swayed in Thomas's direction by a misplaced and retrogressive sense of racial solidarity that precluded blacks from treating Hill's charge—embraced as it was mostly by white middle-class feminists—as serious enough to warrant harming the career of an upwardly-mobile black man. Yet it seems self-evident that while little was known of the real story of Anita Hill at the time, the public instinctively judged her case against Thomas as insufficiently persuasive to deny him confirmation, and rejected the opposition's premise that a cloud of doubt was itself grounds for disqualification. As a political strategy, the GOP's depiction of Hill as deluded provided a comfortable way to support Thomas while avoiding calling Hill an outright liar.[45]

Thomas, for his part, had abandoned the posturing and legalistic answers of the first round of hearings and emerged in that instant as the forceful and impassioned man his friends recognized as the real Clarence Thomas. But Thomas was also reserved, stubborn, and possessed of a deep sense of personal dignity; he therefore refused to engage or attack Hill directly, leaving the motive question unanswered, and making him appear as though he might be repressing his own guilt. His demeanor did, however, allow him to avoid the trap of appearing to be victimizing his accuser.

Thomas's keen political instincts, plainly visible in the first round of hearings, were not altogether tossed aside. His characterization of the hearing as a "high-tech lynching"—which left many of the strategists who had helped devise the "Souter strategy" for the first round of hearings in a panic that Thomas had blown his chances of confirmation in a burst of emotion—turned out to be politically effective, going over the heads of the civil rights establishment and keeping the majority of black Americans on his side. His critics meanwhile argued that the comparison between his case and actual lynchings betrayed an insensitivity to black history and was rank hypocrisy coming from a man who had spent a good portion of his public career criticizing those who used race to their personal advantage.

Because many observers were swept up by the false image of Hill and her case as presented by the media at the time, it is understandable that Thomas's analogy would be jarring. But on further investigation, it seems clear that the analogy was quite apt. The unsubstantiated charge of a lone accuser—only plausible because it was a charge of sexual misconduct against a black man—obscured the real cause of his vilification, namely his conservative politics. The often frivolous invocation of racial and sexual victimology notwithstanding, sometimes there are real victims, and Thomas was one in this case.

This could be seen even more clearly after the hearings, when every person accused of a sex crime (coincidentally all white liberals) was treated far more fairly by the legal system and even by the press. Whether it was Judge Sol Wachtler in New York, who was accused of harassing a former girlfriend and her daughter, the film director Woody Allen, accused by actress Mia Farrow of child abuse, accused rapist William Kennedy Smith, or Senator Bob Packwood, against whom at this date no fewer than 23 women have filed harassment complaints, society generally reserved judgment until the facts could be determined. In this respect, the Packwood case was most striking. Gloria Steinem said the charges of sexual harassment against the pro-choice Senator should be weighed "in the context" of his public record on women's issues, and Judith Lichtman called for "due process"—a fundamental protection that even the Tailhook offenders received. For Thomas, the reverse was true; in the absence of incriminating facts, he was all the more thoroughly demonized, and thus the public opinion polls turned against him within a year.

Clarence Thomas's life was forever transformed by the leak of Hill's unsubstantiated charge. Forty-three years of scrupulous personal behavior and a strong public record on sexual harassment were destroyed literally in an instant. Because he was tried in the court of public opinion, with no due process or rules of evidence, doubts about his integrity would never be dispelled. No matter how weak the case against him actually was, in the face of the testimony of dozens of women who believed that Thomas was incapable of harassment, and despite the absence of any subsequent evidence, Thomas would be considered guilty until proven innocent. His supposed "acquittal"—confirmation to the court—would come from a body whose judgment was delegitimized by a fraudulent charge that the Senate had not taken sexual harassment "seriously." In the end, the battle to "define" the real Clarence Thomas would be won by those who had already vilified him for years for holding unorthodox views and who would use the sexual harassment charge as ultimate "proof" that Thomas had been devious and corrupt all along.

For Hill, however, the experience of "coming forward" was not so much a transformation as an apotheosis, from minor campus activist to civil rights leader on a level with Rosa Parks. Hill's supporters and her detractors have tended to agree on one point: Hill's new-found fame was a sea change in direction for the seemingly mild-mannered business law professor with no prior political interests. "Anita talked about how her life has changed," Gloria Segal told the Minneapolis–St. Paul *Star-Tribune*. Segal met with Hill to discuss plans for the $250,000 endowed professorship at OU for which Segal, a state legislator from Minneapolis, was raising money. "She was teaching contract law at Oklahoma, but she talked about shifting to how the legal system deals with gender issues."[46] In other quarters, Hill has been criticized for throwing her prior academic career to the winds and "cashing in" on her Senate testimony, receiving in 1992 well over $100,000 in speaking fees and awards.

But Hill's sabbatical proposal for the 1992–93 academic year showed that the opportunity to testify against Thomas merely accelerated a shift that had been underway for some years. The proposal included planning an inter-disciplinary conference on "race, gender and power in America"; writing a manuscript on sexual harassment ("my thesis is that the law, as it has developed through federal policy and case law, places too much emphasis on the behavior of the victim in defining what constitutes harassment," Hill wrote); and raising money to start an institute on the concerns of black women (". . . given where the country is going and where it is today, the idea is worth the further investment of the time it will take to fully explore it. My role in the exploration will be thinking of the areas of concern which can be addressed and defining the best approach for addressing them").[47]

Hill, of course, did not seek so public a role. She had been working with Brudney and the others to save the court from behind-the-scenes, the same way she had been working to save the EEOC in the early 1980s from Thomas's swing to the right. "This was not something I did without a great deal of thought," she later told the *New York Times*. "I considered as many of the implications as I could without even understanding this would happen. I couldn't dream this would happen. But as far as I could think it through, I did. There were many nights I could not sleep. I'd wake up thinking what to do, how to do it. I was very cautious."

But when Nina Totenberg called Hill with a leaked copy of her sworn statement, Hill had few choices remaining. Having committed the charges to paper, she had painted herself into a corner. Hill could have disowned the statement, thereby surrendering the chance to stop the Thomas nomination and undermining her credibility with the Shadow Senate and her friends on the campus in Norman. Or she could confirm that the statement was hers and attempt to make the most convincing case that it was true. In fact, she went beyond her written statement in the hearings to portray Thomas as particularly vile. Since the milder statement had failed to stop Thomas, she may have felt compelled to strengthen it with vivid and loathsome details. As the accuser in a sexual harassment case, even if she had no evidence other than the testimony of Susan Hoerchner, she knew that Thomas could never prove these incidents did *not* occur. This was not much of a choice; Hill therefore pressed ahead, motivated not so much by a vindictive desire to punish or humiliate Thomas, or even a desire to fulfill her own sense of mission, but because her efforts to control the process had failed, and she was left with no alternative.

By the time Hill arrived in Washington to testify, surrounded by the faithful and perhaps beginning to believe her own press notices, she portrayed her purposes in "coming forward" in moralistic terms:

> DECONCINI: What do you see as the most significant thing coming out of this unfortunate experience that you have had to go through now, and I mean the public part of it?
>
> HILL: Other than creating awareness, I see that the information is going to be fully explored, the information that I provided will be fully explored, it will be given a full hearing. In addition, I think that coming out, my coming forward may encourage other people to come forward, other people who have had the same experiences who have not been able to talk about them.
>
> DECONCINI: That would be raising the awareness of sexual harassment in public.
>
> HILL: Raising the awareness, but also giving people courage.

Though Hill had spent the weekend disclaiming under oath any motive for coming forward, when she returned to Oklahoma from Washington, she told a press conference: "I did not feel that I had lost. What these people were saying to me is that 'you made a difference, you took some abuse for doing it, and you made a difference.' " Once trapped into confirming a false story to the media, Hill was apparently able to justify her actions on the utilitarian grounds that they advanced the larger causes of helping legitimate victims of sexual harassment to come forward, whether or not they kept Thomas from taking a seat on the Supreme Court. Hill had told the Judiciary Committee that recounting her story on national television was the last thing she had wanted to do. "What happened and telling the world about it are the two most difficult . . . experiences of my life." No doubt this was so; yet at her press conference in Norman two days later, Hill appeared to have accepted her role as a civil rights activist, saying with moral certitude, "I did what was right, and I'll do it all over again."

Hill's ability to telegraph to a nationwide television audience her conviction that she had done "what was right" in testifying against Thomas accounts more than anything for the indelible mark her appearance has left on the American social and political landscape. On one level, Hill's story is that of a person whose seemingly harmless white lies and rationalizations accumulated over the course of a decade and snowballed into a false story over which she lost control. But on another level, the story is much more than the unanticipated result of fortuitous circumstance, coincidence, and human foible.

The widely felt sense that Hill and Thomas were of equal credibility was based on more than image and appearance and the political manipulations of both sides in the contest. Both were impelled by an unabashed moral conviction: his was the outrage and pathos of a man falsely accused in a forum that denied him any means to clear his name; hers was the serene confidence and altruism of a person with superior moral reasons for doing what she did. When Hill's pattern of complaints about harassment and her political and personal disillusionment with Thomas converged with the opportunity to "save" the Supreme Court and preserve the hard-fought gains of the civil rights movement, her evident sense of historical mission allowed her to suspend normal personal ethics and justified in her mind whatever means were necessary in order to achieve her noble ends.

More important than motivation or state of mind, however, was the question posed at the outset of this inquiry, and to which we must return in summary: the reliability of the two witnesses. Thomas had come through four Senate confirmations and five FBI investigations unscathed. No aspect of Thomas's testimony was at variance with the established facts of the case. Thomas's so-called "evasion" in round one of the hearings—that he had never discussed *Roe* v. *Wade*—failed to produce anyone to contradict him. His testimony about his demeanor in the office was massively corroborated by practically every woman who had ever worked with him. This was a man in whose presence people did not swear, a man who knew his every move was being watched by his political enemies, and who lectured the black men on his staff about the need to combat negative cultural stereotypes.

Everyone who knew both Thomas and Hill believed Thomas, not Hill. Clearly Thomas had no pattern of abusive behavior. During the time Thomas was supposed to have been pressing Hill for dates, he was seriously involved with another woman, even contemplating remarriage. When the Justice Department proposed Anita Hill as a witness to testify in favor of his nomination before she made the sexual harassment charge, Thomas encouraged the idea. When her charge was made behind-the-scenes, Thomas had a chance to back down, to keep his name out of the mud, to keep his life-tenure seat on the D.C. Circuit Court. But he did not. Thomas was either power-mad, as his enemies portrayed him, or else so confident that Hill would have no evidence of something he had never done that *she* would be forced to back down, withdrawing her unfounded charges.

And what of Anita Hill? It is now clear that she did not "come forward" in any meaningful sense of that term. Her case—uncorroborated and unsupported by any co-worker, or anyone else—was not a typical case of sexual harassment. Regardless of how one interprets them, Hill's statements about Thomas during the time that she was allegedly being harassed by him are not consistent with her charge. Hill complained that Thomas "did not even notice me"; she portrayed him as the "ideal boss" who was particularly respectful of women employees; and she asserted he would "make a great father."

Further, Hill either made several false statements under oath or more than a dozen other people were lying. Hill testified that she went with Thomas from Education to the EEOC because she feared she would have been jobless. Yet at the time, she had acknowledged career status and was offered the chance to stay on by Thomas's successor. Hill gave several differing and inconsistent explanations of her telephone contacts with Thomas after she had left the EEOC. She said that she had agreed when making her complaint to the Judiciary Committee that the nominee could be told her name, when in fact she had insisted that he not be told. Hill said she agreed to an FBI investigation the moment it was suggested to her, but she had really backed away from the suggestion, delaying any committee investigation.

Hill denied the sworn testimony of Carlton Stewart and Stanley Grayson that she said Thomas deserved the nomination. Hill told a misleading account of how she attained the teaching post at Oral Roberts University. Hill said she had been asked to take Thomas to the airport, but Charles Kothe said she had volunteered. Hill claimed the FBI agents told her at the beginning of the interview that they would come back for the details, but the agents flatly denied this. Hill accused the FBI agents of mis-recording her statement that Thomas had said if she ever told anyone about the harassment he would ruin her career. But both agents independently said Hill was not telling the truth.

Hill said she had not taught a civil rights course in five years, but she had taught one the prior year. Hill told the committee that she had given a copy of her committee statement only to the committee and to her counsel, but she had also given a copy to Jim Brudney. Hill said she had told only her closest friends of the harassment, yet she later claimed to have told Joel Paul, whom she barely knew. Hill said she had asked her three friends for advice on how to handle the harassment, yet each of them later said she had not done so. Hill said that no one had ever suggested to her in any way that she leave Wald, Harkrader & Ross, but this was flatly contradicted by former partners of the firm.

Despite these contradictions, many people will be tempted to deny their implications and continue to assert Hill's veracity. These people may conclude that notwithstanding her manifold omissions, evasions, and false statements, Anita Hill may still have been telling the truth about what happened behind closed doors between herself and Clarence Thomas. For readers such as these, no amount of evidence is likely to be persuasive. The will to believe her account will outweigh whatever facts have been presented here. For open-minded readers, on the other hand, the evidence presented must weigh heavily against her credibility. If that is our standard of judgment—and in the absence of a confession from either Thomas or Hill, it is the only standard we can usefully employ—the weight of evidence is such that no reasonable person could believe that sexual harassment occurred in this case.

Epilogue

Some readers will be found, no doubt, who simply do not care about the truth of this affair. As was suggested at the outset, these are people who regard the positive social and political results of the Thomas–Hill episode as being so important that their benefits transcend other considerations and justify whatever means may have been necessary to ensure their fulfillment. Clearly the attention that has been subsequently riveted on the long-submerged problem of sexual harassment must be seen as a welcome development. Just as clearly, however, the potential for abuse exists. The final question, therefore, must concern the effects of the Anita Hill story on the handling of this problem in the many other cases that have arisen in its wake.

Though it did not come to the attention of the public at the time of the hearings, the notion that the male Senators "just didn't get it" served the interests of a broader ideological movement to redefine the legal and social relations between the sexes. The phrase epitomized and amplified the feminist argument that American society is a patriarchal system that enshrines a male perspective and relegates women to subordinate roles. Notions of logic, objectivity, equality under law, and the common good are all regarded as reflections of this patriarchal bias.

Certain feminist scholars posit distinct differences between male and female ways of thinking, moral reasoning, and social and political behavior. Writing in the *Southern California Law Review*, for example, law professor Judith Resnik—an adviser to Anita Hill during the hearings, and a member of the Ad Hoc Committee on Public Education on Sexual Harassment—reflects this view when she argues that

383

inherent gender bias makes it literally impossible for most men, especially men in positions of power, to "hear" what women are saying:

> . . . "women's issues" are beginning to be on the agenda of courts. Spe-
> cially-chartered commissions are seeking to learn how gender affects
> decision making, procedure, and outcomes in courts. The conclusions
> reached by some state court task forces on gender bias document that
> the inability of some members of the Senate to hear Anita Hill is par-
> alleled every day in courts around the country, where judges do not lis-
> ten to or hear women. Yet in those courts, as in the Senate, some are
> starting to think about learning how to hear women.

Thus any men, or any women for that matter, who disbelieved Anita
Hill are not so much unpersuaded by the evidence as ideologically
deformed; they just "don't get it." Ann Scales of the University of New
Mexico Law School extends this argument to undermine the fundamental premise of legal reasoning that truth can be objectively determined by logical analysis. "Feminist analysis begins with the
principle that objective reality is a myth. It recognizes that patriarchal
myths are projections of the male psyche," she wrote in the *Yale Law
School*. "Male and female perceptions of value are not shared, and are
perhaps not even perceptible to each other." This kind of reasoning
forms the basis for the argument that women evaluated the Anita Hill
case in a different way from men—an argument belied by national
opinion polls taken at the time of the hearings.

Sexual harassment is currently defined as an unwelcome request
for sexual favors or unwelcome sexual conduct when submission is
made a condition of employment. There are two recognized forms
of harassment: quid pro quo harassment, where an employee is subjected to an adverse employment decision ("sleep with me or forget
that promotion"), and "hostile environment" harassment, where the
workplace is judged so offensive (dirty jokes told continually, pornographic pictures on the walls) as to create a barrier to equal employment opportunity.

Feminist lawyers want to expand the law's reach, beginning with
sexual harassment, and in doing so promote separate sex-based legal
standards and entitlements. The cutting edge of feminist theory in
this area aims to replace the legal standard by which the "hostile environment" is defined by arguing that the subjective reaction of the
(female) complainant should be the determining factor, not the objective (male) or gender-neutral person standard enshrined by
current law. The "gender-neutral person," feminists argue, is a patri-

archal artifact intended to perpetuate male power. Thus the utility to the feminist legal project of Anita Hill, the female victim disbelieved by a panel of male senators, becomes evident.

Catharine MacKinnon, the law professor who has pioneered this broadened legal theory of sexual harassment, has taken the argument so far as to deny the distinction between sex crimes and consensual relations. "Feminism stresses the indistinguishability of prostitution, marriage, and sexual harassment," MacKinnon has written. "Compare victim reports of rape with women's reports of sex. They look a lot alike. . . . In this light the major distinction between intercourse (normal) and rape (abnormal) is that the normal happens so often that one cannot see anything wrong with it. . . . Men see rape as intercourse; feminism observes that men make much intercourse rape. . . . All this makes it difficult to sustain the customary distinctions between violence and sex. . . . If 'no' can be taken as 'yes,' how free can 'yes' be? . . . If sex is normally something men do to women, the issue is less whether there was force and more whether consent is a meaningful concept."

Since all men are seen as rapists in this paradigm, it does not matter whether Hill actually proved her case against Thomas or not. As Hill herself has put it in campus lectures, "women should be supported regardless of proof."

As it happens, MacKinnon is also a leading figure in the movement among some feminists to ban pornography. Hill's testimony has been useful in this crusade as well, insofar as it linked pornographic obsession to the commission of a sex crime. Indeed, MacKinnon was so intent on establishing this link, that (as previously shown in Chapter 7) she may have failed to realize how her own expertise as an authority on pornography revealed that Hill's story was almost certainly fictionalized.

Lowering the standard of evidence to the point envisioned by feminists like MacKinnon means that in a case like that of Hill and Thomas—a case, to all appearances, of his word against hers—the legal presumption always favors the accuser. Though little noticed by the public, such a precedent, once established, works implicitly to undermine the long-established legal presumption that an accused party is innocent until proven guilty. Such was certainly the case with Clarence Thomas. This quiet revolution in American jurisprudence, if allowed to go unchecked, may infringe the rights of the accused in other areas and therefore has important implications for the whole of our legal system.

Sexual harassment—because it happens in private and is therefore difficult to prove—is precisely the sort of unanswerable charge that can sometimes be abused. It therefore requires not the suspension of an objective legal standard of proof, but rather a renewed insistence on adherence to established evidentiary norms. Without such safeguards, as the Hill case amply demonstrates, passion and politics can displace reasoned analysis, and in the event an innocent person's reputation can all too easily be ruined.

Feminist legal theorists will undoubtedly continue to exploit the societal earthquake that Anita Hill's charges set off to press their agenda in the courts. It is no coincidence that these interests dovetail with those of the Shadow Senate, whose ideological zeal produced the Anita Hill scandal in the first place, and whose leaders have employed the same pressure tactics in the last decade that the feminist legal theorists are now deploying in their efforts to secure judicial outcomes. Both belong to a political movement that calls itself liberal, but is really deeply hostile to the Western liberal tradition whose premises inform our major legal and political institutions, viewing that tradition as an ideology that supports a racist and sexist social order. Since these radical utopians believe that they are on the side of history, anyone who opposes their agenda is not merely *wrong*, but *wicked*. Thus to question Hill's account of what occurred between herself and Clarence Thomas is seen not as an attempt to explore a reasonable doubt, but as a profoundly immoral bid to justify an evil and oppressive social order.

It is precisely this conviction that existing legal and political procedures are illegitimate that justified to the Shadow Senate, and Anita Hill herself, the abrogation of those procedures in order to stop Clarence Thomas. The leaking of Hill's charges, and the failure of anyone, including the Senate Republicans, to see the leakers brought to justice, has set a new low in the tactics that official Washington seems willing to tolerate. How that dynamic may change with a Democrat in the White House remains to be seen. In the short term, even with the White House and the Senate in the hands of the same party, there seems little prospect that the retail politics of the confirmation process—and the naked political pressures on judges themselves—will abate.

The ultimate consequences of this unbridled pursuit of "any means necessary" to attain political ends also remains to be seen. As with the Watergate and Iran–Contra scandals, when laws are violated and lies are told in the service of a "higher" good, the body politic and the social fabric suffer. The public learns from such events that in politics, only the morality of ends has any significance. But the framers of our Constitution understood that morality lies in the *means,* not the ends. The procedural guarantees that govern legal and judicial as well as political outcomes are not mere arbitrary obstacles set up to block virtuous impulses; they are the soul of our democracy and the bulwark of our freedom. Thus when Anita Hill's totally unsubstantiated charge, rejected by an overwhelming majority of Americans only a year before, became enshrined in popular culture as "the truth," Clarence Thomas was not the only party who was harmed. The American people were also harmed, since as a result of this lamentable episode the public's faith and trust in the integrity of the Senate and the Supreme Court have been perhaps irreparably tarnished.

Afterword
The Debate About
The Real Anita Hill

Writing and publishing The Real Anita Hill had been an education, calling to mind the story Abraham Lincoln used to tell about the man who was tarred, feathered and run out of town on a rail. He was heard to say "Were it not for the honor I would have rather walked."

Well, not completely so. After all, The Real Anita Hill is a best seller, exceeding the expectations of everyone. Three months on the New York Times list, it is now in its seventh printing. And hearing from people who have read The Real Anit.. Hill is gratifying. They tell me they came away with a much better understanding of what happened and why than they possibly could have gotten from the press accounts, whether contemporaneous or after the fact.

And that's what I want to talk about today: What it's like to write and publish a book which, I was to discover, so fundamentally challenged the premises of the prevailing political and media culture.

That's certainly not what I set out to do. Rather, I wrote the book for the best of market reasons. I was convinced that the reading public had an appetite for more hard information and informed speculation—emphasis on the word informed—on the many important questions that the Senate hearings left unanswered. Such basic ques-

This is the text of a lecture delivered by the author on several college campuses in the Fall of 1993.

tions as who told the truth—Clarence Thomas or Anita Hill? And what had really happened between these two people when they worked together ten years ago?

I make the point in the book that the press corps had taken the position that such answers were and are unknowable. Nor would reporters ask such crucial questions as what political forces in Washington produced Anita Hill and her sexual harassment charges.

That, I came to understand, was because the press was part of the story. In the book, I describe the Shadow Senate—an alliance of special-interest groups and unelected Senate staffers forged by ideology, inclination, and sympathy to fight the judges wars. Many of the important press players are part and parcel of that alliance—wittingly or unwittingly. How else to explain that so far as the facts and the evidence of the Thomas-Hill case were concerned, I had the field virtually to myself?

To be sure, reporters started out concerned with the facts, when they sought to prove Anita Hill's charges of sexual harassment. On the morning the hearings opened, reporters were seen lingering outside EEOC headquarters, offering cash bribes to agency employees for old personnel directories, in an attempt to find other female employees of Judge Thomas who could attest to a pattern of such behavior on his part, or who might know something to back up Hill's charges. This exercise was an implicit acknowledgment that sexual harassers tend to be repeat offenders, as well as the fact that victims often provide some form of convincing corroboration. In this case, the reporters found nothing of the sort.

Even after the hearings ended with Thomas's confirmation, people from at least five major news organizations continued this effort. One might have thought that Thomas's bill of health could be considered clean, after four prior Senate confirmations; five FBI checks; dozens of reporters stealing into his garage to pore over old books and papers; and finally, the three-day Senate show trial.

Covering judges as politicians, of course, is the unfortunate legacy of the brutal political campaign successfully waged by the opponents of the Bork nomination in 1987. Now it may be said that the reporters were simply doing their jobs, following the anti-Thomas leads provided by the interest groups and like-minded Senate staff. Perhaps so. Journalists, after all, are supposed to be professional skeptics.

But the journalistic sin in the Thomas-Hill case was both one of commission *and* omission. When the press continued to dog Justice Thomas for months even after he was confirmed and found *no* other women to charge him; *no* support for Anita Hill's version of events from third parties; *no* evidence of Thomas's alleged obsession with pornography; not *one* contradiction in his sworn testimony— their collective news sense should have suggested that they might turn a skeptical eye on Anita Hill's account.

Yet this is precisely the point at which they decided the controversy could not be resolved through further journalistic inquiry, closed their notebooks, and went on to the next story.

Why was this so? While those reporters who did not pursue the story further are perhaps best qualified to respond to this question, I can offer my own view. From the moment Anita Hill burst into the headlines, many in the media regarded her as the victim in this case, before knowing anything about her or her allegations, or trying to find out.

Should anyone doubt this, one need only consult the front-page editorials at the time by Maureen Dowd in the New York Times, promoting the notion that the committee of white men simply didn't take Hill's charge seriously—a patent falsehood refuted in the Senate record itself, which apparently none of my colleagues took the trouble to read.

In Dowd's view, any attempt to assess Hill's credibility or to check into her background would be seen as victimizing the victim all over again.

Secondly, Hill's allegations came to represent something much larger than whether or not Clarence Thomas sexually harassed her. As the media saw it, the controversy was about everything *but* the specifics of Hill's allegations: Hill's testimony clearly encouraged other women to come forward with sexual harassment claims; motivated women to run for office; and may have even jumpstarted the feminist movement, or, at least, radical feminist legal theory.

The notion that the male senators "just didn't get it" served the interests of this broader ideological movement to redefine the legal and social relations between the sexes. The phrase epitomized and amplified the radical feminist argument that American society is a patriarchal system that enshrines a male perspective and relegates women to subordinate roles. Notions of logic, objectivity, equality under law, even of the common good, are all regarded as reflections of this patriarchal bias. Using sexual harassment law as a primary vehicle, the aim of this movement is the promotion of sex-based legal standards and entitlements—and the false image of Anita Hill fostered in the press was quite useful toward that end.

Thirdly, and I think most importantly, much of the press was quite simply biased by ideology against Clarence Thomas by the time Anita Hill's allegations surfaced. Ever since Thomas appeared on the Washington scene in the early 1980's and began to challenge the quota strategies of the civil rights coalition, he had been seen as a dangerous example of a non-conforming black, a traitor to his race. His record at the EEOC was attacked and distorted, and his views were caricatured. This reached a fever pitch during the confirmation fight, when Thomas's qualifications were denigrated and his personal life was laid bare.

But despite all of this scrutiny, the political opposition could not find the silver bullet. Thus, Thomas's strength as a nominee forced Anita Hill into play—coaxed and coached by his long-time ideological enemies. No wonder that by this time the press corps was willing to take it as a matter of faith that Clarence Thomas—that pawn in a bid for "conservative" control of the courts—was capable of just about any abomination.

The startling lack of evidence did not matter. Thomas would be convicted in theory, if not in fact.

In the face of these beliefs and prejudices, any attempt to examine the facts of the sexual harassment case was seen by the opinion elite as a distraction from the "real" issues at stake—a view that would later be reaffirmed in the hysterical condemnation of my book.

In the year following Thomas's confirmation a journalistic boycott on the knowable questions of fact was imposed, together with a public relations campaign by those hoping to capitalize politically on Anita Hill's testimony. Sure enough, a year after the hearings, polls showed that public perception of Thomas and Hill had reversed from the time of the hearings, when two-thirds of both men and women said they believed Thomas, not Hill. Now, more Americans believed Anita Hill than Clarence Thomas.

In short, Anita Hill's supporters had succeeded in muscling history.

And then this new consensus was challenged by the publication of The Real Anita Hill.

As those of you who have read the book know, I did not ask whether Justice Thomas should have been named or confirmed to the Supreme Court; nor did I question whether sexual harassment is a serious issue. Rather, I sought to determine whether or not sexual harassment occurred in this particular instance.

After a painstaking analysis of the record and dozens of interviews, I realized that the conventional wisdom about this case was insupportable:

- Anita Hill did not "come forward" on her own;
- her charges were carefully considered by the Senate Judiciary Committee—she herself was responsible for any delay because she wanted to accuse Thomas anonymously;
- Anita Hill had a whole host of motives to try to stop the nomination, from personal rejection to political opposition;
- Hill is not, as she was widely represented, a political conservative and a sexual innocent;
- despite the presence of four witnesses, Hill really had no firm corroboration for her charge;
- and so, contrary to the feminist line, this was not a "typical" case of sexual harassment;
- and finally—and much to my surprise, frankly—as I began to check, I found that Hill's testimony was shot through with provably false and misleading statements.

To be sure, no one can know with absolute certainty what may or may not have happened between two people, behind closed doors, with no witnesses. But if *any* of this information had been known at the time of the hearings, our view of this issue would have been radically altered. Certainly Anita Hill would not have been subsequently lionized as the "Rosa Parks of sexual harassment."

The Real Anita Hill received an initial boost from George Will, Thomas Sowell, Bill Buckley, Mona Charen, Rush Limbaugh, among others, and was excerpted in the Wall Street Journal, National Review and the American Spectator. Clearly, many conservatives saw in the book a well-researched, fact-based vindication of their belief that Justice Thomas had told the truth in denying Anita Hill's charges and had fallen victim to an eleventh hour plot to derail his nomination for political reasons. Their assessment was later derided as predictable by liberal critics of the book, and perhaps it was—though, as we will see, it was not nearly as predictable as the liberal criticism itself.

Less predictable was the response—or the lack thereof—in the nation's newsrooms. With the exception of the Boston Globe, no newspaper saw fit to run a story about the book's charges or conclusions. Early on, a reporter for Reuters called to schedule an interview, but he later cancelled, saying his editors did not want to be the first ones to run with the story—quite the opposite of the usual reporter's instinct. Other editors apparently had similar fears.

USA Today's editors passed, pronouncing the book "boring," an ironic testament to the fact that the book had turned out to be the opposite of what may have been expected: It was a sober analysis of the facts rather than sensational tabloid fare.

The editors of the Washington Post assured my publisher that they had the book—but they said they didn't know what to do with it. When it was eventually passed from the news department to the Style section, the Post sent it to several people before finding someone willing to write about it.

US News passed as well, saying the book had not proven anything. This was the same magazine that had promoted a book on the subject by Tim Phelps, the Newsday reporter who originally broke the story of Hill's allegations, though his book broke no new ground whatsoever. The Phelps book, however, did have one redeeming quality: It reflected the now-dominant media line—the presumption was reversed to strongly favor the accuser, though not one scintilla of evidence to support or justify that presumption was provided.

Imagine, for a moment, if the shoe had been on the other foot: A book is published exposing an effort to torpedo a Clinton Supreme Court nominee in which aides to Senator Hatch conspired with the Heritage Foundation to coax a piece of uncorroborated dirt out of a completely reluctant witness, broke Senate rules and violated the Privacy Act by leaking the confidential allegation to the Washington Times, and finally lied about all this to a Congressional investigator. Would this not have been another Iran-Contra scandal?

But then I suppose one could not have expected reporters who had covered the hearings to put on hairshirts and confess that they had either missed certain crucial aspects of this story, or in other cases—such as that of National Public Radio's Nina Totenberg—had actively misrepresented or covered them up.

It was left, therefore, to a number of independent liberal book critics to pierce the silence of the media about The Real Anita Hill. Christopher Lehmann-Haupt, the senior daily book reviewer for the New York Times, was the first to report that the book—which he called "must reading for anyone remotely touched by this case"—

fingered Senator Paul Simon and former Howard Metzenbaum staffer Jim Brudney as the leakers of Hill's allegations.

That review and others that followed—notably reviews by David Garrow, the Pulitzer-Prize winning biographer of Martin Luther King, in Newsday, and Jonathan Groner in the Washington Post— suggested that the book had been persuasive, at least to the extent of opening up a reasonable doubt on the previously closed question of Anita Hill's credibility. Groner, for example, wrote that the book was "a serious work of investigative journalism that builds a case quietly and incrementally . . . the first salvo in a long and salutary search for the truth . . ."

When I read those reviews, I knew I was going to pay for them. This was an example of the unsettling dynamic involved in publishing a book that challenges the liberal orthodoxy: The more the book succeeded, the uglier things were bound to get.

Initially, the strategy of the book's opponents was to ignore it. They refused to comment or debate me on the book's contents. In terms of generating reader interest, this created a massive problem because the television networks adopted an unofficial policy on The Real Anita Hill. I could not appear without an Anita Hill partisan denouncing me simultaneously. By refusing to debate, they could thereby censor me.

When I asked my publisher whether the mandatory presence of an opponent was not somewhat unusual for a short book-promotion spot on one of the morning talk shows, I was told it was very unusual—though it was not unheard of for a "conservative" book. By way of comparison, Tim Phelps made the rounds of all of the major talk shows, never once appearing with a Clarence Thomas supporter. More recently, one might look at the treatment accorded Joe McGuinness and his biography of Senator Kennedy. About this book, there was not much of a controversy: everyone, left, right and center, agreed that it was a bad book with little or no journalistic merit. Yet McGuinness appeared everywhere, unchaperoned, simply by virtue of being the author of a "controversial" book.

Yet even after I agreed to accept this double standard for conservative authors, I was booked and cancelled on the Larry King show several times.

When it became clear that The Real Anita Hill would win a mainstream audience, the strategy changed. The first shot across the bow was fired by Anna Quindlen in the New York Times, who filed a column the day before the Lehmann-Haupt review was scheduled to appear.

While conceding my point that the press did not do its job either during or after the hearings, Quindlen attempted to simply dismiss all of the new evidence in my book on the grounds that it was offered by a conservative author. This was the beginning of a campaign to change the subject—as Deirdre English would later put it in The Nation—from The Real Anita Hill to the Real David Brock.

No effort would be made to distinguish between fact and interpretation; my facts were assumed to be wrong simply because of their source. The aim was to de-legitimize the whole book by attacking my credentials as a journalist and stigmatizing me as a hired gun for the right-wing.

In other words, I was not to be allowed to participate in respectable public discourse on this matter. When I finally did appear on the Today show, in a debate with Harvard law professor Charles Ogletree, who had been one of Anita Hill's lawyers, Katie Couric seemed concerned not with the substance of my case, but rather with my alleged politics: "You do, though, Mr. Brock have some innate conservative biases don't you?"

As a columnist for the Chicago Tribune later put it, this was like dismissing All The President's Men out of hand simply because Woodward and Bernstein were liberals.

Ironically, the assertion of Thomas's total innocence of the sexual harassment charge, which is the conclusion I reach in the book, is not an article of faith among conservatives—though for some reason the liberal mind finds it impossible to believe that someone of generally conservative views could approach this subject fairly. This attempt to caricature the right was later confounded by a highly critical review of The Real Anita Hill in National Review. Surely if there was a monolithic conservative line on this complex subject, the magazine would not have published such a piece.

As for personal bias, I do not know Clarence Thomas, nor—prior to writing this book—did I know anyone who knew Clarence Thomas.

The book grew out of an assignment from the American Spectator in November 1991 to write about the leak of Hill's allegations to the press. At the time, I had been working on a book on the inner-workings of Congress. I'd never written about the Supreme Court or even about the contentious social issues that come before it. Surely it was never my intention to take sides as to whether

Thomas or Hill was telling the truth; watching the hearings, I was as confused and uncertain about that as the next person.

In short, I went where the story took me, not the other way around. When I interviewed dozens of people, I had no idea what they would tell me about the relationship between Thomas and Hill ten years ago. Had I discovered evidence for a theory that the truth lay somewhere between the two opposed accounts, that is the book I would have written. Had I amassed a case that Thomas was guilty, I would have written that book.

What incentive could I possibly have had to do otherwise? If I had discovered as many discrepancies in the testimony of Clarence Thomas as I did in Anita Hill's testimony—and believe me, despite the skepticism of my critics, I tried—the book would have been front-page news, I would have gotten the Larry King booking that I'm still waiting for, and I would have been in contention for the Pulitzer Prize. The problem is that the discrepancies are simply not there—they are all on the other side.

In any event, the effort to paper over the facts by charging bias did not do the trick. The facts were going to have to be dealt with after all.

This task fell to Jane Mayer and Jill Abramson, two reporters for the Wall Street Journal, who published a lengthy review of The Real Anita Hill in the New Yorker. The two are writing their own book on this subject—normally considered a disqualifying conflict-of-interest in the book-reviewing business. But as I've previously noted, there has been nothing normal about the reception of this book, including the suspension of professional ethics and fair play.

Should anyone be tempted to accept the New Yorker reviewers' depiction of themselves as dispassionate reporters, one should note that they not only failed to disclose that they are writing a competing book, but also that (according to their publisher's catalogue) their book is to be entitled "Strange Justice: The Selling of Clarence Thomas."

The plot thickened when the Washington Post's media critic revealed that Mayer and Abramson at first resisted the assignment, but eventually succumbed to telephone calls and faxes from the New Yorker's executive editor, Hendrick Hertzberg, who was eager to discredit the book. Hertzberg had written two highly-charged, not to say wildly speculative, articles at the time of the hearings in support of Anita Hill and defying unnamed conservatives to come up with a plausible defense of Clarence Thomas.

By the way, Hertzberg—a former speechwriter for Jimmy Carter—
is one of the many writers and editors who have moved easily from
partisan positions in government into the journalistic world while
somehow escaping the label "liberal journalist."

My response to the New Yorker is too detailed to summarize here.
Suffice it to say that the review was not a review at all. There was no
effort to refute my main arguments—only a pastiche of hair-splitting
cavils, presented as a catalogue of alleged factual errors.

Despite an exhaustive effort that included re-interviewing many
of my sources, the reviewers were unable to show that the book was
inaccurate in any serious respect. I submitted an eight-page reply to
the magazine, rebutting the review point by point and acknowledging one error: Relying on previously published news accounts, I
wrote that Catharine MacKinnon had been one of Anita Hill's
many feminist advisers. She was not. Of course, one mistake in a
non-fiction book of more than 400 pages is probably a remarkable
feat of precision.

Perhaps that is why, as a reviewer in The New Republic later
observed, the New Yorker vitiated the empirical spirit of its review by
refusing to publish my rebuttal. And the authors refused repeated
invitations to appear with me on national television to debate.

But the reviewers did more than simply string together alleged
"errors"; they launched what the Washington Post media critic
called a "fierce liberal counterattack" on my motives and character
by suggesting *willful* manipulation of the facts. If true, such a charge
would make it unnecessary for anyone to engage with my arguments
or consider the evidence for them. The message was clear: Don't
review or read this dishonest book.

In this respect, the review and its aftermath brought to mind the
confirmation struggle itself, when the Senate committee and the
media did everything possible to avoid a genuine discussion about
judicial philosophy, engaging instead in personal attacks and emotional appeals disguised as substantive debate.

The review appeared on a Monday, and I was frankly astonished
at the velocity with which it was embraced as the antidote to my poi-
sonous book by our more liberal columnists, who suddenly and
simultaneously found their voice.

Ellen Goodman of the Boston Globe, I'm told, had been carrying
around The Real Anita Hill for several weeks evidently wishing to
write about it but unsure what tack to take. She had even remarked

on its balance tone—which apparently made it difficult to dismiss as an ideological hatchet-job. Within hours of the New Yorker's arrival in the mail, a Goodman column was filed titled "Anita Hill—The Untrue Story."

Within 48 hours, Molly Ivins, Garry Wills, the Village Voice and others piled on. Pat Schroeder circulated copies of the 8-page review to every member of the House of Representatives. On Friday morning, the Times published a column by Anthony Lewis called "Sleaze With Footnotes." The level of animosity had clearly reached a boiling point: The book was flatly called a lie, its author a person of no integrity—in short, the kind of vilification heretofore reserved for conservative Supreme Court nominees.

Chillingly, the Lewis column seemed designed to smear anyone who had written anything good about the book as much as it was directed at me. These reviewers and columnists, it was said, had unquestioningly accepted the factual assertions in my book and were therefore complicit in my manipulations.

Ironically, Lewis and the other columnists were accepting and repeating many of the plainly wrong assertions in the New Yorker—ranging from quotes from documents that are not actually in those documents, to my alleged failure to request interviews with certain subjects, despite footnotes clearly indicating otherwise.

One of the most egregious misrepresentations—picked up by Lewis and many others—had to do with a $5,000 grant I accepted from the conservative Olin Foundation to support a research assistant. The foundation had twice informed the New Yorker reviewers of the amount of the grant, but the writers chose not to report it, preferring the word "bankrolled" to describe the contribution. For the record, the book was actually bankrolled in the way books usually are—by a generous advance from Macmillan Publishing.

Readers of the Wall Street Journal editorial page later learned that Lewis had himself accepted $5,000 for a speaking engagement at the U.S. Air Force Academy from the same Olin Foundation. As if that were not enough, in subsequent private correspondence, Lewis conceded that he had bothered only to "breeze hastily" through the book before roundly condemning it.

Before the controversy was over, there would be many more such outrages. The American Lawyer published a highly favorable review of the book through its regular reviewing process. The magazine then took the unprecedented step of publishing a second review trashing it. The book was listed as a best-seller in Boston in the conservative-leaning Boston Herald, but it never made the liberal Boston Globe's list—even though they monitor the same stores.

There were also problems in the bookstores. Some posted the Molly Ivins column—titled "Save Yourself $24.95"—beside the displays, an odd way to sell books. A bookstore owner quoted in the New York Times compared The Real Anita Hill to Mein Kampf.

Efforts to answer my critics were unsuccessful—and not only at the New Yorker. The Times rejected an op-ed written by me, and, I am told, the newspaper even suppressed a 2000-word critic's notebook column by Lehmann-Haupt in which he defended his review against the New Yorker's criticism.

By now, it was clear that this was more a political campaign than a literary dispute. Indeed, it has caused me to reassess whether it was ever possible to do what I set out to do—to strip away the heavy layers of racial and sexual politics and emotionalism that have enveloped this episode.

On the one hand, I do believe the publication of The Real Anita Hill has shifted the ground of debate onto issues of fact. After all, the widely cited New Yorker review had to present itself as precisely the thing the media had avoided all along—a factual critique of the case—and in a sense a debate over the inconsistencies of the testimony of Hill's corroborating witnesses and other such "arcana" from the hearing is just the kind of debate I wanted to provoke.

Should the journalistic boycott on the facts now be lifted, I think this is a healthy development. I am quite confident that a fact war is one that Anita Hill's supporters can never win. That is why, I think, in her many public appearances in the two years since the hearings, Anita Hill has refused to discuss any aspect of her case but the metaphysical.

As for the culture war, I am less sanguine.

In a fundamental sense, Thomas versus Hill is one of those historical controversies—like the Dreyfus affair and the Hiss-Chambers case—that mark the fault-line in a culture, the place where moral, social and political values clash.

At the time of the hearings, many wondered what explained the strong impression of sincerity made by the two main witnesses in the case. The answer, it seems to me, is that each was voicing a significant general truth—hers, about the routine victimization of women by sexual harassment; and his, about the evils of character assassination to which Thomas, as a black conservative, was especially vulnerable.

Thomas and Hill have come to represent a symbolic opposition that is both intensely personal and much larger than themselves.

There can be no question as to which of these truths our press corps finds more compelling, and which side in the culture war the press is rooting for—indeed enlisted in. I would describe it not as a media conspiracy but rather a cultural consensus—which may in some ways be more dangerous.

This, I think, explains the root and branch rejection of the book by critics who felt the need to discredit not only me but also those reviewers who had found any merit in my book. Questioning of the cultural consensus could not be permitted.

This also, I think, explains why I've had the Anita Hill story virtually to myself for all these many months. While I reject the idea that my political leanings pre-determined my findings and conclusions, it is surely true that someone outside the establishment press had to be the first to break the taboo and pose these difficult questions publicly.

If this means that I will be called a "conservative commentator," as Nina Totenberg referred to me recently on NPR, rather than a journalist, so be it. But I am no more a conservative than Nina Totenberg, Tim Phelps, Hendrick Hertzberg, and Mayer and Abramson are liberals, and it is only a measure of their hypocrisy that they hide behind a false claim to impartiality, while impugning the motives of those with whom they disagree.

I only ask that my work be judged by the same standards as theirs—on its merits, where what used to be called "the facts" are acknowledged, and their interpretation is then subject to *civil* discussion.

The last round of commentary on my book seemed to confirm that I would not be afforded this courtesy—though the reviews did cheer me nonetheless. Recall that prior to the publication of The Real Anita Hill, the cultural consensus held that Anita Hill was a victim of sexual harassment by Clarence Thomas, who committed perjury to win a seat on the Supreme Court.

Just after the hearings, Harvard sociologist Orlando Patterson published a New York Times op-ed in which he said the truth was likely to be found somewhere between the two stories. He speculated that Thomas "may well have said what he is alleged to have said but he did so as a man not unreasonably attracted to an aloof woman who is esthetically and socially very similar to himself, who had made no secret of her own deep admiration for him. With his mainstream cultural guard down, Judge Thomas on several misjudged occasions may have done something completely out of the cultural frame of his white, upper-middle class work world, but immediately recognizable to Professor Hill and most women of Southern working-class backgrounds, white or black."

Patterson went on to say that he was "convinced that Professor Hill perfectly understood the psycho-cultural context in which Thomas allegedly regaled her with his Rabelaisian humor, which is precisely why she never filed a charge against him." He concluded, therefore, that Hill's testimony was "disingenuous and unfair" and that Thomas was "justified in denying making the remarks on the utilitarian grounds that any admission would have immediately incurred the self-destructive and grossly unfair punishment."

Not surprisingly, Patterson was vilified at the time by the feminist establishment for taking such a heretical position. He subsequently recanted.

Writing about The Real Anita Hill in the New York Review, Kathleen Sullivan of Stanford University first returned to the opening line of criticism of the book, which, she charged, amounted to little more than an "ideological vendetta" on my part. But she then went on to rehabilitate Patterson's middle-ground cultural theory, which he himself had disavowed, implicitly acknowledging that Hill deceived the Senate and the public with her testimony against Thomas.

Finally, Jean Bethke-Ehlstain, writing in the New Republic, made many of the same arguments I maue in the book—for example that most sexual harassers have multiple and identifiable track records of abuse and that Thomas emphatically did *not*; that the nominee was the victim of a confirmation process gone horribly wrong—that permitted, even encouraged, character assassination as an expression of political opposition; that to win the battle for public opinion, Hill contrived to misrepresent herself as helpless, while she was actually quite ambitious; and that Hill's testimony was, at bottom, a political statement right out of contemporary feminist theory. Bethke-Ehlstain also favorably cited the Patterson article.

At the same time, Bethke-Ehlstain did not acknowledge anywhere in the review that these very points were in fact made by me. On the contrary, she did everything she could rhetorically to distance herself from The Real Anita Hill and its "right-wing" author.

Progress, I guess, is made one step at a time.

NOTES

Introduction. The Woman of the Year

1. Statement by Jeffrey Burke Santinover, M.D., obtained independently by the author.
2. E.J. Dionne, "On Once and Future Supreme Court Nominees," *Washington Post,* June 19, 1992, p. 25.
3. Christine A. Littleton, "Dispelling Myths About Sexual Harassment: How the Senate Failed Twice," *Southern California Law Review,* March 1992, pp. 1419–1429.
4. William Raspberry, "Southern Conservatives Change Their Stripes," *The Oregonian,* October 18, 1991, p. C7.
5. Maureen Dowd, "The Thomas Nomination: The Senate and Sexism; Panels Handling of Harassment Allegation Renews Questions About an All-Male Club," *New York Times,* October 8, 1992, p. 1.
6. "Men Still Don't Get It!," *Newsday,* October 15, 1992, p. 1.
7. Robert Suro, "A Private Person in a Storm," *New York Times,* October 11, 1991, p. 1.
8. Jon D. Hull, "A Real Straight Arrow," *Time,* October 21, 1991, p. 44.
9. Eloise Salholz, "Did America 'Get It' ?," *Newsweek,* December 28, 1992, pp. 20–22.
10. That the "Year of the Woman" was directed toward electing more liberal Democrats to the Senate, not only more women, seemed to escape notice. Emily's List, for example, does not support all women candidates, only women candidates who share the group's views on abortion rights. In 1990 eight women had run for the Senate, more than the number in 1992, but women's groups sat on their hands because six of the women in 1990 were Republicans. Two of them—Lynn Martin in Illinois and Susan Engletier in Wisconsin—would have replaced two of the men on the Judiciary Committee, Democrats Paul Simon of Illinois and

Herb Kohl of Wisconsin. See Bob Dole, "Is America Ignoring GOP Women?," *Washington Post*, May 31, 1992, p. C5.

11. Salholz, *Newsweek*.

12. Alan Riding, "France Rethinks Its Wink at Sex Harassment," *New York Times*, May 3, 1992, p. 9.

13. Quoted in Deborah Sontag, "Anita Hill and Revitalizing Feminism," *New York Times*, April 26, 1992, p. 31.

14. "For Thousands in State, Anita Hill's Testimony Isn't Over," Minneapolis *Star Tribune*, October 30, 1992.

15. See Michele Landsberg, "The Rebirth of Feminism," *Toronto Star*, May 2, 1992, p. G1.

16. Text of Michael McWilliams letter to ABA members.

17. Bob Cohn, "At Least He's Read Roe Now," *Newsweek*, October 5, 1992, p. 58.

18. Toni Morrison, Ed., *Race-ing Justice, En-gendering Power* (New York: Pantheon Books, 1992), p. 276.

19. Transcript of Nina Totenberg's McClatchy Lecture at Stanford University by National Public Radio, May 7, 1992.

20. Quoted in "Sen. Simon says Hill, not Thomas, told truth," *USA Today*, June 29, 1992, p. 5a.

21. *Village Voice*, April 14, 1992, p. 1.

22. See Ruth Marcus, "Thomas is Lectured on Roots, Responsibilities," *Washington Post*, March 13, 1992, p. A23.

23. "Justice Thomas, the Freshman," *New York Times* editorial, July 5, 1992. Another striking manifestation of the demonization of Thomas relating to his work on the court is the unprecedented phenomenon of prospective Supreme Court clerks, who traditionally apply to all of the Justices, specifically excepting Justice Thomas from their applications.

24. Lance Morrow, "Truth in the Ruins," *Time*, October 28, 1991, p. 104.

25. Orlando Patterson, "Race, Gender, and Liberal Fallacies," reprinted in *Court of Appeal*, edited by Robert Chrisman and Robert L. Allen (New York: Ballantine Books, 1992), p. 160, from the *New York Times*, October 20, 1991, p. E15; Camille Paglia, "The Strange Case of Clarence Thomas and Anita Hill," *Philadelphia Inquirer*, October 21, 1991, p. A15.

26. Jacquelyne Johnson Jackson, " 'Them Against Us': Anita Hill v. Clarence Thomas," in Robert Chrisman and Robert L. Allen, eds., *Court of Appeal*, p. 101.

27. Susan King, *Los Angeles Times*, TV Times, October 11–17, 1992, p. 8.

28. Jill Abramson, "Image of Anita Hill Brighter in Hindsight, Galvanizes Campaigns," *Wall Street Journal*, October 5, 1992, p. 1.

29. Salholz, *Newsweek*.

30. Abramson, *Wall Street Journal*.

31. Thomas C. Palmer, Jr., "Women May Be Getting the Last Word," *Boston Globe*, June 7, 1992, p. 81.

32. Abramson, *Wall Street Journal*.

33. Statement of Senator Mitch McConnell to the U.S. Senate, Congressional Record, October 24, 1991, p. S15125.
34. Neil A. Lewis, "Investigation Fails to Find Discloser of Hill Accusation," *New York Times*, May 6, 1992, p. 18.
35. Nowhere is this popular view more comprehensively elucidated than in the aforementioned book of ideologically charged essays edited by Toni Morrison, *Race-ing Justice, En-gendering Power*. The volume will provide a useful foil as its various myths are deconstructed, the facts of Hill's case re-examined, and the record finally corrected.

1. The Shadow Senate

1. Letter from Senator Joseph R. Biden, Jr., to Senators Orrin Hatch, Alan Simpson, Charles Grassley, and Hank Brown, October 11, 1991, responding to their written request of October 10, 1991.
2. Nellie Y. McKay, "Remembering Anita Hill and Clarence Thomas: What Really Happened When One Black Woman Spoke Out," in Toni Morrison, ed., *Race-ing Justice* (New York: Pantheon Books, 1992), p. 272.
3. Statement by Senator Al Gore to the U.S. Senate, *Congressional Record*, October 15, 1991, p. S14666.
4. Statement by Senator Strom Thurmond to the U.S. Senate, *Congressional Record*, October 7, 1991, p. S14466.
5. Thomas L. Jipping and Phyllis Berry-Myers, "Declaration of Independence: Justice Clarence Thomas, One Year Later," Free Congress Foundation, October, 1992.
6. Statement by Senator Bill Bradley to the U.S. Senate, *Congressional Record*, October 15, 1991, p. S14646.
7. This exchange and other direct quotations from the Senate hearings are found in *Nomination of Judge Clarence Thomas*, Senate Judiciary Committee hearings (Washington, D.C.: Government Printing Office, October 11–13, 1991).
8. Paul Simon, *Advice and Consent* (Bethesda, MD: National Press Books, 1992), p. 78.
9. This account is drawn from interviews with White House and Justice Department officials in April and May 1992.
10. James Rowley, "Thomas Nomination Fills Quota, Senate Majority Leader Says," Associated Press dispatch, July 8, 1991.
11. Transcript of interview of Susan Jane Hoerchner by the U.S. Senate Committee on the Judiciary, October 10, 1991. This document was sealed by the committee and never made public. It was obtained independently by the author.
12. Portions of the FBI's file on Clarence Thomas's background investigation, no part of which has ever been publicly revealed, were obtained independently by the author.

13. Transcript of interview of Gary Liman Phillips by the U.S. Senate Committee on the Judiciary, October 12, 1991. This document was sealed by the committee and not made public. It was obtained independently by the author.

14. In the Senate staff interview, Phillips revealed that he and Hill had a mutual friend named Keith Henderson, a former Senate Judiciary Committee staffer. He said he did not speak to Henderson about the Hill allegations until mid-September, well after the story reached Washington. Phillips also said that through a Yale law school classmate, Jeff Cunard, he was introduced to Morgan Frankel, a graduate of the same Yale law class as Hill, Hoerchner, and Phillips. Frankel, an assistant legal counsel in the Office of the Senate Legal Counsel, an adjunct of Senate Majority Leader George Mitchell's office, and Cunard, an attorney in private practice in Washington, contacted Phillips after Anita Hill's allegations became public and suggested that Phillips approach the Judiciary Committee about testifying for Hill.

15. This passage and other quotations from the Fleming report are found in *Report of Temporary Special Independent Counsel* (Washington, D.C.: Government Printing Office, 1992), Document 102–20, Parts I & II, May 13.

16. Fleming apparently believes it was more likely that Phillips, rather than Hoerchner, was responsible for the transmission of the story to the Alliance for Justice. Fleming's sole source for his account of the dinner party is the deposition of Metzenbaum aide Bonnie Goldstein, who recounted to Fleming what she said Aron had told her. Hoerchner, however, might still have been the source. She asked for, and was granted, permission by Hill to talk about the matter with other parties. She may have spoken to Aron directly or to someone else in Washington who could have conceivably been the dinner party guest. Aron told the *ABA Journal* that the Alliance was told about Hill by a former Yale classmate of Hill—which could be a reference to either Phillips or Hoerchner. On October 13, 1991, the *New York Times* reported, "Today an official of the Alliance for Justice said the group had received a tip from a fellow Yale Law School graduate of Professor Hill that a former employee of Clarence Thomas had been subjected to sexual harassment by him." Neil A. Lewis, "Judge's Backers Seek to Undercut Hill," p. 28. Both Phillips and Hoerchner fitted this description. Tim Phelps appears to think Hoerchner was the source. "The first, unconfirmed news about Anita Hill was provided to the Alliance by one of the law professor's *woman* classmates at Yale, who has remained anonymous." Tim Phelps and Helen Winternitz, *Capitol Games* (New York: Hyperion, 1992), p. 124. Hoerchner has stated: "I did not bring the story to Washington." Letter of Susan J. Hoerchner to author, June 18, 1991. Aron and Phillips declined to be interviewed.

17. Walter V. Robinson, "White House Readying Campaign for Thomas," *Boston Globe,* July 28, 1991, p. 1.

18. See, generally, Robert Bork, *The Tempting of America* (New York: Free Press, 1990); Ethan Bronner, *Battle for Justice* (New York: W.W. Norton & Company, 1989); Terry Eastland, *Energy in the Executive* (New York: Free Press, 1992); Orrin Hatch, "The Politics of Picking Judges," *Journal of Law and Politics,* Fall 1989, pp. 35–53, and "Special Interest Groups Threaten to Destroy Independence of the Judiciary," text of Senate speech, August 1, 1991; Patrick McGuigan and Jeffrey P. O'Connell, editors, *The Judges War* (Washington, D.C.: Free Congress Research and Education Foundation, 1987); Patrick McGuigan and Dawn M. Weyrich, *Ninth Justice* (Washington, D.C.: Free Congress Foundation, 1990); Michael Pertschuk and Wendy Schaetzel, *The People Rising* (New York: Thunder's Mouth Press, 1989); and Laurence H. Silberman, "The Clarence Thomas Confirmation: A Retrospective," text of speech delivered at a Federalist Society conference, Mayflower Hotel, Washington, D.C., June 13, 1992.

19. Alliance for Justice, "Highlights of Past Work," December 1991.

20. *Ibid.*

21. Memorandum from Nan Aron and George Kassouf of the Alliance for Justice to Fred Abramson of the ABA Standing Committee on the Federal Judiciary, September 22, 1989. The ABA's guidelines are found in *What It Is and How It Works,* American Bar Association, Standing Committee on the Federal Judiciary, March 1991.

22. Controversy erupted in 1987, when the ABA awarded Judge Bork its highest rating, "well-qualified." Four members of the fifteen-member Standing Committee, however, found Bork "unqualified," triggering angry attacks from Republican Senators, who charged that the votes were politically inspired. The ABA practice of providing the names to the Alliance prior to nominations being made was eventually ended after heated Republican objections.

23. Dan Trigoboff, "Bush Judicial Nominees Blasted," *ABA Journal,* March 1991, p. 20.

24. This was actually less damning than it appeared. Both Justice Rehnquist and Justice O'Connor received "qualified" ratings from the ABA. It was the two "not qualified" votes that made Thomas's rating the lowest in history. "The committee did not undertake any examination or consideration of Judge Thomas' political ideology or his views on any issues that might come before the court," the committee report said. The report, submitted September 14, 1991, to the Senate Judiciary Committee, is reprinted in *Legal Times,* September 23, 1991, pp. 12–13.

25. *Ibid.,* in *Legal Times,* p. 12.

26. Orrin Hatch, "Judge Thomas Is Well Qualified," text of Senate speech, July 11, 1991.

27. Interview of Alan Simpson, May 4, 1992.

28. Verveer is now an aide to Hillary Clinton.

29. Seidman later joined the Clinton–Gore campaign as manager of its Little Rock "war room" and then won a deputy's position on Clinton's transition team. She is now the top deputy to George Stephanopoulous in the White House.

30. Statement by Senator Howard Metzenbaum to the U.S. Senate, *Congressional Record,* June 16, 1992, p. S8239.

31. Dan Vukelich, "Senate Panel Charges Misfeasance," *Washington Times,* March 31, 1989, p. 36.

32. "Age Discrimination: Liars Figure and Figures Lie," Coalitions for America, September 16, 1991.

33. "The NAACP Announces Opposition to Judge Thomas's Nomination," public announcement, August 7, 1991.

34. Interviews of Ricky Silberman, March 17 and April 15, 1992.

35. See Isaiah J. Poole, "Ideologies Clash as Senators Size Up Reagan EEOC Nominee," *Washington Times,* March 5, 1986, p. 7, and Mary Thornton, "Senate Panel Rejects EEOC Nomination," *Washington Post,* May 21, 1986, p. 23.

36. Interview of Jeffrey Zuckerman, March 26, 1992.

37. Larry J. Sabato, *Feeding Frenzy* (New York: Free Press, 1991), p. 140.

38. "Marijuana Culpa," *Washington City Paper,* January 17–23, 1988, p. 20. Totenberg was not the best choice to be policing other people's morals. A January 1992 profile of Totenberg headlined "Queen of Leaks" in *Vanity Fair* exposed Totenberg's ripoff of a story about Judge Ginsburg's alleged "resumé enhancement" from the *Legal Times,* a weekly newspaper that covers legal affairs. On a Friday afternoon, Totenberg called the *Legal Times* to track down a tip that the paper had a juicy story for its Monday edition on Ginsburg. The reporter, Aaron Freiwald, told *Vanity Fair* that he walked a copy of the piece over to Totenberg and struck a deal that she could use it in exchange for attribution. The newspaper regularly leaked its exclusive stories to other media as a promotional device. Totenberg was on the radio an hour later broadcasting the story—without attribution. Totenberg told the magazine that she already had the story before Freiwald gave her his piece, but she admitted to "one or two language overlaps." Ann Louise Bardach, "Nina Totenberg: Queen of the Leaks," *Vanity Fair,* January 1992, pp. 46–57.

39. Howard Kurtz, "The Legal Reporter's Full Court Press," *Washington Post,* October 10, 1991, p. D1.

40. Albert R. Hunt, "Tales of Ignominy: Beyond Thomas and Hill," *Wall Street Journal,* October 28, 1991, p. 14.

41. Transcript of 1992 McClatchy Lecture, National Public Radio Public Affairs, May 7, 1992.

42. Phelps and Winternitz, *Capitol Games,* p. 17.

43. Interview of Clint Bolick, March 21, 1992.
44. Timothy M. Phelps, " 'Real Clarence Thomas' Revealed," *Newsday,* September 14, 1991.
45. Charging that a nominee's religion would skew his jurisprudence, and endorsing the *Roe* v. *Wade* litmus test of the abortion rights groups, Phelps wrote in *Capitol Games,* "It is legitimate to ask, for example, whether we want to give a potentially deciding vote on the issue of separation of church and state to a man who attends a fundamentalist church. It is entirely legitimate for women's groups to ask whether Thomas would throw out what they consider to be a basic right to choose an abortion." (p. 69)
46. See, generally, Bork, *Tempting of America;* Bronner, *Battle for Justice;* Suzanne Garment, "The War Against Robert H. Bork," *Commentary,* January 1988, pp. 17–26; Mark Gitenstein, *Matters of Principle* (New York: Simon & Schuster, 1992); Linda Greenhouse, "What Went Wrong," *New York Times,* October 7, 1987, p. B10; Al Kamen and Edward A. Walsh, "Bork Lays Out Philosophy," *Washington Post,* September 16, 1987, p. 1; McGuigan and Weyrich, *Ninth Justice;* and Stuart Taylor, Jr., "A Committed Conservative," *New York Times,* July 2, 1987, p. 1, and "Senate Liberals Will Try to Block Nominee on Ideological Grounds," *New York Times,* July 5, 1987, p. E1.
47. Interview of Orrin Hatch, March 9, 1992.
48. Isaiah J. Poole, "NAACP Sees Bork Vote as a 'Litmus Test,' " *Washington Times,* July 7, 1991, p. 4.
49. Aric Press, "Bork's Last Stand," *Newsweek,* October 19, 1987, pp. 26–27. See also Stuart Taylor, Jr., "Debate Continues on Accusations of Distortion in Ads Against Bork," *New York Times,* October 21, 1987, p. 23.
50. The sterilization case had involved the American Cyanamid Company, whose manufacturing process was putting lead into the air of the workplace. The company could not remove the lead from the air, and when it was discovered that fetuses of pregnant workers could be damaged, the company was required by federal law to remove women of childbearing age from the site. It offered them the possibility of transfer, but job openings were limited and at lower pay.

   The company also informed the women that a sterilization procedure would be provided by the company. Five of them availed themselves of that option. Later the women sued, claiming that the offering of hysterectomies constituted an "unsafe condition of the workplace" under the Occupational Safety and Health Act. A three-judge panel of the D.C. Circuit ruled unanimously, in an opinion written by Judge Bork, that this did not constitute an "unsafe working condition," within the specific meaning of that statute. The Bork opinion noted, however, that even if the company's action did not violate that statute, it might well be illegal under other laws. It might, for instance, constitute a form of employment discrimination. A finding that a particular law does not provide a remedy in a particular case simply does not mean, as Bork's opponents insinuated, that the judge was against workplace safety, had an antipathy for labor, or favored female sterilization.

51. For an extensive discussion of this matter, see Terry Eastland, "The Tempting of Justice Kennedy," *The American Spectator,* February 1993, pp. 32–37. Circuit Judge Silberman addressed the general problem in his 1992 Federalist Society speech prior to the June abortion case: "Federal judges have instead appeared particularly prone to listen very carefully to the views of what has been described as the 'new class,' or lately, the 'chattering classes.' In the United States, that very much means the press. . . . It seems that the primary objective of the [New York] *Times'* legal reporters is to put activist heat on recently appointed Supreme Court justices. Tom Sowell has described this technique as the 'Greenhouse effect,' after the *Times'* leading court reporter [Linda Greenhouse]. Their Washington second stringer, Mr. Neil Lewis, covers our court, and his reporting is so obviously distorted and tendentious that it reads as if it were a cross between the columns of his namesakes, Anthony and Flora Lewis."

52. Statement by Senator Mitch McConnell to the U.S. Senate, *Congressional Record,* October 7, 1991, p. S14478.

53. Interview of Harry Singleton, March 9, 1992.

54. Interview of Senate Labor Committee staffer, March 9, 1992.

55. Elaine Sciolino, "Polite and Yet Dogged, an Ohio Senator Gives Opponents Heartburn," *New York Times,* October 25, 1991, p. 12.

56. Martin Tolchin, "After Warning, Bork Witness Fell Silent," *New York Times,* October 18, 1987, p. 36.

57. See, generally, Julie Johnson, "Congressmen Deal Blows to Nomination for Top Civil Rights Post," *New York Times,* July 21, 1989, p. 38; Ruth Marcus, "Civil Rights Groups' Split Could Give Lucas a Boost," *Washington Post,* May 4, 1989, p. 21, and "Senate Committee Delays Lucas Vote," *Washington Post,* July 28, 1989, p. 7; Jerry Seper, "Supporters, Critics, Head for Showdown over Lucas Nomination," *Washington Times,* May 15, 1989, p. 3; and Philip Shenon, "2 Top Rights Groups Oppose Nominee for Justice Department Job," *New York Times,* May 10, 1989, p. 1.

58. Metzenbaum used the tactic in 1984 against Edwin Meese, President Reagan's nominee for Attorney General. Suzanne Garment reported in her book *Scandal* (New York: Times Books, 1991), pp. 86–87: "A man named Roy C. Meyers, an aide to Senate Judiciary Committee member Howard H. Metzenbaum, flew out to Meese's home territory of California to search for damaging information on the nominee. At first he found none. But a former Senate investigator eventually steered Meyers toward records on Meese's sale of his San Diego home, which he had left upon moving to Washington at the start of the Reagan Administra-

tion. When Meese appeared before the Senate Judiciary Committee for his confirmation hearings in March 1984, committee Democrats began asking Meese about charges that his financial dealings were unethical. Metzenbaum asserted that Meese, when selling the San Diego house, was given bank loans on specially favorable terms in return for getting federal jobs for two Californians connected with the bank." An independent counsel was later appointed to investigate Meese, and he found no evidence of criminal wrongdoing.

59. William Safire, "Myths of the Confirmation," *New York Times,* October 17, 1991, p. 27.
60. Sciolino, "Polite Yet Dogged," p. 12.
61. Interviews with Senate Judiciary Committee and Senate Labor Committee staff, April and May 1992.
62. "House of Lords v. Thomas," *Wall Street Journal* editorial, July 30, 1991.
63. See *Nomination of Robert H. Bork to be Associate Justice,* Hearings, Senate Judiciary Committee (Washington, D.C.: Government Printing Office, 1989).

2. The Borking of Clarence Thomas

1. Quoted in Lydia Martin, "NOW Official: Thomas Must Not Make Court," *Miami Herald,* July 8, 1991, p. 18.
2. Quoted in Associated Press dispatch, July 5, 1991.
3. Quoted in "Racial Correctness," *Wall Street Journal* editorial, August 1, p. 12.
4. For more on political tensions within the black community, see, generally, Dorothy J. Gaiter, "Black Conservatives Wield Growing Clout Beyond Their Number," *Wall Street Journal,* July 3, 1991, p. 1; Pam Richtler and Sam Fulwood III, "Conservative Black Thinkers Gain Visibility," Los Angeles Times–Washington Post News Service, as printed in *The Oregonian,* July 17, 1991, p. 3; and Elizabeth Wright, "Black America and the Thomas Nomination," *Wall Street Journal,* July 24, 1991, p. A10.
5. In addition to interviews, the portrait of Thomas and quotations from his speeches are drawn from L. Gordon Crovitz, editor, *Clarence Thomas: Confronting the Future* (Washington, D.C.: Regnery Gateway, 1992); Howard Kurtz, "Clarence Thomas: Skirting the Controversy on Civil Rights Policy," *Washington Post,* September 22, 1986, p. 15; Bill McAllister, "Under Thomas EEOC Relinquished Rights Role," *Washington Post,* September 10, 1991, p. 1; Phelps and Winternitz, *Capitol Games;* Isaiah J. Poole, "EEOC: An Agency on the Defensive," *Insight,* March 3, 1986, pp. 26–27; Aric Press and Bob Cohn, "Judging Thomas: The Life and Contradiction of the Supreme Court Nominee," *Newsweek,* September 16, 1991, pp. 18–28; Charles Shanor, "Thomas' Record at the EEOC,"

Washington Post, September 9, 1991, p. 15; Shelby Steele, "Thomas Refuses Victim's Mantle," *Los Angeles Times,* August 11, 1991, p. M5; Karen Tumulty, "Clarence Thomas' Life Was Born out of Ashes," Los Angeles Times–Washington Post News Service, as printed in *The Oregonian,* July 7, 1991, p. 5; Juan Williams, "A Question of Fairness," *Atlantic Monthly,* February 1987, pp. 71–82; "A Unique Contribution to America: An Analysis of President George Bush's Nomination of Clarence Thomas to be an Associate Justice of the Supreme Court of the U.S.," Coalitions for America, July 1991; and "Clarence Thomas Rises from Poverty to Supreme Court Nominee," *Jet,* July 22, 1991, p. 1.

6. Bolick interview.
7. Interview of John Marini, March 31, 1992.
8. Singleton interview.
9. Interview of Jeffrey Zuckerman, March 26, 1992.
10. Zuckerman interview.
11. Bill McAllister, "EEOC Chief Faces Scrutiny as a Court Nominee," *Washington Post,* February 5, 1991, p. 1.
12. Llewellyn Rockwell, "Cultural Revolutions," *Chronicles,* January 1992, p. 5.
13. Interview of Joe Schutt, April 23, 1991.
14. Marini interview.
15. Ricky Silberman interviews. Like all government agencies, the EEOC is comprised of a large career bureaucracy that does not change when a new administration comes to office. In the case of the EEOC, most of the career employees that Thomas inherited had been at the agency since the 1960s and 1970s. The career bureaucracy most often has a policy agenda of its own, and it is the task of the political appointees of any administration to try to impose direction on that bureaucracy.
16. Interview of Phyllis Berry-Myers, April 2, 1991.
17. Bolick interview.
18. "The EEOC Is Thriving," *Washington Post* editorial, August 1, 1987, p. 22.
19. Public statement of Willie King, undated.
20. Interview of Dick Leon, June 6, 1992.
21. Interview of Laurence Silberman, April 21, 1992.
22. Ruth Marcus, "14 in House Assail Judgeship Choice," *Washington Post,* July 18, 1989, p. 15.
23. "Thomas Rises from Poverty," *Jet,* July 22, 1991.
24. Associated Press dispatch, "Reagan Wants Confirmation of Bork to be Apolitical," as printed in the *Washington Post,* July 5, 1987, p. 4.
25. Quoted in Steve Allen, "More Equal than Others," United Seniors Newsletter no. 10, July 1991, p. 5. In early July Allen wrote presciently: "Before he is confirmed to the Supreme Court, he will endure a smear campaign like nothing we have seen in this country."

26. Haywood Burns, "Clarence Thomas, A Counterfeit Hero," *New York Times,* July 9, 1991, p. A15.

27. Quoted in Arch Puddington, "Clarence Thomas and the Blacks," *Commentary,* February 1992, pp. 28–33.

28. *Ibid.*

29. Barbara Reynolds, "Thomas Nomination Another Sour Note," *USA Today,* July 5, 1991, p. 9, and "Thomas May Have Last Laugh After All," *USA Today,* September 13, 1991, p. 9.

30. Jack E. White, "The Pain of Being Black," *Time,* September 16, 1991, pp. 25–27.

31. Adam Clymer, "About That Flag on the Judge's Desk," *New York Times,* July 19, 1991, p. 13.

32. Quoted in Puddington, "Thomas and Blacks."

33. *Ibid.*

34. "Rethinking Black Concerns," *Wall Street Journal* editorial, July 16, 1992, p. 10.

35. For more on race and the Thomas nomination, see, generally, Edith Efron, "Native Son: Why a Black Supreme Court Nominee Has No Rights White Men Respect," *Reason,* February 1992, pp. 23–32; Steven A. Holmes, "A Changed Landscape for Southern Democrats," *New York Times,* September 8, 1991, p. 22; Ruth Marcus, "Anti-Bork Forces Find Thomas a Different Fight," *Washington Post,* August 3, 1991, p. 1; and Robert Suro, "Thomas's Foes Off to Slow Start, Say Swaying Public Will Be Hard," *New York Times,* September 8, 1991, p. 1.

36. Interview with Black Caucus member, January 14, 1992. See also "Congressional Black Caucus Statement in Opposition to the Nomination of Judge Clarence Thomas to the Supreme Court," July 18, 1991, and Tom Kenworthy, "Black Caucus Is Low-Key Thomas Foe," *Washington Post,* September 17, 1991, p. 6.

37. Interview with an EEOC official who requested anonymity.

38. On July 31, just before the August 1 scheduled meeting of the NAACP board to vote on the Thomas nomination, the organization's highly critical staff report was leaked to the *New York Times.* (Steven A. Holmes, "NAACP Report Assaults Thomas Views on Equality Issues," p. A1). The report, a draft of which was also obtained by the author, was never publicly released. It would later be revealed that Anita Hill's main legal adviser, Harvard Professor Charles Ogletree, was a principal drafter of the secret NAACP report, which, in one instance, altered a quote from one of Thomas's writings to make the point it wanted to make.

39. Al Kamen and Michael Ishikoff, "A Distressing Turn: Activists Decry What Process Has Become," *Washington Post,* October 12, 1991, p. 1.

40. Statement of the Leadership Conference on Civil Rights Opposing the Confirmation of Judge Clarence Thomas to the U.S. Supreme Court, Ralph G. Neas, Executive Director, August 7, 1991.

41. Margaret Bush Wilson, "NAACP Is Wrong on Thomas," *Washington Post,* August 6, 1991, p. 15.

42. Quoted in Judi Hasson, "Black Conservatives: Caucus Out of Touch," *USA Today,* July 19, 1991, p. 3.

43. See "Emancipation from the NAACP," *Wall Street Journal* editorial, August 9, 1991, p. 8, and Lynne Duke, "NAACP Warns Unit Backing Thomas," *Washington Post,* August 9, 1991, p. 1.

44. "See You Next Year," *Wall Street Journal* editorial, August 6, 1991, p. 16.

45. Interview of the Reverend Henry Delaney, July 17, 1992.

46. Interview of Tom Jipping, March 25, 1992.

47. See "Organizations Supporting Clarence Thomas' Nomination to the Supreme Court," Coalitions for America, September 19, 1991.

48. Ruth Marcus, "Groups Take Turns Taking Sides on Court Nominee," *Washington Post,* July 31, 1991, p. 18.

49. Judith Colp, "The GOP's Own Dennis the Menace," *Washington Times,* July 10, 1992, p. E1.

50. The ad neglected to mention Howard Metzenbaum, the man who delighted in making ethics charges against Republican nominees. In 1984 Metzenbaum had accepted a $250,000 finder's fee for making a phone call to grease the way for the sale of a Washington hotel. Embarrassed by the publicity surrounding the payment, Metzenbaum returned the money. In 1991 he was sued for fraud in the sale of the Little Tavern hamburger restaurant, which he had owned with his daughter and business partners. The suit claimed that Metzenbaum had misrepresented the financial condition of the chain at sale, and owed back taxes as well.

51. Interview of Gary Bauer, April 24, 1992.

52. See statement of the Alliance for Justice on the Nomination of Clarence Thomas to the Supreme Court of the U.S., July 29, 1991, and "Coalitions for America Exposes Questionable Tactics in Thomas Opposition," Coalitions for America, July 29, 1991.

53. Quoted in Fred Strasser, "Lawyers Line Up for Fall Hearing," *National Law Journal,* July 22, 1991, p. 1.

54. "Toward Justice Thomas," *Wall Street Journal* editorial, July 25, 1991, p. 8.

55. Reported by Clarence Thomas, *Nomination of Judge Clarence Thomas,* Senate Judiciary Committee Hearings (Washington, D.C.: Government Printing Office, 1991), October 11, 12, and 13.

56. Ricky Silberman interviews.

57. Interview of Floyd Hayes, March 25, 1992.

58. Juan Williams, "Open Season on Clarence Thomas," *Washington Post,* October 10, 1991, p. 23. After this piece appeared the *Post,* in a note to readers, said that an allegation of "verbal sexual harassment" had been made against Williams shortly before the column was published. Williams denied the charge, which may have been an indication of the kind of vituperation anyone may face who steps forward to defend

Thomas against the liberal special interest groups. See "Columnist Faces Harassment Charges," *USA Today,* October 19, 1991.

59. Bolick interview.
60. Ricky Silberman interviews.
61. These and other charges against Thomas are summarized in Phelps and Winternitz, *Capitol Games,* and "Thomas: The Water Torture Test," *Newsweek,* July 22, 1991, p. 19.
62. Ann Devroy, "Thomas Tried Marijuana While a College Student," *Washington Post,* July 11, 1991, p. 1.
63. Cheryl Arvidson, "Speeches of Court Nominee Cite Admiration for Farrakhan," *Dallas Times Herald,* July 12, 1991, p. 1.
64. Question and Answer in *Catholic Twin Circle,* July 20, 1991, reprinted from an interview with Thomas in 1989.
65. Wayne Woodlief, "Former In-Law: Thomas Is Supreme," *Boston Herald,* July 4, 1991, p. 1.
66. Kamen and Ishikoff, "Distressing Turn."
67. *Ibid.*
68. Phelps and Winternitz, *Capitol Games,* p. 147.
69. See Walter V. Robinson, "Files Suggest Illicit Thomas Travel," *Boston Globe,* September 7, 1991, p. 1, and "Panel Urged to Examine Thomas's Use of Trip Funds," *Boston Globe,* September 9, 1991, p. 1.
70. Judi Hasson, "Ethics Charges Leveled at Thomas," *USA Today,* July 22, 1991, p. 3, and Tony Mauro, "History Suggests Thomas Ethics Flap May Bear Watching," *USA Today,* July 23, 1991, p. 6.
71. Letter from Senator Hank Brown to Kate Michelman, July 17, 1991.
72. Lewis Lehrman, "Natural Right and the Right to Life," *American Spectator,* April 1987, pp. 21–23.
73. Timothy Phelps, "A Clue to Thomas' Views," *Newsday,* July 3, 1991, p. 6.
74. "Gov. Wilder Is Questioning Role of Thomas's Religion," *Wall Street Journal,* July 3, 1991, p. 8.
75. Quoted in Helen Kennedy, "Liberals Troubled by Nomination," *Boston Herald,* July 2, 1991, p. 2.
76. See *Clarence Thomas Hearings,* Senate Judiciary Committee, unpublished transcript, September 19, 1991, p. 33. Simon's observation was true, but not relevant to Thomas's jurisprudence. Never before had an issue been made of a judicial candidate's personal religious views.
77. Ricky Silberman interviews.
78. David Brock, "Fighting Words: Reagan Says Bork," *Insight,* July 20, 1987, pp. 8–12.
79. In 1968 President Johnson's plan to elevate Justice Abe Fortas to Chief Justice was withdrawn amid charges of political cronyism. Fortas had remained an adviser to Johnson while on the court. President Nixon nominated Clement F. Haynsworth to fill the seat of Fortas, who resigned in a financial scandal in 1969. During the confirmation hearings, it was re-

vealed that Judge Haynsworth had purchased stock in a corporation after he had decided, but before he had announced, the ruling in a suit involving that corporation. Nixon tried again with G. Harrold Carswell, but research on Carswell's record showed that 60 percent of his published opinions had been reversed by higher courts; his decisions in many areas of law were criticized as mediocre, confused, and ignorant of precedent.

There were a few nominees defeated for essentially political reasons, usually concerning race relations, but these were anomalies. George Woodward, nominated by President James Polk, was defeated largely because he had endorsed the American Nativist Agenda, favoring discrimination against immigrants. President James Buchanan's nomination of Secretary of State Jeremiah Black was scuttled in part because the nominee opposed the outright abolition of slavery. Both Nixon nominees, Haynsworth and Carswell, were attacked for harboring racist sentiments. Senator Strom Thurmond showed that the race question could cut both ways by leading a filibuster against Abe Fortas over his endorsement of a landmark Supreme Court decision on racial integration.

80. Quoted in "Coalitions for America Warns Against Double Standard," Coalitions for America, September 13, 1991.
81. Quoted in Doug Bandow, "The Democrats' Abortion Litmus Test," *Wall Street Journal,* July 29, 1992, p. 11.
82. "Clarence Thomas, P.O.W.," *Wall Street Journal* editorial, September 18, 1991, p. 14.
83. Bolick interview.
84. Ricky Silberman interviews.
85. Singleton interview.
86. See *Confirmation of Judge David Souter* (Washington, D.C.: Government Printing Office, 1990).
87. Hatch interview.
88. See statement of Kate Michelman, July 2, 1991, and Michelman briefing, July 16, 1991.
89. Ricky Silberman interviews.
90. These and other quotations and exchanges are from *Clarence Thomas Hearings,* Senate Judiciary Committee (Washington, D.C.: Government Printing Office, 1992).
91. "Judge Thomas and *Roe v. Wade,*" *Washington Post* editorial, September 13, 1991, p. 24.
92. Quoted in *Wall Street Journal* editorial, "Thomas Said That? Never Mind," December 2, 1991, p. A12.
93. Mary McGrory, "BCCI: Politics and Politesse," *Washington Post,* October 27, 1991, p. C1.
94. Richard L. Berke, "Senate Vote on Thomas Faces Delay," *New York Times,* October 2, 1991, p. 20.
95. Simon, *Advice and Consent,* p. 41.

96. Phelps and Winternitz, *Capitol Games*, p. 195.
97. Michael Thelwell, "False, Fleeting, Perjured Clarence: Yale's Brightest and Blackest Go To Washington," in Toni Morrison, ed., *Race-ing Justice*, p. 105.
98. E. J. Dionne, Jr., "Souter Splintered Liberal Coalition," *Washington Post*, October 2, 1990, p. 3. Souter was asked by Biden: "Let us say that a woman and/or her mate uses . . . a birth control device and it fails. Does she still have a constitutional right to choose not to become pregnant?" Souter answered, "I think for me to start answering that question, in effect, is for me to start discussing the concept of *Roe v. Wade*." Senator Herb Kohl then asked Souter: "Do you have an opinion on *Roe v. Wade?*" Souter answered: "I have not got any agenda on what should be done with *Roe v. Wade*, if that case were brought before me. I will listen to both sides of that case. I have not made up my mind and I do not go on the Court saying I must go one way or I must go another way."
99. Bauer interview.
100. Quoted in Kenneth B. Noble, "In Petition, Lawyers and Scholars Urge Senate to Reject Judge Bork," *New York Times*, September 15, 1987, p. 27, and Stuart Taylor, Jr., "At Hearing on Bork, Words of Warning," *New York Times*, September 22, 1987, p. B6.
101. Interviews with White House officials, May and June 1992.
102. Letter from William T. Coleman, Jr., to President Bush, October 31, 1989.
103. Interview with Lovida Coleman, April 29, 1992.
104. See "An Analysis of the Views of Judge Clarence Thomas," NAACP Legal Defense and Educational Fund, Inc., August 13, 1991. The report also found fault with Thomas on the grounds that in his early years he "most often quoted Langston Hughes and Martin Luther King's *Why We Can't Wait*; in his later years he emphasized Ayn Rand and Alan [sic] Bloom's *Closing of the American Mind*." This was a complete distortion of Thomas's critical comments about Rand and Bloom in a speech to the Pacific Research Institute: "But why should Bloom's aristocratic view of American life—in many ways more aristocratic than Ayn Rand's—be so popular?" Significantly, the group did not offer any criticism of Thomas's EEOC record.
105. Interviews with sources close to Coleman and the court, June and July 1991. Coleman declined to be interviewed.
106. Interviews with Senate Judiciary Committee staffers, May and June 1992.
107. Garry Sturgess, "Senate Mulls Thomas's Controversial Case," *Legal Times*, September 30, 1991, p. 1.
108. See, generally, "Who Mediates a Bench Battle? Appeals Court Split Along Political Lines in Rift over Opinion Leak," *Washington Post*, March 2, 1992, p. 15, and statements of Chief Judge Mikva, Judge David B. Sentelle, and Judge Laurence H. Silberman.

109 *Lamprecht* v. *FCC,* D.C. Circuit, No. 88-1395 (decided February 19, 1992).

110. See Gordon Crovitz, "Another Anti-Thomas Leaker Likely to Evade Justice," *Wall Street Journal,* February 26, 1992, p. 13.

3. The Tempting of Anita Hill

1. Marjorie Williams, "From Women, an Outpouring of Anger," *Washington Post,* October 9, 1991, p. 1.
2. Margaret Carlson, *Time,* October 21, 1991.
3. Judith Resnik, "Hearing Women," *Southern California Law Review,* March 1992, pp. 1333–1345.
4. Barbara Ransby, "The Gang Rape of Anita Hill and the Assault Upon Women of African Descent," in Robert Chrisman and Robert L. Allen, eds., *Court of Appeal,* p. 174. This book is a collection of forty-one essays that originally appeared in the Winter 1991–Spring 1992 issue of *The Black Scholar: Journal of Black Studies and Research.* Ransby overlooked the fact that the term "high-tech lynching" was Thomas's own, not an invention of white conservatives.
5. *Ibid.,* p. 98.
6. From "Confidential Document Request for Judge Clarence Thomas," reprinted in part in "Thomas's Judges: A Collection of Speed Readers?," *Wall Street Journal* editorial, September 5, 1991, p. 14.
7. See "Thomas in the Coliseum," *Wall Street Journal* editorial, September 5, 1991, p. 14.
8. Unless otherwise noted, details on Senate staff activities in this chapter are drawn from *Report of Temporary Special Independent Counsel, Pursuant to Senate Resolution 202,* Document 120-20, May 13, 1991, Parts I & II, and a chronology of Judiciary Committee staff contacts with Anita Hill released by Senator Biden and reprinted in the *Congressional Record,* October 8, 1991, pp. S14545–46.
9. Statement by Senator Howard Metzenbaum to the U.S. Senate, *Congressional Record,* October 7, 1991, p. S14473.
10. Quoted in Neil A. Lewis, "Judge's Backers Seek to Undercut Hill," *New York Times,* October 13, 1991, p. 28.
11. Interview of Senator Hank Brown, April 21, 1992.
12. Interview of Diane Holt, April 3, 1992.
13. Interview of Armstrong Williams, April 3, 1992.
14. According to a report in the Washington *Afro-American* newspaper, which could not be independently substantiated, Brudney and Hill "were not only best friends, but were roommates" at Yale. Hamil Harris, "Hill and Metzenbaum Staffer Shared Home," Washington *Afro-American,* October 19, 1991, p. 1. Though there is no evidence to support such a conclusion, conspiracy theorists might be tempted to conclude that these close links preclude coincidence.

15. Statement by Senator Hank Brown to the U.S. Senate, *Congressional Record*, October 15, 1991, pp. S14653–54.
16. Tom Squitieri and Sam Meddis, "Hill Assured Thomas Would Withdraw 'Quietly,' " *USA Today*, October 9, 1991, p. 1.
17. Statement by Senator Malcolm Wallop to the U.S. Senate, *Congressional Record*, October 24, 1991, p. S15126.
18. Statement by Senator Jack Danforth to the U.S. Senate, *Congressional Record*, October 8, 1991, p. S14568.
19. "Thomas Fallout," *Legal Times*, November 11, 1991, p. 23.
20. Sarah E. Wright, "The Anti-Black Agenda," in Robert Chrisman and Robert L. Allen, eds., *Court of Appeal*, p. 228.
21. Ricky Silberman, text of a speech to the Federalist Society in Washington, October 16, 1992.
22. Al Kamen, "Biden Calls Pressuring Hill 'Immoral,' " *Washington Post*, October 10, 1991, p. 14.
23. Statement by Senator Kit Bond to the U.S. Senate, *Congressional Record*, October 24, 1991, p. S15123.
24. Lewis, "Judge's Backers Seek to Undercut Hill."
25. In a speech given after the hearings, Ross said: "Somehow, I think, the recent hearings might have proceeded very differently, and had a different result, if fourteen of the women sitting in this room had been on the Senate Judiciary Committee." Ross went on to decry the "workplace hierarchy," the "cultural mythologizing of women," and a "boys will be boys" approach to jurisprudence. She also called for "unlimited compensatory and punitive damages" for sexual harassment victims. Susan Deller Ross, "Proving Sexual Harassment," text of speech at the Forum for Women State Legislators, San Diego, November 15, 1991, reprinted in *Southern California Law Review*, March 1992, pp. 1452–1457.
26. Hill's statement is reproduced in the Fleming report. It has never been established if this document was a sworn statement. Hill told Fleming that the statement was notarized, but she claimed that she could not locate the original. The telefaxed copy appeared to bear the markings of a notary's seal. Given Hill's concern with confidentiality, it is unclear why she faxed the document.
27. Statement by Senator Orrin Hatch to the U.S. Senate, *Congressional Record*, October 7, 1991, p. S14452.
28. Richard L. Berke, "Thomas's Accuser Assails Handling of Her Complaint," *New York Times*, October 8, 1991, p. 1.
29. Transcript of Totenberg NPR broadcast, "Weekend Edition," October 6, 1991. Emphasis added.
30. Text of Totenberg lecture at Stanford University.
31. Transcript of *Good Morning America*, #1559, June 4, 1992, p. 7.
32. Statement by Senator Nancy Kassebaum to the U.S. Senate, *Congressional Record*, October 15, 1991, p. S14661.
33. The White House had decided not to forewarn Thomas about the charge

before the FBI arrived for the interview. Later in the day, Timothy Flanigan, a top Justice Department official handling the nomination, went to see Thomas at his home on another matter, and they also discussed the Hill allegation. Flanigan said he was convinced of Thomas's total innocence because in his experience, Thomas had had a "low guilt threshold." Throughout the summer, when Thomas was criticized by the opposition on various fronts, for example on the issue of his tax returns, "he would always wonder if he had done something wrong," Flanigan said. "But in this case, he just knew the story was totally false. He kept saying 'Anita? Anita?' Then he said 'I've got to get my name back.' "

34. Simon, *Advice and Consent*, pp. 103–31.
35. Gloria Borger, *U.S. News and World Report*, October 21, 1991, pp. 32–36. Emphasis added.
36. Mark Gitenstein, *Matters of Principle* (New York: Simon and Schuster, 1992) p. 340.
37. Hatch interview.
38. Simpson interview.
39. Quoted in Lynne Duke, "Charges Ignite Lobbying Groups," *Washington Post*, October 8, 1991, p. 9
40. Abramson and Shribman, *Wall Street Journal*, p. 1.
41. Dowd, *New York Times*, p. 1.
42. Gitenstein, *Matters of Principle*, p. 342.
43. Abramson and Shribman, *Wall Street Journal*, p. 1.
44. An adviser to Biden, Tribe was the author of the 1986 book *God Save This Honorable Court*, which laid out the case for an expanded advice and consent role for the Senate in judicial nominations. Tribe's book encouraged Senators to vote down nominees on political grounds—a defensible position. Yet the Senators could not bring themselves to admit what they were doing, thus producing the destructive borking phenomenon: Bork was "strange," Thomas was "unstable."
45. Fred Strasser, "Committee Handled the Allegations by the Book, but Not Aggressively," *National Law Journal*, October 21, 1991, p. 1.
46. Bruce Fein, "The Thomas–Hill Leak Probe," *ABA Journal*, June 1992, p. 54.
47. Statement by Senator Joseph Biden to the U.S. Senate, *Congressional Record*, October 8, 1991, p. S14567.
48. Statement by Senator Howard Metzenbaum to the U.S. Senate, *Congressional Record*, October 7, 1991, p. S14473.

4. Trial by Leak

1. Timothy M. Phelps, "Doubting Thomas, Panel Casts Tie Vote," *Newsday*, September 28, 1991, p. 7.
2. Statement by Senator Nancy Kassebaum to the U.S. Senate, *Congressional Record*, October 15, 1991, p. S14661.

3. Statement by Senator Thad Cochran to the U.S. Senate, *Congressional Record,* October 24, 1991, p. S15127.

4. Letter from Judith Lichtman to members of the U.S. Senate, October 15, 1991.

5. Unless otherwise noted, the sequence of events leading up to the leak is drawn from the Fleming report.

6. Simon, *Advice and Consent,* p. 105.

7. Interview with Chicago woman who requested anonymity, June 19, 1992, and interview of John Danforth, March 19, 1992.

8. Quoted in "Find the Character Assassins," *Washington Times* editorial, October 10, 1991, p. C2.

9. Quoted in Helen Dewar, "Senate Opens Debate on Thomas Nomination," *Washington Post,* October 4, 1991, p. 14.

10. Quoted in Judi Hasson, "Thomas Nomination: Watching the Clock," *USA Today,* September 30, 1991, p. 3.

11. Quoted in Aaron Epstein, "Split Vote on Thomas Looks Possible," Knight-Ridder News Service, September 26, 1991.

12. Quoted in "Thomas Likely to Win Seat on Top Court," *Wall Street Journal,* September 30, 1991, p. A14.

13. Statement by Senator Orrin Hatch to the U.S. Senate, *Congressional Record,* October 8, 1991, p. S14521.

14. Statement by Senator Robert Dole to the U.S. Senate, *Congressional Record,* October 8, 1991, p. S14539.

15. Statement by Senator Alan Simpson to the U.S. Senate, *Congressional Record,* October 7, 1991, p. S14474.

16. Timothy M. Phelps, "Sex Harassment Allegation: The Charge Against Thomas," *Newsday,* October 6, 1991, p. 7

17. Phelps and Winternitz, *Capitol Games,* p. 229.

18. *Ibid.,* p. 230.

19. By his own admission in *Advice and Consent,* Simon used a similar construction in describing Hill's charge on the telephone on October 2 with Kate Michelman that he evidently used with Phelps the same day.

20. Phelps, "Sex Harassment Allegation," p. 7.

21. The two versions are reprinted in the Fleming report, pp. 31–32.

22. Phelps and Winternitz, *Capitol Games,* p. 233. Should there be any doubt on this point, Phelps dispelled it once and for all in a press packet that accompanied *Capitol Games.* In the release, entitled "A Conversation with Timothy Phelps and Helen Winternitz," Phelps stated: "I finally got the details of her allegations, *and the FBI report,* not because someone wanted to use me against Thomas, but because I pushed hard to get the information." [Emphasis added.]

23. Fleming discounted other textual evidence from Phelps's story that indicated his source had seen the FBI report. Phelps reported: "Hill told the FBI that Thomas repeatedly discussed sexual matters with her in a

suggestive way." He also reported that "the FBI interviewed the unidentified friend who corroborated her account." Fleming, a Senate employee, was led to dismiss these obvious clues and conclude that Phelps's source had not seen the FBI report on the grounds that only Senators had seen the FBI report and all of the Senators denied leaking the story. This seems to have been a conclusion based on political convenience rather than the evidence.

24. Statement by Senator Howard Metzenbaum to the U.S. Senate, *Congressional Record,* October 24, 1991, p. S15133. When first apprised of the leak, Hatch had told Phelps, "I'm going to kill Metzenbaum and Neas."

25. In his book *Advice and Consent,* Simon hailed Phelps's skills as a journalist. Other than the five senators, Biden staffers Harriet Grant and Jeff Peck, who brought the file to each Senator for his review, might have read it on the sly. Given their general respect for committee procedures, this is not likely. Moreover, neither of them spoke with Phelps before he broke the story. The three Senate staffers who did speak with Phelps before he broke the story—Metzenbaum aides Bill Corr, Chris Harvie, and Kennedy aide Ricki Seidman—did not have access to the FBI report.

26. Phelps declined to comment on this or any other aspect of his reportage.

27. Transcript of Totenberg NPR broadcast, "Weekend Edition," October 6, 1991. Phelps reported: "Simon said he and most other Members of the Senate Judiciary Committee were not aware of the allegations when they voted on the nomination, though he has since read the FBI report." This sentence is interesting on two counts: Not only does it show Simon misstating the fact that he had not seen the FBI report before voting; it also indicates that Phelps knew Simon had in fact read the FBI file.

28. Paul M. Rodriguez and George Archibald, "Panelists Say Simon Was the One," *Washington Times,* October 23, 1991, p. 1.

29. Statement of Paul Simon, as transcribed and released to author by David Carle, Simon's press secretary.

30. Statement of Nina Totenberg before Senate special independent counsel Peter E. Fleming, Jr., February 24, 1992.

31. Bill Gertz and Gene Grabowski, "Leahy Confesses Leak Led Him to Step Down," *Washington Times,* July 29, 1987, p. 1.

32. Jill Hodges, "Hill Urges Attorneys to Take Lead in Eliminating Sexual Harassment in the Workplace," Minneapolis *Star-Tribune,* October 29, 1992, p. 1.

33. Fleming's theory relies on a quote from Totenberg's NPR producer, William Buzenberg, who told *Vanity Fair* (Bardach, "Totenberg: Queen of Leaks," p. 48) that Totenberg "had the [Hill] affidavit five days before she spilled the beans"—which would have been Tuesday, October 1. Fleming attributes Totenberg's failure to confront Hill with the statement until Saturday to a purported doubt on Totenberg's part that she had an authentic document. Fleming further speculates that the explanation for Totenberg's uncertainty about the document in her posses-

sion could have been that it was neither signed nor dated. The only un-signed and undated copy of Hill's statement was the one that she had faxed to Brudney on September 25. This theory, however, is not per-suasive. The best way for Totenberg to have overcome any doubt about the authenticity of the document would have been for her to confront Hill with it as soon as possible. But Totenberg did not do this. She waited five days. It is far more plausible that Totenberg did not confront Hill with the statement until Saturday because she did not obtain the state-ment until Saturday, after Seidman told Brudney that Totenberg was looking for it. Totenberg was quoted in the *Washington Post* as follows: "But Totenberg says she spent four days seeking corroboration from Hill's friends and employers, and that she had several off-the-record conversations with Hill *before she obtained the affidavit* [emphasis added] and persuaded Hill to speak publicly." Howard Kurtz, "The Legal Re-porter's Full Court Press," *Washington Post,* October 10, 1991, p. D1. Furthermore, on Tuesday, October 1, the day that Buzenberg said he thought Totenberg got the statement, no one knew when the floor vote on the nomination would occur. It was expected to come as soon as Fri-day, October 4. Therefore, Totenberg would not have sat on the state-ment for four days, until Saturday, October 5, if she had obtained it earlier.

34. According to Harriet Grant's deposition by special counsel Fleming, the committee's copy was kept at all times in her safe and was not photo-copied. Seidman was Brudney's link to Totenberg; Grant, however, never spoke with Totenberg directly or indirectly and therefore could not have been the source of the leak.

35. Simon would be guilty of lying to Congress, but not of perjury, since his statement to Fleming, unlike Brudney's and the others', was not under oath. Simon, like Metzenbaum, refused to be interviewed by Fleming, only providing a written statement. Metzenbaum's denial that his staff was involved in the leak may have reflected the Senator's ignorance about what Brudney may have done, or it may have been a false state-ment to Congress.

36. Statement by Senator Howard Metzenbaum to the U.S. Senate, *Con-gressional Record,* October 7, 1991, p. S14473.

37. Adam Clymer, "Delaying the Vote: How Senators Reached Accord," *New York Times,* October 10, 1991, p. B15.

38. Simpson interview.

39. See, generally, " 'Tree Time,' " *American Lawyer,* December 1991, pp. 45–51, and Phelps, *Capitol Games,* pp. 293–296.

5. In Her Own Words

1. Paul M. Barrett and Jill Abramson, "Unsolved Mysteries," *Wall Street Jour-nal,* October 14, 1991, p. 1.

2. Phelps and Winternitz, *Capitol Games,* p. 433.

3. Lynne Duke, "Hill Says Racial Perceptions Undercut Her Credibility," *Washington Post,* October, 1992, p. A10.
4. Statement by Senator Orrin Hatch to the U.S. Senate, *Congressional Record,* October 8, 1991, p. S14452.
5. Statement by Senator Strom Thurmond to the U.S. Senate, *Congressional Record,* October 7, 1991, p. S14466.
6. Claudia Brodsky Lacour, "Doing Things with Words: 'Racism,' as Speech Act and the Undoing of Justice," in Toni Morrison, ed., *Race-ing Justice,* p. 149.
7. The document was obtained by the author.
8. Hill's inability to obtain a political appointment will be discussed in Chapter 8.
9. Interview with Phyllis Berry-Myers, April 2, 1992.
10. Interview with Andrew Fishel, March 31, 1992.
11. Singleton interview. Singleton had given essentially the same information that he recounted in this interview in a sworn affidavit to the Judiciary Committee during Anita Hill's testimony. But when Specter tried to use it as the basis for questioning Hill, the question was disallowed by Biden. At one point in an exchange with Hill, Specter said, "Harry Singleton, in fact, according to an affidavit provided, was prepared to retain you as one of his attorney advisers." Senator Metzenbaum then interrupted, calling the Singleton affidavit "a back door way of approaching the question of how many witnesses each side will bring forth." Specter responded quite correctly that the affidavit "goes to the heart of the credibility of what the witness has testified to."

Biden then ruled that Hill could be questioned about Singleton, but Singleton's sworn statement could neither be introduced nor referred to in any way. Biden explained, "It would be appropriate to ask her about Mr. Singleton. But it is inappropriate to represent what Mr. Singleton says via an affidavit. There is a distinction. So, you can ask anything you want. You can ask her what Santa Claus said or didn't say, whether she spoke to him or not, but it's inappropriate to introduce an affidavit from Santa Claus prior to every member in this Committee having an opportunity to check it out, for the following reason: we may find that Santa Claus is not real."

The public, therefore, would never find out that Singleton's testimony directly contradicted Hill's. Though the Singleton affidavit was circulated to the media by Thomas's supporters, its content was not reported. Singleton was not called as a witness for Thomas. Both sides had agreed to limit the number of witnesses to a certain number; once the testimony began, events moved so quickly that many officials were unaware of the Singleton affidavit until it was too late to change the witness line-up.

As a result of the Singleton controversy, the committee adopted a rule under whch no new information could be introduced into the hearing from affidavits or statements until such documents had been in the committee's possession for 24 hours. Given the short time span during which the hearings were conducted, this inevitably meant that relevant information might be excluded from the hearing.

12. Holt's testimony was later corroborated by Anna Jenkins, who had been an EEOC secretary in the chairman's office at the time of Thomas's appointment. Jenkins testified: "Upon Judge Thomas's arrival at the agency, I worked directly for him as his secretary until his confidential assistant Diane Holt and legal assistant Anita Hill came on board. He brought them from the Department of Education. Prior to Anita Hill joining the staff, she appeared quite anxious to work for the EEOC. In fact she called Judge Thomas several times to inquire about the status of her appointment. I recall the first day Miss Hill reported to work at the EEOC. She was pleased and excited about being able to pick an office with a big picture window overlooking the Watergate Hotel and Potomac River."

13. Sarah E. Wright, *Court of Appeal,* p. 225.

14. Statement by Senator Connie Mack to the U.S. Senate, *Congressional Record,* October 15, 1991, p. S14700.

15. Statement by Senator John Danforth to the U.S. Senate, *Congressional Record,* October 8, 1991, p. S14538.

16. Copies of Thomas phone logs obtained by author.

17. Quoted in Michael Wines, "Stark Conflict Marks Accounts Given by Thomas and Professor," *New York Times,* October 10, 1991, p. B14.

18. Interview with Charles Kothe, April 9, 1992.

19. Statement of Carlton R. Stewart, October 7, 1991. Statement of Stanley E. Grayson, October 7, 1991.

20. Quotes from Hill's press conference are from the Reuters transcript report, October 9, 1991, pp. 1–2.

21. Kevin W. Saunders letter to Thomas, January 31, 1989.

22. Thomas letter to Kothe, May 21, 1983.

23. Written statement of Charles Kothe to the Senate Judiciary Committee, October 9, 1991.

24. *Ibid.* If the Thomas letter had been merely a formality, as Hill stated, and if in fact he had sexually harassed her, she might have been expected to go to someone other than Thomas—another EEOC supervisor, or her supervisor at the law firm of Wald, Harkrader & Ross where she worked before joining the Thomas staff—for a recommendation.

25. Statement by Senator Orrin Hatch to the U.S. Senate, *Congressional Record,* October 15, 1991, p. S14681.

26. Statement by Senator Charles Grassley to the U.S. Senate, *Congressional Record,* October 15, 1991, p. S14628.

27. The agents' statements are contained in the Thomas FBI file and were obtained by the author.

28. When Senator Howell Heflin asked Hill about this telephone call with Henderson, Hill denied ever speaking to him about this matter.

> HEFLIN: Well, do you know whether or not there was a conversation between Keith Henderson and some other staffer in which they were discussing the affidavit and saying that there were certain possibilities, which included the possibility that Clarence Thomas might withdraw his name?
>
> HILL: That might have happened, but I haven't talked with Keith Henderson about that.

However, in Gary Phillips' confidential interview with Senate lawyers, he corroborated that Henderson had spoken to Hill:

> Q: When did you know that she had told someone other than you about her allegations?
>
> A: I had a conversation with Keith Henderson and he told me that he had spoken to Anita and that Anita had told him that she had been contacted by Senate staff and that she had agreed to provide them with the information that she had told me about, and that she had done so with the idea that the matter would be handled discreetly by the Senate Judiciary Committee.

29. Specter's dramatic statement—"flat-out perjury"—only confused the issue, drawing attention away from a crucial aspect of the entire affair: Brudney's inducement of Hill's initial charge.
30. It is possible that Hill considered Brudney to be her "counsel" but if this was so an even more serious question would be raised as to how a staffer of a governmental body that had called for the testimony of a witness could also be functioning as that witness's lawyer.
31. Transcript of NBC *Today* interview with Anita Hill, October 8, 1991.
32. Transcript of telephone interview of John William Carr by the U.S. Senate Committee on the Judiciary, October 10, 1991. This document was sealed by the committee and not made part of the public record. It was obtained independently by the author.

6. Judge Hoerchner's Amnesia

1. Interviews with former Yale classmates of Susan Hoerchner, on the condition of anonymity.
2. Hoerchner letter to author, June 18, 1992.
3. These details are drawn from Hoerchner's interview with Senate Judiciary Committee staff.
4. Tracy Wood, "Hill's Friend Had a Role in 2nd Harassment Case," *Los Angeles Times,* October 11, 1991, p. A13.

5. Interviews with associates of Judge Foster, April and May 1992.
6. In the staff interview, Hoerchner said she believed Thomas had "an attitude about power," which "really showed a disregard for general principles of equal opportunity or the rights of individuals."
7. Napolitano declined to be interviewed, but in an interview months later, she referred to this interpretation of Hoerchner's account, first published by the author in the *American Spectator,* in March 1992 as "the far-right theory of Anita Hill. He's taken a couple of isolated lines totally out of context of the rest of the deposition." As Napolitano should well know, this criticism is not valid. Napolitano then went on to concede that Hoerchner "did get a little mixed up about dates." Doug MacEachern, "Seems Everyone Is Checking Out Anita Hill Slam Piece," *Mesa Tribune,* Arizona, October 14, 1992, p. B1. Hoerchner also declined to be interviewed, but in her letter to the author she wrote that while "I did not remember the date of the conversation with Professor Hill . . . there is no doubt in my mind that at the time of the conversation, Professor Hill was working for Clarence Thomas."
8. Interview with Judith Hope, June 10, 1992.
9. According to Bush Administration and Senate sources who spoke with Hope at the time, these two people were, respectively, former Wald, Harkrader partners Jodi Bernstein and Donald Bucklin, neither of whom would comment on the conversations.
10. Fred Strasser and Marianne Lavelle, "Legal Team Assembles to Advise Hill," *National Law Journal,* October 21, 1991, p. 1.
11. This was Robert Shack, according to sources who spoke with Hope at the time. He declined to be interviewed.
12. Details about the Wald firm come from Jill Abramson, "How Two D.C. Firms Toughed Out the Downturn," *The American Lawyer,* December 1983, pp. 72–75; L. J. Pendlebury, "Wald, Harkrader, to Merge," *Legal Times,* March 23, 1987, p. 1; and W. John Moore, "More Defections Reported at Wald, Harkrader," *Legal Times,* January 6, 1986, p. 2.
13. Interviews with former Wald, Harkrader partners, most of whom did not wish to be identified for fear of jeopardizing their current legal practices.
14. Ricky Silberman interviews.
15. Singleton interview.
16. Berry-Myers interview.
17. Hardy's knowledge of the circumstances under which Hill left the firm may have been what Thomas meant when he said in his testimony: "We wouldn't be here today if Gil Hardy were alive."
18. Interviews with friends of Burke who wished to remain unidentified. Burke did not know Hope, and had not spoken with her about the Anita Hill matter.
19. Affidavit of John L. Burke, Jr., October 13, 1991.

20. Interview with David Berz, April 14, 1992.
21. Interview with Larry Thompson, June 5, 1992.
22. Affidavit of Donald H. Green, October 14, 1991. Green's affidavit appears in the *Congressional Record,* October 15, 1991, p. S14701.
23. See, for example, Jim McGee, "Hill's Departure from Law Firm Disputed," *Washington Post,* October 15, 1991, p. 5.
24. Neither Wald nor Green agreed to be interviewed.
25. Annual report of the Women's Legal Defense Fund, 1990–91.
26. Danforth interview.
27. Holt interview.
28. Stewart interview.
29. Quoted in Susan Dianne Rice and Yvonne Schibsted, *Los Angeles Daily Journal,* November 27, 1992. Hoerchner has made the most of her newfound fame. "People recognize me and come up to me and say very nice things, and they pick up the tab in restaurants. It is very gratifying, and a little intimidating or awe-inspiring," she told the *Long Beach Press-Telegram* (November 27, 1991, p. B1).
30. Leon interview.

7. The Myth of the Typical Case

1. Tamar Lewin, "Professor's Description of Events Called Typical," *New York Times,* October 8, 1991, p. 22.
2. Jill Smolowe, "She Said, He Said," *Time,* October 21, 1991, p. 39.
3. EEOC, "Policy Guidance on Current Issues of Sexual Harassment," October 25, 1988, pp. 6–13. According to a report in the *National Journal,* ". . . women's legal advocacy groups generally have credited the Equal Employment Opportunity Commission in Clarence Thomas's tenure with helping to develop one of the policies key to enforcing the law." (Marianne Lavelle, "Thomas' EEOC Worked On Key Harassment Case," Oct. 21, 1991).
4. Billie Wright Dziech, "Colleges Must Help to Unravel the Bewildering Complexities of Sexual Harassment," *Chronicle of Higher Education,* November 13, 1991, pp. B1–3.
5. "4 Testify Hill Spoke Years Ago of Harassment," *Washington Post,* October 14, 1991, p. 1.
6. June Jordan, "Can I Get a Witness?," in Robert L. Chrisman and Robert L. Allen, eds., *Court of Appeal,* p. 121.
7. Stuart Lefstein, "It's Not Too Late for the Crucible," *ABA Journal,* May 1992, p. 5.
8. Carr declined to be interviewed.
9. "Toward Justice Thomas," *Wall Street Journal* editorial, July 25, 1991, p. A8.
10. See Statement of the Association of the Bar of the City of New York, Sep-

tember 6, 1991, and Daniel Wise, "City Bar Withholds Approval of Thomas for High Court Seat," *New York Law Journal*, Sept. 9, 1991, p. 1.

11. See "Statement of Goals of New York Law Firms and Corporate Legal Departments for Increasing Minority Representation and Retention," Association of the Bar of the City of New York, September 24, 1991.

12. Paul declined to be interviewed. The quote is from the transcript of the telephone interview of Joel R. Paul by the U.S. Senate Committee on the Judiciary, October 10, 1991, obtained independently by the author.

13. Interview with former EEOC staffer, May 26, 1992. Roggerson declined comment.

14. Williams interview.

15. Transcript of telephone interview of Ellen Wells by the U.S. Senate Committee on the Judiciary, October 10, 1991, obtained independently by the author.

16. Interview of Ronald Langston, April 3, 1992.

17. Stephen Chapman, "The Senate's Duty: Confirm Clarence Thomas," *Chicago Tribune*, October 15, 1991, p. 17.

18. Statement by Sam Nunn to the U.S. Senate, October 15, 1991, p. S14690.

19. Margaret A. Burnham, "The Supreme Court Appointment Process and the Politics of Sex and Race," in Toni Morrison, ed., *Race-ing Justice*, pp. 290–319.

20. Adam Clymer, "Conflict Emerges Over a 2nd Witness," *New York Times*, October 11, 1991, p. 1.

21. See also David A. Firestone, "Another Accuser: Wright Waiting to Testify," *Newsday*, October 10, 1991, p. 5, and Guy Gugliotta, "Other Women Alleges Thomas Pushed for Date," *Washington Post*, October 14, 1991, p. 17.

22. Lynda Edwards, "Gag Rule," *Spy*, March 1992, pp. 40–47.

23. Garry G. B. Trudeau, *Doonesbury*, May 25 and 26, 1992.

24. Transcript of Totenberg address from NPR Public Affairs.

25. Phelps and Winternitz, *Capitol Games*, p. 368.

26. Gloria Borger and Ted Gest, "The Untold Story," *U.S. News and World Report*, October 12, 1992, p. 37. The witness to whom Simon referred was a woman named Rose Jourdain, a former Thomas speechwriter at the EEOC, who gave an unsworn statement to the Senate Judiciary Committee after Wright was asked if she could corroborate any part of the statement. Jourdain, whom Wright later referred to as a "mother figure," did not, however, corroborate any of Wright's specific charges. The details in Jourdain's statement—she remembered, for example, Wright telling her that Thomas had said "you have hair on your legs and it turns me on"—were not contained in Wright's own statement. Furthermore, like Wright, Jourdain was a disgruntled former employee of Thomas who had been fired at the same time as Wright for failing to complete her work assignments. "Rose was writing a book, and she worked on her book all day. She never did any work," Diane Holt recalled. Jourdain at-

tributed the firing to political differences with Thomas, according to Phelps in *Capitol Games,* pp. 362–64.

27. Simon, *Advice and Consent,* p. 118. Simon also falsely claimed that Wright "had charged sexual harassment" and concluded: "In retrospect, we made a mistake in not hearing her."

28. It is not clear if the column was or was not intended for publication. Wright contradicted herself on this point, and she declined to be interviewed.

29. Telephone interview of Angela Denise Wright by the U.S. Senate Committee on the Judiciary, October 10, 1991. The Wright interview is part of the official record of the hearings. *Nomination of Judge Clarence Thomas,* Senate Judiciary Committee Hearings (Washington, D.C.: GPO, 1991), October 11, 12, and 13.

30. Interviews with former co-workers of Wright, April and May 1992.

31. Letter from Kate Semerad to Senator Strom Thurmond, October 10, 1991, furnished to the author.

32. Written statement of Jay F. Morris, former deputy administrator, AID, *Congressional Record,* October 15, 1991, p. S14678.

33. Interview of Pamela Talkin, March 25, 1992.

34. Phelps and Winternitz, *Capitol Games,* p. 368, and interview with Charles Ogletree, July 13, 1992.

35. Simpson interview.

36. Borger and Gest, "Untold Story," p. 36. In addition to resurrecting and mischaracterizing Wright's charge against Thomas, the magazine also claimed that a third sexual harassment charge had been lodged against Thomas by Sukari Hardnett. This was also false. Hardnett, a former legal assistant to Chairman Thomas, submitted an affidavit to the Judiciary Committee on October 14, the day before the Senate vote on the nomination. "Women know when there are sexual dimensions to the attention they are receiving. And there was never any doubt about that dimension in Clarence Thomas's office," Hardnett wrote. She provided no specifics to describe this "dimension," however. She also stated plainly: "I am not claiming that I was the victim of sexual harassment." Hardnett said she eventually resigned from the EEOC because she found working on Thomas's staff "unpleasant." Diane Holt, however, said in a written statement to the Judiciary Committee that Hardnett was fired from the staff after failing on more than one occasion to pass the bar exam. Co-workers of Hardnett during the period said she had never complained to anyone about the working environment in the agency. Barbara Lawrence, who shared an office with Hardnett at the time, said, "Thomas was like our mentor. He was very nice to all of us and spent a lot of time with us. I know he spent a lot of time trying to help her. But I know there was nothing more to it than that. I saw them every day." According to David Savage in *Turning Right: The Making of the Rehnquist*

Supreme Court (New York: John Wiley & Sons, 1992), pp. 433–34, Hardnett had met with Nan Aron of the Alliance for Justice earlier in the summer to discuss her concerns about Thomas. This was apparently an unsuccessful effort by Aron to obtain corroboration for Hill's nascent charge. Hardnett declined to be interviewed.

37. Stephanie Saul, "X-Rated Justice?," *Newsday,* June 2, 1991, p. 7.
38. Simon, *Advice and Consent,* pp. 120–21.
39. Steven Roberts, "The Crowning Thomas Affair," *U.S. News and World Report,* September 16, 1991.
40. Coleman interview. Roberts declined to discuss the sourcing of the piece.
41. Singleton interview.
42. Coleman's letter to Leahy was placed in the *Congressional Record,* October 4, 1991, p. S14423.
43. Neil A. Lewis, "Judge's Backers Seek to Undercut Hill," *New York Times,* October 13, 1991, p. 28.
44. Written statement of Lovida Coleman furnished to the author.
45. Donahue transcript #3314, October 14, 1991, "Clarence Thomas: A Nation Divided."
46. Catharine MacKinnon suggested an explanation for one of these details, the totally mystifying Coke can story. Hill alleged that Thomas, in the middle of a meeting in his office, walked over to a can of Coke sitting on a table and asked her, "Who put pubic hair on my Coke?" MacKinnon told Donahue, ". . . a great many women, unlike a great many men, may not have seen this pornography. They do not know that in pornography, Coke cans are used to penetrate women. That's what the pubic hair is doing."
47. Williams interview.
48. Leon interview.
49. Bolick interview.
50. Stewart interview.
51. Packwood, at Michelman's urging, opposed the Thomas nomination.
52. Ricky Silberman interviews.
53. Marini interview.
54. Quoted in Michael Ross, "Effect of Hill's 'Passing' of Lie Test Uncertain," *Los Angeles Times,* October 14, 1991, p. 1.
55. Hatch interview.
56. Peter G. Gosselin, "Hill Passed Lie Detector Test, Her Lawyers Say," *Boston Globe,* October 14, 1991, p. 1.
57. See, generally, "He Said/She Said Dispute: Truth Eludes Even Experts," *Los Angeles Times,* October 12, 1991, p. 1; Robert F. Howe, "Do Lie Detectors Always Tell the Truth?," *Washington Post,* June 3, 1991, p. 16; Edwin Chen, "Hill Legal Team Uses Lie Detector," *Los Angeles Times,* October 14, 1991, p. 1; and Michael Isikoff, "Hill's

Story Said to Pass Polygraph Examination," *Washington Post,* October 14, 1991, p. 1.

58. Martin Fletcher and Nick Nuttall, "Polygraph Test Spotlights Political Undercurrents," *Financial Times,* London, October 15, 1991, "Overseas News."

59. Carleton R. Bryant, "Polygraph Backs Hill; Examiner in Question," *Washington Times,* October 14, 1991, p. 1.

60. Polygraph Examination Report, American International Security Corporation, Paul K. Minor, President, October 13, 1991.

61. News conference transcript.

62. " 'Tree' Time," *American Lawyer,* December 1991, pp. 45–51.

63. Ross, "Effect of Hill's 'Passing' of Lie Test Uncertain," p. 1.

64. Bryant, "Polygraph Backs Hill," p. 1.

65. Quoted in "Credibility Gulch," *Wall Street Journal* editorial, October 15, 1991, p. A22.

8. The Search for a Motive

1. Joseph Albright, "Some Reasons to Trust Thomas or Believe Hill," *Atlanta Constitution,* October 15, 1991, p. A7. The other five pillars of Hill's case, according to this analysis, were the testimony of Susan Hoerchner, John Carr, Ellen Wells, and Joel Paul; and the fact that Hill passed a polygraph test. All five pillars have been dealt with in previous chapters.

2. Simon, *Advice and Consent,* p.139.

3. Phelps and Winternitz, *Capitol Games,* p. 348.

4. Wanheema Lubiano, "Black Ladies, Welfare Queens, and State Minstrels, Ideological War by Narrative Means," in Toni Morrison, ed., *Racing Justice,* pp. 340–341.

5. Borger and Gest, "Untold Story."

6. Virginia I. Postrel, "What a Year of Revisionist PR Can Buy," *Los Angeles Times,* October 18, 1992, p. M5.

7. This sequence is discussed in Chapter 6.

8. Hill was the sole attorney-adviser to Thomas. Patricia Healey handled management issues, while Lori Saxon was Thomas's confidential assistant. Both Healey and Saxon, in addition to Holt, submitted statements to the Judiciary Committee in support of Thomas during the Hill hearings.

9. This assertion was patently false, as demonstrated in Chapter 5.

10. NPR transcript.

11. Neil A. Lewis, "Law Professor Accuses Thomas of Sexual Harassment," *New York Times,* October 7, 1991, p. 1.

12. Laurence Silberman interview.

13. Jarvis affidavit.
14. Hill affidavit.
15. Hill's support came exclusively from people who did not know Thomas and therefore had no evidence of their interaction in a professional or personal setting, whereas most of Thomas's supporters knew both Hill and Thomas quite well. Indeed, two of Thomas's witnesses were close friends of Hill: Diane Holt and Nancy Fitch. Hill's witnesses were best described as former friends and fleeting acquaintances. There appeared to be wide support for Hill among the student body in Oklahoma, but this was irrelevant to the case. Most of the students who appeared at her campus press conference did not know her and were pressed to appear and sign statements of support by Hill's faculty friends. Kirk A. Olson, a third-year law student, told the *National Law Journal*, "It's very pro-Hill down here, understandably. People are afraid to speak up and say anything derogatory about her." A petition backing Hill's word in the sexual harassment case circulated among the law faculty, but it had to be watered down to a general endorsement of her character to attract broad support. Still, six faculty members refused to sign. An organized campaign among Yale alumni produced sixty-five signatures on a statement of "unhesitating and unwavering support" from people who may—or may not—have known Hill more than fifteen years before.
16. Williams interview.
17. Holt interview.
18. Singleton interview.
19. Interview with former Hill classmate, June 3, 1992.
20. Interview with former EEOC staffer, May 26, 1992.
21. Lubiano, p. 350.
22. This issue is discussed at length in Chapter 5.
23. Hill's explanation was directly contradicted by Harry Singleton in Chapter 5.
24. Dziech, "Colleges Must Help."
25. Affidavit of John N. Doggett, undated.
26. Interview with Janet Dorsey, March 24, 1992.
27. Fishel interview.
28. Berry-Myers interview. When Berry-Myers made a similar comment to a reporter from the *New York Times* after the story of Hill's allegations broke, Hill, in a press conference, claimed that she did not know Berry-Myers, and Berry-Myers did not know her. Berry-Myers and Hill, however, worked together at both Education and the EEOC. When challenged during her Senate testimony on this seeming discrepancy, Hill said that she had meant that Berry-Myers did not know her well enough to draw conclusions about her social interests.
29. Interview of Barbara Lawrence, November 16, 1992.

30. Singleton interview.
31. Dorsey interview.
32. Lawrence interview.
33. Interview with EEOC staffer, April 16, 1992.
34. This subject was explored in Chapter 7.
35. Duncan has declined to comment publicly on the scandal. But she did tell the FBI that she did not credit Hill's charge against Thomas.
36. Williams letter to Thurmond, October 7, 1991, reprinted in the *Congressional Record,* October 7, p. S14467. Just as the White House overlooked the importance of Singleton's testimony, it seems in retrospect that Williams should have been called as a witness. Williams was on a proposed witness list, but he was struck by the White House because he had made comments to the press earlier in the summer that were seen as unhelpful to the nominee. When asked by a reporter for the *Washington Post* why Thomas had married Ginni Thomas, Williams commented that many black women did not find Thomas physically attractive. Williams had also been the author of the controversial Farrakhan speech that made headlines in July.
37. Manning Marable, "Clarence Thomas and the Crisis of Black Political Culture," in Toni Morrison, ed., *Race-ing Justice,* p. 77.
38. Williams interview.
39. Holt's recollection did not seem consistent with Hill's testimony that she and Thomas had left the EEOC office together on her last day at work and gone directly to dinner, at a location Hill said she could not recall. "I reluctantly agreed to accept that invitation but only if it was at the very end of a working day," Hill testified. Thomas testified that there was no such dinner.
40. Shirley E. Perlman, Kevin McCoy, and Steve Wick, "Far From her Roots," *Newsday,* October 11, 1991, p. 18.
41. This fact was developed by NBC's Andrea Mitchell, who reported, "Jarvis also said that Hill had never mentioned sexual harassment to her even though they lived together when it was allegedly taking place," NBC Nightly News, October 12, 1991, transcript prepared by Burrelle's Information Services.
42. Jon D. Hull, "A Real Straight Arrow," *Time,* October 21, 1991.
43. Robert Suro, "A Private Person in a Storm," *New York Times,* October 11, 1991, p. 1.
44. David A. Maraniss and Jim McGee, "After the Thomas Hearings," *Washington Post,* October 20, 1991, p. 1.
45. Bardach, "Totenberg: Queen of Leaks."
46. NPR transcript of Totenberg speech.
47. Women's Legal Defense Fund, "Summary of the Record on Sexual Harassment Allegations," October 15, 1991.

48. Manning Marable, in *Race-ing Justice,* p. 69.
49. Michael Thelwell, in *ibid.,* p. 123. In an interview, Judge Bork said he remembered that Anita Hill had taken one of his classes at Yale, but he does not recall her speaking during the term. "Certainly I was neither her friend nor mentor," Bork said.
50. Cornel West, "Black Leadership and the Pitfalls of Racial Reasoning," in Toni Morrison, ed. *Race-ing Justice,* pp. 390–401.
51. Brown interview. Some Thomas opponents later speculated that Biden's ruling was intended to protect Thomas, not Hill. They surmised that if Hill had answered fully, she may have revealed that Thomas did have a legal opinion of *Roe* v. *Wade,* contrary to his sworn testimony.
52. Lally Weymouth, "Some Clues to Anita Hill's Motive," *Wall Street Journal,* Nov. 26, 1991, p. A16. Weymouth is a regular columnist for the *Washington Post,* which was not interested in publishing this column.
53. C-SPAN transcript, Brian Lamb and Tim Phelps, October 15, 1991.
54. Phelps and Winternitz, *Capitol Games,* p. 353.
55. *Ibid.,* p. 348.
56. Shirley E. Perlman, Kevin McCoy, and Steve Wick, "Far From Her Roots," *Newsday,* October 11, 1991, p. 4.
57. Jill Nelson, "No Regrets," *Essence,* March 1992, pp. 55–119.

9. The Real Anita Hill

1. Interview of Helen Jones, July 1, 1992.
2. As with many of the sources with information about Hill, this professor spoke only on the condition of anonymity. This is a measure of how politically correct supporting Hill has become in university and legal circles.
3. Interview of John Eidsmoe, May 22, 1992.
4. Quoted in Gertha Coffee, "Friends See Hill Sticking to Her Guns," *The Atlanta Journal/Atlanta Constitution,* October 11, 1991, p. C1.
5. Interview with Keith Lapayude, April 29, 1992.
6. Interview of William Michael Roberts, May 20, 1992.
7. Interview with Leo Whinery, April 13, 1992.
8. Affidavit of Todd A. Cone, obtained from Senate Judiciary Committee sources by the author.
9. Many of the letters were placed in the *Congressional Record* by Simpson on October 15, 1991, pp. S14675-81. In fairness to Simpson, the committee's rule under which all material had to be introduced meant that he had little or no time to introduce the information officially.
10. Patrick McGuigan, "Hill and OU Law: Politically Correct," *Daily Oklahoman,* October 12, 1991, p. 14.
11. Tuttle interview.
12. Tuttle interview.

13. Interview with Jim Wagoner, August 22, 1992.

14. Felicity Barringer, "Anita Hill Offers Her Version of Senate Hearings," *New York Times,* October 17, 1992, p. A6.

15. Linda Lyons, "Anita on Color," *Metro Norman,* May 1992, p. 13.

16. Interview of Dennis Olson, March 31, 1992.

17. See Harry F. Tepker, " 'The Defects of Better Motives': Reflections on Mr. Meese's Jurisprudence of Original Intention," *Oklahoma Law Review,* Volume 39:23, 1986; Tepker, "Justice Brennan, Judge Bork and A Jurisprudence of Original Values," *Oklahoma Law Review,* Volume 43, Winter 1990.

18. Interview with EEOC staffer who declined to be identified.

19. Letter from Mary Constance T. Matthies to Senate Judiciary Committee, October 12, 1991, reprinted in the *Congressional Record,* October 15, 1991, p. S14675.

20. They did not come forward publicly at the time because they were embarking on legal careers and feared negative repercussions.

21. Interview of Alvin Harrell, August 11, 1992.

22. Jon D. Hull, *Time.*

23. Pemberton, p. 189.

24. Nellie Y. McKay, *Race-ing Justice,* pp. 276–277.

25. Matthew Schofield, "Hill's Story Sounded Familiar to Wichita Woman," *Kansas City Star,* October 15, 1991, p. 1.

26. Interview of Justice Department official.

27. Affidavit of Lawrence Thomas Shiles, filed with the Senate Judiciary Committee, obtained from Senate sources by the author. The affidavit was also referred to in Borger and Gest, *U.S. News and World Report,* p. 35; and Phelps, *Capitol Games,* p. 353.

28. Interview of Lawrence Shiles, June 3, 1992.

29. Interview of Jeff Londoff, December 13, 1991. Stewart declined comment.

30. Ogletree interview. The fact that the students joked that the hairs were pubic at the time was confirmed by other students in the class. But this may have simply been a sexist and even racist joke made about the sole black female professor in the school.

31. Interview with former student of Hill, December 13, 1991. This story was not consistent with the notion that Hill lifted "Long Dong Silver" from the 1988 Kansas case. If the student was telling the truth, Hill would have had to come across "Long Dong" before she mentioned it to him in 1984.

32. Simpson interview. The student in question apparently told the same story to a reporter for *Newsweek,* Bob Cohn, who wrote an article in *The New Republic* about his attempts to follow up the Thomas–Hill story after the hearings. "A fourth [ORU] student claimed Hill had made sexually provocative comments to him—he said he later 'fantasized about

the world's kinkiest law professor'—but he wouldn't sign a committee affidavit or let me use his name because he said he feared his law practice might suffer." Bob Cohn, "On the Thomas–Hill Dirt Trail," January 6 and 13, 1992, pp. 16–18. Shiles was unable to corroborate the "Long Dong" detail, but he did say that it was well known in the school that Hill "had the hots" for this particular student.

33. Holt interview.
34. He is now a professor at another law school, and a well-respected member of his state bar and local community. He declined to be identified so as not to jeopardize his career.
35. The source's presence at the table was verified independently by one of the faculty members who was often present.
36. The fact that one of Hill's close friends—Professor Shirley Wiegand— had tried a sodomy case was independently corroborated. In January 1992, Wiegand spoke to the gay and lesbian section of the American Association of Law Schools about her role in litigating the case, a challenge to the constitutionality of Kentucky's anti-sodomy statute, while she was in private practice in Lexington in 1986.
37. Phillips interview transcript.
38. Paul Richtler and Douglas Frantz, "Lives of Thomas, Accuser Eerily Similar," *Los Angeles Times,* October 15, 1991, p. A15.
39. Phelps, *Capitol Games,* p. 146.
40. Jake Thompson, "Earlier talks held no hint of harassment allegations," *Kansas City Star,* October 8, 1991, p. A8.
41. Sharon La Franiere, "Despite Achievement, Thomas Felt Isolated," *Washington Post,* September 9, 1991, p. 1.
42. Gil Hardy's death in 1989 would have made it possible for Hill to implement Hoerchner's suggestion without fear of getting caught.
43. Quoted in Phelps, *Capitol Games,* pp. 419–420.
44. Margot Habiby, "Prof Says Thomas Not Best Choice," *Oklahoma Daily,* September 19, 1991, p. 1.
45. Republican Senators were apparently not the only ones who did not believe Hill. On Sunday evening after the hearings concluded, Senator Biden encountered two of Thomas's witnesses, Janet Brown and Pamela Talkin, in the Senate corridor. Biden told the pair, "I believe him, not her." Senator Hatch had a similar encounter with another liberal Democrat on the Judiciary Committee, whom he declined to name. This Senator told Hatch on Friday evening that he did not believe Hill for a moment but was voting against Thomas because he did not like Thomas's views on certain issues.
46. Jim Parsons, "Minnesotans' Efforts to Get Endowed Chair for Anita Hill Thrive," Minneapolis *Star Tribune,* June 1, 1992, p. 1.
47. University of Oklahoma Application for Sabbatical Leave of Absence, Anita F. Hill, Law School, March 13, 1992. The proposal was approved

after Dean David Swank, who had allowed Hill to use the law center as a staging ground for her press conferences at the time of the Thomas hearings, countermanded the recommendation of Committee A in the law school that ranked Hill's sabbatical request third in terms of priority. Swank jumped Hill's proposal to first in priority, according to a letter from Dean Swank to Provost Richard Gibson, dated March 26, 1992.

INDEX